T0324233

MATHEMATICAL TOOLS IN COMPUTER GRAPHICS WITH C# IMPLEMENTATIONS

MATHEMATICAL TOOLS IN COMPUTER GRAPHICS WITH C# IMPLEMENTATIONS

Alexandre Hardy & Willi-Hans Steeb

University of Johannesburg, South Africa

World Scientific

NEW JERSEY · LONDON · SINGAPORE · BEIJING · SHANGHAI · HONG KONG · TAIPEI · CHENNAI

Published by

World Scientific Publishing Co. Pte. Ltd.

5 Toh Tuck Link, Singapore 596224

USA office: 27 Warren Street, Suite 401-402, Hackensack, NJ 07601

UK office: 57 Shelton Street, Covent Garden, London WC2H 9HE

British Library Cataloguing-in-Publication Data
A catalogue record for this book is available from the British Library.

**MATHEMATICAL TOOLS IN COMPUTER GRAPHICS
WITH C# IMPLEMENTATIONS**

ISBN-13 978-981-279-102-3
ISBN-10 981-279-102-7
ISBN-13 978-981-279-103-0 (pbk)
ISBN-10 981-279-103-5 (pbk)

Printed in Singapore.

Preface

Computer graphics is applied in many different fields including the entertainment industry, medical and geographic visualization and industrial design. Successful development of computer graphics programs and algorithms requires knowledge from a diverse set of fields to be combined and applied effectively. The most important part of any computer graphics algorithm is the underlying mathematical tools that are used to analyze and develop the algorithm. This book introduces computer graphics from a mathematical perspective. The basic computer graphics principles are introduced as well as more advanced topics. The mathematical techniques are developed in detail. Selected topics include: basic transforms, curves, surfaces and subdivision surfaces. New techniques such as wavelets, fractals, parameterization and fluid simulation are also included. Throughout a large portion of the text a new curve and surface algorithm are developed to illustrate the use of mathematics to develop computer graphics algorithms. C# implementations for many of the algorithms are provided throughout the book. The C# implementation allows the reader to obtain practical knowledge along with the theoretical knowledge.

The provided C# implementations can be downloaded from our websites for use in other software projects.

Book websites
http://eve.uj.ac.za/gfxbook
http://issc.uj.ac.za

Email addresses of the authors
alexandre.hardy@gmail.com
steebwilli@gmail.com
whsteeb@uj.ac.za

Contents

List of Figures

Notation

$\mathbb{N}$	the set of natural numbers
$\mathbb{Z}$	the set of integer numbers
$\mathbb{Q}$	the set of rational numbers
$\mathbb{R}$	the set of real numbers
$\mathbb{C}$	the set of complex numbers (of the form $a + bi$, $a, b \in \mathbb{R}$)
$\mathbb{R}^n$	the Cartesian product space, i.e. $\mathbb{R}^n = \{ (x_0, x_1, \ldots, x_{n-1}) \mid x_j \in \mathbb{R} \}$
z	complex number
$\bar{z}$	complex conjugate of $z \in \mathbb{C}$
i	$i = \sqrt{-1}$
I_n	$n \times n$ unit matrix
M^T	transpose of the matrix M
$|M|$, $\det(M)$	determinant of the matrix M
$\mathbf{x} = (x_0 \ x_1 \ \ldots \ x_{n-1})^T$	column vector $\mathbf{x} \in \mathbb{R}^n$
$\mathbf{x}^T$	row vector $\mathbf{x} \in \mathbb{R}^n$
$\mathbf{0}$	zero column vector
$\mathbf{n}$	normal vector
$\mathbf{t}$	tangent vector
$\|\mathbf{x}\|$	Euclidean norm of $\mathbf{x}$, $\|\mathbf{x}\| = \sqrt{\mathbf{x}^T \mathbf{x}}$
$\langle \mathbf{x}, \mathbf{y} \rangle$	the inner product (scalar product) of $\mathbf{x}$ and $\mathbf{y}$
$\mathbf{x} \cdot \mathbf{y}$	dot product, an inner product defined by $\mathbf{x}^T \mathbf{y} = \sum_{k=0}^{n-1} x_k y_k$, where $\mathbf{x}, \mathbf{y} \in \mathbb{R}^n$
$\mathbf{x} \times \mathbf{y}$	the vector product (cross product) of $\mathbf{x} \in \mathbb{R}^3$ and $\mathbf{y} \in \mathbb{R}^3$,

$\mathrm{ang}(\mathbf{a}, \mathbf{b}, \mathbf{c})$	the angle between the vectors $\mathbf{a} - \mathbf{b}$ and $\mathbf{c} - \mathbf{b}$
$[0, 1]$	unit interval
δ_{jk}	Kronecker delta, 1 if $j = k$, 0 otherwise
I_n	$n \times n$ identity matrix
t	curve parameter
u, v	surface parameters
C^k	continuity of a curve or surface
G^k	geometric continuity of a curve or surface
$\lfloor x \rfloor$	floor of $x \in \mathbb{R}$, the largest y such that $y \in \mathbb{Z}$ and $y \leq x$
$\lceil x \rceil$	ceiling of $x \in \mathbb{R}$, the smallest y such that $y \in \mathbb{Z}$ and $y \geq x$
$\otimes$	Kronecker product

Chapter 1

Vectors, Matrices and Transforms

In this chapter we discuss the basic building blocks of objects in computer graphics. It is not only important to find a way to represent objects, but it is also very important to be able to manipulate the objects in some fashion. The building blocks for objects and transforms are vectors and matrices. We will postpone descriptions of curves and surfaces to later chapters, in this chapter we focus on points as the primary means to describe objects, and how to transform these points in some way. For further details consult the tutorials on the matter by Goldman [45, 47, 44]. Buss [8] derives these transforms in detail. Affine transforms are described in detail by Steeb [122].

To begin we describe the vector space in which vectors reside.

1.1   Vector Spaces

A vector space V is a set on which the operations of addition and scalar multiplication are defined. The set V associated with the operations of addition and scalar multiplication is said to form a *vector space* if the following properties are satisfied

- If $\mathbf{x} \in V$ and $\mathbf{y} \in V$ then $\mathbf{x} + \mathbf{y} \in V$.

- $\mathbf{x} + \mathbf{y} = \mathbf{y} + \mathbf{x}$ (*Commutative*).

- $\mathbf{x} + (\mathbf{y} + \mathbf{z}) = (\mathbf{x} + \mathbf{y}) + \mathbf{z}$ (*Associative*).

1

- There is a zero vector $\mathbf{0}$ in V such that $\mathbf{0} + \mathbf{x} = \mathbf{x} + \mathbf{0} = \mathbf{x}$ for all $\mathbf{x} \in V$.

- For each $\mathbf{x} \in V$, there is a $-\mathbf{x} \in V$, called the negative of $\mathbf{x}$ such that $\mathbf{x} + (-\mathbf{x}) = (-\mathbf{x}) + \mathbf{x} = \mathbf{0}$.

- if α is any scalar and $\mathbf{x} \in V$, then $\alpha\mathbf{x} \in V$.

- $\alpha(\mathbf{x} + \mathbf{y}) = \alpha\mathbf{x} + \alpha\mathbf{y}$.

- $(\alpha + \beta)\mathbf{x} = \alpha\mathbf{x} + \beta\mathbf{x}$.

- $\alpha(\beta\mathbf{x}) = (\alpha\beta)(\mathbf{x})$.

- $1\mathbf{x} = \mathbf{x}$.

Here we consider the vector space $V = \mathbb{R}^n$, and the scalars are therefore in $\mathbb{R}$. We consider the vectors as column vectors. Thus $\mathbf{x}^T$ denotes a row vector, where ^{T} denotes the *transpose*.

We can define a *scalar product* in $\mathbb{R}^n$ as

$$\langle \mathbf{x}, \mathbf{y} \rangle := \mathbf{x} \cdot \mathbf{y} = \mathbf{x}^T \mathbf{y} = \sum_{i=0}^{n-1} x_i y_i$$

where $\mathbf{x} = (x_0 \ x_1 \ \ldots \ x_{n-1})^T$ and $\mathbf{y} = (y_0 \ y_1 \ \ldots \ y_{n-1})^T$. The scalar product implies the *Euclidean norm* defined as

$$\|\mathbf{x}\| := \sqrt{\langle \mathbf{x}, \mathbf{x} \rangle} = \sqrt{\sum_{i=0}^{n-1} x_i^2}.$$

The *Euclidean distance* between the vectors $\mathbf{x}$ and $\mathbf{y}$ is then given by

$$\|\mathbf{x} - \mathbf{y}\| = \sqrt{\langle \mathbf{x} - \mathbf{y}, \mathbf{x} - \mathbf{y} \rangle} = \sqrt{\sum_{i=0}^{n-1} (x_i - y_i)^2}.$$

We typically work with the vector spaces $\mathbb{R}^2$ and $\mathbb{R}^3$. The operators in $\mathbb{R}^2$ (the extension to $\mathbb{R}^3$ is similar) are

- $(x_0 \ x_1)^T + (y_0 \ y_1)^T := (x_0 + y_0 \ x_1 + y_1)^T$,

- $\alpha(x_0 \ x_1)^T := (\alpha x_0 \ \alpha x_1)^T$

where $\mathbf{x} = (x_0 \ x_1)^T$ and $\mathbf{y} = (y_0 \ y_1)^T$ are vectors in $\mathbb{R}^2$ and $\alpha \in \mathbb{R}$.

Two vectors are called *perpendicular* to each other if $\langle \mathbf{x}, \mathbf{y} \rangle = 0$. For example, the vectors

$$\mathbf{x} = \begin{pmatrix} 1 \\ 1 \\ -1 \end{pmatrix}, \qquad \mathbf{y} = \begin{pmatrix} -1 \\ 0 \\ -1 \end{pmatrix}$$

are perpendicular. A vector $\mathbf{x}$ is called *normalized* if $\|\mathbf{x}\| = 1$.

Note that $\mathbf{x}\mathbf{y}^T$ provides the square matrix

$$\mathbf{x}\mathbf{y}^T = \begin{pmatrix} x_0 \\ x_1 \\ \vdots \\ x_{n-1} \end{pmatrix} (y_0 \ y_1 \ \cdots \ y_{n-1})$$

$$= \begin{pmatrix} x_0 y_0 & x_0 y_1 & \cdots & x_0 y_{n-1} \\ x_1 y_0 & \ddots & & \vdots \\ \vdots & & \ddots & \vdots \\ x_{n-1} y_0 & x_{n-1} y_1 & \cdots & x_{n-1} y_{n-1} \end{pmatrix}.$$

In $\mathbb{R}^3$ the *vector product* (also called the *cross product*) plays an important role. Given two vectors $\mathbf{x}$ and $\mathbf{y} \in \mathbb{R}^3$ one defines

$$\mathbf{x} \times \mathbf{y} := \begin{pmatrix} x_1 y_2 - x_2 y_1 \\ x_2 y_0 - x_0 y_2 \\ x_0 y_1 - x_1 y_0 \end{pmatrix}.$$

The vector $\mathbf{x} \times \mathbf{y}$ is perpendicular to the plane spanned by the vectors $\mathbf{x}$ and $\mathbf{y}$. We have the properties

$$\mathbf{x} \times (\mathbf{y} + \mathbf{z}) = \mathbf{x} \times \mathbf{y} + \mathbf{x} \times \mathbf{z}$$

$$\mathbf{x} \times \mathbf{y} = -\mathbf{y} \times \mathbf{x}$$

$$\mathbf{x} \times (\mathbf{y} \times \mathbf{z}) + \mathbf{z} \times (\mathbf{x} \times \mathbf{y}) + \mathbf{y} \times (\mathbf{z} \times \mathbf{x}) = \mathbf{0} \quad (\textit{Jacobi identity}).$$

We also have the *vector identity*

$$\mathbf{x} \times (\mathbf{y} \times \mathbf{z}) \equiv (\mathbf{x} \cdot \mathbf{z})\mathbf{y} - (\mathbf{x} \cdot \mathbf{y})\mathbf{z}.$$

1.2   Points and Vectors

In the following, we refer to points and vectors in $\mathbb{R}^2$ and $\mathbb{R}^3$. It is important to note that vectors and points differ. Vectors are quantities with magnitude and direction. Points are locations in the Cartesian space. Points can be represented by vectors, indicating the direction and distance from the origin of the Cartesian plane. However, points and vectors differ in that points can be moved whereas vectors cannot [44]. For example, a normal to a surface (a vector perpendicular to the surface) remains the same, no matter where the surface is, as long as the orientation of the surface remains constant. However, points describing the surface are affected by the position of the surface. We nevertheless often use points as if they were vectors, and vectors as if they were points. To represent a point in $\mathbb{R}^3$ we use the format $(x_0 \ x_1 \ x_2)^T$ which is the vector representing the location of the point relative to the origin. The same notation is used for points in other dimensions. In $\mathbb{R}^2$ we write a vector as $(x_0 \ x_1)^T$.

Matrix transforms can be applied to vectors, so vectors are written in column vector form. The column vector form of the vector $\mathbf{x} \in \mathbb{R}^3$ is given by

$$\mathbf{x} = \begin{pmatrix} x_0 \\ x_1 \\ x_2 \end{pmatrix} \equiv (x_0 \ x_1 \ x_2)^T.$$

Thus we consider $\mathbf{x}$ as a column vector, and $\mathbf{x}^T$ is a row vector. Then $\mathbf{x} = (x_0 \ x_1 \ x_2)^T$, where T denotes the transpose. *Line segments* can now be defined by two points. The line segment is the portion of the line passing through the two points that is between those two points. Let $\mathbf{p}_1$ and $\mathbf{p}_2$ be the two points. Then

$$\mathbf{g} = (1 - \alpha)\mathbf{p}_1 + \alpha\mathbf{p}_2$$

defines points on the line segment where $\alpha \in [0, 1]$.

1.2.1   Homogeneous Coordinates

In several situations it is necessary to differentiate between points and vectors. To do so we embed the vector space $\mathbb{R}^3$ in the vector space $\mathbb{R}^4$ to create the homogeneous coordinate system.

Definition 1.1. *If u_0, u_1, u_2, $w \in \mathbb{R}$ and $w \neq 0$, then $(u_0 \ u_1 \ u_2 \ w)^T$ is a homogeneous coordinate representation of the point $(u_0/w \ u_1/w \ u_2/w)^T$. The points $(u_0 \ u_1 \ u_2 \ 0)^T$ are so called "points at infinity", and are often used to represent vectors.*

We now have separate representations for points and vectors. Points have the form $(u_0 \ u_1 \ u_2 \ w)^T$ with $w \neq 0$. Vectors have the form $(u_0 \ u_1 \ u_2 \ 0)^T$. Vectors and points in $\mathbb{R}^4$ form a *Grassmann space* [46]. The homogeneous form of vectors and points will prove to be useful when defining various transforms.

1.3   Representing Objects by Points

Most objects can be represented by a set of points P. These points may describe points on the surface of the object, or may be used as control values to describe a surface. There may be additional parameters describing the surface, but we do not consider those parameters here.

Perhaps the simplest form of object is a polygonal mesh. The polygonal mesh is further described by a set of polygons created from the point set P. These polygons can be described by a set of faces F where each element of F is a set of edges that describe that face. The edges are simply described by $(\mathbf{p}_1, \mathbf{p}_2)$ where $\mathbf{p}_1, \mathbf{p}_2 \in P$.

With this simple representation it becomes obvious that only positional information is stored in P. F stores only connectivity information. Thus any transform applied to the points in P will transform the whole object in some way.

We typically use affine transforms to transform the points, and this is the topic of the next section.

1.4   Affine Transformations

1.4.1   Introduction and Definitions

We would like to be able to transform a curve or surface and not be forced to manually calculate the new curve or surface. For example, during an animation sequence, we would like to be able to rotate an object, continuously changing the camera angles and render the object accordingly. Affine transforms will allow us to do this. We first introduce transforms, and in particular affine transforms.

A *transform* on $\mathbb{R}^n$ is any mapping $A : \mathbb{R}^n \mapsto \mathbb{R}^n$. That is, each point $\mathbf{x} \in \mathbb{R}^n$ is mapped to exactly one point, $A(\mathbf{x})$, also in $\mathbb{R}^n$. The first transform we discuss is the linear transform.

Definition 1.2. *Let $A : \mathbb{R}^n \mapsto \mathbb{R}^n$ be a transform. A is a linear transform if and only if*

(a) *For all $\alpha \in \mathbb{R}$ and all $\mathbf{x} \in \mathbb{R}^n$, $A(\alpha \mathbf{x}) = \alpha A(\mathbf{x})$.*

(b) *For all $\mathbf{x}, \mathbf{y} \in \mathbb{R}^n$, $A(\mathbf{x} + \mathbf{y}) = A(\mathbf{x}) + A(\mathbf{y})$.*

This implies that $A(\mathbf{0}) = \mathbf{0}$ since $A(0 \cdot \mathbf{x}) = 0 \cdot A(\mathbf{x})$. An example of a linear transform is the identity transform given by $I(\mathbf{x}) = \mathbf{x}$. It is easy to verify that the identity transform satisfies requirements (a) and (b).

Another transform that is important, is translation.

Definition 1.3. *A transform A is a translation if there exists $\mathbf{u} \in \mathbb{R}^n$ so that for all $\mathbf{x} \in \mathbb{R}^n$, $A(\mathbf{x}) = \mathbf{x} + \mathbf{u}$. A translation moves all vectors or points by a fixed distance, in a fixed direction.*

We can now proceed to define an affine transform.

Definition 1.4. *An affine transform is a transform that can be written as $A(\mathbf{x}) = T(L(\mathbf{x}))$ where L is a linear transform and T is a translation. This can also be written as*

$$A = T_{\mathbf{u}} L$$
$$A(\mathbf{x}) = L(\mathbf{x}) + \mathbf{u}.$$

If A is an affine transform then $\mathbf{u}$ and L are uniquely determined by A. From this point on, we discuss points in $\mathbb{R}^3$ because these are the points that we are interested in. Most of the discussion is equally relevant to other dimensions. Any linear transform can be represented by a 3×3 matrix of the form [8]

$$L = \begin{pmatrix} \ell_{11} & \ell_{12} & \ell_{13} \\ \ell_{21} & \ell_{22} & \ell_{23} \\ \ell_{31} & \ell_{32} & \ell_{33} \end{pmatrix}.$$

We now describe a few common transforms and their matrix representations.

1.4.2　Scaling

It is sometimes necessary to change the size of an object. If we assume that the object is centered at the origin, then scaling is given by

$$S = \begin{pmatrix} s & 0 & 0 \\ 0 & s & 0 \\ 0 & 0 & s \end{pmatrix}$$

for points in $\mathbb{R}^3$. To scale a point we apply the matrix S to the point $\mathbf{u} \in \mathbb{R}^3, \mathbf{u} = (u_0 \ u_1 \ u_2)^T$ to get

$$Su = S\begin{pmatrix} u_0 \\ u_1 \\ u_2 \end{pmatrix} = \begin{pmatrix} s & 0 & 0 \\ 0 & s & 0 \\ 0 & 0 & s \end{pmatrix}\begin{pmatrix} u_0 \\ u_1 \\ u_2 \end{pmatrix} = \begin{pmatrix} su_0 \\ su_1 \\ su_2 \end{pmatrix}.$$

It is not necessary to scale evenly in all directions, in this case we obtain the non-uniform scaling matrix

$$S = \begin{pmatrix} s_x & 0 & 0 \\ 0 & s_y & 0 \\ 0 & 0 & s_z \end{pmatrix}.$$

1.4.3 Translation

Translations cannot be written as 3×3 matrices, however. To allow a single representation (matrices) for affine transforms, we can use the homogeneous coordinate system. The homogeneous representation allows us to represent an affine transform as a matrix. Translations can also be applied with homogeneous coordinates. A translation by $\mathbf{u} = (u_0 \ u_1 \ u_2)^T$ is given by the 4×4 matrix

$$T_{\mathbf{u}} = \begin{pmatrix} 1 & 0 & 0 & u_0 \\ 0 & 1 & 0 & u_1 \\ 0 & 0 & 1 & u_2 \\ 0 & 0 & 0 & 1 \end{pmatrix}.$$

It is clear that points will be translated by T, but $T\mathbf{v} = \mathbf{v}$ where $\mathbf{v}$ is a vector of the form $(v_0 \ v_1 \ v_2 \ 0)^T$.

Linear transforms can also be represented as transforms on homogeneous coordinate systems. A linear transform for homogeneous coordinates has the form

$$L = \begin{pmatrix} \ell_{11} & \ell_{12} & \ell_{13} & 0 \\ \ell_{21} & \ell_{22} & \ell_{23} & 0 \\ \ell_{31} & \ell_{32} & \ell_{33} & 0 \\ 0 & 0 & 0 & 1 \end{pmatrix}.$$

Affine transforms can be represented as a combination of a linear transform and a translation. Any affine transform can thus be represented by the matrix product $A = TL$ in the homogeneous coordinate system.

1.4.4 Rotation

Rotation in the Cartesian plane in $\mathbb{R}^2$ is easily derived. A typical situation is illustrated in figure 1.1. In this diagram $\mathbf{r} = (r_0 \ r_1)^T$ is rotated anti-

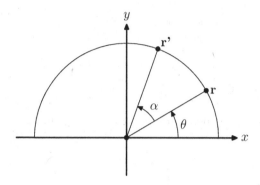

Figure 1.1: Rotation in the two-dimensional Cartesian plane.

clockwise by an angle of α to obtain $\mathbf{r}' = (r_0' \ r_1')^T$. It is clear that $r_0 = r\cos\theta$ and $r_1 = r\sin\theta$. We also have

$$
\begin{aligned}
r_0' &= r\cos(\theta + \alpha) \\
&= r\cos\theta\cos\alpha - r\sin\theta\sin\alpha \\
&= r_0\cos\alpha - r_1\sin\alpha.
\end{aligned}
$$

Likewise we can compute r_1' by

$$
\begin{aligned}
r_1' &= r\sin(\theta + \alpha) \\
&= r\cos\theta\sin\alpha + r\sin\theta\cos\alpha \\
&= r_0\sin\alpha + r_1\cos\alpha.
\end{aligned}
$$

The transform can be written as the orthogonal matrix

$$
R_{z,\alpha} = \begin{pmatrix} \cos\alpha & -\sin\alpha \\ \sin\alpha & \cos\alpha \end{pmatrix}
$$

so that

$$
\begin{pmatrix} r_0' \\ r_1' \end{pmatrix} = R_{z,\alpha} \begin{pmatrix} r_0 \\ r_1 \end{pmatrix}.
$$

Note that

$$
R_{z,-\alpha} = \begin{pmatrix} \cos\alpha & \sin\alpha \\ -\sin\alpha & \cos\alpha \end{pmatrix}.
$$

The Euler Transform

The previous section rotates in the Cartesian plane, which is essentially rotation around the z-axis. The same derivation can be applied to rotate around the x- or y-axes. The rotation matrices are given by

$$R_{x,\alpha} = \begin{pmatrix} 1 & 0 & 0 \\ 0 & \cos\alpha & -\sin\alpha \\ 0 & \sin\alpha & \cos\alpha \end{pmatrix}$$

and

$$R_{y,\alpha} = \begin{pmatrix} \cos\alpha & 0 & \sin\alpha \\ 0 & 1 & 0 \\ -\sin\alpha & 0 & \cos\alpha \end{pmatrix}.$$

The *Euler transform* is defined as $E(\alpha, \beta, \gamma) := R_{z,\gamma} R_{x,\beta} R_{y,\alpha}$. The angles α, β and γ define yaw, pitch and roll angles. The Euler transform is often used to represent the orientation of an object. However, the Euler transform suffers from *gimbal lock*. That is, a degree of freedom can be lost in some cases. Instead of using the Euler transform, we introduce a general rotation matrix and use concatenated transforms to specify rotations.

General Rotation

To rotate a vector $\mathbf{v}$ by an angle θ around an arbitrary axis specified by the unit vector $\mathbf{u} = (u_0 \ u_1 \ u_2)^T$ (i.e. $\|\mathbf{u}\| = 1$) we consider the transform on the parallel and perpendicular components of the vector. Let $\mathbf{v} = \mathbf{v}_1 + \mathbf{v}_2$, where $\mathbf{v}_1$ is parallel to $\mathbf{u}$ and $\mathbf{v}_2$ is perpendicular to $\mathbf{u}$. We have

$$\mathbf{v}_1 = \mathbf{u}(\mathbf{u}^T\mathbf{v}) = (\mathbf{u}\mathbf{u}^T)\mathbf{v}.$$

We can thus define the 3×3 projection matrix

$$\mathbf{P_u} := \mathbf{u}\mathbf{u}^T = \begin{pmatrix} u_0 \\ u_1 \\ u_2 \end{pmatrix} \begin{pmatrix} u_0 & u_1 & u_2 \end{pmatrix} = \begin{pmatrix} u_0^2 & u_0 u_1 & u_0 u_2 \\ u_0 u_1 & u_1^2 & u_1 u_2 \\ u_0 u_2 & u_1 u_2 & u_2^2 \end{pmatrix}$$

and thus we have $\mathbf{v}_1 = \mathbf{P_u}\mathbf{v}$ and $\mathbf{v}_2 = (I_3 - \mathbf{P_u})\mathbf{v}$, where I_3 is the 3×3 identity matrix. Now $\mathbf{v}_1$ is unaffected by rotation around $\mathbf{u}$ so $R_{\theta,\mathbf{u}}\mathbf{v}_1 = \mathbf{v}_1$. To rotate $\mathbf{v}_2$ we create a vector $\mathbf{v}_3$ perpendicular to $\mathbf{v}_1$ and $\mathbf{u}$, namely

$$\mathbf{v}_3 = \mathbf{u} \times \mathbf{v}_2 = \mathbf{u} \times \mathbf{v}.$$

The vectors $\mathbf{v}_1$, $\mathbf{v}_3$ and $\mathbf{u}$ form an orthogonal basis in $\mathbb{R}^3$ which can be used to rotate $\mathbf{v}_2$. Since $\|\mathbf{v}_2\| = \|\mathbf{v}_3\|$ we have

$$R_{\theta,\mathbf{u}}\mathbf{v}_2 = (\cos\theta)\mathbf{v}_2 + (\sin\theta)\mathbf{v}_3.$$

This is a straightforward 2D rotation using the axis system we have built with $\mathbf{v}_2$ and $\mathbf{v}_3$ as axes. We can now apply the rotation to $\mathbf{v}$ by determining the effect on $\mathbf{v}_1$ and $\mathbf{v}_2$ to determine the form of the rotation matrix

$$\begin{aligned}
R_{\theta,\mathbf{u}}\mathbf{v} &= R_{\theta,\mathbf{u}}\mathbf{v}_1 + R_{\theta,\mathbf{u}}\mathbf{v}_2 \\
&= \mathbf{v}_1 + (\cos\theta)\mathbf{v}_2 + (\sin\theta)\mathbf{v}_3 \\
&= \mathbf{P}_{\mathbf{u}}\mathbf{v} + (\cos\theta)(I_3 - \mathbf{P}_{\mathbf{u}})\mathbf{v} + (\sin\theta)(\mathbf{u}\times\mathbf{v}).
\end{aligned}$$

Considering the skew-symmetric matrix

$$M_{\mathbf{u}\times} = \begin{pmatrix} 0 & -u_3 & u_2 \\ u_3 & 0 & -u_1 \\ -u_2 & u_1 & 0 \end{pmatrix}$$

we have

$$\begin{aligned}
R_{\theta,\mathbf{u}}\mathbf{v} &= [\mathbf{P}_{\mathbf{u}} + (\cos\theta)(I_3 - \mathbf{P}_{\mathbf{u}}) + (\sin\theta)M_{\mathbf{u}\times}]\mathbf{v} \\
&= [(1-\cos\theta)\mathbf{P}_{\mathbf{u}} + (\cos\theta)I_3 + (\sin\theta)M_{\mathbf{u}\times}]\mathbf{v}
\end{aligned}$$

which after simplification and conversion to a homogeneous matrix yields the rotation matrix of Goldman [43]

$$R_{\theta,\mathbf{u}} := \begin{pmatrix} (1-c)u_0^2 + c & (1-c)u_0u_1 - su_2 & (1-c)u_0u_2 + su_1 & 0 \\ (1-c)u_0u_1 + su_2 & (1-c)u_1^2 + c & (1-c)u_1u_2 - su_0 & 0 \\ (1-c)u_0u_2 - su_1 & (1-c)u_1u_2 + su_0 & (1-c)u_2^2 + c & 0 \\ 0 & 0 & 0 & 1 \end{pmatrix}$$

with $c := \cos\theta$ and $s := \sin\theta$.

1.4.5 Concatenation of Transforms

It would be very convenient if we could apply a series of transforms in succession. For example, rotation transforms always rotate around the origin. To rotate an object around an axis designated by the starting point $\mathbf{p}_1$ and end point $\mathbf{p}_2$,

- Translate the object to the origin, that is apply the transform $T_{-\mathbf{p}_1}$.

- Rotate the object around the axis $\mathbf{u} = \mathbf{p}_2 - \mathbf{p}_1$.

- Finally, translate the object back to its original position using $T_{\mathbf{p}_1}$.

Since these transforms can all be represented by 4×4 matrices on the homogeneous coordinate system the entire transform is simply

$$M = T_{\mathbf{p}_1} R_{\mathbf{u},\theta} T_{-\mathbf{p}_1}.$$

To apply many transforms at the individual stages of an animation requires only matrix multiplication to keep one 4×4 matrix up to date.

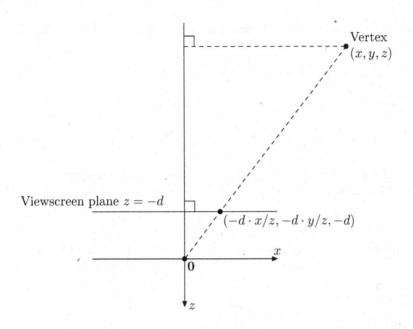

Viewscreen plane $z = -d$

Figure 1.2: Projection onto a plane.

1.4.6 Projection

It is necessary to project points in $\mathbb{R}^3$ onto points in $\mathbb{R}^2$ to render points on a computer screen. If we consider the diagram in figure 1.2 we see that the transformed coordinate can be calculated using similar triangles to get

$$x' = -\frac{d \cdot x}{z}$$

$$y' = -\frac{d \cdot y}{z} \, .$$

What remains is the decision regarding the z-component. Since we are looking down the negative z-axis, the notion of distance is not preserved by $z' = z$. Also, we would like lines to map to lines when applying the perspective transform. This is useful for hardware to be able to linearly interpolate the calculated depth values. We use the following pseudo-distance function pd [45] which has the required properties

$$pd(z) := A + B/z$$

where A and B has to be determined. We can define a view volume using the values l, r, t, b, n and f. These values define the left, right, top, bottom, near and far planes of a view frustum. Our target is to produce the canonical view volume (a unit cube), so

$$pd(-n) = A - B/n = 1, \qquad pd(-f) = A - B/f = -1.$$

Solving these two linear equations for A and B yields

$$A = \frac{-(f+n)}{f-n}, \qquad B = \frac{-2fn}{f-n}.$$

Using the homogeneous coordinate representation we can multiply by $-z$ without affecting the point which is represented. Thus we obtain

$$(x \ y \ z \ 1)^T \mapsto (d \cdot x \ d \cdot y \ - A \cdot z - B \ - z)^T.$$

The perspective division will yield the desired coordinates. Using the fact that $(x \ y \ z \ w)^T$ is the same point as $(x/w \ y/w \ z/w \ 1)^T$ we have

$$(x/w \ y/w \ z/w \ 1)^T \mapsto (d \cdot x/w \ d \cdot y/w \ - A \cdot (z/w) - B \ - z/w)^T.$$

Multiplying by w gives

$$(x \ y \ z \ w)^T \mapsto (d \cdot x \ d \cdot y \ - (A \cdot z + B \cdot w) \ - z)^T.$$

The transform can be represented by the 4×4 matrix

$$P = \begin{pmatrix} d & 0 & 0 & 0 \\ 0 & d & 0 & 0 \\ 0 & 0 & -A & -B \\ 0 & 0 & -1 & 0 \end{pmatrix}.$$

Projections are also useful for projecting the shadow of an object onto a plane. First the scene must be transformed so that the plane onto which the shadow is cast is parallel to the xy-plane and at a distance d from the origin. The above projection matrix can then be applied to create a shadow of the object casting shadow. Finally, the resulting shadow polygon is transformed back into world space. Using the values from the view frustum (figure 1.3) to scale and translate the points into the canonical view volume, we obtain the *perspective projection matrix*

$$P = \begin{pmatrix} \frac{2n}{r-l} & 0 & 0 & \frac{r+l}{r-l} \\ 0 & \frac{2n}{t-b} & 0 & \frac{t+b}{t-b} \\ 0 & 0 & \frac{-(f+n)}{f-n} & \frac{-2fn}{f-n} \\ 0 & 0 & -1 & 0 \end{pmatrix}.$$

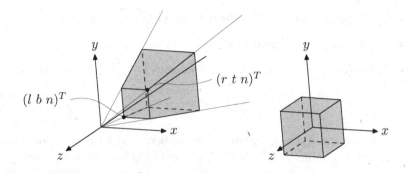

Figure 1.3: The view frustum and canonical view volume.

1.5 Quaternions

Quaternions have proven to be useful for representing rotations of objects [119]. Quaternions are an extension to the complex number system. In the complex number system, each number has the form $a + bi$ where a, $b \in \mathbb{R}$ and $i^2 = -1$. The coefficient a is known as the real coefficient, and b is known as the imaginary coefficient. In the quaternion number system, numbers have the form $a + bi + cj + dk$, where a, b, c, $d \in \mathbb{R}$. In this case there are three imaginary coefficients, namely b, c and d.

The imaginary portion of the quaternion has the following properties

$$i^2 = j^2 = k^2 = -1 \text{ and } ij = k,\ jk = i,\ ki = j,\ ji = -k,\ kj = -i,\ ik = -j.$$

To simplify notation, we often write $a + bi + cj + dk$ as $(u, \mathbf{v})$ with $u = a$ and $\mathbf{v} = bi + cj + dk$. Quaternions have the following properties

- Two quaternions are equal if their components are equal.

- $\alpha(u, \mathbf{v}) = (\alpha u, \alpha \mathbf{v})$.

- Multiplication is given by

$$q_1 q_2 = (u_1 u_2 - \mathbf{v}_1 \cdot \mathbf{v}_2, u_1 \mathbf{v}_2 + u_2 \mathbf{v}_1 + \mathbf{v}_1 \times \mathbf{v}_2).$$

  This formula is easily verified by applying the identities defining quaternions.

- The norm of a quaternion q is defined as $\|q\| := \sqrt{a^2 + b^2 + c^2 + d^2}$.

- A quaternion q is a unit quaternion if $\|q\| = 1$.

- Quaternions have the distributivity property $q(r+s) = qr + qs$.

- The conjugate is defined as $q^* := (u, -\mathbf{v})$.

- The inverse q^{-1} of a quaternion q satisfies $q^{-1}q = 1$. It follows that

$$q^{-1} = \frac{q^*}{\|q\|^2}.$$

Quaternions are useful in computer graphics because unit quaternions can be used to rotate points or vectors. A conventional homogeneous point or vector is represented in the usual way, where the real component is the homogeneous coordinate, and the vector describing the point (or vector) are used as imaginary coefficients. To rotate around the axis (unit vector) $\mathbf{u}$ by an angle of 2θ, construct the unit quaternion $q = (\cos\theta, \sin\theta\mathbf{u})$. The homogeneous coordinate p (represented as a quaternion) is rotated by calculating $p' = qpq^{-1} = qpq^*$. Compound rotations can also be applied. The useful property $(q_1q_2)^* = q_2^*q_1^*$ allows a single quaternion to be used to represent rotations by multiple quaternions.

Quaternions offer an alternative solution to representing rotations. One of the advantages of quaternions is relative simplicity of the calculation. Matrices may also be multiplied in the same way, however. In addition, matrices can represent translation (which quaternions cannot do). So what are the advantages of quaternions? Possible advantages are

- **Simple representation** - Quaternions only require four real values to describe a rotation. A rotation matrix requires a minimum of nine values to be stored.

- **Numerical stability** - A unit quaternion is a rotation. If the quaternion is not a unit quaternion, it can be normalized. We thus have a technique to ensure that compound rotations remain rotations.

- **Spherical linear interpolation** - We can easily interpolate between quaternions, providing a smooth transition from one orientation to another. Conventional linear interpolation should not be used, however. Rather spherical linear interpolation should be used. Spherical linear interpolation is given by [138]

$$\text{slerp}(q, p, \alpha) = \frac{\sin((1-\alpha)\psi)}{\sin\psi}q + \frac{\sin(\alpha\psi)}{\sin\psi}p$$

where ψ is the angle between p and q. We have

$$\cos\psi = p \cdot q = p_aq_a + p_bq_b + p_cq_c + p_dq_d$$

where

$$p = p_a + p_b i + p_c j + p_d k \text{ and } q = q_a + q_b i + q_c j + q_d k.$$

In terms of animation, it is easy to construct a quaternion to indicate the direction in which a camera should be looking. Once the destination direction has been determined, we can use spherical linear interpolation to smoothly transition from the one view to another.

It is also possible to obtain an equivalent matrix representation with *Pauli matrices*. It is not necessary to exclusively use one technique or the other. The 4×4 matrix that performs the identical transform to a quaternion $q = q_w + q_x i + q_y j + q_z k$ is

$$R_q = \begin{pmatrix} 1 - 2(q_y^2 + q_z^2) & 2(q_x q_y - q_w q_z) & 2(q_x q_z + q_w q_y) & 0 \\ 2(q_x q_y + q_w q_z) & 1 - 2(q_x^2 + q_z^2) & 2(q_y q_z - q_w q_y) & 0 \\ 2(q_x q_z - q_w q_y) & 2(q_y q_z + q_w q_x) & 1 - 2(q_x^2 + q_y^2) & 0 \\ 0 & 0 & 0 & 1 \end{pmatrix}.$$

1.6 C# Implementation

We have a *vector class* to represent points and vectors in the homogeneous coordinate system. We overload the $+$, $-$ and $*$ operators to allow us to use these vectors within the C# program. We have chosen $*$ to represent the dot product, since the "." already has an associated meaning in C#. We overload the ^ operator to implement the vector product. Further calculations such as reflection and transmission, which will be used for raytracing have also been included.

```
// Vector.cs
using System;

public class Vector {
    public double x,y,z,w;

    public Vector() { x=0.0; y=0.0; z=0.0; w=1.0; }

    public Vector(Vector v) { x=v.x; y=v.y; z=v.z; w=v.w; }

    public Vector(double x,double y,double z) {
        this.x=x;this.y=y;this.z=z;this.w=1.0; }

    public Vector(double x,double y,double z,double w) {
        this.x=x;this.y=y;this.z=z;this.w=w; }
```

```
public object Clone() {
    Object o=new Vector(x,y,z,w);
    return o; }

public override bool Equals(object b) {
    if((((Vector)b).x==x)&&(((Vector)b).y==y)&&
    (((Vector)b).z==z)&&(((Vector)b).w==w)) return true;
    else return false; }

public static Vector operator+(Vector a,Vector v) {
    return new Vector(a.x+v.x,a.y+v.y,a.z+v.z,a.w); }

public static Vector operator-(Vector a,Vector v) {
    return new Vector(a.x-v.x,a.y-v.y,a.z-v.z,a.w); }

//dot product
public static double operator*(Vector a,Vector v) {
    return a.x*v.x+a.y*v.y+a.z*v.z; }

public static Vector operator*(double c,Vector v) {
    return new Vector(c*v.x,c*v.y,c*v.z,v.w); }

//cross product
public static Vector operator^(Vector a,Vector v) {
    Vector r=new Vector();
    r.x=a.y*v.z-a.z*v.y;
    r.y=a.z*v.x-a.x*v.z;
    r.z=a.x*v.y-a.y*v.x;
    r.w=a.w;
    return r; }

//componentwise multiply
public static Vector operator%(Vector a,Vector v) {
    Vector r=new Vector();
    r.x=a.x*v.x; r.y=a.y*v.y; r.z=a.z*v.z; r.w=a.w*v.w;
    return r; }

public static Vector operator*(Vector a,double c) {
    return new Vector(c*a.x,c*a.y,c*a.z,a.w); }

public static Vector operator/(Vector a,double c) {
    return new Vector(a.x/c,a.y/c,a.z/c,a.w); }

//unary minus
public static Vector operator-(Vector v) {
    return new Vector(-v.x,-v.y,-v.z,v.w); }

//unary plus
public static Vector operator+(Vector v) { return v; }

public double norm() { return Math.Sqrt(x*x+y*y+z*z); }
```

```
    public void normalize() {
        double s=norm();
        if(s!=0.0) { x/=s;y/=s;z/=s; }}

    public static Vector reflect(Vector v,Vector n) {
        Vector r=2.0*(v*n)*n-v;
        return r; }

    public static Vector transmit(Vector i,Vector n,
        double n1,double n2) {
        Vector t;
        double w,r,k;
        if(n*i>0.0) { n=-n; r=n1; n1=n2; n2=r; }
        r=n1/n2; w=-i*n*r; k=1.0+(w-r)*(w+r);
        //check for total internal reflection
        if(k<0.0) return reflect(-i,n);
        k=Math.Sqrt(k); t=r*i+(w-k)*n; t.normalize();
        return t;}

    public override string ToString() {
        return String.Format("({0},{1},{2},{3})",x,y,z,w);}
};
```

The following *matrix class* is used for matrix transforms as applied to homogeneous vectors. We overload the $+$, $-$ and $*$ operators. The $*$ operator is used for matrix multiplication. In addition, the transforms presented in this chapter are also implemented. The matrix can be applied directly to a vector to transform the vector.

```
//Matrix.cs
using System;

public class Matrix {
    private double[,] mat;

    //constructor
    public Matrix() {
        //create identity matrix
        int row, col;
        mat=new double[4,4];
        for(row=0;row<4;row++)
            for(col=0;col<4;col++)
                if(row==col) mat[row,col]=1.0;
                else mat[row,col]=0.0;
    }

    public object Clone() {
        Matrix m=new Matrix();
```

```
        int row,col;
        for(row=0;row<4;row++)
            for(col=0;col<4;col++) m[row,col]=mat[row,col];
        return (object)m; }

    public override bool Equals(object b) {
        Matrix m=(Matrix)b;
        int row,col;
        for(row=0;row<4;row++)
            for(col=0;col<4;col++)
                if(m[row,col]!=mat[row,col]) return false;
        return true; }

    //index operator, to retrieve and set values in the matrix
    public double this[int row,int col] {
        get { return mat[row,col]; }
        set { mat[row,col]=value;} }

    //arithmetic operators
    public static Matrix operator+(Matrix a,Matrix b) {
        int row,col;
        Matrix r=new Matrix();
        for(row=0;row<4;row++)
            for(col=0;col<4;col++)
                r[row,col]=a[row,col]+b[row,col];
        return r; }

    public static Matrix operator-(Matrix a,Matrix b) {
        int row, col;
        Matrix r=new Matrix();
        for(row=0;row<4;row++)
            for(col=0;col<4;col++)
                r[row,col]=a[row,col]-b[row,col];
        return r; }

    public static Matrix operator*(Matrix a,Matrix b) {
        int row, col;
        Matrix r=new Matrix();
        for(row=0;row<4;row++)
            for(col=0;col<4;col++) {
                r[row,col]=0;
                for(int i=0;i<4;i++) r[row,col]+=a[row,i]*b[i,col];
            }
        return r; }

    public static Vector operator*(Matrix a,Vector v) {
        Vector r=new Vector();
        r.x=v.x*a[0,0]+v.y*a[0,1]+v.z*a[0,2]+v.w*a[0,3];
        r.y=v.x*a[1,0]+v.y*a[1,1]+v.z*a[1,2]+v.w*a[1,3];
        r.z=v.x*a[2,0]+v.y*a[2,1]+v.z*a[2,2]+v.w*a[2,3];
        r.w=v.x*a[3,0]+v.y*a[3,1]+v.z*a[3,2]+v.w*a[3,3];
```

```csharp
        return r; }

public Matrix Transpose() {
    int row, col;
    Matrix m=new Matrix();
    for(row=0;row<4;row++)
        for(col=0;col<4;col++) m[row,col]=mat[col,row];
    return m; }

public static Matrix Translate(Vector t) {
    Matrix m=new Matrix();
    m[0,3]=t.x; m[1,3]=t.y; m[2,3]=t.z;
    return m; }

public static Matrix Scale(double s) {
    Matrix m=new Matrix();
    m[0,0]=s; m[1,1]=s; m[2,2]=s;
    return m; }

public static Matrix Scale(double sx,double sy,double sz) {
    Matrix m=new Matrix();
    m[0,0]=sx; m[1,1]=sy; m[2,2]=sz;
    return m; }

//general rotation around the vector axis
public static Matrix Rotate(Vector axis,double angle) {
    Matrix r=new Matrix();
    double c=Math.Cos(angle);
    double s=Math.Sin(angle);
    axis.normalize();
    r[0,0]=(1.0-c)*axis.x*axis.x+c;
    r[1,0]=(1.0-c)*axis.x*axis.y+s*axis.z;
    r[2,0]=(1.0-c)*axis.x*axis.z-s*axis.y; r[3,0]=0.0;
    r[0,1]=(1.0-c)*axis.x*axis.y-s*axis.z;
    r[1,1]=(1.0-c)*axis.y*axis.y+c;
    r[2,1]=(1.0-c)*axis.y*axis.z+s*axis.x; r[3,1]=0.0;
    r[0,2]=(1.0-c)*axis.x*axis.z+s*axis.y;
    r[1,2]=(1.0-c)*axis.y*axis.z-s*axis.x;
    r[2,2]=(1.0-c)*axis.z*axis.z+c;
    r[3,2]=0.0; r[0,3]=0.0; r[1,3]=0.0;
    r[2,3]=0.0; r[3,3]=1.0;
    return r; }

public static Matrix Projection(double n,double f,
        double t,double b,double l,double r) {
    Matrix m=new Matrix();
    m[0,0]=2.0*n/(r-l); m[1,0]=0.0; m[2,0]=0.0; m[3,0]=0.0;
    m[0,1]=0.0; m[1,1]=2.0*n/(t-b); m[2,1]=0.0; m[3,1]=0.0;
    m[0,2]=0.0; m[1,2]=2.0*n/(t-b); m[2,2]=-(f+n)/(f-n); m[3,2]=-1.0;
    m[0,3]=(r+l)/(r-l); m[1,3]=(t+b)/(t-b);
    m[2,3]=-2.0*f*n/(f-n); m[3,3]=0.0;
```

```
        return m; }

    //method to display the matrix
    public override string ToString() {
        String s="\n";
        for(int i=0;i<4;i++)
            s+=String.Format("/{0},{1},{2},{3}/\n",
                mat[i,0],mat[i,1],mat[i,2],mat[i,3]);
        return s; }
};
```

The *quaternion class* describes rotations in terms quaternions, but also allows the equivalent matrix transform to be produced from the quaternion. Once again, we have overloaded the necessary operators to allow quaternions to be used seamlessly within C#.

```
//Quaternion.cs
using System;

public class Quaternion {
    //w - real, x, y, z - imaginary
    public double x, y, z, w;

    public const double eps=1e-7;
    public const double pi=Math.PI;
    public const double halfpi=(pi/2.0);

    public Quaternion() { x=0.0; y=0.0; z=0.0; w=1.0; }

    public Quaternion(Vector axis,double theta) {
        Vector a=axis;
        double s,c;
        a.normalize();
        s=Math.Sin(pi*theta/180.0/2.0);
        c=Math.Cos(pi*theta/180.0/2.0);
        x=a.x*s;y=a.y*s;z=a.z*s;w=c; }

    public Quaternion(double x,double y,double z,double w) {
        this.x=x; this.y=y; this.z=z; this.w=w; }

    public object Clone() {
        object o=new Quaternion(x,y,z,w);
        return o; }

    public override bool Equals(object b) {
        if((((Quaternion)b).x==x)&&(((Quaternion)b).y==y)&&
           (((Quaternion)b).z==z)&&(((Quaternion)b).w==w))
            return true;
        else return false; }
```

```
public static Quaternion operator+(Quaternion a,Quaternion v)
{ return new Quaternion(a.x+v.x,a.y+v.y,a.z+v.z,a.w+v.w); }

public static Quaternion operator-(Quaternion a,Quaternion v)
{ return new Quaternion(a.x-v.x,a.y-v.y,a.z-v.z,a.w-v.w); }

public static Quaternion operator*(Quaternion a,Quaternion r){
  Quaternion m=new Quaternion();
  m.x=a.y*r.z-a.z*r.y+r.w*a.x+a.w*r.x;
  m.y=a.z*r.x-a.x*r.z+r.w*a.y+a.w*r.y;
  m.z=a.x*r.y-a.y*r.x+r.w*a.z+a.w*r.z;
  m.w=a.w*r.w-a.x*r.x-a.y*r.y-a.z*r.z;
  return m;  }

public static Quaternion operator+(Quaternion a,double c) {
  return new Quaternion(a.x,a.y,a.z,a.w+c);  }

public static Quaternion operator-(Quaternion a,double c) {
  return new Quaternion(a.x,a.y,a.z,a.w-c);  }

public static Quaternion operator*(Quaternion a,double c) {
  return new Quaternion(c*a.x,c*a.y,c*a.z,c*a.w);  }

public static Quaternion operator*(double c,Quaternion v) {
  return new Quaternion(v.x*c,v.y*c,v.z*c,v.w*c);  }

public static Quaternion operator+(double x,Quaternion v) {
  return new Quaternion(v.x,v.y,v.z,v.w+x);  }

public static Quaternion operator-(double x,Quaternion v) {
  return new Quaternion(-v.x,-v.y,-v.z,x-v.w);  }

public static Quaternion operator/(Quaternion a,double c) {
  return new Quaternion(a.x/c,a.y/c,a.z/c,a.w/c);  }

//unary minus
public static Quaternion operator-(Quaternion a) {
  return new Quaternion(-a.x,-a.y,-a.z,-a.w);  }

//unary plus
public static Quaternion operator+(Quaternion a) {
  return a; }

public Matrix toMatrix() {
  double s,xs,ys,zs,wx,wy,wz,xx,xy,xz,yy,yz,zz;
  double div=(x*x+y*y+z*z+w*w);
  Matrix mat=new Matrix();
  if(div!=0.0){ s=2.0/(div); } else s=0.0;
  xs=x*s; ys=y*s; zs=z*s; wx=w*xs; wy=w*ys; wz=w*zs;
  xx=x*xs; xy=x*ys; xz=x*zs; yy=y*ys; yz=y*zs; zz=z*zs;
  mat[0,0]=1.0-(yy+zz); mat[1,0]=xy+wz; mat[2,0]=xz-wy;
```

```
    mat[0,1]=xy-wz; mat[1,1]=1.0-(xx+zz); mat[2,1]=yz+wx;
    mat[0,2]=xz+wy; mat[1,2]=yz-wx; mat[2,2]=1.0-(xx+yy);
    mat[0,3]=0.0; mat[1,3]=0.0; mat[2,3]=0.0; mat[3,3]=1.0;
    mat[3,0]=0.0; mat[3,1]=0.0; mat[3,2]=0.0;
    return mat;  }

public Quaternion conj() {
  return new Quaternion(-x,-y,-z,w);  }

public static Quaternion slerp(Quaternion p,Quaternion q,double t) {
  double omega,cosom,sinom,sclp,sclq;
  Quaternion qt=new Quaternion();
  if(p.dist(q)>p.dist(-q))  q=-q;
  cosom=p.x*q.x+p.y*q.y+p.z*q.z+p.w*q.w;
  if((1.0+cosom)>eps) {
    if((1.0-cosom)>eps) {
      omega=Math.Acos(cosom); sinom=Math.Sin(omega);
      sclp=Math.Sin((1.0-t)*omega)/sinom;
      sclq=Math.Sin(t*omega)/sinom;
    } else {sclp=1.0-t; sclq=t;  }
    qt.x=sclp*p.x+sclq*q.x; qt.y=sclp*p.y+sclq*q.y;
    qt.z=sclp*p.z+sclq*q.z; qt.w=sclp*p.w+sclq*q.w;
  } else {
    qt.x=-p.y; qt.y=p.x; qt.z=-p.w; qt.w=p.z;
    sclp=Math.Sin((1.0-t)*halfpi);
    sclq=Math.Sin(t*halfpi);
    qt.x=sclp*p.x+sclq*qt.x; qt.y=sclp*p.y+sclq*qt.y;
    qt.z=sclp*p.z+sclq*qt.z;  }
  return qt;  }

public double dist(Quaternion q) { return (this-q).norm();  }

public double norm() { return Math.Sqrt(x*x+y*y+z*z+w*w);  }
public void normalize() { double s=norm(); x/=s; y/=s; z/=s; w/=s;  }

public override string ToString() {
  return String.Format("({0},{1},{2},{3})",x,y,z,w);  }
};
```

Chapter 2

Lighting

In a real environment, the appearance of an object is not determined solely by the attributes of the object. Lights in the environment create shadows and give clues to the shape of the surface. It is not always feasible to compute the lighting accurately at every point on the object, in these situations shading algorithms can be used to achieve the speed or accuracy required.

2.1 Shading

Shading refers to the process whereby the interior color of the polygon is inferred (on a per pixel level) using the properties of the vertices. This allows us to treat polygonal objects as if they were curved (if necessary) and adds to the perceived shape of the object. There are two main shading techniques, namely

- *Gouraud Shading* — The colors computed at the vertices of the polygon are interpolated, perhaps using the Bresenham algorithm (see chapter 3). The color of a pixel is thus a linear combination of the colors at the vertices. For a line with colors c_1 and c_2 at the end points, this would be $(1-\alpha)c_1 + \alpha c_2$, where the parameter $0 \leq \alpha \leq 1$ is computed from the current screen coordinates.

- *Phong Shading* — The normal vectors at the vertices of the polygon are interpolated. The interpolated normal vector is then used in the lighting model (per pixel lighting). It is desirable to have a unit normal vector, so interpolation of the normal vector would be of the form

$$\mathbf{n}_\alpha = \frac{(1-\alpha)\mathbf{n}_0 + \alpha\mathbf{n}_1}{\|(1-\alpha)\mathbf{n}_0 + \alpha\mathbf{n}_1\|}.$$

Since Phong shading applies the lighting model per pixel, whereas Gouraud shading applies the lighting model per vertex, the results for Phong shading are usually superior. Gouraud shading is much faster and usually implemented in hardware. Two polygons, one very large, and another quite small can map to precisely the same location on screen due to viewing transforms. In this case, a slanted large polygon would be expected to vary in color differently to a smaller slanted polygon mapped to the same coordinates. These algorithms do not take this into account. A later section on interpolation will address this issue. One way to partially address this issue with Phong shading, is to interpolate the x and y components of the normal, and calculate the z-component so that the resulting vector is normalized.

Complex, curved objects can be approximated by polygons. If the normals at the vertices are adjusted so that they match the normals of the curved surface, Phong or Gouraud shading will enhance the appearance that the object is indeed curved.

2.1.1   Affine Transforms and Normal Vectors

Using the homogeneous coordinate system, normal vectors can be represented as $(n_x \ n_y \ n_z \ 0)^T$. Since the last component is zero, a 4×4 matrix can be used to transform both points and normals. For rigid body transforms, no translation will be applied to the normals.

Linear transforms do not necessarily maintain angles between lines however (but rigid body transforms do), so after the transform the normal vector may not be perpendicular to the surface. It is possible to determine the transform that will leave the normal perpendicular to the surface. The following theorem provides the transform to be applied to surface normals so that they will remain perpendicular to the surface.

Theorem 2.1. *Let B be a linear transformation represented by the real invertible 3×3 matrix M. We have $(M^T)^{-1} = (M^{-1})^T$. Let $N := (M^{-1})^T$. Let P be a plane and the vector $\mathbf{n}$ be orthogonal to P. Then the vector $N\mathbf{n}$ is orthogonal to the image $B(P)$ of the plane P under the map B.*

Proof. Suppose $\mathbf{x}$ is a vector lying in the plane P. Then

$$\mathbf{n} \cdot \mathbf{x} = \mathbf{n}^T \mathbf{x} = 0.$$

We need to show that

$$(N\mathbf{n}) \cdot (M\mathbf{x}) = 0.$$

This follows from

$$(N\mathbf{n}) \cdot (M\mathbf{x}) = ((M^{-1})^T \mathbf{n}) \cdot (M\mathbf{x})$$
$$= ((M^{-1})^T \mathbf{n})^T (M\mathbf{x})$$
$$= (\mathbf{n}^T M^{-1})(M\mathbf{x})$$
$$= \mathbf{n}^T (M^{-1} M)\mathbf{x}$$
$$= \mathbf{n}^T \mathbf{x}$$
$$= 0$$

as required. We use the fact that matrix multiplication is associative and $\mathbf{x}^T \mathbf{y} \equiv \mathbf{x} \cdot \mathbf{y}$.

2.2 Local Lighting Models

For the moment we restrict our attention to local lighting models. That is, we do not consider the overall effect of the environment, but rather consider the direct application of some light to the surface of an object. These algorithms are thus known as local lighting models due to the fact that no inter-reflection and other global lighting effects are taken into account. In other words, only the lighting contribution made by identified light sources are used in the calculations. Direct reflections from a light source to the eye is calculated but not light reflecting off other surfaces. Global lighting models address these problems.

2.3 The Phong Lighting Model

We ignore color for a large part of the following discussions. The color of light is determined by the frequency composition of the light. It is not necessary to consider all frequencies, rather certain important frequencies are selected and the lighting model is applied to these frequencies. Superposition is then used to combine the results. This means that we can use a color model such as RGB by individually calculating the color components (Red, Green, and Blue frequencies) for each surface or light and then simply use the resulting combined color for the color of the pixel. Both the Phong lighting model and Cook-Torrance lighting model are local lighting models. These models attempt to model lighting in a physically accurate way, but do not use physics based modeling. Only point light sources (emitting light equally in all directions) are dealt with, but we show later how this can be adapted for spot lights and directional lights. The model considers several properties of the light and object material. Each of these is discussed below.

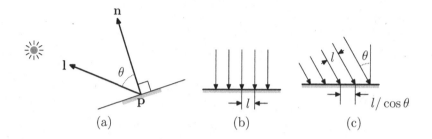

Figure 2.1: Diffuse reflection.

2.3.1 Emissive Properties

The object may not be considered a light source, but may emit light of its own. This means that the object will be visible even if there is no light source present. The intensity of the emitted light will be indicated by I_e.

2.3.2 Ambient Reflection

Ambient light refers to lighting of the object due to indirect lighting. In other words reflections of light from other objects. However, this is an approximation. A general level of ambient light I_a is contributed by each light to the scene. It may also be necessary to specify a general level of ambient light $I_{a,global}$ irrespective of the number of lights in the scene. The fraction of ambient light reflected by the model is indicated by ρ_a. The total reflected ambient light for a single light is given by

$$I_a = \rho_a I_a^{in}.$$

2.3.3 Diffuse Reflection

Diffuse reflection models matt surfaces. It models light that is reflected equally in all directions. The position of the viewer is, therefore, irrelevant. The position of the light source does affect the perceived intensity. Figure 2.1 (a) illustrates the information required to compute diffuse reflection. The intensity with respect to diffuse reflection for a single light is given by

$$I_d := \rho_d I_d^{in} \cos\theta = \rho_d I_d^{in}(\max(\mathbf{l} \cdot \mathbf{n}, 0))$$

where

- I_d^{in} is the diffuse intensity of the light source.

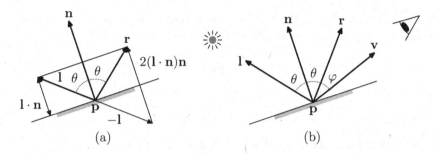

Figure 2.2: Specular reflection and the reflection vector.

- ρ_d is the diffuse reflectivity coefficient of the material, the fraction of light that is reflected in a diffuse fashion. It depends on the wavelength of the incident light.

- **l** and **n** are unit vectors.

- **n** is the normal vector to the surface.

- **l** is in the direction of the light source.

- θ is the angle between the surface normal at the point, and the line from the point to the light source ($0 \leq \theta \leq \frac{\pi}{2}$).

We normally measure light intensity in terms of energy flux per unit area. If we observe what happens in the figure 2.1 (b) and (c), we see that if the light reflects off the surface at an angle, then the density of light rays hitting a unit area decreases. We associate the density of light rays hitting an area with the intensity at that location. In this example we measure the density by looking at the distance between the light rays. This explains the cosine term. This is known as *Lambert's Law* of radiation.

2.3.4 Specular Reflection

The specular reflection component models glossy surfaces, and in particular the specular highlight due to the light reflected from the light source. In this case light is not reflected equally in all directions. The light is reflected most in the vicinity of the reflection vector

$$\mathbf{r} = 2(\mathbf{l} \cdot \mathbf{n})\mathbf{n} - \mathbf{l}.$$

The reflection vector is easily determined from figure 2.2 (a). The position of the viewer influences the perceived intensity. The closer the viewer is to the reflection vector, the brighter the perceived lighting. The specular reflection for a single light is given by (refer to figure 2.2 (b))

$$I_s := \rho_s I_s^{in} (\cos \varphi)^f = \rho_s I_s^{in} (\max(\mathbf{v} \cdot \mathbf{r}, 0))^f$$

where

- I_s^{in} is the specular component of the light source.

- ρ_s is the specular reflectivity coefficient of the material.

- $\mathbf{l}$, $\mathbf{r}$, $\mathbf{v}$ and $\mathbf{n}$ are unit vectors described in figure 2.2 (b).

- f is a factor that determines the size of the specular highlight (or reflectivity). f is determined experimentally.

- $\mathbf{r}$ is the direction of the reflected ray.

- $\mathbf{v}$ is the direction of the viewer.

We can avoid calculating the reflection vector if we note that there is a (approximate) correspondence between the angle between $\mathbf{v}$ and $\mathbf{r}$, and the angle between $\mathbf{n}$ and $\mathbf{h}$, where

$$\mathbf{h} = \frac{\mathbf{l} + \mathbf{v}}{\|\mathbf{l} + \mathbf{v}\|}.$$

The specular contribution is then given by

$$I_s = \rho_s I_s^{in} (\cos \phi)^f = \rho_s I_s^{in} (\max(\mathbf{h} \cdot \mathbf{n}, 0))^f$$

with

$$(\mathbf{v} \cdot \mathbf{r})^f \approx (\mathbf{h} \cdot \mathbf{n})^{4f}.$$

Figure 2.3 shows different coefficients for the Phong model. In the left hand image, the specular reflection coefficient increases from left to right, the diffuse reflection coefficient increases from top to bottom. In the right hand image, the specular reflection coefficient increases from left to right, the specular highlight coefficient f increases from top to bottom.

2.3.5 Multiple Colored Light Sources

We can specify a materials properties in terms of ρ_s and ρ_d to get the right balance between matte and glossy surface. We can also specify how the light from the light source reacts with glossy and specular surfaces by specifying I_s^{in} and I_d^{in}. Although we would not realistically expect light to consist of a diffuse component and a specular component, it may be

Figure 2.3: Phong lighting model.

useful to model lights that emit white light with a blue element. If we consider different frequencies of light, then each frequency coefficient can be represented by a vector. Each component of the vector is the coefficient (response) to that frequency. For example, a blue matte object could be specified by $\rho_d = (0.0\ 0.0\ 0.9)^T$, $\rho_s = (0.0\ 0.0\ 0.1)^T$ and $f = 8$ assuming an RGB color model. Effects of multiple lights are additive so we have

$$\mathbf{I} = \mathbf{I}_e + \rho_a \bullet \mathbf{I}_{a,global}^{in} + \rho_a \bullet \sum_{i=1}^{k} \mathbf{I}_a^{in,i}$$

$$+ \rho_d \bullet \sum_{i=1}^{k} \mathbf{I}_d^{in,i}(\mathbf{l}_i \cdot \mathbf{n}) + \rho_s \bullet \sum_{i=1}^{k} \mathbf{I}_s^{in,i}(\mathbf{r}_i \cdot \mathbf{v})^f$$

where $\bullet$ denotes componentwise multiplication, i.e.

$$(r_1\ g_1\ b_1)^T \bullet (r_2\ g_2\ b_2)^T := (r_1 r_2\ g_1 g_2\ b_1 b_2)^T.$$

Naturally, we only keep the diffuse contribution if $\mathbf{l}_i \cdot \mathbf{n} > 0$, otherwise the light is behind the surface. Likewise, we only keep the specular contribution for each light if $\mathbf{r}_i \cdot \mathbf{v} > 0$ and $\mathbf{l}_i \cdot \mathbf{n} > 0$.

2.3.6 Attenuation

Since light is an electromagnetic wave, we know that the energy flux from a light decreases with distance. This is known as *attenuation*. To model attenuation we multiply the contribution of each light source by

$$d = \frac{1}{a_c + a_l \|\mathbf{l}\| + a_q \|\mathbf{l}\|^2}$$

where

- l is the position of the light source relative to the point being lit.

- a_c is the constant attenuation factor.

- a_l is the linear attenuation factor.

- a_q is the quadratic attenuation factor.

We can then choose attenuation that is suitable for our needs (but not necessarily realistic).

2.4 Lights

All the lighting equations so far have assumed that the light comes from a point source. It is also possible to create directional lights and spot lights with very little effort. A directional light is assumed to be infinitely far away, thus all light rays are assumed to be parallel. It is therefore not necessary to know where the light is located, but simply the direction of the light.

Using homogeneous coordinates we can differentiate between point lights and directional lights. A point light is represented by a point in homogeneous coordinates and is thus affected by translation. A directional light on the other hand, is represented by a vector in homogeneous coordinates. The directional light is thus only affected by linear transforms (such as rotation), and not by translation.

2.4.1 Spot Lights

Spot lights are similar to point lights, except they have a direction on which the light is pointed and an exponential falloff factor which describes how tight the beam is. For each spotlight we can calculate the constant

$$c_{spot} = \max(-\mathbf{l} \cdot \mathbf{l}_{dir}, 0)^{c_{exp}}$$

where

- $\mathbf{l}_{dir}$ is the direction in which the spotlight is pointing.

- c_{exp} is the factor controlling the tightness of the beam.

Each spotlight's contribution is multiplied by c_{spot} to take into account the directional and falloff characteristics of the light.

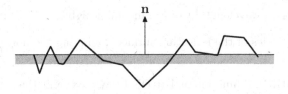

Figure 2.4: Microfacets.

2.5   Transparent Objects

If objects are transparent, then we should use a coefficient of transparency ρ_t and coefficient of reflectivity ρ_r to model the characteristics of the object. Now the color of the surface will be $\rho_r \mathbf{I} + \rho_t \mathbf{T}$, where $\mathbf{T}$ is the intensity of the transmitted light. Since the light arriving at an object must be transmitted, reflected or absorbed a guideline for the choice of ρ_r and ρ_t is $\rho_r + \rho_t = 1$, $0 \leq \rho_r, \rho_t \leq 1$, but this may be adjusted to obtain the desired effects.

2.6   Cook-Torrance Model

The Cook-Torrance lighting model can better represent a wider range of surface materials. It uses a microfacet model for the surface of the object. The object surface is assumed to consist of many facets that are perfect mirrors as illustrated in figure 2.4. These facets are much smaller than the eye can see. If we model the interaction between the light and the facets, we model how the surface appears when lit. This lighting model tends to handle rough, metallic surfaces and changes in reflection due to grazing angles (angles nearly perpendicular to the normal) better than the Phong model.

2.6.1   Bidirectional Reflectivity

We would like to describe how light from a source in the direction of the unit vector $\mathbf{l}$ is reflected in the direction of a unit vector $\mathbf{v}$. We can use a single BRIDF (*Bidirectional reflected intensity distribution* function) to do so.

The parameters to the BRIDF function are

- the incoming direction $\mathbf{l}$.

- the outgoing direction $\mathbf{v}$.

- the color or wavelength λ of the incoming light.

- the properties of the reflecting surface, including the normal and orientation.

We write the BRIDF function as BRIDF(l,v,λ) and omit the surface properties. The BRIDF function returns the ratio of the intensity of the outgoing light in direction $\mathbf{v}$ to the intensity of the incoming light pointed to by l.

BRIDF has the potential to model more surface characteristics, such as *anisotropic surfaces*. Anisotropic surfaces have different reflective characteristics dependent on the direction of the incoming light. This may be caused by parallel grooves on the surface or other artifacts. Examples of anisotropic surfaces include some types of cloth (velvet), CD's, hair, feathers and fur. Although BRIDF has the potential to simulate a wide range of materials, physical attributes such as *subsurface scattering, polarization* and *diffraction* are not taken into account. Note that the Phong lighting model is a simple example of BRIDF.

2.6.2   Cook-Torrance Model

The Cook-Torrance model considers a surface to consist of small flat pieces called facets. The assumption is made that light hitting a microfacet is either reflected or can enter into the surface. The reflection is presumed to be a perfect reflection. Light that enters the surface is presumed to reflect many times internally before exiting the surface, in an unpredictable direction. This is considered to be the diffuse reflection.

The Cook-Torrance model also considers various components of the light.

- Ambient lighting - computed in the same way as the Phong model.

- Diffuse lighting - computed in the same way as the Phong model.

- Specular lighting - This term considers the microfacets of the surface. The intensity is calculated by

$$I_s = \frac{(\mathbf{n} \cdot l)}{(\mathbf{n} \cdot \mathbf{v})} \rho_s \, F(l, \mathbf{v}, \lambda) \, G(l, \mathbf{v}) \, D(l, \mathbf{v}) I_s^{in}$$

where

  - ρ_s is a scalar constant.
  - I_s^{in} is the intensity of the incoming light.

- $(\mathbf{n} \cdot \mathbf{l})$ is used to calculate the intensity of light hitting a unit area of the surface.

- $(\mathbf{n} \cdot \mathbf{v})$ is used to calculate the intensity of light leaving a unit area of the surface.

- $D(\mathbf{l}, \mathbf{v})$ is the microfacet distribution term, or the fraction of microfacets that are oriented correctly for the specular reflection from $\mathbf{l}$ to $\mathbf{v}$.

- $G(\mathbf{l}, \mathbf{v})$ is the geometric term and measures the effect that shadowing and masking have on the outgoing light.

- $F(\mathbf{l}, \mathbf{v}, \lambda)$ is the Fresnel coefficient. This is a useful term for modeling lighting at grazing angles, possibly making the light more specular at grazing angles (near perpendicular to the normal).

2.6.3   Microfacet Distribution Term

The amount of light reflected in the direction $\mathbf{v}$ is assumed to be proportional to the number of microfacets correctly oriented for a mirror reflection in that direction. We use the halfway vector

$$\mathbf{h} = \frac{\mathbf{l} + \mathbf{v}}{\|\mathbf{l} + \mathbf{v}\|}$$

for this calculation. For perfect reflection the microfacet normal must be equal to $\mathbf{h}$. Let $\psi = \cos^{-1}(\mathbf{h} \cdot \mathbf{n})$, where $\mathbf{n}$ is the surface normal (not the microfacet normal), so that we can write $D = D(\psi)$ for the percentage of light reflected in direction $\mathbf{v}$. Possible functions include

- The *Gaussian distribution* function

$$D(\psi) = ce^{-\psi^2/m^2}$$

- The *Beckmann distribution*

$$D(\psi) = \frac{1}{\pi m^2 \cos^4 \psi} e^{-(\tan^2 \psi)/m^2}$$

where c and m are positive constants selected for the material. Sometimes 4 is used instead of π for the Beckmann distribution function.

2.6.4   Geometric Surface Occlusion Term

This term takes into account shadowing and masking caused by the microfacets. To simplify the calculation, we assume that $\mathbf{v}$, $\mathbf{l}$ and $\mathbf{n}$ are coplanar,

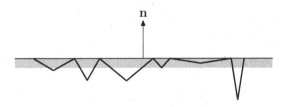

Figure 2.5: V shaped grooves.

and that the facets form symmetrical V shaped grooves (not necessarily of the same depth) as shown in figure 2.5. The tops of the grooves are assumed to be at the same height.

Figure 2.6 shows the different masking and shadowing combinations that can occur. In each diagram, 6 rays represent the full incoming light. If there are less rays, they have been shadowed or masked as illustrated. We do not need to take into account different V shaped grooves, only those that reflect perfectly need be considered. The fraction of V shaped grooves that do not reflect perfectly are removed by the Microfacet Distribution Term (D). The classic Cook-Torrance model, takes the minimum of light that is not shadowed, and light that is not masked. We instead follow the approach that Buss [8] recommends. To calculate the amount of shadowing and masking we need to use the following lemma by Blinn [8].

Lemma 2.1. *We consider figure 2.7. Let $\|AB\|$ be the distance from A to B, then*

$$\frac{\|BC\|}{\|AC\|} = \frac{2(\mathbf{n} \cdot \mathbf{h})(\mathbf{n} \cdot \mathbf{v})}{(\mathbf{h} \cdot \mathbf{v})}.$$

Proof. We define $\mathbf{h}'$ as the unit vector normal to the opposite side of the groove. Since the groove is symmetric, is is clear that $\mathbf{h}'$ is the reflection of $\mathbf{h}$ around the normal to the surface $\mathbf{n}$ so that $\mathbf{h}' = 2(\mathbf{n} \cdot \mathbf{h})\mathbf{n} - \mathbf{h}$. From the symmetry of the groove and the law of sines we have

$$\frac{\|AB\|}{\|AC\|} = \frac{\|AB\|}{\|AD\|} = \frac{\sin \alpha}{\sin \beta}.$$

We also have

$$\sin \alpha = \cos \left(\frac{\pi}{2} - \alpha \right) = -\mathbf{v} \cdot \mathbf{h}'$$

and

$$\sin \beta = \cos \left(\frac{\pi}{2} - \beta \right) = \mathbf{v} \cdot \mathbf{h}.$$

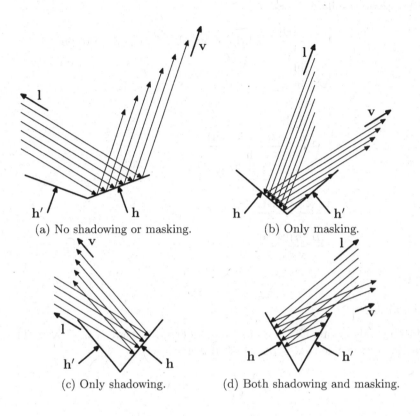

(a) No shadowing or masking.   (b) Only masking.

(c) Only shadowing.   (d) Both shadowing and masking.

Figure 2.6: Shadowing and masking.

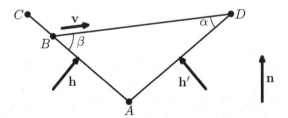

Figure 2.7: Blinn's geometric lemma.

Using these results we obtain

$$\frac{\|BC\|}{\|AC\|} = 1 - \frac{\|AB\|}{\|AC\|} \quad \text{(ratio of lengths must add up to one)}$$

$$= 1 - \frac{\sin \alpha}{\sin \beta}$$

$$= 1 + \frac{\mathbf{v} \cdot \mathbf{h'}}{\mathbf{v} \cdot \mathbf{h}}$$

$$= 1 + \frac{\mathbf{v} \cdot (2(\mathbf{n} \cdot \mathbf{h})\mathbf{n} - \mathbf{h})}{\mathbf{v} \cdot \mathbf{h}}$$

$$= \frac{\mathbf{v} \cdot \mathbf{h} + \mathbf{v} \cdot (2(\mathbf{n} \cdot \mathbf{h})\mathbf{n} - \mathbf{h})}{\mathbf{v} \cdot \mathbf{h}}$$

$$= \frac{\mathbf{v} \cdot (2(\mathbf{n} \cdot \mathbf{h})\mathbf{n})}{\mathbf{v} \cdot \mathbf{h}}$$

$$= \frac{2(\mathbf{n} \cdot \mathbf{h})(\mathbf{v} \cdot \mathbf{n})}{\mathbf{v} \cdot \mathbf{h}}$$

as required.

Masking

Masking only occurs if $\mathbf{v} \cdot \mathbf{h'} < 0$. Figure 2.6(b) illustrates this clearly. The fraction of the side that is not masked is given by

$$\frac{2(\mathbf{n} \cdot \mathbf{h})(\mathbf{n} \cdot \mathbf{v})}{(\mathbf{h} \cdot \mathbf{v})} \quad \text{(lemma)}.$$

Shadowing

Shadowing only occurs if $\mathbf{l} \cdot \mathbf{h'} < 0$. Figure 2.6(c) illustrates this clearly. The fraction of the side that is not in shadow is given by

$$\frac{2(\mathbf{n} \cdot \mathbf{h})(\mathbf{n} \cdot \mathbf{l})}{(\mathbf{h} \cdot \mathbf{l})} \quad \text{(lemma)}.$$

If there is no shadowing or masking then $G = 1$. If there is only masking then

$$G = \frac{2(\mathbf{n} \cdot \mathbf{h})(\mathbf{n} \cdot \mathbf{v})}{(\mathbf{h} \cdot \mathbf{v})}.$$

If there is only shadowing, then according to Buss [8], there is no decrease in the intensity of the reflected light. Any light that is shadowed by the edge of one facet will be reflected by the facet just before it. So in this case $G = 1$.

If there is shadowing and masking, then the decrease in intensity is the amount of masking of the unshadowed light so that

$$G = \frac{2(\mathbf{n} \cdot \mathbf{h})(\mathbf{n} \cdot \mathbf{v})}{(\mathbf{h} \cdot \mathbf{v})} \div \frac{2(\mathbf{n} \cdot \mathbf{h})(\mathbf{n} \cdot \mathbf{l})}{(\mathbf{h} \cdot \mathbf{l})} = \frac{\mathbf{n} \cdot \mathbf{v}}{\mathbf{n} \cdot \mathbf{l}}$$

since $\mathbf{h} \cdot \mathbf{v} = \mathbf{h} \cdot \mathbf{l}$ and $\mathbf{h}$ is the half vector of $\mathbf{v}$ and $\mathbf{l}$. G should be computed such that $0 \leq G \leq 1$, so this formula is only applied if $\mathbf{n} \cdot \mathbf{v} < \mathbf{n} \cdot \mathbf{l}$. Our final formula for coplanar $\mathbf{n}$, $\mathbf{l}$ and $\mathbf{v}$ is thus

$$G = \begin{cases} 1 & \text{if } \mathbf{v} \cdot \mathbf{h}' \geq 0 \text{ or } \mathbf{n} \cdot \mathbf{v} \geq \mathbf{n} \cdot \mathbf{l} \\ \frac{2(\mathbf{n} \cdot \mathbf{h})(\mathbf{n} \cdot \mathbf{v})}{(\mathbf{h} \cdot \mathbf{v})} & \text{if } \mathbf{v} \cdot \mathbf{h}' < 0 \text{ and } \mathbf{l} \cdot \mathbf{h}' \geq 0 \\ \frac{\mathbf{n} \cdot \mathbf{v}}{\mathbf{n} \cdot \mathbf{l}} & \text{if } \mathbf{v} \cdot \mathbf{h}' < 0, \mathbf{l} \cdot \mathbf{h}' < 0 \text{ and } \mathbf{n} \cdot \mathbf{v} < \mathbf{n} \cdot \mathbf{l}. \end{cases}$$

If the vectors are not coplanar, we project the normal onto the plane created by $\mathbf{v}$ and $\mathbf{l}$ to get

$$\mathbf{n}_0 = \frac{(\mathbf{n} \cdot \mathbf{l})\mathbf{l} + (\mathbf{n} \cdot \mathbf{v})\mathbf{v} - (\mathbf{v} \cdot \mathbf{l})(\mathbf{v} \cdot \mathbf{n})\mathbf{l} - (\mathbf{v} \cdot \mathbf{l})(\mathbf{l} \cdot \mathbf{n})\mathbf{v}}{1 - (\mathbf{v} \cdot \mathbf{l})^2}.$$

We use $\mathbf{m} = \frac{\mathbf{n}_0}{\|\mathbf{n}_0\|}$ instead of $\mathbf{n}$ in the calculation of G. Although the geometric term is only applied to specular reflection in the Cook-Torrance model, it can be applied to diffuse reflection as well for non-Lambertian surfaces.

2.6.5 Fresnel Term

The Fresnel equations describe what fraction of incident light is specularly reflected from a flat surface. For a particular wavelength λ, this can be defined in terms of a function $\mathcal{F}$

$$F(\mathbf{l}, \mathbf{v}, \lambda) = \mathcal{F}(\psi, \eta)$$

where $\psi := \cos^{-1}(\mathbf{l} \cdot \mathbf{h})$, and η is the index of refraction of the surface. For materials that are not electrically conducting we have

$$\mathcal{F} = \frac{1}{2} \left(\frac{\sin^2(\psi - \theta)}{\sin^2(\psi + \theta)} + \frac{\tan^2(\psi - \theta)}{\tan^2(\psi + \theta)} \right)$$

which applies to unpolarized light. *Snell's law* is given by

$$\frac{\sin \psi}{\sin \theta} = \eta$$

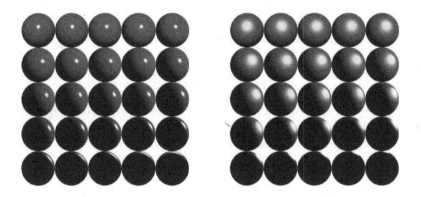

Figure 2.8: Phong compared to Cook-Torrance lighting model.

where θ is the angle of the refracted ray with respect to the surface. If we let $c = \cos\psi$ and $g = \sqrt{\eta^2 + c^2 - 1}$ we find that $g = \eta\cos\theta$,

$$\frac{\sin(\psi - \theta)}{\sin(\psi + \theta)} = \frac{(g - c)}{(g + c)}$$

and

$$\frac{\cos(\psi - \theta)}{\cos(\psi + \theta)} = \frac{c(g - c) + 1}{c(g + c) - 1}.$$

The *Fresnel equation* becomes

$$\mathcal{F} = \frac{1}{2}\frac{(g - c)^2}{(g + c)^2}\left(1 + \frac{[c(g + c) - 1]^2}{[c(g - c) + 1]^2}\right).$$

If $\eta > 1$ then g is well defined. If $\eta < 1$ then we have total internal reflection and we should set $\mathcal{F} = 1$. Conducting materials need an imaginary component (*the extinction coefficient*) in the index of refraction and are not considered here. Obviously η depends on the wavelength. For example, some values for η for different wavelengths and materials are listed in [8]. Figure 2.8 compares Phong shading on the left and Cook-Torrance shading on the right.

2.6.6 Beer-Lambert Law

The *Beer-Lambert* law describes how light is absorbed by a translucent material through which it is travelling. The equations that govern absorption are

$$A = \alpha\ell c$$
$$I_1 = 10^{-A}I_0$$

where

- A is the absorbance.

- I_0 is the intensity of the the light entering the material.

- I_1 is the intensity of the light exiting the material.

- ℓ is the distance the light travels through the material.

- c is the concentration of the material that absorbs the light.

- α is the absorption coefficient of the material given by

$$\alpha = 4\pi k\lambda.$$

- λ is the wavelength of the light.

- k is the extinction coefficient of the material (for the wavelength under consideration).

For computer graphics purposes, where an artist must decide what values to use, it is sufficient to simply choose an acceptable value of α for each wavelength that is modelled.

2.7   C# Implementation

We make use of a `Colour` class to represent colors in the lighting model. The standard C# classes to represent color are insufficient since they cannot handle a wide range of colors. For lighting, it is important that we be able to represent colors that cannot be rendered on the screen. These colors will then be transformed later to values that can be rendered on the screen. We use the alternative spelling `Colour` to differentiate our color class from that of C#. The methods `HSVtoRGB` and `RGBtoHSV` are adapted from *Computer Graphics: Principles and Practice*, by Foley, van Dam, Feiner and Hughes [38].

```
// Colour.cs
using System;

public class Colour {
    public double r,g,b,a;
    public Colour() { r=g=b=a=0.0; }
    public Colour(double r,double g,double b) {
        this.r=r; this.g=g; this.b=b; this.a=1.0; }
```

```
public Colour(double r,double g,double b,double a) {
   this.r=r; this.g=g; this.b=b; this.a=a; }

public object Clone() {
   object o=new Colour(r,g,b,a);
   return o; }

public override bool Equals(object x) {
   if((((Colour)x).r==r)&&(((Colour)x).g==g)&&
   (((Colour)x).b==b)&&(((Colour)x).a==a)) return true;
   else return false; }

public static Colour operator+(Colour c1,Colour c2) {
   return new Colour(c1.r+c2.r,c1.g+c2.g,c1.b+c2.b); }

public static Colour operator-(Colour c1,Colour c2) {
   return new Colour(c1.r-c2.r,c1.g-c2.g,c1.b-c2.b); }

//componentwise multiply
public static Colour operator*(Colour c1,Colour c2) {
   return new Colour(c1.r*c2.r,c1.g*c2.g,c1.b*c2.b,c1.a*c2.a); }

public static Colour operator*(double c,Colour c2) {
   return new Colour(c*c2.r,c*c2.g,c*c2.b,c2.a); }

public static Colour operator*(Colour c1,double c) {
   return new Colour(c*c1.r,c*c1.g,c*c1.b,c1.a); }

public static Colour operator/(Colour c1,double c) {
   return new Colour(c1.r/c,c1.g/c,c1.b/c,c1.a); }

public static Colour operator-(Colour c1) { //unary minus
   return new Colour(-c1.r,-c1.g,-c1.b,c1.a); }

public static Colour operator+(Colour c1) { //unary plus
   return new Colour(c1.r,c1.g,c1.b,c1.a); }

public Colour clamp() {
   Colour ret=new Colour();
   ret.r=(r>1.0)?1.0:r;
   ret.g=(g>1.0)?1.0:g;
   ret.b=(b>1.0)?1.0:b;
   ret.r=(ret.r<0.0)?0.0:ret.r;
   ret.g=(ret.g<0.0)?0.0:ret.g;
   ret.b=(ret.b<0.0)?0.0:ret.b;
   return ret;      }

public double norm() { return Math.Sqrt(r*r+g*g+b*b); }

public Colour normalize() {
   Colour ret=new Colour();
```

```
    if((r>1.0)||(g>1.0)||(b>1.0)){
        if((r>=g)&&(r>=b)) ret.r=1.0; ret.g=g/r; ret.b=b/r;
        else if((g>=r)&&(g>=b)) ret.r=r/g; ret.g=1.0; ret.b=b/g;
        else ret.r=r/b; ret.g=g/b; ret.b=1.0;
    } else ret.r=r; ret.g=g; ret.b=b;
    return ret; }

private Colour RGBtoHSV() {
    double max, min;
    double h=0.0, s, v;
    max=max3(r,g,b); min=min3(r,g,b); v=max;

    s=(max!=0.0)?((max-min)/max):0.0;
    if(s==0.0) h=-360.0;
    else {
        double delta=min-max;
        if(r==max) h=(g-b)/delta;
        else if(g==max) h=2.0+(b-r)/delta;
        else if(b==max) h=4.0+(r-g)/delta;
        h*=60.0;
        if(h<0.0) h+=360.0;
    }
    h/=360.0;
    return new Colour(h,s,v,a); }

private Colour HSVtoRGB() {
    double h=r, s=g, v=b;
    double rt=0.0, gt=0.0, bt=0.0;
    h*=360.0;
    if(s==0.0) {
        if(h<0.0) rt=gt=bt=v;
        else { //Error! This should never happen!
            rt=gt=bt=0.0;
        }
    } else {
        double f, p, q, t;
        int i;
        if(h>=360.0) h-=360.0;
        h/=60.0;
        i=(int)Math.Floor(h);
        f=h-i;
        p=v*(1.0-s); q=v*(1.0-(s*f)); t=v*(1.0-(s*(1.0-f)));
        switch(i) {
            case 0:  rt=v; gt=t; bt=p; break;
            case 1:  rt=q; gt=v; bt=p; break;
            case 2:  rt=p; gt=v; bt=t; break;
            case 3:  rt=p; gt=q; bt=v; break;
            case 4:  rt=t; gt=p; bt=v; break;
            case 5:  rt=v; gt=p; bt=q; break;
        }
    }
```

```
    return new Colour(rt,gt,bt,a); }

private static double max3(double a,double b,double c) {
    if((a>=b)&&(a>=c)) return a;
    if((b>=a)&&(b>=c)) return b;
    return c; }

private static double min3(double a,double b,double c) {
    if((a<=b)&&(a<=c)) return a;
    if((b<=a)&&(b<=c)) return b;
    return c; }

public double R { get { return r; } set { r = value; } }

public double G { get { return g; } set { g = value; } }

public double B { get { return b; } set { b = value; } }

public double A { get { return a; } set { a = value; } }

public double Cyan { get { return 1.0-r; } set { r = 1.0-value; } }

public double Magenta { get { return 1.0-g; } set { g = 1.0-value; } }

public double Yellow { get { return 1.0-b; } set { a = 1.0-value; } }

public double Hue {
    get { Colour hsv=RGBtoHSV(); return hsv.r; }
    set { Colour hsv=RGBtoHSV(); hsv.r=value;
        Colour rgb=hsv.HSVtoRGB();
        r=rgb.r; g=rgb.g; b=rgb.b; } }

public double Saturation {
    get { Colour hsv=RGBtoHSV(); return hsv.g; }
    set { Colour hsv=RGBtoHSV(); hsv.g=value;
        Colour rgb=hsv.HSVtoRGB();
        r=rgb.r; g=rgb.g; b=rgb.b;} }

public double Value {
    get { Colour hsv=RGBtoHSV(); return hsv.b; }
    set { Colour hsv=RGBtoHSV(); hsv.b=value;
        Colour rgb=hsv.HSVtoRGB();
        r=rgb.r; g=rgb.g; b=rgb.b;} }

public override string ToString() {
    return String.Format("Colour({0},{1},{2})", r, g, b);}
};
```

The Material abstract class allows various lighting models to be used without regard to the particular implementation. Common attributes for lighting models have been moved into the Material class.

```
//Material.cs
using System;

abstract public class Material
{
    public Material() {
        pd=0.5; ps=0.4; pa=0.1; pe=0.0;
        diffuse=new Colour(1.0,0.0,0.0);
        specular=new Colour(1.0,1.0,1.0);
        emissive=new Colour(1.0,0.0,0.0);
        ambient=new Colour(1.0,0.0,0.0);
        pt=0.0; pr=0.0; ir=1.0;
    }

    abstract public Colour Light(Vector n,Vector l,Vector v,
        Colour Ia,Colour Id,Colour Is);
    public Colour diffuse, specular, emissive, ambient;
    public double pd, ps, pa, pe;
    //transmission
    public double pt;
    //index of refraction
    public double ir;
    //reflection
    public double pr;
}
```

The Phong lighting model implements the Material interface and so can be used as a Material for objects. The required coefficients are specified when the object is instantiated.

```
//Phong.cs
using System;

public class Phong: Material
{
    public double f;

    public override Colour Light(Vector n,Vector l,Vector v,
        Colour Ia,Colour Id,Colour Is) {
        Vector r;
        Colour c, e, a;
        e=pe*emissive;
        a=pa*Ia*ambient;
        n=(Vector)n.Clone(); l=(Vector)l.Clone();
        v=(Vector)v.Clone();
        n.normalize(); l.normalize(); v.normalize();
        r=Vector.reflect(l,n);
        if(n*l<0.0) {
            Id=new Colour(0.0,0.0,0.0);
```

```
            Is=new Colour(0.0,0.0,0.0);
        }
        if(r*v<0.0) Is=new Colour(0.0,0.0,0.0);
        c=e+a+pd*diffuse*Id*(n*l)
            +ps*specular*Is*Math.Pow(r*v,f);
        return c;
    }

    public Phong()
    {
        pd=0.5; ps=0.4; pa=0.1; pe=0.0;
        f=20.0;
        diffuse=new Colour(1.0,1.0,1.0);
        specular=new Colour(1.0,1.0,1.0);
        emissive=new Colour(1.0,1.0,1.0);
        ambient=new Colour(1.0,1.0,1.0);
    }

    public object Clone() {
        Phong ph=new Phong();
        ph.pd=pd; ph.ps=ps; ph.pa=pa; ph.pe=pe; ph.f=f;
        ph.diffuse=(Colour)diffuse.Clone();
        ph.specular=(Colour)specular.Clone();
        ph.emissive=(Colour)emissive.Clone();
        ph.ambient=(Colour)ambient.Clone();
        object o=ph;
        return o; }

    public override string ToString() {
        return "Material::Phong()";}
}
```

The Cook-Torrance model also implements the Material interface.

```
//CookTorrance.cs
using System;

public class CookTorrance: Material
{
    public Colour eta;
    public double f,m,c;

    private double Beckmann(double psi) {
        double c,d,t;
        double e=Math.E;
        c=Math.Cos(psi);
        d=1.0/(Math.PI*m*m*c*c*c*c);
        t=Math.Tan(psi)/m;
        return d*Math.Pow(e,-t*t);
    }
```

```csharp
private double Gaussian(double psi)
{ return c*Math.Pow(Math.E,-psi*psi/(m*m)); }

private double Geometric(Vector v,Vector h,Vector hd,
    Vector l,Vector n) {
    double vhd, nv, nl, lhd, vl;
    Vector m=new Vector();
    double s;

    vl=v*l; nl=n*l; nv=v*n;
    s=1.0-(v*l)*(v*l);
    m.x=nl*l.x+nv*v.x-vl*nv*l.x-vl*nl*v.x;
    m.y=nl*l.y+nv*v.y-vl*nv*l.y-vl*nl*v.y;
    m.z=nl*l.z+nv*v.z-vl*nv*l.z-vl*nl*v.z;
    m.x/=s; m.y/=s; m.z/=s;
    if(Math.Abs(m*m)<1e-7) m=n;
    m.normalize();
    n=m;
    vhd=v*hd; lhd=l*hd;
    nv=n*v; nl=n*l;
    if((vhd>=0.0)||(nv>=nl)) return 1.0;
    if((vhd<0.0)&&(lhd>=0.0))return 2.0*(n*h)*(n*v)/(h*v);
    if((vhd<0.0)&&(lhd<0.0)&&(nv<nl))return nv/nl;
    return 0.0;
}

private double sqr(double x) { return x*x; }

private double Fresnel(double psi,double F) {
    double c,g;
    double eta;
    eta=(1.0+Math.Sqrt(F))/(1.0-Math.Sqrt(F));
    if(eta<1.0) return 1.0;
    c=Math.Cos(psi);
    g=Math.Sqrt(eta*eta+c*c-1.0);
    return 0.5*sqr(g-c)/sqr(g+c)*(1.0+sqr(c*(g+c)-1.0)/
        sqr(c*(g-c)+1.0));
}

Colour cook_torrance(Colour Is,Vector lpos,
                    Vector n,Vector v) {
    Colour cs;
    Vector h, hd;
    Colour F=new Colour();
    double psi;
    double D, G;

    n=(Vector)n.Clone();
    lpos=(Vector)lpos.Clone();
    v=(Vector)v.Clone();
    lpos.normalize(); n.normalize(); v.normalize();
```

```
    h=lpos+v;
    h.normalize();
    hd=Vector.reflect(h,n);
    hd.normalize();

    psi=h*n;
    if(psi>=0.0) { psi=Math.Acos(psi); D=Beckmann(psi); }
    else { D=0.0; }
    if(lpos*n<0.0) D=0.0;
    G=Geometric(v,h,hd,lpos,n);
    psi=lpos*h;
    if(psi>=0.0) {
        psi=Math.Acos(psi);
        F.r=Fresnel(psi,eta.r);
        F.g=Fresnel(psi,eta.g);
        F.b=Fresnel(psi,eta.b);
    } else { F.r=F.g=F.b=0.0; }
    cs=(n*lpos)/(n*v)*ps*F*G*D*Is;
    return cs;
}

public override Colour Light(Vector n,Vector l,Vector v,
    Colour Ia,Colour Id,Colour Is) {
    Vector r;
    Colour c, e, a;
    e=pe*emissive; a=pa*Ia*ambient;
    n.normalize(); l.normalize(); v.normalize();
    r=Vector.reflect(l,n);
    if(n*l<0.0) {
        Id=new Colour(0.0,0.0,0.0);
        Is=new Colour(0.0,0.0,0.0);
    }
    if(r*v<0.0) Is=new Colour(0.0,0.0,0.0);
    c=e+a+pd*diffuse*Id*(n*l)+cook_torrance(Is,l,n,v);
    return c;
}

public CookTorrance()
{
    pd=0.5; ps=0.4; pa=0.1; pe=0.0;
    m=0.4; c=0.25;
    diffuse=new Colour(1.0,0.0,0.0);
    specular=new Colour(1.0,1.0,1.0);
    emissive=new Colour(1.0,0.0,0.0);
    ambient=new Colour(1.0,0.0,0.0);
    eta=new Colour(0.38,0.88,0.93);
}

public object Clone() {
    CookTorrance ct=new CookTorrance();
    ct.pd=pd; ct.ps=ps; ct.pa=pa; ct.pe=pe;
```

```
    ct.m=m; ct.c=c;
    ct.diffuse=(Colour)diffuse.Clone();
    ct.specular=(Colour)specular.Clone();
    ct.emissive=(Colour)emissive.Clone();
    ct.ambient=(Colour)ambient.Clone();
    object o=ct;
    return o; }

  public override string ToString() {
    return "Material::CookTorrance()";}
}
```

The main program makes use of these classes to render a sphere under various lighting conditions. The sphere is rendered under an orthographic projection.

```
//MainForm.cs
using System;
using System.Windows.Forms;
using System.Drawing;

namespace DefaultNamespace
  public class MainForm : Form
  {
    private bool mustpaint=false;
    private PictureBox render;
    private Colour matt=new Colour(1.0,0.0,0.0);
    private Colour spec=new Colour(1.0,1.0,1.0);
    //IDE generated code omitted...
    void CmdRenderClick(object sender,EventArgs e)
    { mustpaint=true; render.Invalidate(); }

    void Plot(Graphics gfx,double x,
      double y,double r,double g,double b) {
      Pen pen=new Pen(Brushes.Black);
      pen.Color=Color.FromArgb(255,
        (int)(r*255),(int)(g*255),(int)(b*255));
      gfx.DrawLine(pen,(int)x,(int)y,(int)x+1,(int)y);
    }

    void RenderPaint(object sender,PaintEventArgs e)
    {
      int x, y;
      double rx, ry, rz;
      Material mat=new CookTorrance();
      Vector n;
      Vector l=new Vector(-100,100,100);
      Vector v=new Vector(0,0,100);
      if(mustpaint) {
        for(y=0;y<256;y++) {
```

```
for(x=0;x<256;x++) {
  //The window is 256×256, convert
  //the coordinates to lie in the range -1 to 1
  rx=x/255.0; ry=y/255.0;
  rx-=0.5; ry-=0.5; rx*=2.0; ry*=2.0;
  //and compute the corresponding coordinate on the shere with radius 1
  rz=Math.Sqrt(1.0-rx*rx+ry*ry);
  n=new Vector(rx,ry,rz);

  if(rx*rx+ry*ry<1.0) {
    //inside the sphere
    Colour c=mat.Light(n,l-n,v-n,
      new Colour(1.0,1.0,1.0),
      new Colour (1.0,1.0,1.0),
      new Colour(1.0,1.0,1.0));
    Plot(e.Graphics,x,y,c.R,c.G,c.B);
  }
}
}
  mustpaint=false;
}
}

void CmdMaterialClick(object sender,EventArgs e)
{
  colorDlg.ShowDialog();
  Color c=colorDlg.Color;
  matt=new Colour(c.R/255.0,c.G/255.0,c.B/255.0);
  cmdMaterial.BackColor=c;
}

void CmdSpecularClick(object sender,EventArgs e)
{
  colorDlg.ShowDialog();
  Color c=colorDlg.Color;
  spec=new Colour(c.R/255.0,c.G/255.0,c.B/255.0);
  cmdSpecular.BackColor=c;
}
}
}
```

Chapter 3

Rasterization

Images are displayed on the screen by selecting colors for specific grid positions. The screen is usually divided up into square picture elements (pixels) at a specific resolution, for example 1024×768. Images that are generated by the computer must be mapped onto this grid in some fashion. The process of converting objects to colors on a grid (for display) is known as rasterization. Most of the algorithms presented are optimized for speed and do not necessarily compute accurate value.

3.1   Pixels

Most primitives are represented by several points and attributes. However, it is important to note that pixels and points are not the same thing. A point has no area, whereas a pixel does have area. Lines also have no area, and so lines cannot be drawn accurately by a raster display. The line drawing algorithms presented here will ignore this fact and represent the line by a number of pixels that the line passes through. The image can be improved if we employ anti-aliasing techniques and represent the line as a quadrilateral with a defined area.

3.2   Drawing Lines

In this section we introduce a formulation of a line segment, and a fast algorithm for rasterizing the line segment.

In general, a line in the 2D Cartesian plane is given by

$$ax + by = d$$

where either $a \neq 0$ or $b \neq 0$ or both nonzero. If $b \neq 0$ we have $y = mx + c$ with $m = -a/b$ and $c = d/b$. Thus m is the gradient and c is the intersection with the y-axis. If the line is defined by two points $\mathbf{p}_1 = (x_1 \; y_1)^T$ and $\mathbf{p}_2 = (x_2 \; y_2)^T$ with $x_1 \neq x_2$, then

$$m = \frac{y_2 - y_1}{x_2 - x_1}$$

and $c = y_1 - mx_1$. Since integer operations are usually faster than floating point operations, it is desirable to have an algorithm to draw lines that requires only integer arithmetic. This implicit formula for a line can be used to develop an algorithm to quickly draw lines without requiring floating point operations. This algorithm is known as the Bresenham algorithm.

3.2.1 Bresenham's Algorithm for Lines

Assume that the line will be rasterized in the first quadrant, and that $m < 1$. The other situations can be handled by reflection. Therefore $y_2 - y_1 < x_2 - x_1$. Let $\Delta x := x_2 - x_1$ and $\Delta y := y_2 - y_1$. Since $\Delta x > \Delta y$ it is natural to take each position on the grid in the x direction and determine the corresponding y-coordinate for the point on the line. We thus have the following algorithm

```
m=(y2-y1)/(x2-x1); c=y1-m*x1;
for(x=x1;x<=x2;x++) { y=m*x+c; plot(x,y); }
```

Observe that this algorithm only works for floating point variables. Note that when $x = x_1$ then $y = y_1$ describes a point on the line. Also note that $m(x + 1) \equiv mx + m$. It is thus possible to determine the initial value for y and adjust this value with each iteration. The algorithm can now be written as

```
m=(y2-y1)/(x2-x1); y=y1;
for(x=x1;x<=x2;x++) { plot(x,y); y=y+m; }
```

The algorithm still relies on floating point variables. To allow integer variables to be used note that

$$m(x + 1) = \frac{\Delta y}{\Delta x}(x + 1) = \frac{(\Delta y)x + \Delta y}{\Delta x}.$$

Let $y = y_i + \frac{r}{\Delta x}$. If $r < \Delta x$, then y can be taken to be y_i for the purposes of rasterization. However, if $r > \Delta x$, then the raster position will need to be updated to reflect r. At the beginning of the iteration $r = 0$. At each step, it is necessary to update the remainder by Δy, and since $\Delta y < \Delta x$ we seldom have that $r > \Delta x$. If $r > \Delta x$, then y must advance 1 raster position, and r must be reduced to reflect the accurate remainder. The algorithm then becomes

```
dx=x2-x1; dy=y2-y1;
r=0; y=y1;
for(x=x1;x<=x2;x++) { plot(x,y); r=r+dy;
    if(r>dx) { y=y+1;r=r-dx; }
}
```

Note that we do not set $r = 0$, instead we maintain the accuracy by subtracting exactly 1 from $\frac{r}{\Delta x}$. This algorithm only increments y to obtain $y = y_i$ if $y_i = \lfloor m x_i \rfloor$. It is customary to round up when the fractional value reaches 0.5. The refined algorithm is given by

```
dx=x2-x1; dy=y2-y1;
r=dx/2; y=y1;
for(x=x1;x<=x2;x++) { plot(x,y); r=r+dy;
    if(r>dx) { y=y+1;r=r-dx; }
}
```

r is chosen so that $\frac{r}{\Delta x} \approx 0.5$ when the algorithm begins, thus providing identical results to rounding.

3.3   Drawing Circles

A similar derivation can be used to develop an algorithm that draws circles with only integer arithmetic. As a starting point we use the implicit formula for a circle centered at the origin with radius r

$$x^2 + y^2 = r^2.$$

Bresenham's Algorithm for drawing circles avoids floating point arithmetic so that a circle can be drawn with only integer operations.

3.3.1   Bresenham's Algorithm for Circles

Once again we only consider the first quadrant, and in particular the first 45° of the circle. In this case we use an alternative derivation. When drawing the first 45°, we start at the coordinate $(r\ 0)^T$. At each iteration, the y-coordinate will be increased. On the other hand, it may or may not be necessary to decrease the x-coordinate. The error (or distance) relative to the circle of any point in the Cartesian plane is defined by

$$e(x, y) := x^2 + y^2 - r^2.$$

Points on the circle have an error of 0 while points not on the circle have a nonzero error value. The increase in error due to increasing the y-component is

$$e(x, y+1) - e(x, y) = 2y + 1$$

whereas the increase in error due to decreasing the x-component and increasing the y-component is given by

$$e(x-1, y+1) - e(x, y) = 2y - 2x + 2.$$

The best choice is to choose the change in coordinates that produces the smallest absolute error. The following algorithm draws a complete circle making use of appropriate reflections.

```
x=r; y=0; e=0;
while(y<=x) {
    circleplot(x,y);
    e1=e+2*y+1; e2=e+2*y-2*x+2;
    if(abs(e2)<abs(e1)) { e=e2;x=x-1; } else { e=e1; }
    y=y+1;
}
```

The `circleplot` function fills pixels at $(\pm x \quad \pm y)^T$ and $(\pm y \quad \pm x)^T$, thus `circleplot` is defined by

```
plot(x,y); plot(-x,y); plot(x,-y); plot(-x,-y);
plot(y,x); plot(-y,x); plot(y,-x); plot(-y,-x);
```

The multiplication performed at every iteration of the loop can be eliminated by observing that

$$e_1 = e + d_1(x, y)$$
$$e_2 = e + d_2(x, y)$$

with $d_1(x, y) = 2y + 1$ and $d_2(x, y) = 2y - 2x + 2$. Note that

$$d_1(x, y+1) - d_1(x, y) = 2$$
$$d_1(x-1, y+1) - d_1(x, y) = 2$$
$$d_2(x, y+1) - d_2(x, y) = 2$$
$$d_2(x-1, y+1) - d_2(x, y) = 4.$$

The final circle algorithm is given by

```
x=r; y=0; e=0;
d1=1; d2=2-2*r;
while(y<=x) {
   circleplot(x,y);
   e1=e+d1; e2=e+d2;
   if(abs(e2)<abs(e1)) { e=e2; x=x-1; d2=d2+2; }
   else { e=e1; }
   y=y+1; d1=d1+2; d2=d2+2;
}
```

3.4 Filling

It is not sufficient to just draw lines. To obtain realistic graphics it is necessary to be able to fill polygons. Since color or lighting attributes need to be interpolated across the polygon we only develop an algorithm to fill a triangle. Foley et al. [38] describes the general case. However, all polygons can be constructed from triangles. Assume we have the vertices

$$\mathbf{v}_0 = (x_0 \ y_0)^T, \qquad \mathbf{v}_1 = (x_1 \ y_1)^T, \qquad \mathbf{v}_2 = (x_2 \ y_2)^T$$

that define the triangle. To rasterize the triangle, we rasterize each of the edges of the triangle and store the minimum and maximum x values for each line. It is possible to avoid these storage costs by first sorting the vertices into ascending order according to the y-coordinate.

A polygon is convex if all points on the line connecting any two points in the polygon are still in the polygon. Each scanline will intersect the triangle exactly twice since triangles are *convex polygons*, once entering the triangle, and once exiting the triangle. Only two edges need to be tested in this case. However, if we test all edges, then the vertex at which two edges meet will be counted twice. The solution is to disregard one of the edges from the intersect test. Alternatively, since we need a minimum and maximum value, we can simply use the minimum and maximum values of all edges that intersect the scanline.

A rudimentary algorithm for filling a triangle is given by

```
ymin=min(y0,y1,y2);
ymax=max(y0,y1,y2);
for(y=ymin;y<ymax;y++) {
   xm1=linemin(x0,y0,x1,y1,y);
   xm2=linemin(x0,y0,x2,y2,y);
```

```
        xm3=linemin(x1,y1,x2,y2,y);
        xc1=linemax(x0,y0,x1,y1,y);
        xc2=linemax(x0,y0,x2,y2,y);
        xc3=linemax(x1,y1,x2,y2,y);
        xmin=min(xm1,xm2,xm3);
        xmax=max(xc1,xc2,xc3);
        hfill(y,xmin,xmax);
    }
```

The functions `linemin` and `linemax` are modified versions of Bresenham's algorithm that are defined to return the minimum x-coordinate and maximum x-coordinate that are filled by the algorithm for a particular y-coordinate. For y-coordinates that are not on the line segment, `linemin` and `linemax` return some suitable value that will never be the minimum or maximum. Typically we implement `linemin` and `linemax` as a single function so that the Bresenham algorithm can run effectively. Note that the Bresenham algorithm need not execute for an edge if $y < y_s$ and $y > y_e$ where y_s is the start of the edge and y_e denotes the end of the edge. The function `hfill` simply draws to the pixels that satisfy $x_{min} \leq x \leq x_{max}$, that is

```
    for (x=xmin;x<=xmax;x++) plot(x,y);
```

3.4.1 Gouraud Shading

It is not satisfactory to simply fill a triangle with a constant color. This form of shading (known as *flat shading*) is not very realistic. Light from the environment seldom results in a constant color across the surface of an object. One method to overcome the constant color, is to compute the color of the object at the vertices of the triangle and interpolate the values across the triangle. We concentrate on this algorithm here since it is possible to implement the algorithm efficiently without floating point numbers.

During the fill procedure, colors are interpolated along the edges in a similar fashion to how the coordinates are computed with Bresenham's algorithm. These values are then interpolated by `hfill` to produce the color in the center of the triangle. The Bresenham algorithm needs to be modified to determine the change of value to accommodate larger steps. Assume that the line is once again in the first quadrant and that $\Delta x \geq \Delta y$.

```
    dx=x2-x1; dv=v2-v1;
    r=dx/2; i=dv/dx;
    dv=dv-i*dx; v=v1;
```

```
for(x=x1;x<=x2;x++) {
   r=r+dv;
   if(r>dx){ v=v+1;r=r-dx; }
   v=v+i;
}
```

In this algorithm the values to be interpolated are stored in v_1 and v_2. The algorithm determines the integer portion of the increment i which is added at each step. The fractional portion of the increment is represented by r and must be computed modulo Δx. As soon as the fractional part adds up to a value large enough, an integral contribution is made. If the values are floating point values it probably makes more sense to use a more accurate floating point algorithm rather than something similar to Bresenham's algorithm.

3.5 Rasterization in C#

It is important to take note of the theory behind rasterization so that future techniques can be developed. However, these algorithms are already implemented in C#. In this section we discuss some of the methods available for rasterization in C#.

To draw some object on a window, it is necessary to handle the *paint* event of the window. The paint event receives a `PaintEventArgs` parameter which describes which part of the window needs to be repainted, and also provides a `Graphics` object which can be used for rasterization. Most of the classes required are included in `System.Drawing`.

An alternative is to override the `OnPaint` method of the `Form` as follows

    `protected override void OnPaint(PaintEventArgs e);`

The `Graphics` object provides several methods for rasterizing geometric shapes. For example, a line is rendered with the method

    `void Graphics.DrawLine(Pen pen,int x1,int y1,int x2,int y2);`

The `Graphics` object also has methods that accept floating point values for the coordinates. These methods can anti-alias the drawing primitives more accurately than their integer counterparts if anti-aliasing is enabled. The `Graphics` method requires a `Pen` object to describe how the line is drawn. The pen usually describes the color used for drawing. Colored pens can be created using the `Color class`. For example, to select a black pen, specify `new Pen(Color.black)`. Several predefined colors exist, but it is also possible to specify a color based on red, green and blue components. To create such a pen, specify

```
Pen pen=new Pen(Color.FromArgb(r,g,b,t));
```

where r, g, b specify the color and t determines the transparency of the pen. The t component can be omitted. These components are in the range 0-255. So

```
Color.FromArgb(0,0,0)
```

specifies black and

```
Color.FromArgb(255,255,255)
```

specifies white.

Several rasterization methods are available including

```
void Graphics.DrawRectangle(Pen pen,int x,int y,
                            int width,int height);
void Graphics.DrawEllipse(Pen pen,int x,int y,
                            int width,int height);
void Graphics.DrawArc(Pen pen,int x,int y,int width,
          int height,int start_angle,int sweep_angle);
void Graphics.DrawPolygon(Pen pen,PointF[] points);
```

DrawPolygon accepts an array of PointF objects that represent ordered pairs of x- and y-coordinates that define points in the two-dimensional Cartesian plane. It is possible to fill rectangles, polygons and ellipses with

```
void Graphics.FillRectangle(Brush br,int x,int y,
                            int width,int height);
void Graphics.FillEllipse(Brush br,int x,int y,
                            int width,int height);
void Graphics.FillPolygon(Brush br,PointF[] points);
```

Instead of requiring a Pen object, fill routines require a Brush object. The Brush object allows primitives to be filled with patterns or images. We concentrate on fixed colors. In this case we can create a brush with

```
Brush brush=new SolidBrush(Color.FromArgb(r,g,b,a));
```

3.5.1   Drawing Pixels

The C# `Graphics` object does not support drawing pixels directly to the form. To simulate drawing pixels a line of less than 1 pixel in length, or a rectangle with area less than 1 pixel can be drawn. If a full pixel is used, then the primitive overlaps the adjacent pixel and two or more pixels are rendered instead of one. Drawing a pixel can thus be accomplished by

```
g.DrawLine(pen,x,y,x+0.5f,y);
```

or

```
g.DrawRectangle(pen,x,y,0.5f,0.5f);
```

The parameters x and y are of type `float`.

3.6   Bresenham's Algorithms in C#

In this section we present the Bresenham algorithms in C#. First we need a definition of `plot` to place a color in a pixel.

```
void plot(Graphics g,int x,int y) {
    Pen pen=new Pen(Color.Black);
    g.DrawLine(pen,x,y,x+0.5f,y);
}
```

For the circle, a function is needed to plot multiple points based on symmetry to cover all the quadrants.

```
void circleplot(Graphics g,int x,int y,int xc,int yc) {
    plot(g,x+xc,y+yc); plot(g,-x+xc,y+yc);
    plot(g,x+xc,-y+yc); plot(g,-x+xc,-y+yc);
    plot(g,y+yc,x+xc); plot(g,-y+yc,x+xc);
    plot(g,y+yc,-x+xc); plot(g,-y+yc,-x+xc);
}
```

There are two functions to draw lines, based on the gradient of the line. These functions are `linex` and `liney`. In addition, we make sure that the coordinates are in ascending order for the appropriate function, and determine whether the line ascends or descends. This value is stored in the `inc` variable.

```
void linex(Graphics g,int x1,int y1,int x2,int y2) {
    int dx,dy,r,x,y;
    int inc=1;
    if(x2<x1) { x=x2;x2=x1;x1=x2; y=y2;y2=y1;y1=y; }
```

```
    dx=x2-x1; dy=y2-y1;
    r=dx/2; y=y1;
    if(dy<0) { inc=-1; dy=-dy; }
    for(x=x1;x<=x2;x++){
        plot(g,x,y); r=r+dy;
        if(r>dx) { y=y+inc; r=r-dx; }
    }


}
```

The function `liney` is similar to `linex`, the roles of the x- and y-axes have simply been swapped.

```
void liney(Graphics g,int x1,int y1,int x2,int y2) {
    int dx,dy,r,x,y;
    int inc=1;
    if(y2<y1) { x=x2;x2=x1;x1=x2; y=y2;y2=y1;y1=y; }
    dx=x2-x1; dy=y2-y1;
    r=dy/2; x=x1;
    if(dx<0) { inc=-1; dx=-dx; }
    for(y=y1;y<=y2;y++){
        plot(g,x,y); r=r+dx;
        if(r>dy) { x=x+inc; r=r-dy; }
    }

}
```

The `line` function examines the gradient and determines which of `linex` and `liney` should be invoked.

```
void line(Graphics g,int x1,int y1,int x2,int y2) {
    int dx,dy;
    dx=x2-x1; dy=y2-y1;
    if(dx<0) dx=-dx;
    if(dy<0) dy=-dy;
    if(dx>dy) linex(g,x1,y1,x2,y2);
    else liney(g,x1,y1,x2,y2);
}
```

The `circle` function follows directly from the algorithm developed. The circle algorithm is derived for a circle centered at the origin. Instead of deriving a new algorithm for arbitrary circles, we can simply offset all points by a fixed amount to draw circles at various locations. Both `circle` and circleplot accept the parameters x1 and y1 that represent the center of the circle.

```
void circle(Graphics g,int x1,int y1,int r) {
    int x,y,d1,d2,e1,e2,e;
    x=r; y=0; e=0;
    d1=1; d2=2-2*r;
    while(y<=x){
        circleplot(g,x,y,x1,y1);
        e1=e+d1; e2=e+d2;
        if((Math.Abs(e2)<Math.Abs(e1))) {
            e=e2; x=x-1; d2=d2+2;
        } else { e=e1; }
        y=y+1; d1=d1+2; d2=d2+2;
    }
}
```

The required graphics object is provided by the paint event handler. Several lines and circles are drawn in the event handler.

```
void MainFormPaint(object sender,PaintEventArgs e) {
    line(e.Graphics,20,20,100,50);
    line(e.Graphics,20,50,100,20);
    line(e.Graphics,40,60,100,250);
    circle(e.Graphics,150,150,100);
}
```

3.7 Fractals

A *fractal* is "a rough or fragmented geometric shape that can be subdivided in parts, each of which is (at least approximately) a reduced/size copy of the whole" [90]. Fractal is derived from the Latin *fractus* meaning "broken" or "fractured" and was first used by Benoît Mandelbrot in 1975 to describe such structures. These structures usually possess self-similar properties and infinite detail. That is, on examination of smaller parts of the structure it appears that the smaller part has the same structure as the whole fractal object with subtle differences, ad infinitum. Fractals are thus useful for representing natural objects that have a self-similar structure, for example leaves, trees or terrain.

Fractal structures are characterized by a fractal dimension D. There are several measures of fractal dimension, two such measures are the *Hausdorff dimension* and *capacity* [125]. Suppose the fractal consists of all points

$x \in X$, where $X \subset \mathbb{R}^n$. A cover of X is a collection of balls (perhaps infinitely many) whose union contains X. The diameter of a cover $\mathcal{A}$ is the maximum diameter of the balls in $\mathcal{A}$. The smaller the maximum diameter, the better the cover approximates the set X. The cover can be used to measure the Hausdorff dimension. Let

$$\alpha(d, \epsilon) := \inf_{\substack{\mathcal{A}=\text{cover of } X \\ \text{diam } \mathcal{A} \leq \epsilon}} \sum_{A \in \mathcal{A}} (\text{diam } A)^d$$

and

$$\alpha(d) := \lim_{\epsilon \to 0} \alpha(d, \epsilon).$$

There is a unique d_0 such that

$$d < d_0 \Rightarrow \alpha(d) \to \infty$$
$$d > d_0 \Rightarrow \alpha(d) \to 0.$$

The quantity d_0 is defined to be the Hausdorff dimension of X.

Definition 3.1. *A fractal is a set for which the Hausdorff dimension strictly exceeds the topological dimension.*

The *topological dimension* is given by the *Lebesgue covering dimension*. To describe the topological dimension, it is necessary to define a refinement of a cover. A refinement of a cover C is another cover C' such that each ball in C' is contained in a ball of C. Refinements create a smaller cover in some sense (and thus more detailed). Suppose the fractal consists of all points $x \in X$, then the fractal has topological dimension m if every covering C of X has a refinement C' such that every point of X occurs in at most $m + 1$ balls in C'.

For many of the examples, the fractals are constructed out of line segments, the line segments are of topological dimension 1. However, the Hausdorff dimension lies somewhere between 1 and 2 for these figures.

Since real natural structures have finite self-similarity (eventually everything reduces to molecules and atoms) it is not necessary to evaluate fractal structures completely accurately. A finite precision (or number of iterations) is sufficient to achieve useful results. In this section we examine a few fractal structures.

3.7.1   Mandelbrot Set

The *Mandelbrot set* [90] is determined by the convergence of the recursion relation

$$z_{n+1} = z_n^2 + c, \quad n = 0, 1, 2, \ldots$$

Figure 3.1: Mandelbrot Set.

where c is the coordinate in the complex plane under consideration and $z_0 = c$. If the function converges, then the point is in the Mandelbrot set. If $z = x + iy$ $(x, y \in \mathbb{R})$ and $c = p + iq$ $(p, q \in \mathbb{R})$, then

$$z^2 + c \equiv x^2 - y^2 + p + (2xy + q)i.$$

Letting $z_n = x_n + iy_n$ the recursion relation can be rewritten as

$$x_{n+1} = x_n^2 - y_n^2 + p \quad y_{n+1} = 2x_n y_n + q, \quad n = 0, 1, 2, \ldots$$

In practice it is not necessary to determine absolutely whether the function converges. Rather, if the function has not diverged after a fixed number of iterations, then the point is assumed to be in the set. The series will diverge if $\|z_n\| > 2$. Figure 3.1 shows that the Mandelbrot set is clearly self-similar. The imaginary component corresponds to the vertical axis, and the real component corresponds to the real axis. The range over which the image was produced is $-2 \le x \le 2$ and $-2 \le y \le 2$. More colorful versions of the Mandelbrot set are obtained by coloring the contours of the number of iterations required to determine if the set converges. The contours are colored so as to provide a pleasing image.

The C# code renders to a bitmap first, and not directly to the screen. This is because the Mandelbrot set can take some time to compute. Thereafter the image is simply displayed. The variables a and b define the vertical and horizontal resolution of the bitmap.

```
// Mandelbrot.cs
private double xmin=-2.0, xmax=2.0;
private double ymin=-2.0, ymax=2.0;
private System.Drawing.Bitmap img;
```

```
public void mandelbrot() {
  int a=400, b=400, kmax=200, m=4;
  double x0, y0, dx, dy, x, y, r, p, q;
  dx=(xmax-xmin)/((double)a-1.0);
  dy=(ymax-ymin)/((double)b-1.0);

  for(int nx=0;nx<=a;nx++){
    for(int ny=0;ny<=b;ny++){
      int k=0;
      x0=xmin+nx*dx; y0=ymin+ny*dy;
      r=0; p=x0; q=y0;
      while((k++<=kmax)&&(r<m)) {
        x=x0; y=y0;
        x0=x*x-y*y+p; y0=2.0*x*y+q; r=x0*x0+y0*y0;
      }
      if(r>m){
        if(k<20) k*=10;
        if(k>255) k=255;
        img.SetPixel(nx,ny,Color.FromArgb(255,k,255-k,k));
      } else { img.SetPixel(nx,ny,Color.Black); }
    }
  }
}

void MainFormPaint(object sender,PaintEventArgs e)
  e.Graphics.DrawImage(img,0,0);
}
```

3.7.2   Julia Set

The *Julia set* is similar to the Mandelbrot set, but c is selected as constant instead. The Julia set is mostly studied for the map $f(z) = z^2 + c$, where $c \in \mathbb{C}$. Complex numbers belong to this particular Julia set if the sequence

$$z_{n+1} = z_n^2 + c, \qquad n = 0, 1, 2, \ldots$$

converges with c a predetermined complex constant and z_0 the point in the complex plane under evaluation. The divergence criteria is the same as that for the Mandelbrot set. Figure 3.2 illustrates some interesting choices for c. Once again color images can be produced by drawing colored contours of the number of iterations required before divergence. The Julia set also takes some time to compute and so the set is rendered to a bitmap first, before display.

// Julia.cs
```
private double xmin=-2.0, xmax=2.0;
```

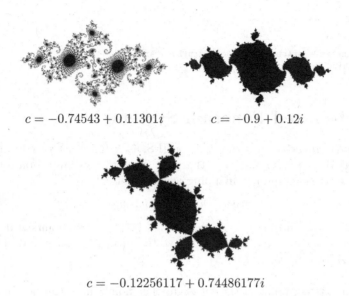

$c = -0.74543 + 0.11301i$ $\qquad$ $c = -0.9 + 0.12i$

$c = -0.12256117 + 0.74486177i$

Figure 3.2: Julia Set.

```
private double ymin=-2.0, ymax=2.0;
private System.Drawing.Bitmap img;

public void julia() {
  int a=400, b=400, kmax=200, m=4;
  double x0, y0, dx, dy, x, y, r;
  double p=-0.9, q=0.12;
  dx=(xmax-xmin)/((double)a-1.0);
  dy=(ymax-ymin)/((double)b-1.0);

  for(int nx=0;nx<=a;nx++){
    for(int ny=0;ny<=b;ny++){
      int k=0;
      x0=xmin+nx*dx; y0=ymin+ny*dy;
      r=0.0;
      while((k++<=kmax)&&(r<m)) {
        x=x0; y=y0;
        x0=x*x-y*y+p; y0=2.0*x*y+q; r=x0*x0+y0*y0;
      }
      if(r>m){
        if(k<20) k*=10;
        if(k>255) k=255;
        img.SetPixel(nx,ny,Color.FromArgb(255,k,255-k,k));
      } else { img.SetPixel(nx,ny,Color.Black); }
    }
  }
}
```

```
}

void MainFormPaint(object sender,PaintEventArgs e)
{ e.Graphics.DrawImage(img,0,0); }
```

3.8   Iterated Function Systems

An *iterated function system* [125], or IFS, is a finite set of contractive mappings $W = \{w_1, w_2, \ldots, w_n\}$ that map from the domain X onto itself. A contractive mapping is a mapping w such that

$$d(w(x), w(y)) < sd(x, y)$$

where d is a distance metric on X, and $s < 1$. The set of points A defined by the contractive mappings W all have the property that if $x \in A$ then $w_i(x) \in A$ for each $w_i \in W$.

Given an existing point in the set A, further points in A can be obtained by applying one of the contractive mappings to that point. If the original point is not in the set, then the contractive mappings gradually produce points closer to A. A is thus an *attractor* for the IFS.

An example of an IFS is a model of the fern leaf [3]. The fern leaf can be produced using the contractive mappings

$$w_1 = \begin{pmatrix} 0.00 & 0.00 & 0.00 \\ 0.00 & 0.16 & 0.00 \\ 0.00 & 0.00 & 1.00 \end{pmatrix}$$

$$w_2 = \begin{pmatrix} 0.20 & -0.26 & 0.00 \\ 0.23 & 0.22 & 1.60 \\ 0.00 & 0.00 & 1.00 \end{pmatrix}$$

$$w_3 = \begin{pmatrix} -0.15 & 0.28 & 0.00 \\ 0.26 & 0.24 & 0.44 \\ 0.00 & 0.00 & 1.00 \end{pmatrix}$$

$$w_4 = \begin{pmatrix} 0.85 & 0.04 & 0.00 \\ -0.04 & 0.85 & 1.60 \\ 0.00 & 0.00 & 1.00 \end{pmatrix}$$

which are given in homogeneous form for coordinates in the xy-plane. To render the set, we select the starting point $(0\ 0)^T$ and repeatedly choose one of the transforms to apply at random. Each point is plotted to create the image. The result is illustrated in figure 3.3. The paint event of C# is used to render the fern directly to the window in the following C# code.

Figure 3.3: IFS Fern.

```
//Fern.cs
  void MainFormPaint(object sender,Forms.PaintEventArgs e)
{
  int n, i;
  Random rnd=new Random();
  double x, y, xn, yn, r;
  float sx, sy;
  Pen pen=new Pen(Color.Black);
  n=20000; x=0.0; y=0.0;
  for(i=0;i<n;i++) {
    r=rnd.NextDouble();
    if(r<0.02) { xn=0.0; yn=0.16*y; }
    else if(r<=0.17) { xn=0.2*x-0.26*y; yn=0.23*x+0.22*y+1.6; }
    else if(r<=0.3) { xn=-0.15*x+0.28*y; yn=0.26*x+0.24*y+0.44;}
    else { xn=0.85*x+0.04*y; yn=-0.04*x+0.85*y+1.6; }
    x=xn; y=yn;
    sx=(float)((x/12.0+0.5)*Width);
    sy=(float)(y/12.0+0.15f);
    sy=(1.0f-sy)*Height;
    e.Graphics.DrawLine(pen,sx,sy,sx+0.5f,sy);
  }
}
```

3.9 L-Systems and Fractals

One of the defining features of fractals is self similarity. It is then natural to define self similar structures which converge to fractal figures. One way of defining these self-similar figures, is *Lindenmayer systems* [102] or

Figure 3.4: Tree generated with an L-System.

L-Systems for short. L-Systems are specified by a grammar consisting of a series of symbols, and productions. The symbols in the L-System describe some action or part of the figure. The productions describe how to produce the next iteration of the figure. In the limit, the figure may produce a fractal. A simple L-System to describe a tree would have productions looking something like

$$B \rightarrow BbB.$$

The initial tree is described by B. At each iteration, the branch is split into two branches of type B, with one normal branch b left over. The branches of type b will not split again. This L-System only provides the structure of the tree. An example of a tree after several iterations is shown in figure 3.4. Each branch is rotated a random amount to produce the irregular shape. After three productions the tree is described by

$$B \rightarrow BbB \rightarrow BbBbBbB \rightarrow BbBbBbBbBbBbBbB$$

which describes a trunk, first and second level branches.

The *Hilbert curve* is a fractal that can be produced by the L-System productions

$$L \rightarrow +RF - LFL - FR+$$
$$R \rightarrow -LF + RFR + FL-$$

The symbol + indicates a clockwise rotation of $90°$ and $-$ indicates an anticlockwise rotation of $90°$. F indicates that a line must be drawn in the current direction, 1 unit in length. R and L are ignored when drawing the Hilbert curve and are only used in productions. The initial string used

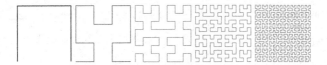

Figure 3.5: First four steps in the construction of the Hilbert curve.

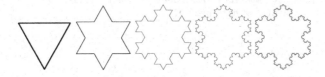

Figure 3.6: First five steps in the construction of the Koch snowflake.

to produce the curve is simply L. Examples of successive iterations of the Hilbert curve are illustrated in figure 3.5.

The *Koch snowflake* can also be produced by an L-System. The productions are given by

$$F \rightarrow F + F - -F + F$$

The initial string describing the snowflake is given by $F - -F - -F$. Once again F indicates that a line should be drawn in the current direction, $+$ indicates a clockwise rotation of $60°$ and $-$ indicates an anticlockwise rotation of $60°$. Several iterations in the production of the Koch snowflake are illustrated in figure 3.6. The Koch curve has infinite length even though it encloses a simply connected region in the xy-plane. The Hausdorff dimension of the Koch snowflake is

$$S = \frac{\ln(4)}{\ln(3)}.$$

The C# code to implement these L-System fractals is given below.

```
//LSystem.cs
using System;
using System.Collections.Generic;
using System.Drawing;
using System.Windows.Forms;

namespace lsystem
  public partial class MainForm
  {
    double scale, angle=90;
    string[] rules, patterns;
```

```csharp
string lsystem;
double startx=10.0, starty=10.0;
int maxdepth=5;

public static void Main(string[] args)
{
  Application.EnableVisualStyles();
  Application.SetCompatibleTextRenderingDefault(false);
  Application.Run(new MainForm());
}

public MainForm()
{
  //Hilbert curve
  rules=new string[2]; patterns=new string[2];
  rules[0]="L"; rules[1]="R";
  patterns[0]="+RF-LFL-FR+";
  patterns[1]="-LF+RFR+FL-";
  angle=90; lsystem="L";
  scale=300.0; startx=10.0; starty=10.0;

  //Koch snowflake
  rules=new string[1]; patterns=new string[1];
  rules[0]="F"; patterns[0]="F+F-F+F";
  angle=60; lsystem="F-F-F";
  scale=30.0; startx=200.0-scale*4; starty=200.0;
}

void LSystem(Graphics g) {
  string current=lsystem;
  string next=lsystem;
  bool found;
  int depth=0;
  while(depth<maxdepth) {
    current=next; next="";
    for(int i=0;i<current.Length;i++){
      found=false;
      for(int j=0;j<rules.Length;j++) {
        if(current[i]==rules[j][0]) {
          next=next+patterns[j]; found=true;
        }
      }
      if(!found) next=next+current[i];
    }
    depth++;
  }
  DrawLSystem(next,g);
}

void DrawLSystem(string ls,Graphics g) {
  double dx=scale/Math.Pow(2,maxdepth), dy=0.0;
```

```
double rx, ry, x=startx, y=starty;
Pen pen=new Pen(Color.Black);
for(int i=0;i<ls.Length;i++) {
  if(ls[i]=='F') {
    g.DrawLine(pen,(float)x,(float)y,(float)(x+dx),(float)(y+dy));
    x+=dx; y+=dy;
  }
  if(ls[i]=='+') {
    rx=dx; ry=dy;
    double radian=Math.PI*angle/180.0;
    dx=rx*Math.Cos(radian)-ry*Math.Sin(radian);
    dy=rx*Math.Sin(radian)+ry*Math.Cos(radian);
  }
  if(ls[i]=='-') {
    rx=dx; ry=dy;
    double radian=Math.PI*angle/180.0;
    dx=rx*Math.Cos(-radian)-ry*Math.Sin(-radian);
    dy=rx*Math.Sin(-radian)+ry*Math.Cos(-radian);
  }
 }
}

void MainFormPaint(object sender,PaintEventArgs e)
{ LSystem(e.Graphics); }
 }
}
```

3.10 Kronecker Product and Fractals

The *Kronecker product* of matrices (also known as the *tensor product* or *direct matrix product*) has been used in a variety of fields. The Kronecker product can also be used in image processing and related fields. Here we describe how the Kronecker product can be used in the construction of fractals.

3.10.1 Definitions

Let A be an $m \times n$ matrix and B be an $r \times s$ matrix. The *Kronecker product* [122, 126] of A and B is defined as the $(m \cdot r) \times (n \cdot s)$ matrix

$$A \otimes B := \begin{pmatrix} a_{11}B & a_{12}B & \cdots & a_{1n}B \\ a_{21}B & a_{22}B & \cdots & a_{2n}B \\ \vdots & \vdots & \ddots & \vdots \\ a_{m1}B & a_{m2}B & \cdots & a_{mn}B \end{pmatrix}.$$

For example, let

$$A = \begin{pmatrix} 1 & 1 \\ 0 & 1 \end{pmatrix}.$$

Then

$$A \otimes A = \begin{pmatrix} 1 & 1 & 1 & 1 \\ 0 & 1 & 0 & 1 \\ 0 & 0 & 1 & 1 \\ 0 & 0 & 0 & 1 \end{pmatrix}.$$

The Kronecker product is associative

$$(A \otimes B) \otimes C = A \otimes (B \otimes C).$$

The Kronecker product is also distributive

$$(A + B) \otimes C = A \otimes C + B \otimes C$$

for A and B both $m \times n$ matrices and C a $p \times q$ matrix. Let $c \in \mathbb{C}$. Then

$$((cA) \otimes B) = c(A \otimes B) = (A \otimes (cB)).$$

Let A be an $m \times n$ matrix, B be a $p \times q$ matrix, C be a $n \times r$ matrix and D be a $q \times s$ matrix then

$$(A \otimes B)(C \otimes D) = (AC) \otimes (BD)$$

where AC, BD denote matrix multiplication.

The *multiple Kronecker product* is defined in a recursive fashion as

$$\otimes_{i=1}^{k} A_i = (\otimes_{i=1}^{k-1} A_i) \otimes A_k$$
$$= A_1 \otimes A_2 \otimes \cdots \otimes A_k$$

where $\otimes_{i=1}^{1} A_i = A_1$. We can represent or approximate a given matrix A by the sum of several Kronecker products

$$A \cong \sum_{i=1}^{p} A_{i1} \otimes A_{i2} \otimes \cdots \otimes A_{ik}.$$

This is called the multiple Kronecker product sum approximation of the matrix A. Images and fractals can thus be represented by this multiple Kronecker product.

3.10.2   Kronecker Product Fractals

Many fractals have a self-similar nature, and so can be constructed from a union of self-similar sets. A closed, bounded self-similar set of the Euclidean plane $\mathbb{R}^2$ is a set of the form $A = A_1 \cup A_2 \cup \cdots \cup A_k$ with each of the sets A_i non-overlapping with A and congruent to A.

The simplest example of such a set, is perhaps the middle-third *Cantor set*. The Cantor set is obtained by starting with a line segment, and removing the middle third. The middle third of each of the remaining two segments is then also removed, and the process is continued ad infinitum. It is clear that the two remaining segments are self-similar to the original segment, scaled by a factor of $\frac{1}{3}$. We can express the middle-third Cantor set using the Kronecker product. Let $\mathbf{x} = (1\ 0\ 1)^T$ which represents the fact that the middle third is removed. The operation can be applied again to the remaining two segments by applying the Kronecker product

$$\mathbf{x} \otimes \mathbf{x} = (1\ 0\ 1\ 0\ 0\ 0\ 1\ 0\ 1)^T.$$

Thus each 1 has been replaced by a copy of the original vector. The middle-third Cantor set is thus given by

$$\bigotimes_{i=1}^{\infty} \mathbf{x}.$$

An approximation is given by $\bigotimes_{i=1}^{n} \mathbf{x}$. This set can be visualized if each entry 0 is identified with a black pixel and an entry 1 with a white pixel.

Other self-similar fractals can be produced in the same way. For any matrix produced in this fashion, each 0 entry is identified by a black pixel and each 1 entry is identified by a white pixel. For example, the *Sierpinski carpet* is obtained by taking a square, and dividing the square into 9 equal squares. The middle square is removed, and the process is repeated on the 8 remaining squares. The Sierpinski carpet can thus be generated from the defining matrix

$$X = \begin{pmatrix} 1 & 1 & 1 \\ 1 & 0 & 1 \\ 1 & 1 & 1 \end{pmatrix}$$

using the Kronecker product. The resulting approximation for $n = 7$ is shown in figure 3.7. To compute the Kronecker product fractal in C# we first need to implement the *Kronecker product*.

Figure 3.7: Sierpinski carpet after seven iterations of the Kronecker product.

//Kronecker.cs

```
double[,] Kronecker(double[,] M,double[,] N) {
    int i,j,k,l;
    double[,] R;
    R=new double[M.GetLength(0)*N.GetLength(0),
    M.GetLength(1)*N.GetLength(1)];
    for(i=0;i<M.GetLength(0);i++){
        for(j=0;j<M.GetLength(1);j++){
            for(k=0;k<N.GetLength(0);k++){
                for(l=0;l<N.GetLength(1);l++){
                    R[i*N.GetLength(0)+k,j*N.GetLength(1)+l]=M[i,j]*N[k,l];
                }
            }
        }
    }
    return R;
}
```

Now, the Kronecker product function can be used to create the Sierpinski carpet through iteration. The paint method invokes the function that generates the fractal, and then draws the resulting matrix on the screen using rectangles.

```
void SierpinskiCarpet(Graphics g) {
    double[,] J;
    double[,] R;
    J=new double[3,3];
    J[0,0]=1.0; J[0,1]=1.0; J[0,2]=1.0;
    J[1,0]=1.0; J[1,1]=0.0; J[1,2]=1.0;
    J[2,0]=1.0; J[2,1]=1.0; J[2,2]=1.0;
    R=new double[1,1]; R[0,0]=1.0;
    for(int i=0;i<5;i++) R=Kronecker(J,R);
```

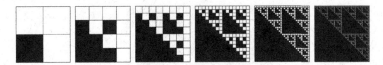

Figure 3.8: First six iterations of the Kronecker product to produce the Sierpinski triangle.

```
   DrawMatrix(R,g);
 }

 void DrawMatrix(double[,] R,Graphics g) {
   float dx=400.0f/R.GetLength(1);
   float dy=400.0f/R.GetLength(0);
   for(int x=0;x<R.GetLength(1);x++){
     for(int y=0;y<R.GetLength(0);y++){
       int b=(int)(R[y,x]*255);
       Brush brush=new SolidBrush(Color.FromArgb(b,b,b));
       g.FillRectangle(brush,x*dx,y*dy,dx,dy);
     }
   }
 }

 void MainFormPaint(object sender,PaintEventArgs e)
 { SierpinskiCarpet(e.Graphics); }
```

The *Sierpinski triangle* can be generated in the same way with the matrix

$$X = \begin{pmatrix} 1 & 1 \\ 0 & 1 \end{pmatrix}.$$

The stages in creation of the fractal (each step is displayed) are visible in figure 3.8.

Gray scale fractal images can be produced if the elements of the matrix are allowed to take on values between 0 and 1. For example, the matrix

$$X = \begin{pmatrix} 1.0 & 0.5 & 1.0 \\ 0.5 & 1.0 & 0.5 \\ 1.0 & 0.5 & 1.0 \end{pmatrix}$$

produces figure 3.9.

Obviously nonfractal images can be generated. For example the Kronecker product sum

$$\left(\bigotimes_{i=1}^{n} X \right) \otimes B$$

Figure 3.9: Kronecker product fractal: Gray scale fractal.

Figure 3.10: First four iterations of checkerboard generated by Kronecker products.

with matrices

$$X = \begin{pmatrix} 1 & 1 \\ 1 & 1 \end{pmatrix} \quad \text{and} \quad B = \begin{pmatrix} 0 & 1 \\ 1 & 0 \end{pmatrix}$$

generates a checkerboard (figure 3.10).

Chapter 4

Curves

4.1 Introduction

In this chapter we discuss existing curves and interpolation techniques. A few of the important properties that we desire for curves are introduced and proven where necessary. In particular we examine continuity and affine invariance. Affine invariance is of particular importance for the simple manipulation of curves and surfaces. The discussion is by no means meant to be exhaustive, we discuss primarily curves that will be of interest to us later on, and variations of these curves. Refer to the books by Buss [8] and Watt & Watt [138] for a more comprehensive treatment. In the next section we introduce transformations for manipulating curves, and then we proceed to discuss some of the more popular curves and splines in computer graphics. Before we do that, we discuss some properties of parametric curves.

Plane curves can be described in explicit form $y = f(x)$ (as a function graph) or implicitly as a set of points that satisfy an equation

$$f(x, y) = 0$$

and in parametric form

$$\mathbf{r}(t) = (x(t) \ y(t))^T.$$

Restrictions need to be placed on f so that the solutions do not fill the entire plane. *Algebraic curves* are curves defined by f such that f is a polynomial function in two variables. Equations of the first degree define straight lines while equations of the second degree define ellipses, parabolas or hyperbolas. Space curves in $\mathbb{R}^3$ can be defined as intersections of two surfaces $f(x_0, x_1, x_2) = 0$ and $g(x_0, x_1, x_2) = 0$. For example, the intersection of the two surfaces $x_0^2 + x_1^2 + x_2^2 = 1$ and $x_2 - 1/2 = 0$ is a circle. *Parametric curves* place restrictions on f by defining the curve in terms of some parameter, say t. The curve can then be written as

$$\mathbf{r}(t) = (x_0(t) \ x_1(t) \ x_2(t))^T$$

where $x_0(t)$, $x_1(t)$ and $x_2(t)$ are continuous functions defined on some interval $a \leq t \leq b$. Each value of $a \leq t \leq b$ defines a point on the curve. The curve is defined to be the set of all such points. However, there are still some parametric curves that are space filling, for example the Peano curve.

In most cases we assume that $\mathbf{r}(t)$ can be differentiated at least twice.

4.2 Affine Invariance

Given a curve defined by

$$\sum_{k=0}^{n-1} f_k(t)\mathbf{x}_k, \quad t \in [0,1]$$

we would like to investigate what happens when an affine transform is applied to the curve. It would be desirable if the affine transform applied to points generated by the curve, produces precisely the same curve as transforming the points $\mathbf{x}_k$ and then calculating the resulting curve. If the curve has this property, that is

$$A \sum_{k=0}^{n-1} f_k(t)\mathbf{x}_k = \sum_{k=0}^{n-1} f_k(t) A\mathbf{x}_k$$

then the curve is said to be *affine invariant* [138]. If the basis functions $f_k(t)$ of the curve satisfy the property $\sum_{k=0}^{n-1} f_k(t) = 1$ for $t \in [0,1]$ then the curve is affine invariant.

Theorem 4.1. *Let C be a curve defined by*

$$\sum_{k=0}^{n-1} f_k(t)\mathbf{x}_k, \quad t \in [0,1].$$

If the basis functions $f_k(t)$ are a partition of unity, that is

$$\sum_{k=0}^{n-1} f_k(t) = 1, \quad t \in [0,1]$$

*then C is affine invariant. That is, for any affine transform $A = TL$ where
L is a linear transform and T is a translation by $\mathbf{u}$ we have*

$$A \sum_{k=0}^{n-1} f_k(t)\mathbf{x}_k = \sum_{k=0}^{n-1} f_k(t)A\mathbf{x}_k.$$

Proof. We provide the proof by Buss [8]. We begin with the affine transform
applied to each point of the curve

$$A \sum_{k=0}^{n-1} f_k(t)\mathbf{x}_k = L\left(\sum_{k=0}^{n-1} f_k(t)\mathbf{x}_k\right) + \mathbf{u}$$

$$= \left(\sum_{k=0}^{n-1} Lf_k(t)\mathbf{x}_k\right) + \mathbf{u}, \quad \text{by definition 1.2(b)}$$

$$= \left(\sum_{k=0}^{n-1} f_k(t)L\mathbf{x}_k\right) + \mathbf{u}, \quad \text{by definition 1.2(a)}.$$

Using the property $\sum_{k=0}^{n-1} f_k(t) = 1$ of the basis functions we get

$$A \sum_{k=0}^{n-1} f_k(t)\mathbf{x}_k = \sum_{k=0}^{n-1} f_k(t)L\mathbf{x}_k + \left(\sum_{k=0}^{n-1} f_k(t)\right)\mathbf{u}$$

$$= \sum_{k=0}^{n-1} (f_k(t)L\mathbf{x}_k + f_k(t)\mathbf{u})$$

$$= \sum_{k=0}^{n-1} f_k(t)\,(L\mathbf{x}_k + \mathbf{u})$$

$$= \sum_{k=0}^{n-1} f_k(t)A\mathbf{x}_k$$

as required.   □

We now have one of the most significant properties for parametric curves
at our disposal, so we discuss some common parametric curves and indicate
if this property holds or not.

4.3 Convex Hull

It is useful if a curve lies within its *convex hull*. To be able to determine if
this is so, we need a formal definition of a convex hull.

Definition 4.1. *Let* $\mathbf{p}_1$, $\mathbf{p}_2$, ..., $\mathbf{p}_k$ *be points, and* a_1, a_2, ..., a_k *be real numbers. Then*

$$\sum_{j=1}^{k} a_j \mathbf{p}_j$$

is a linear combination of $\mathbf{p}_1$, $\mathbf{p}_2$, ..., $\mathbf{p}_k$. *If* $\sum_{j=1}^{k} a_j = 1$ *then this is called an affine combination of* $\mathbf{p}_1$, $\mathbf{p}_2$, ..., $\mathbf{p}_k$. *If* $\sum_{j=1}^{k} a_j = 1$ *and* $a_j \geq 0$ *then this is called a weighted average of* $\mathbf{p}_1$, $\mathbf{p}_2$, ..., $\mathbf{p}_k$.

Now we define a convex set.

Definition 4.2. *Let* A *be a set of points in* $\mathbb{R}^d$. *The set* A *is convex if and only if for any two points* $\mathbf{x}$ *and* $\mathbf{y}$ *in* A, *the line segment joining* $\mathbf{x}$ *and* $\mathbf{y}$ *is entirely in* A.

Finally we have the definition of a convex hull.

Definition 4.3. *The convex hull of* A *is the smallest convex set containing* A.

The convex hull of a set is the set of points that are weighted averages of points in that set. Thus

$$chull(A) := \left\{ \mathbf{x} \,|\, \mathbf{x} = \sum_{j=1}^{k} a_j \mathbf{p}_j, \, \mathbf{p}_j \in A, \, \sum_{j=1}^{k} a_j = 1, \, a_j \geq 0 \right\}$$

is a definition of the convex hull, where $A = \{\mathbf{p}_1, \mathbf{p}_2, \ldots, \mathbf{p}_k\}$.

4.4   Lagrange Interpolation

Perhaps the simplest form of interpolation is *Lagrange interpolation* [101]. Lagrange interpolation is given by

$$\mathbf{q}(t) = \sum_{k=0}^{n} L_k^n(t) \mathbf{x}_k$$

with

$$L_k^n(t) = \prod_{\substack{j=0 \\ j \neq k}}^{n} \frac{(t - t_j)}{(t_k - t_j)}$$

where t_j are the parameter values at which the values $\mathbf{x}_k$ should be interpolated. The basis functions $L_k^n(t)$ are *cardinal*. That is

$$L_k^n(t_j) = \delta_{j,k}$$

where $\delta_{j,k}$ is the *Kronecker delta* given by

$$\delta_{j,k} = \begin{cases} 0, & j \neq k \\ 1, & j = k. \end{cases}$$

The functions $L_k^n(t)$ are a partition of unity. Thus curves produced by Lagrange interpolation are affine invariant. However, Lagrange interpolation does not satisfy the convex hull property. If $t_j = j$, $j \in \mathbb{Z}$, then we have uniform Lagrange interpolation. The uniform Lagrange interpolation basis functions are shown in figure 4.1. Points on the curve can be efficiently calculated using Neville's algorithm [101].

Example. An example of Lagrange interpolation is shown in figure 4.2. The coordinates for interpolation are given by

$$\begin{aligned} \mathbf{x}_0 &= (1\ 1)^T & t_0 &= 0 \\ \mathbf{x}_1 &= (2\ 3)^T & t_1 &= 1 \\ \mathbf{x}_2 &= (4\ -1)^T & t_2 &= 2 \\ \mathbf{x}_3 &= (4.6\ 1.5)^T & t_3 &= 3. \end{aligned}$$

A significant problem with Lagrange interpolation, is oscillation. Figure 4.2 begins to show this behavior, we see that the curve extends a fair distance beyond $\mathbf{x}_1$ and $\mathbf{x}_2$. Typically we would like the curve to be more confined. By confined, we mean that the area of the convex hull of the curve should not be much greater than the area of the convex hull of the control points. In the next sections we discuss some of the more popular curves and how they may be used to interpolate points.

4.4.1 C# Implementation

Parametric curves are represented by the abstract class **Curve**. This class defines a method **evaluate** that all curves must implement.

```
// Curve.cs
public abstract class Curve {
```

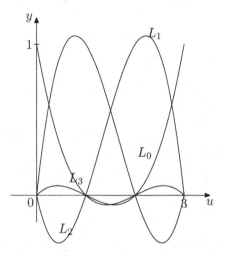

Figure 4.1: Basis functions for uniform Lagrange interpolation of degree 3.

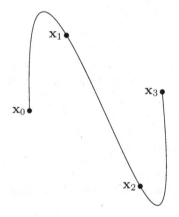

Figure 4.2: Uniform Lagrange interpolation of 4 points.

```
        public abstract Vector evaluate(Vector[] p,double t);
}
```

The main program adds points to an array for each point clicked and then queries a `Curve` to obtain points on the curve. These points are connected with line segments. The curve can be changed by replacing the curve object with an appropriate curve.

```
//CurveDraw.cs
using System;
using System.Collections.Generic;
using System.Drawing;
using System.Windows.Forms;

namespace curves
{
    public partial class MainForm
    {
        public Vector[] points;
        public Curve curve;
        [STAThread]
        public static void Main(string[] args)
        {
            Application.EnableVisualStyles();
            Application.SetCompatibleTextRenderingDefault(false);
            Application.Run(new MainForm());
        }

        public MainForm()
        {
            InitializeComponent();
            points=new Vector[0];
            curve=new Harmonic();
        }

        void MainFormMouseUp(object sender,MouseEventArgs e)
        {
            int n=points.GetLength(0);
            Vector v=new Vector(e.X,e.Y,0.0);
            Array.Resize(ref points,n+1);
            points[n]=v;
            Invalidate();
        }

        void MainFormPaint(object sender,PaintEventArgs e)
        {
            int n=points.GetLength(0);
            double t;
            Vector v,vnext;
            Pen pen=new Pen(Color.Black);
```

```
Brush b=new SolidBrush(Color.Black);
for(int i=0;i<n;i++) {
    e.Graphics.FillRectangle(b,(float)points[i].x-2.0f,
        (float)points[i].y-2.0f,4.0f,4.0f);
}
t=0.0;
v=curve.evaluate(points,t);
t+=0.001;
for(;t<=1.0;t+=0.001) {
    vnext=curve.evaluate(points,t);
    e.Graphics.DrawLine(pen,(float)v.x,(float)v.y,
        (float)vnext.x,(float)vnext.y);
    v=vnext;
}
t=1.0;
vnext=curve.evaluate(points,t);
e.Graphics.DrawLine(pen,(float)v.x,(float)v.y,
    (float)vnext.x,(float)vnext.y);
}

void CmdClearClick(object sender,EventArgs e)
{
    points=new Vector[0];
    Invalidate();
}
}
}
```

Lagrange interpolation is implemented by overriding the evaluate method of Curve.

//Lagrange.cs
```
public class Lagrange:Curve {
    public static double L(int n,int k,double t) {
        double l=1.0, tj, tk;
        tk=k/(n-1.0);
        for(int j=0;j<n;j++) {
            if(j!=k) { tj=j/(n-1.0); l*=(t-tj)/(tk-tj); }
        }
        return l;
    }

    public override Vector evaluate(Vector[] p,double t) {
        Vector r=new Vector();
        int n=p.GetLength(0);
        for(int i=0;i<n;i++) r+=L(n,i,t)*p[i];
        return r;
    }
}
```

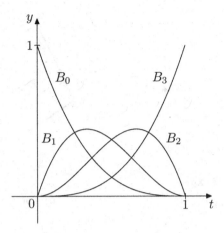

Figure 4.3: Basis functions for Bézier curves of degree 3.

4.5 Bézier Curves

Bézier curves [5] are one of the most popular representations for curves. Most of the common curves can be represented as Bézier curves. A Bézier curve of degree n is given by

$$\mathbf{q}(t) = \sum_{k=0}^{n} B_k^n(t)\mathbf{x}_k \qquad (4.1)$$

where the functions $B_k^n(t)$ are the *Bernstein polynomials* defined by

$$B_k^n(t) := \binom{n}{k} t^k (1-t)^{n-k} . \qquad (4.2)$$

The most popular Bézier curves, are Bézier curves of degree 3. The basis functions for degree 3 Bézier curves are displayed in figure 4.3. Bézier curves interpolate the end points $\mathbf{x}_0$ and $\mathbf{x}_n$. The Bernstein polynomials have a number of useful properties. These properties are discussed in the following sections.

4.5.1 Affine Invariance

The Bernstein polynomials are a partition of unity, in other words

$$\sum_{k=0}^{n} B_k^n(t) = 1.$$

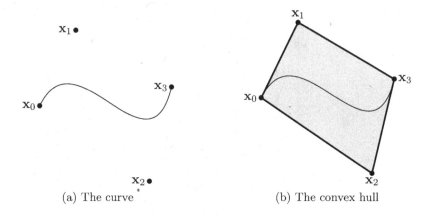

(a) The curve   (b) The convex hull

Figure 4.4: A Bézier curve and its convex hull.

This is easily seen by application of the *binomial theorem* [134]

$$\sum_{k=0}^{n} B_k^n(t) = \sum_{k=0}^{n} \binom{n}{k} t^k (1-t)^{n-k} = (t + (1-t))^n = 1.$$

From theorem 4.1 it is clear that Bézier curves are affine invariant. Figure 4.4(a) shows an example of a Bézier curve.

4.5.2 Convex Hull

It is easy to see from figure 4.3, and in general, that $0 \leq B_k^n(t) \leq 1$ for $t \in [0,1]$. A point on the Bézier curve $q(t) = \sum_{k=0}^{n} B_k^n(t) x_k$ is thus a *weighted average* [8] of the points x_k. The convex hull of the curve $q(t)$ is the set of all weighted averages of x_k. The Bézier curve thus lies in the convex hull of the points x_k. The convex hull is easily defined by a polygon created from the points x_k (not necessarily in order). This will prove useful when considering how to draw Bézier curves and surfaces. The convex hull of the Bézier curve illustrated in figure 4.4(a) is displayed in figure 4.4(b).

4.5.3 Derivative at Edges

The derivative of $q(t)$ given by eq. 4.1 with respect to the parameter t is

$$q'(t) = \sum_{k=0}^{n} B_k'(t) x_k$$

$$= \sum_{k=0}^{n} \left(\frac{d}{dt} \binom{n}{k} t^k (1-t)^{n-k} \right) \mathbf{x}_k$$

$$= \sum_{k=0}^{n} \binom{n}{k} (kt^{k-1}(1-t)^{n-k} - t^k(n-k)(1-t)^{n-k-1}) \mathbf{x}_k$$

$$= \sum_{k=0}^{n} \binom{n}{k} kt^{k-1}(1-t)^{n-k} \mathbf{x}_k - \sum_{k=0}^{n} \binom{n}{k} t^k(n-k)(1-t)^{n-k-1} \mathbf{x}_k .$$

In the sum on the right hand side, the term given by $k = n$ is 0,

$$\mathbf{q}'(t) = \sum_{k=0}^{n} \binom{n}{k} kt^{k-1}(1-t)^{n-k} \mathbf{x}_k - \sum_{k=0}^{n-1} \binom{n}{k} t^k(n-k)(1-t)^{n-k-1} \mathbf{x}_k$$

and once again on the left hand side, the term given by $k = 0$ is 0. Thus

$$\mathbf{q}'(t) = \sum_{k=1}^{n} \binom{n}{k} kt^{k-1}(1-t)^{n-k} \mathbf{x}_k - \sum_{k=0}^{n-1} \binom{n}{k} t^k(n-k)(1-t)^{n-k-1} \mathbf{x}_k .$$

We alter the index in the left hand sum to begin at zero,

$$\mathbf{q}'(t) = \sum_{k=0}^{n-1} \binom{n}{k+1} (k+1)t^k(1-t)^{n-k-1} \mathbf{x}_{k+1}$$

$$- \sum_{k=0}^{n-1} \binom{n}{k} t^k(n-k)(1-t)^{n-k-1} \mathbf{x}_k .$$

To simplify the expression we use the identities

$$\binom{n}{k+1}(k+1) \equiv n\binom{n-1}{k}, \qquad \binom{n}{k}(n-k) \equiv n\binom{n-1}{k}$$

so that

$$\mathbf{q}'(t) = \sum_{k=0}^{n-1} n\binom{n-1}{k} t^k(1-t)^{n-k-1} \mathbf{x}_{k+1}$$

$$- \sum_{k=0}^{n-1} n\binom{n-1}{k} t^k(1-t)^{n-k-1} \mathbf{x}_k$$

$$= \sum_{k=0}^{n-1} n\binom{n-1}{k} t^k(1-t)^{n-k-1} (\mathbf{x}_{k+1} - \mathbf{x}_k)$$

$$= n \sum_{k=0}^{n-1} B_k^{n-1}(t)(\mathbf{x}_{k+1} - \mathbf{x}_k) . \qquad (4.3)$$

Hence the derivative of a Bézier curve is also a Bézier curve. Furthermore, we have

$$\mathbf{q}'(0) = n(\mathbf{x}_1 - \mathbf{x}_0) \quad \text{and} \quad \mathbf{q}'(1) = n(\mathbf{x}_n - \mathbf{x}_{n-1}). \qquad (4.4)$$

Thus we have an immediate form for the derivative at the end points. This will prove to be useful in defining curves that are piecewise continuous.

4.5.4   Piecewise Continuous Bézier Curves

We can construct Bézier curves of arbitrary degree. However, it becomes more difficult to control the curve since the Bézier curve is only guaranteed to interpolate the end points. Instead, it is often sufficient to create several Bézier curves that are piecewise continuous. That is, the curves are continuous, and at the points where they join, there is continuity. There are different kinds of continuity that can be considered.

Definition 4.4. *Let $k \geq 0$. A function $\mathbf{f}(u)$ is C^k continuous if $\mathbf{f}$ has the kth derivative defined and continuous everywhere in the domain of $\mathbf{f}$. C^0 continuity is simply the usual definition of continuity. $\mathbf{f}$ is C^∞ continuous if $\mathbf{f}$ is C^k continuous for all $k \geq 0$.*

Definition 4.5. *A function $\mathbf{f}(u)$ is G^1 continuous provided $\mathbf{f}$ is continuous and there is a function $t = t(u)$ that is continuous and strictly increasing such that the function $\mathbf{g}(u) = \mathbf{f}(t(u))$ has a continuous, nonzero first derivative everywhere in its domain.*

Usually we use C^1 continuity, but G^1 continuity sometimes offers better control. It is easy to see that we can obtain C^1 continuity between two Bézier curves $\mathbf{q}(t)$ and $\mathbf{r}(t)$ defined as

$$\mathbf{q}(t) = \sum_{k=0}^{n} B_k^n(t)\mathbf{q}_k$$

and

$$\mathbf{r}(t) = \sum_{k=0}^{n} B_k^n(t)\mathbf{r}_k$$

by requiring that $\mathbf{q}'(1) = \mathbf{r}'(0)$. Using equation 4.4, we require that

$$\mathbf{q}_n - \mathbf{q}_{n-1} = \mathbf{r}_1 - \mathbf{r}_0.$$

For G^1 continuity we can require that

$$\mathbf{q}_n - \mathbf{q}_{n-1} = s(\mathbf{r}_1 - \mathbf{r}_0).$$

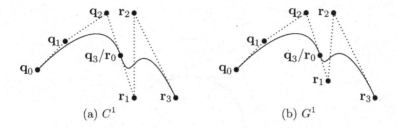

Figure 4.5: Piecewise continuous Bézier curves.

We have assumed that $\mathbf{q}(t)$ will occur before $\mathbf{r}(t)$, as is demonstrated by our choice of control points. This example is easily adapted to Bézier curves of different degree. We can now construct a piecewise smooth curve (C^1) from m Bézier curves $\mathbf{q}^j(t)$, $j = 1, \ldots, m$, of degree n, by requiring that

$$\mathbf{q}_n^j - \mathbf{q}_{n-1}^j = \mathbf{q}_1^{j+1} - \mathbf{q}_0^{j+1}, \quad \text{for } j = 1, \ldots, m-1. \tag{4.5}$$

The continuous curve can then be defined by

$$\mathbf{Q}(t) = \begin{cases} \mathbf{q}^1(t \cdot m), & t \in [0, \frac{1}{m}) \\ \mathbf{q}^2(t \cdot m - 1), & t \in [\frac{1}{m}, \frac{2}{m}) \\ \quad\vdots \\ \mathbf{q}^m(t \cdot m - (m-1)), & t \in [\frac{m-1}{m}, 1]. \end{cases}$$

The control points of $\mathbf{Q}(t)$ are simply the control points of $\mathbf{q}^j(t)$, $j = 1, \ldots, m$, with the restriction 4.5. A C^1 piecewise smooth Bézier curve is illustrated in figure 4.5(a), and a G^1 piecewise smooth Bézier curve is illustrated in figure 4.5(b) with $s = 0.6$.

4.5.5 Rendering

To render a Bézier curve $\mathbf{q}(t)$ we can simply choose a number of values $t_j \in [0, 1]$, $j = 0, \ldots, m$, so that $t_j < t_{j+1}$ and render line segments from $\mathbf{q}(t_j)$ to $\mathbf{q}(t_{j+1})$. We usually select equally spaced t_j. As $m \to \infty$ we get closer to the correct Bézier curve. Repeated evaluation of the Bernstein polynomial (equation 4.2) can be expensive. The next result can increase the speed at which points on Bézier curves can be evaluated.

de Casteljau's Method

de Casteljau's method [138] allows us to evaluate the points on a Bézier curve by repeated linear interpolation. If the control points of the curve

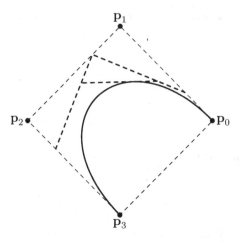

Figure 4.6: de Casteljau's method.

are $\mathbf{p}_i$ for $i = 0, 1, \ldots, n$, which defines a Bézier curve of degree n, then we define

$$\mathbf{p}_i^r(t) := (1 - t)\mathbf{p}_i^{r-1}(t) + t\mathbf{p}_{i+1}^{r-1}(t) \qquad (4.6)$$

with $r = 1, \ldots, n$, $i = 0, \ldots, n - r$, and $\mathbf{p}_i^0(t) = \mathbf{p}_i$.

The Bézier curve is then given by $\mathbf{q}(t) = \mathbf{p}_0^n(t)$. The repeated linear interpolation as demonstrated in figure 4.6 is an efficient technique to draw Bézier curves. The figure illustrates a degree 3 Bézier curve, where de Casteljau's algorithm is used to calculate the point for $t = 0.3$. Dashed lines show the control polygon, and dark dashed lines connect the points between which repeated linear interpolation took place. Although de Casteljau's method can increase speed, we still do not know at how many points the Bézier curve needs to be evaluated to obtain acceptable results. The next section discusses how Bézier curves may be subdivided until a desired level of accuracy is obtained.

Recursive Subdivision

We now investigate a technique that allows us to break Bézier curves down into sub-portions until we have a curve that can be approximated by a line for the desired level of accuracy. If we have a Bézier curve $\mathbf{q}(t)$ of degree n, then

$$\mathbf{q}_1(t) = \mathbf{q}(t/2) \qquad \text{and} \qquad \mathbf{q}_2 = \mathbf{q}((t + 1)/2)$$

are both Bézier curves of degree n. We have then successfully divided the curve in two. Drawing a Bézier curve can now be achieved by recursively subdividing the Bézier curve in two until the portions of the Bézier curves are as close to a straight line as we need. One way to determine if the curve is close enough to a straight line, is to define an error value δ. If

$$\|\mathbf{q}(0.5) - \frac{1}{2}(\mathbf{p}_0 + \mathbf{p}_n)\| < \delta \qquad (4.7)$$

then we assume the distance from the curve to the line will be less than δ pixels, and can thus be approximated by a straight line segment. This test may fail on occasion, another test that can be used is to determine how far the interior points of the control polygon are from the line connecting the first and last control point. Now we prove that the two portions of the curve are indeed Bézier curves (from [8]).

Theorem 4.2. *Let $\mathbf{q}_1(t) = \mathbf{q}(t_0 t)$ and $\mathbf{q}_2(t) = \mathbf{q}(t_0 + (1 - t_0)t)$, where $t_0 \in [0, 1]$ determines the parameter value at which the curve should be split. If $t_0 = 0.5$ then the curve is split in two in such a way that the parameter values are divided equally between the curves. If the curve is defined over $t \in [0, 1]$ then the subdivided curve $\mathbf{q}_1$ will be $\mathbf{q}$ defined over $t \in [0, t_0]$, and $\mathbf{q}_2$ will be $\mathbf{q}$ defined over $t \in [t_0, 1]$.*

a) The curve $\mathbf{q}_1(t)$ is equal to the degree n Bézier curve with control points $\mathbf{p}_0^0$, $\mathbf{p}_0^1$, $\mathbf{p}_0^2$, $\ldots$, $\mathbf{p}_0^n$.

b) The curve $\mathbf{q}_2(t)$ is equal to the degree n Bézier curve with control points $\mathbf{p}_0^n$, $\mathbf{p}_1^{n-1}$, $\mathbf{p}_2^{n-2}$, $\ldots$, $\mathbf{p}_n^0$.

We use $\mathbf{p}_i^j$ as defined in equation 4.6.

Proof. Only part (a) will be proven. We provide the proof by Buss [8]. We want to show that

$$\mathbf{q}(t_0 t) = \sum_{j=0}^{n} B_j^n(t)\mathbf{p}_0^j(t_0)\,.$$

This is equivalent to showing that

$$\sum_{i=0}^{n} B_i^n(t_0 t)\mathbf{p}_i = \sum_{j=0}^{n} B_j^n(t) \sum_{i=0}^{j} B_i^j(t_0)\mathbf{p}_i$$

$$= \sum_{j=0}^{n} \sum_{i=0}^{j} B_j^n(t) B_i^j(t_0)\mathbf{p}_i$$

$$= \sum_{i=0}^{n} \sum_{j=i}^{n} B_j^n(t) B_i^j(t_0)\mathbf{p}_i\,.$$

In the last step, we just swapped the order of the summation as described in [73]. The coefficients of $\mathbf{p}_i$ should be equal, so we must show that

$$B_i^n(t_0 t) = \sum_{j=i}^{n} B_j^n(t) B_i^j(t_0).$$

Using the definition of the Bernstein polynomials (equation 4.2) we get

$$\binom{n}{i}(t_0 t)^i(1 - t_0 t)^{n-i} = \sum_{j=i}^{n} \binom{n}{j}\binom{j}{i} t^j t_0^i (1-t)^{n-j}(1-t_0)^{j-i}.$$

We have the identity

$$\binom{n}{j}\binom{j}{i} \equiv \binom{n}{i}\binom{n-i}{j-i}$$

and dividing by $\binom{n}{i}(t_0 t)^i$ on both sides gives

$$(1 - t_0 t)^{n-i} = \sum_{j=i}^{n} \binom{n-i}{j-i} t^{j-i}(1-t)^{n-j}(1-t_0)^{j-i}.$$

Thus we find

$$\sum_{j=i}^{n} \binom{n-i}{j-i} t^{j-i}(1-t)^{n-j}(1-t_0)^{j-i} = \sum_{j=0}^{n-i} \binom{n-i}{j} t^j (1-t)^{n-j-i}(1-t_0)^j$$

$$= \sum_{j=0}^{n-i} \binom{n-i}{j}(1-t)^{n-j-i}(t - t_0 t)^j$$

$$= ((t - t_0 t) + (1-t))^{n-i}$$

$$= (1 - t_0 t)^{n-i}$$

using the binomial theorem.   □

This theorem provides us with the ability to subdivide a Bézier curve into two Bézier curves of the same degree. Furthermore, the parameter values for the two curves produced are still between 0 and 1. In addition, we can compute the new control points for these curves. Using the convex hull property or equation 4.7, we can subdivide the Bézier curves until the terminating criteria is satisfied. In this case we can draw a line from $\mathbf{p}_0$ to $\mathbf{p}_n$. Figure 4.7 shows the result when figure 4.4 is subdivided.

We now have an efficient technique for drawing Bézier curves. In the next section, we consider the effect of homogeneous coordinates on Bézier curves.

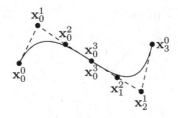

Figure 4.7: Subdivision of figure 4.4 into two Bézier curves.

4.5.6   Rational Bézier Curves

A Bézier curve is rational if its control points are specified by homogeneous coordinates. If we define the Bézier curve in terms of homogeneous coordinates, then each control point $\mathbf{x}_k$ becomes $(w_k\mathbf{x}_k\ \ w_k)^T$. The Bézier curve is then given by

$$\mathbf{q}(t) = \sum_{k=0}^{n} B_k^n(t)(w_k\mathbf{x}_k\ \ w_k)^T.$$

The point $\mathbf{q}(t)$ is also a homogeneous coordinate. The point that $\mathbf{q}(t)$ represents is given by

$$\frac{\sum_{k=0}^{n} w_k B_k^n(t)\mathbf{x}_k}{\sum_{k=0}^{n} w_k B_k^n(t)}.$$

The w_k terms act as weighting factors, and specify how much influence a point has on the curve. The extra weighting factors allows us to draw conic sections, which we are unable to do with conventional Bézier curves. The books by Farin [32] and Lasser [65] provide more details regarding rational Bézier curves.

4.5.7   Bézier Curves: Conic Sections

Rational Bézier curves can be used to draw conic sections. In this section we briefly illustrate how a segment of a circle can be drawn using a rational Bézier curve of degree 3. Figure 4.8 shows the right side of a circle and the control points required to draw the curve.

4.5.8   C# Implementation

```
//Bezier.cs
using System;
```

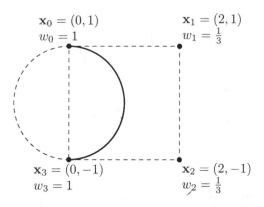

Figure 4.8: Section of a circle, drawn with a rational Bézier curve.

```
public class Bezier:Curve {
    public static double B(int n,int k,double t) {
        double tnk, tk, num=1.0, den=1.0;
        int b, j;
        n=n-1;
        tk=Math.Pow(t,k);
        tnk=Math.Pow(1.0-t,n-k);
        if(n-k>k) b=n-k; else b=k;
        //prefactor part of the combination out, so that the numbers aren't so large
        for(j=b+1;j<=n;j++) num*=j;
        for(j=1;j<=n-b;j++) den*=j;
        return tk*tnk*num/den;
    }

    public override Vector evaluate(Vector[] p,double t) {
        Vector r=new Vector();
        int n=p.GetLength(0);
        for(int i=0;i<n;i++) r+=B(n,i,t)*p[i];
        return r;
    }
}
```

4.6   Catmull-Rom Splines

Catmull-Rom splines [13] interpolate the control points $\mathbf{x}_1, \ldots, \mathbf{x}_{n-1}$ using piecewise degree 3 Bézier curves. For Catmull-Rom splines the parameter values are chosen so that $t \in [0, n]$ and $\mathbf{q}(i) = \mathbf{x}_i$ for $i = 1, \ldots, n - 1$. The interpolation points are placed at parameter values $t_i = i$. The derivatives of the curve at each point are approximated by the line joining the previous and next point. We define

$$\mathbf{l}_i := \frac{1}{2}(\mathbf{x}_{i+1} - \mathbf{x}_{i-1}). \tag{4.8}$$

We then define

$$\mathbf{x}_i^+ := \mathbf{x}_i + \frac{1}{3}\mathbf{l}_i \quad \text{and} \quad \mathbf{x}_i^- := \mathbf{x}_i - \frac{1}{3}\mathbf{l}_i.$$

The segment of the curve is defined by a Bézier curve of degree 3 with control points $\mathbf{x}_i$, $\mathbf{x}_i^+$, $\mathbf{x}_{i+1}^-$, and $\mathbf{x}_{i+1}$. The curve is piecewise continuous by construction.

4.7   Bessel-Overhauser Splines

If the control points for a Catmull-Rom spline are not placed uniformly then curves are not always as smooth as we would expect. This is because equation 4.8 does not take into account the distance between the control points. So, the larger the distance between the control points, the greater the "velocity", causing apparent overshoots to occur. If we place the control points at non-uniform parameter values t_i, then this effect can be reduced. We define

$$\mathbf{v}_{i+\frac{1}{2}} := \frac{\mathbf{x}_{i+1} - \mathbf{x}_i}{t_{i+1} - t_i}$$

and

$$\mathbf{v}_i := \frac{(t_{i+1} - t_i)\mathbf{v}_{i-\frac{1}{2}} + (t_i - t_{i-1})\mathbf{v}_{i+\frac{1}{2}}}{t_{i+1} - t_{i-1}}.$$

The interpolation points are defined much the same as with Catmull-Rom splines except we change the definition of $\mathbf{x}_i^+$ and $\mathbf{x}_i^-$ to

$$\mathbf{x}_i^+ := \mathbf{x}_i + \frac{1}{3}(t_{i+1} - t_i)\mathbf{v}_i \quad \text{and} \quad \mathbf{x}_i^- := \mathbf{x}_i - \frac{1}{3}(t_i - t_{i-1})\mathbf{v}_i.$$

With suitable choices for t_i, the resulting curve is pleasing even when control point distance varies.

4.8   Tension-Continuity-Bias Splines

Catmull-Rom splines do not give much control over the curvature at interpolation points. To improve the control we can introduce *tension, continuity* and *bias* controls to affect the tangents and the $\mathbf{x}_i^+$ and $\mathbf{x}_i^-$ control points. We introduce left and right first derivatives for an interpolation point $\mathbf{x}_i$ as follows

$$Dx_i^- := \lim_{t \to t_i^-} \frac{\mathbf{q}(t_i) - \mathbf{q}(t)}{t_i - t} = 3(\mathbf{x}_i - \mathbf{x}_i^-),$$

$$Dx_i^+ := \lim_{t \to t_i^+} \frac{\mathbf{q}(t) - \mathbf{q}(t_i)}{t - t_i} = 3(\mathbf{x}_i^+ - \mathbf{x}_i).$$

We can now determine values for $\mathbf{x}_i^+$ and $\mathbf{x}_i^-$ using the above equations to get

$$\mathbf{x}_i^+ = \mathbf{x}_i + \frac{1}{3}Dx_i^+ \quad \text{and} \quad \mathbf{x}_i^- = \mathbf{x}_i - \frac{1}{3}Dx_i^-.$$

For Catmull-Rom splines Dx^- and Dx^+ are defined by

$$Dx_i^+ := \frac{1}{2}(\mathbf{v}_{i-\frac{1}{2}} + \mathbf{v}_{i+\frac{1}{2}})$$
$$Dx_i^- := Dx_i^+$$

where $\mathbf{v}_{i-\frac{1}{2}} = \mathbf{p}_i - \mathbf{p}_{i-1}$ and $\mathbf{v}_{i+\frac{1}{2}} = \mathbf{p}_{i+1} - \mathbf{p}_i$. To obtain more control we add a parameter t to control the tension, or tightness of the curve. We also introduce a continuity parameter c. If $c = 1$ then the curve is continuous. Lastly, we introduce a bias parameter b. The bias parameter weights $\mathbf{v}_{i-\frac{1}{2}}$ and $\mathbf{v}_{i+\frac{1}{2}}$ differently to cause overshoot or undershoot. The final formula for tension-continuity-bias splines is then

$$Dx_i^- = \frac{(1-t)(1-c)(1+b)}{2}\mathbf{v}_{i-\frac{1}{2}} + \frac{(1-t)(1+c)(1-b)}{2}\mathbf{v}_{i+\frac{1}{2}}$$
$$Dx_i^+ = \frac{(1-t)(1+c)(1+b)}{2}\mathbf{v}_{i-\frac{1}{2}} + \frac{(1-t)(1-c)(1-b)}{2}\mathbf{v}_{i+\frac{1}{2}}.$$

These parameters can be applied globally to the entire curve, or locally to certain interpolation points.

We have discussed a variety of piecewise continuous curves that are G^1 or C^1 continuous. Next we consider cubic curves that are piecewise continuous (C^2) by design.

4.9   Uniform B-Splines

Piecewise continuous Bézier curves have C^1 continuity as we have defined them. We now investigate piecewise continuous cubic curves, since these are the most common. It is possible to follow a similar process to derive

B-splines of higher degree. We aim to produce curves that are C^2. The ith segment in the cubic B-spline will be denoted by $\mathbf{q}_i$. Four control points specify the curve. The control points are $\mathbf{x}_i$, $\mathbf{x}_{i+1}$, $\mathbf{x}_{i+2}$ and $\mathbf{x}_{i+3}$. We have assumed that the cubic spline will share control points.

We begin by considering the curve $\mathbf{q}_i$ with basis functions $B_k(t)$ and control points $\mathbf{x}_i$, $\mathbf{x}_{i+1}$, $\mathbf{x}_{i+2}$ and $\mathbf{x}_{i+3}$. The curve is given by

$$\mathbf{q}_i(t) = \sum_{k=0}^{3} B_k(t)\mathbf{x}_{i+k} \, .$$

The curve $\mathbf{q}_{i+1}(t)$ is defined similarly. We want to define the basis functions $B_k(t)$ so that we have C^0, C^1 and C^2 continuity between adjacent curves. For C^0 continuity we require that

$$\mathbf{q}_i(1) = \mathbf{q}_{i+1}(0) \, .$$

It follows that

$$\sum_{k=0}^{3} B_k(1)\mathbf{x}_{i+k} = \sum_{k=0}^{3} B_k(0)\mathbf{x}_{i+k+1} \, .$$

The control points can take on arbitrary values so the coefficients of the control points should be equal. Requiring C^1 and C^2 continuity we get

$$
\begin{array}{lll}
B_0(1)=0 & B_0'(1)=0 & B_0''(1)=0 \\
B_1(1)=B_0(0) & B_1'(1)=B_0'(0) & B_1''(1)=B_0''(0) \\
B_2(1)=B_1(0) & B_2'(1)=B_1'(0) & B_2''(1)=B_1''(0) \\
B_3(1)=B_2(0) & B_3'(1)=B_2'(0) & B_3''(1)=B_2''(0) \\
0=B_3(0) & 0=B_3'(0) & 0=B_3''(0) \, .
\end{array}
$$

So we have 15 equations in 16 unknowns. We need an extra constraint to solve the system of equations. Since the affine invariance property is useful, we require that $\sum_{k=0}^{3} B_k(0) = 1$. Solving the system of equations yields

$$B_0(t) = \frac{1}{6}(1 - t)^3$$

$$B_1(t) = \frac{1}{6}(3t^3 - 6t^2 + 4)$$

$$B_2(t) = \frac{1}{6}(-3t^3 + 3t^2 + 3t + 1)$$

$$B_3(t) = \frac{1}{6}t^3 \, .$$

The basis functions for each curve segment is shown in figure 4.9. This is

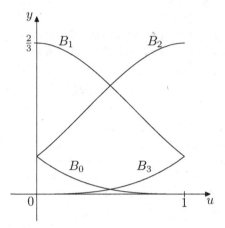

Figure 4.9: Basis functions of B-splines of degree 3.

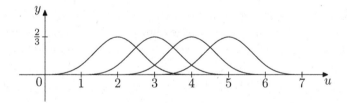

Figure 4.10: Blending functions of B-splines of degree 3.

the definition for one segment. We have several segments placed in sequence and use a parameter T to define the curve globally, and t will be used to determine the local parameter for a segment. We thus have $T \in [0, n-2]$, where there are n control points, and $t = T - i$ for a particular segment. We can now define the *blending functions* that will be used throughout the curve as

$$N_i(T) = \begin{cases} B_3(t_0), & i-3 \le T < i-2 \\ B_2(t_1), & i-2 \le T < i-1 \\ B_1(t_2), & i-1 \le T < i \\ B_0(t_3), & i \le T < i+1 \\ 0, & \text{otherwise.} \end{cases}$$

We have to select an appropriate t_j for the basis functions. t_j is calculated from the global parameter T by $t_j = T - i + 3 - j$. We can see that the correct basis functions are selected by noting that $N_0(t) = B_0(t_3)$ for $t \in [0,1]$, and $N_1(t) = B_1(t_2)$, and so forth. The entire curve can now be defined as

$$\mathbf{q}(t) = \sum_{i=0}^{n} N_i(t)\mathbf{x}_i, \quad t \in [0, n-2].$$

The maximum parameter is clearly $n-2$ since each segment i is defined by the control points $\mathbf{x}_i$, $\mathbf{x}_{i+1}$, $\mathbf{x}_{i+2}$ and $\mathbf{x}_{i+3}$. So the last segment is segment $n-3$, and the last value of T with nonzero value for $N_{n-3}(T)$ is the maximum T such that $n-3 \le T < n-3+1$ so that $T < n-2$. The blending functions are illustrated in figure 4.10. It is interesting to note that the support of each of the functions N_i is $(i, i+4)$. We only need to calculate the contribution of the blending functions with nonzero value for a particular value of t. The curve can then be defined by

$$\mathbf{q}(t) = \sum_{i=j}^{j+3} N_i(t)\mathbf{x}_i, \quad t \in [j, j+1], 0 \le j \le n-3.$$

This indicates that there is a large degree of local control. In other words, it is possible to edit one portion of a curve without influencing remote portions of the curve. Figure 4.12 illustrates a cubic B-spline. The usefulness of B-splines is apparent in comparison to the Bézier curve of high degree (using the same control points) illustrated in figure 4.11. We now turn our attention to the properties of the blending functions.

4.9.1 Affine Invariance

For B-splines to be affine invariant, we need the blending functions to be a partition of unity. That is

$$\sum_{i=0}^{n} N_i(t) = 1 \,.$$

We note that the blending functions are translates of each other. This means $N_i(t) = N_0(t-i)$. We also note, once again, the local support of the functions $N_i(t)$. So, for a particular value of t, there are only four blending functions that are (possibly) nonzero. These functions are translates of each other, and therefore, they must be the four basis functions. We expect this because of the construction of the curve from piecewise continuous segments. We simply compute the sum of the basis functions to find

$$B_0(t) + B_1(t) + B_2(t) + B_3(t) = 1 \,.$$

4.9.2 Convex Hull

It is clear from figure 4.10, that the blending functions are such that $N_i(t) \geq 0$. All points on the curve are weighted averages of the control points. Thus the control points form the convex hull for the curve.

4.9.3 Cox-de Boor Formula

For Bézier curves we have the de Casteljau method to evaluate points on the curve without the need to evaluate the expensive Bernstein polynomials. In the case of B-splines the *Cox-de Boor formula* provides an efficient means to evaluate points on a B-spline. The Cox-de Boor formula is given by

$$N_{i,1}(t) = \begin{cases} 1, & \text{if } t_i \leq t \leq t_{i+1} \\ 0, & \text{otherwise.} \end{cases}$$

$$N_{i,k}(t) = \frac{t - t_i}{t_{i+k-1} - t_i} N_{i,k-1}(t) + \frac{t_{i+k} - t}{t_{i+k} - t_{i+1}} N_{i+1,k-1}(t)$$

for $i = 0, \ldots, n-k$ and $k = 2, \ldots, d$, where d is one more than the degree of the curve. The *de Boor algorithm* in [8] allows us to determine the points on a B-spline using repeated linear interpolation. The Cox-de Boor formula also applies to non-uniform B-splines. For uniform cubic B-splines we have $t_i = i$, $i \in \mathbb{Z}$ and $N_i = N_{i,4}$ and the curve

$$\sum_{i=0}^{n-4} N_i(t) \mathbf{x}_i \,.$$

4.9.4   C# Implementation

//BSpline.cs
using System;

```
public class BSpline:Curve {
    public static double B(int n,double t) {
        if(n==0) return 1.0/6.0*Math.Pow(1.0-t,3.0);
        if(n==1) return 1.0/6.0*(3.0*t*t*t-6.0*t*t+4.0);
        if(n==2) return 1.0/6.0*(-3.0*t*t*t+3.0*t*t+3.0*t+1.0);
        if(n==3) return 1.0/6.0*Math.Pow(t,3.0);
        return 0.0;
    }

    public static double N(int n,int i,double t) {
        double tj, T=t*(n-3);
        int b=-1;
        if((i-3.0<=T)&&(T<i-2.0)) b=3;
        if((i-2.0<=T)&&(T<i-1.0)) b=2;
        if((i-1.0<=T)&&(T<i)) b=1;
        if((i<=T)&&(T<i+1.0)) b=0;
        if(b==-1) return 0.0;
        tj=T-i+b;
        return B(b,tj);
    }

    public override Vector evaluate(Vector[] p,double t) {
        Vector r=new Vector();
        int n=p.GetLength(0);
        if(n<4) return r;
        int j=(int)(t*(n-3));
        if(j>n-4) j=n-4;
        for(int i=j;i<=j+3;i++) r+=N(n,i,t)*p[i];
        return r;
    }
}
```

4.10   Non-Uniform B-Splines

The distance between parametric values in a non-uniform B-spline differ from one parameter to the next. For non-uniform splines we create the knot-vector $(t_0, t_1, \ldots, t_k)$ which is used in the Cox-de Boor formula. We define $0/0 := 0$ for the Cox-de Boor formula so that we can have knots with the same value. The support of $N_{i,k}$ is then (t_i, t_{i+k}), where $k-1$ is the degree of the curve. Since

$$\mathbf{q}(t) = \sum_{i=0}^{n} N_i(t)\mathbf{x}_i, \quad t \in [0, n-2]$$

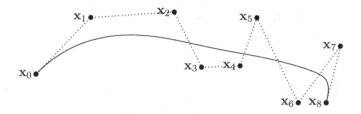

Figure 4.11: Bézier curve of degree 8.

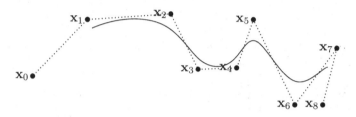

Figure 4.12: B-spline curve of degree 3, using the same control points as figure 4.11.

and $N_{i,k}$ has support (t_i, t_{i+k}), we need $n + k + 1$ knots in the knot vector. Each curve segment is defined by k control points: $\mathbf{x}_i$, $\mathbf{x}_{i+1}$, ..., $\mathbf{x}_{i+k-1}$. The first segment is defined by $\mathbf{x}_0$, $\mathbf{x}_1$, ..., $\mathbf{x}_{k-1}$ and the last segment is defined by $\mathbf{x}_{n-k+1}$, $\mathbf{x}_{n-k+2}$, ..., $\mathbf{x}_n$. We thus have $n - k + 2$ segments. We define $n - k + 3$ knots since we have $n - k + 2$ segments. However, there are $n + k + 1$ knots in the knot vector. The remaining $2k - 2$ knots are usually obtained by repeating the first and last knot $k - 1$ times each. The first and last knot then appear k times. Any knot with multiplicity k is interpolated. As a result, the spline interpolates the first and last control points. That is

$$\mathbf{q}(t_{k-1}) = \mathbf{x}_0 \qquad \text{and} \qquad \mathbf{q}(t_{n+1}) = \mathbf{x}_n \, .$$

We thus define the curve for $t \in [t_{k-1}, t_{n+1}]$. If any knot values (other than the first or last) are duplicated, then continuity is reduced. This adds further power to the non-uniform B-spline representation.

4.11   Interpolating with B-Splines

Although B-splines do not interpolate their control points, it is possible to find a B-spline that interpolates the desired set of points. We use a non-

uniform cubic B-spline to interpolate the first and last points. We assume
uniform distribution of the remaining knots. Assume that we use $n + 1$
control points. We know that multiplicity 4 is required at the end points.
Since we are using cubic splines the curve is defined over $[t_3, t_{n+1}]$. There
is thus $n - 2$ intervals (and thus $n - 2$ segments that we work with). We can
thus interpolate a maximum of $n - 1$ points. Interpolation occurs at the
knot values t_i. We need to solve for the control points x_i, $i = 0, \ldots, n$, of
a B-spline curve, given the points to interpolate p_i, $i = 0, \ldots, n - 2$. Since
there are $n - 2$ distinct segments, we have $n - 1$ parameter values to work
with to solve for $n + 1$ values. For the remaining constraints, we choose to
make the first two, and last two, control points coincident, that is

$$x_0 = x_1 \quad \text{and} \quad x_n = x_{n-1}. \tag{4.9}$$

We know that the support of the blending function $N_{i,4}$ is (t_i, t_{i+4}). We
can thus determine for a parameter value t_i which functions contribute a
nonzero value to the final point on the curve. We thus have

$$q(t_i) = N_{i-3,4}(t_i)x_{i-3} + N_{i-2,4}(t_i)x_{i-2} + N_{i-1,4}(t_i)x_{i-1}$$

since $N_{i-4,4}(t_i) = 0$ and $N_{i,4}(t_i) = 0$. Rewriting this equation using $i \mapsto i + 3$ we get

$$q(t_{i+3}) = N_{i,4}(t_{i+3})x_i + N_{i+1,4}(t_{i+3})x_{i+1} + N_{i+2,4}(t_{i+3})x_{i+2}.$$

We want the curve to interpolate the points p_i at parameter values t_{i+3}.
Thus

$$p_i = q(t_{i+3}) = \alpha_i x_i + \beta_i x_{i+1} + \gamma_i x_{i+2}.$$

with

$$\alpha_i = N_{i,4}(t_{i+3}), \qquad \beta_i = N_{i+1,4}(t_{i+3}), \qquad \gamma_i = N_{i+2,4}(t_{i+3}).$$

Since we are going to require multiplicity 4 at the end points so that the
B-spline curve interpolates the end points, we have

$$x_0 = x_1 = p_0 \quad \text{and} \quad x_n = x_{n-1} = p_{n-2},$$

taking into account the constraints 4.9. We rewrite the equations into
matrix form

$$\begin{pmatrix} 1 & & & & \\ \alpha_1 & \beta_1 & \gamma_1 & & \\ & \ddots & \ddots & \ddots & \\ & & \alpha_{n-3} & \beta_{n-3} & \gamma_{n-3} \\ & & & & 1 \end{pmatrix} \begin{pmatrix} x_1 \\ x_2 \\ \vdots \\ x_{n-2} \\ x_{n-1} \end{pmatrix} = \begin{pmatrix} p_0 \\ p_1 \\ \vdots \\ p_{n-3} \\ p_{n-2} \end{pmatrix}.$$

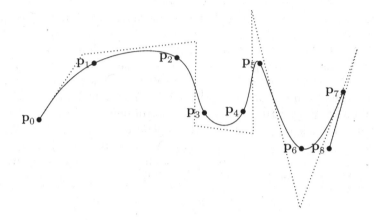

Figure 4.13: Interpolation using B-splines.

All empty entries are 0. The matrix is *tridiagonal* so we can efficiently solve
the equations [127]. Watt & Watt [138] explain the algorithm for efficient
solving in detail. Figure 4.13 illustrates this technique for interpolating
points. Interpolation using chord length parameterization often provides
better results. Watt & Watt [138] provide a heuristic that can be used to
approximate chord length parameterization, that is

$$\frac{t_{i+4} - t_{i+3}}{t_{i+5} - t_{i+4}} = \frac{\|\mathbf{x}_{i+1} - \mathbf{x}_i\|}{\|\mathbf{x}_{i+2} - \mathbf{x}_{i+1}\|}.$$

Another simpler heuristic is provided by Epstein [30], namely $t_i - t_{i-1} = \|\mathbf{x}_i - \mathbf{x}_{i-1}\|$. Further heuristics are discussed by Farin [32].

4.11.1   Periodic Interpolation

Periodic interpolation with cubic B-splines is in many ways simpler than
non-periodic interpolation. In this case we use a uniform cubic B-spline
to interpolate the $n + 1$ points $\mathbf{p}_0, \ldots, \mathbf{p}_n$. We need $n + 1$ control points
to interpolate periodically. As in the non-periodic case, we determine the
functions that contribute a nonzero value to the curve to get

$$\mathbf{p}_i = \mathbf{q}(t_{i+3}) = \alpha_i \mathbf{x}_i + \beta_i \mathbf{x}_{i+1} + \gamma_i \mathbf{x}_{i+2} \tag{4.10}$$

with

$$\alpha_i = N_{i,4}(t_{i+3}), \qquad \beta_i = N_{i+1,4}(t_{i+3}), \qquad \gamma_i = N_{i+2,4}(t_{i+3})$$

so that the curve interpolates at the knot values t_i. The curve is usually
defined over the range $t \in [0, n-1]$. However, this will not make the curve

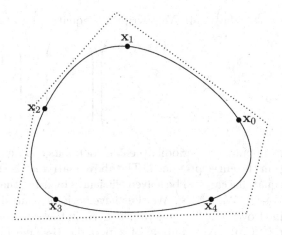

Figure 4.14: Periodic interpolation using B-splines.

periodic. Since the interpolation is periodic, we need an extra segment to join the first and last point of the curve. The curve is thus defined over the range $t \in [0, n]$. The equations 4.10 must be applied in a periodic fashion, that is the subscripts are calculated modulo $n + 1$. The two equations that are influenced are given by

$$\mathbf{p}_{n-1} = \alpha_{n-1}\mathbf{x}_{n-1} + \beta_{n-1}\mathbf{x}_n + \gamma_{n-1}\mathbf{x}_0$$

and

$$\mathbf{p}_n = \alpha_n\mathbf{x}_n + \beta_n\mathbf{x}_0 + \gamma_n\mathbf{x}_1 \, .$$

We rewrite the equations into matrix form

$$
\begin{pmatrix}
\alpha_0 & \beta_0 & \gamma_0 & & & \\
& \alpha_1 & \beta_1 & \gamma_1 & & \\
& & \ddots & \ddots & \ddots & \\
& & & \alpha_{n-2} & \beta_{n-2} & \gamma_{n-2} \\
\gamma_{n-1} & & & & \alpha_{n-1} & \beta_{n-1} \\
\beta_n & \gamma_n & & & & \alpha_n
\end{pmatrix}
\begin{pmatrix}
\mathbf{x}_0 \\
\mathbf{x}_1 \\
\vdots \\
\mathbf{x}_{n-2} \\
\mathbf{x}_{n-1} \\
\mathbf{x}_n
\end{pmatrix}
=
\begin{pmatrix}
\mathbf{p}_0 \\
\mathbf{p}_1 \\
\vdots \\
\mathbf{p}_{n-2} \\
\mathbf{p}_{n-1} \\
\mathbf{p}_n
\end{pmatrix} .
$$

This matrix is not tridiagonal. We rewrite this equation into the form

$$
\begin{pmatrix}
\beta_n & \gamma_n & & & & & \alpha_n \\
\alpha_0 & \beta_0 & \gamma_0 & & & & \\
& \alpha_1 & \beta_1 & \gamma_1 & & & \\
& & \ddots & \ddots & \ddots & & \\
& & & \alpha_{n-2} & \beta_{n-2} & \gamma_{n-2} & \\
\gamma_{n-1} & & & & \alpha_{n-1} & \beta_{n-1}
\end{pmatrix}
\begin{pmatrix}
\mathbf{x}_n \\
\mathbf{x}_0 \\
\mathbf{x}_1 \\
\vdots \\
\mathbf{x}_{n-2} \\
\mathbf{x}_{n-1}
\end{pmatrix}
=
\begin{pmatrix}
\mathbf{p}_n \\
\mathbf{p}_0 \\
\mathbf{p}_1 \\
\vdots \\
\mathbf{p}_{n-2} \\
\mathbf{p}_{n-1}
\end{pmatrix}.
$$

Since the control points are periodic, the control points can be renumbered with no change in the curve produced. The above matrix is also not tridiagonal, but the equations can still be solved efficiently by using the techniques described by Watt & Watt [138]. We thus have periodic control points and the curve defined over $t \in [nk, n + nk]$, $k \in \mathbb{N}$, is the same as the curve defined over $t \in [0, n]$. An example of a periodic B-spline interpolating curve is shown in figure 4.14.

4.12 Non-Uniform Rational B-Splines

Non-uniform rational B-splines (NURBS [39]) are non-uniform B-splines applied to control points specified by homogeneous coordinates. The curve is thus defined by

$$
\mathbf{q}(t) = \sum_{i=0}^{n} N_{i,k}(t)(w_i \mathbf{x}_i \; w_i)^T, \quad t \in [0, n-2].
$$

The point that is represented by $\mathbf{q}(t)$ is then

$$
\frac{\sum_{i=0}^{n} w_i N_{i,k}(t) \mathbf{x}_i}{\sum_{i=0}^{n} w_i N_{i,k}(t)} = \sum_{i=0}^{n} R_{i,k}(t) \mathbf{x}_i
$$

with

$$
R_{i,k}(t) = \frac{w_i N_{i,k}(t)}{\sum_{j=0}^{n} w_j N_{j,k}(t)}.
$$

The extra coordinate w_i adds further flexibility to the curve and allows B-splines to represent conic sections. Razdan and Farin [104] describe interpolation with NURBS.

4.13 Trigonometric Interpolation

In the previous sections, we discussed interpolating points using polynomial functions of a fixed degree. Now we consider trigonometric functions. As we see later, harmonic interpolation is also a form of trigonometric interpolation. For standard trigonometric interpolation [55], we wish to find a function

$$\mathbf{q}(t) = \sum_{k=0}^{n-1} (\mathbf{a}_k \cos kt + \mathbf{b}_k \sin kt) \qquad (4.11)$$

such that $\mathbf{q}(t_k) = \mathbf{x}_k$ for $k = 0,\ldots,n-1$. For simplicity we assume that t_k is equally spaced on $[0, 2\pi]$ (uniform interpolation) so that $t_k = 2\pi k/n$. We can express this equation in terms of a single coefficient using the exponential form of complex numbers $e^{it} \equiv \cos t + i \sin t$ and adding the constraint $\mathbf{b}_k = i\mathbf{a}_k$. The equivalent problem is then to find a function

$$\mathbf{q}(t) = \sum_{k=0}^{n-1} \mathbf{c}_k e^{ikt},$$

such that $\mathbf{q}(t_k) = \mathbf{x}_k$ for $k = 0,\ldots,n$. Since $e^{i(t+2\pi)} = e^{it}e^{2\pi i} = e^{it}$ we have periodic interpolation. We now determine the coefficients $\mathbf{c}_k$. Let

$$w := e^{2\pi i/n}$$

so that $e^{it_k} = w^k$. We now have

$$\mathbf{x}_k = \mathbf{q}(t_k) = \mathbf{c}_0 + \mathbf{c}_1 w^k + \mathbf{c}_2 w^{2k} + \cdots + \mathbf{c}_{n-1} w^{(n-1)k}.$$

These equations hold for $k = 0,\ldots,n-1$ so that we have n equations in n unknowns. Written in matrix form we have

$$\begin{pmatrix} 1 & 1 & 1 & \cdots & 1 \\ 1 & w & w^2 & \cdots & w^{n-1} \\ 1 & w^2 & w^4 & \cdots & w^{2(n-1)} \\ \vdots & \vdots & \vdots & \ddots & \vdots \\ 1 & w^{n-1} & w^{2(n-1)} & \cdots & w^{(n-1)^2} \end{pmatrix} \begin{pmatrix} \mathbf{c}_0 \\ \mathbf{c}_1 \\ \mathbf{c}_2 \\ \vdots \\ \mathbf{c}_{n-1} \end{pmatrix} = \begin{pmatrix} \mathbf{x}_0 \\ \mathbf{x}_1 \\ \mathbf{x}_2 \\ \vdots \\ \mathbf{x}_{n-1} \end{pmatrix}$$

or simply $A\mathbf{c} = \mathbf{x}$. The matrix A is called a *Fourier matrix*. The components of A are

$$A_{lm} = w^{lm}.$$

To solve for $\mathbf{c}$ we calculate A^{-1} so that $\mathbf{c} = A^{-1}\mathbf{x}$. The inverse of A is given by

$$(A^{-1})_{ij} = \frac{1}{n} w^{-ij}$$

which is easily seen by

$$(A^{-1}A)_{ij} = \sum_{k=0}^{n-1} (A^{-1})_{ik} A_{kj} = \frac{1}{n} \sum_{k=0}^{n-1} w^{-ik} w^{kj} = \frac{1}{n} \sum_{k=0}^{n-1} w^{(j-i)k}.$$

If $i = j$ then

$$(A^{-1}A)_{ij} = 1.$$

If $i \neq j$ then

$$(A^{-1}A)_{ij} = \frac{1}{n} \cdot \frac{1 - w^{(j-i)n}}{1 - w^{(j-i)}} = 0$$

since $w^n = 1$. Thus $A^{-1}A = I$. We have

$$\mathbf{c}_k = \frac{1}{n} \sum_{m=0}^{n-1} w^{-km} \mathbf{x}_m = \frac{1}{n} \sum_{m=0}^{n-1} e^{-2\pi ikm/n} \mathbf{x}_m$$

which is the discrete Fourier transform of the points $\mathbf{x}_k$. If $n = 2^m$, then we can use the fast Fourier transform [127] to determine $\mathbf{c}_k$ quickly.

Examining equation 4.11, we see that there are $2n$ unknowns. By using the exponential form of complex numbers we introduced further constraints. To avoid the use of complex numbers we can reduce the number of unknowns. If n is odd and the number of unknowns in equation 4.11 are reduced, then we obtain

$$\mathbf{q}(t) = \mathbf{a}_0 + \sum_{k=1}^{m} (\mathbf{a}_k \cos kt + \mathbf{b}_k \sin kt)$$

with $n = 2m + 1$. There are thus $((n-1)/2) \cdot 2 + 1 = n$ unknowns and n equations if we require that $\mathbf{q}(t_k) = \mathbf{x}_k$ for $k = 0, \ldots, n-1$. Once again we assume $t_j := 2\pi j/n$. Jiaxing [68] shows that the solution to these equations is

$$\mathbf{a}_0 = \frac{1}{2m+1} \sum_{j=0}^{2m} \mathbf{x}_j$$

$$\mathbf{a}_k = \frac{2}{2m+1} \sum_{j=0}^{2m} \mathbf{x}_j \cos(kt_j)$$

$$\mathbf{b}_k = \frac{2}{2m+1} \sum_{j=0}^{2m} \mathbf{x}_j \sin(kt_j) \tag{4.12}$$

so that

$$\mathbf{q}(t) = \frac{1}{2m+1} \left(\sum_{j=0}^{2m} \mathbf{x}_j + 2 \sum_{k=1}^{m} \sum_{j=0}^{2m} \mathbf{x}_j \left(\cos(kt_j) \cos(kt) + \sin(kt_j) \sin(kt) \right) \right)$$

$$= \frac{1}{2m+1} \left(\sum_{j=0}^{2m} \mathbf{x}_j + 2 \sum_{j=0}^{2m} \sum_{k=1}^{m} \mathbf{x}_j \cos k(t - t_j) \right)$$

$$= \frac{1}{2m+1} \sum_{j=0}^{2m} \mathbf{x}_j \left(1 + 2 \sum_{k=1}^{m} \cos k(t - t_j) \right). \tag{4.13}$$

We use the trigonometric identity (shown later in 4.28)

$$1 + 2 \sum_{k=1}^{m} \cos kt \equiv \frac{\sin(m + \frac{1}{2})t}{\sin \frac{1}{2}t},$$

and find that

$$\mathbf{q}(t) = \frac{1}{2m+1} \sum_{j=0}^{2m} \frac{\sin \left((m + \frac{1}{2})(t - t_j) \right)}{\sin \frac{1}{2}(t - t_j)} \mathbf{x}_j$$

$$= \frac{1}{n} \sum_{j=0}^{n-1} \frac{\sin \left(\frac{n}{2}(t - t_j) \right)}{\sin \left(\frac{1}{2}(t - t_j) \right)} \mathbf{x}_j$$

which is known as *Lagrange trigonometric interpolation*. We can also change the parameter to $2\pi u = t$, $u \in [0, 1]$, so that

$$\mathbf{q}(u) = \sum_{j=0}^{n-1} \frac{\sin \pi n(u - j/n)}{n \sin \pi(u - j/n)} \mathbf{x}_j.$$

To see that 4.13 does interpolate the desired points (and thus that the expansion coefficients $\mathbf{a}_k$ and $\mathbf{b}_k$ are in fact the solution we are looking for), we note that if $t = t_j$ then

$$1 + 2 \sum_{k=1}^{m} \cos k(t_j - t_j) = 2m + 1,$$

and if $t \neq t_j$ (and $t = t_k$, $t_j = \frac{2\pi j}{n}$) then

$$\frac{\sin \frac{n}{2}(t_k - t_j)}{\sin \frac{1}{2}(t_k - t_j)} = \frac{\sin \pi(k - j)}{\sin \frac{\pi}{n}(k - j)} = \frac{\sin \pi(\ell)}{\sin \frac{\pi}{n}(\ell)} = 0$$

where $\ell = k - j \in \mathbb{Z}$. Thus $\mathbf{q}(t_j) = \mathbf{x}_j$. Newberry [96] discusses trigonometric interpolation for curve fitting and minimal degree trigonometric polynomials for interpolation in [95]. Newberry also shows how trigonometric polynomials can be used for curves in a general fashion, including approximation.

4.14 METAPOST and Bézier Curves

METAPOST [62] is a useful tool for drawing diagrams. METAPOST will be used to draw many of the Bézier curves for comparison to harmonic interpolation. A significant reason for the choice of METAPOST, is that METAPOST uses piecewise cubic Bézier curves to interpolate the specified points. METAPOST is also a programming language, and so harmonic interpolation is implemented in METAPOST to provide an accurate comparison. The details of how the Bézier control points are selected are given in [61] and [72], we give a brief overview here. Since cubic Bézier curves interpolate their end points, we simply have to discuss how the remaining two control points are selected to create a piecewise continuous Bézier curve. There are many parameters that influence how these control points are selected. We are primarily interested in how the points are selected automatically without extra parameters being specified, since this is the technique that harmonic interpolation will use.

The following discussion is based on the paper by Hobby [61]. We begin by examining a curve segment $\mathbf{q}_i(t)$, that must interpolate $\mathbf{z}_i$ and $\mathbf{z}_{i+1} \in \mathbb{R}^2$. To simplify notation we use the convention

$$\mathbf{z}_i = \begin{pmatrix} x_i & y_i \end{pmatrix}^T.$$

We are given the unit direction vectors $\mathbf{w}_i$ and $\mathbf{w}_{i+1}$ for the end points. $\mathbf{q}_i(t)$ must be defined by

$$\mathbf{q}_i(0) = \mathbf{z}_i, \qquad \mathbf{q}_i(1) = \mathbf{z}_{i+1}, \qquad \mathbf{q}_i'(0) = \alpha\mathbf{w}_i, \qquad \mathbf{q}_i'(1) = \beta\mathbf{w}_{i+1}.$$

Hobby [61] includes tension parameters τ_i and $\bar{\tau}_{i+1}$. We accept that the default value of 1 is used as described in [72]. First we consider a function $\hat{\mathbf{q}}_i(t)$ defined by

$$\hat{\mathbf{q}}_i(0) = \begin{pmatrix} 0 \\ 0 \end{pmatrix}, \qquad \hat{\mathbf{q}}_i(1) = \begin{pmatrix} 1 \\ 0 \end{pmatrix},$$

$$\hat{\mathbf{q}}_i'(0) = \frac{1}{\tau_i}\rho(\theta,\phi)\begin{pmatrix} \cos\theta \\ \sin\theta \end{pmatrix}, \qquad \hat{\mathbf{q}}_i'(1) = \frac{1}{\bar{\tau}_{i+1}}\sigma(\theta,\phi)\begin{pmatrix} \cos\phi \\ -\sin\phi \end{pmatrix}$$

where $\theta = \arg(\mathbf{w}_i) - \arg(\mathbf{z}_{i+1} - \mathbf{z}_i)$ and $\phi = \arg(\mathbf{z}_{i+1} - \mathbf{z}_i) - \arg(\mathbf{w}_{i+1})$. The function $\arg(\mathbf{w}_i)$ maps $\mathbf{w}_i$ to the angle that $\mathbf{w}_i$ makes with the unit vector $(1\ 0)^T$. For example, $\arg\left((1\ 1)^T\right)$ is $\frac{\pi}{4}$. The functions ρ and σ will be determined later. $\mathbf{q}_i(t)$ is then given by

$$\mathbf{q}_i(t) = \mathbf{z}_i + \begin{pmatrix} x_{i+1} - x_i & y_i - y_{i+1} \\ y_{i+1} - y_i & x_{i+1} - x_i \end{pmatrix}\hat{\mathbf{q}}(t).$$

The Bézier curve that satisfies the requirements for $\hat{\mathbf{q}}_t$ has control points

$$\begin{pmatrix} 0 \\ 0 \end{pmatrix}, \quad \frac{\rho(\theta,\phi)}{3\tau_i}\begin{pmatrix} \cos\theta \\ \sin\theta \end{pmatrix}, \quad \begin{pmatrix} 1 - \frac{\sigma}{3}\bar{\tau}_{i+1}\cos\phi \\ \frac{\sigma}{3}\bar{\tau}_{i+1}\sin\phi \end{pmatrix}, \quad \begin{pmatrix} 1 \\ 0 \end{pmatrix}.$$

The curve $\hat{\mathbf{q}}(t)$ is then given by

$$\hat{\mathbf{q}}(t) = \frac{\rho(\theta,\phi)}{\tau_i}t(1-t)^2\begin{pmatrix} \cos\theta \\ \sin\theta \end{pmatrix} + t^2(1-t)\begin{pmatrix} 3 - \sigma/(\bar{\tau}_{i+1}) \\ \sigma/(\bar{\tau}_{i+1}) \end{pmatrix} + t^3\begin{pmatrix} 1 \\ 0 \end{pmatrix}.$$

Now we must choose the functions $\rho(\theta,\phi)$ and $\sigma(\theta,\phi)$ so that $\rho(\theta,\phi) = \sigma(\phi,\theta) = \rho(-\theta,-\phi)$. The functions selected for METAPOST are

$$\rho(\theta,\phi) = \frac{2+\alpha}{1+(1-c)\cos\theta + c\cos\phi}, \quad \sigma(\theta,\phi) = \frac{2-\alpha}{1+(1-c)\cos\phi + c\cos\theta}$$

where

$$\alpha := a(\sin\theta - b\sin\phi)(\sin\phi - b\sin\theta)(\cos\theta - \cos\phi).$$

The constants a, b and c selected are $a = \sqrt{2}$, $b = \frac{1}{16}$ and $c = (3 - \sqrt{5})/2$. At this point we have the tools to create a Bézier curve using the direction specifiers and points to interpolate. We now turn our attention to the entire curve. The goal is to interpolate the points specified, without needing extra information (although extra information can be provided). Thus only the points to interpolate are given, and not the direction vectors. So we need an algorithm to determine the directions of the curve at each point so that the above formulas can be applied. For this, Hobby [61] introduces *mock curvature*. We omit the details, and simply state the techniques used, as explained in [72]. First we note that at each interpolation point, two directions may be specified. One for the incoming curve, and one for the exiting curve. If one of the directions are specified, then the other is simply a duplicate. For our purposes these directions are not specified and must be determined. We consider each of the points $\mathbf{z}_i$, $i = 0,\ldots,n$ and direction vectors $\mathbf{w}_i$, $i = 0,\ldots,n$. Let d_i be the Euclidean distance between $\mathbf{z}_{i+1} - \mathbf{z}_i$ for $i = 0,\ldots,n-1$. We further define

$$\theta_i := \arg(\mathbf{w}_i) - \arg(\mathbf{z}_{i+1} - \mathbf{z}_i), \quad i = 0,\ldots,n-1,$$
$$\phi_i := \arg(\mathbf{z}_i - \mathbf{z}_{i-1}) - \arg(\mathbf{w}_i), \quad i = 1,\ldots,n,$$
$$\psi_i := \arg(\mathbf{z}_{i+1} - \mathbf{z}_i) - \arg(\mathbf{z}_i - \mathbf{z}_{i-1}), \quad i = 1,\ldots,n',$$

with $n' = n$ for periodic interpolation and $n' = n - 1$ for non-periodic interpolation. We have the relation

$$\theta_i + \phi_i + \psi_i = 0, \quad i = 1,\ldots,n-1.$$

For periodic interpolation, all directions can be determined. For non-periodic interpolation the directions at the end points are specified. These are specified by "curl" values. The default value is 1 for the curl at the end points, and this is the value we use. For the inner control points the following equations should hold

$$\frac{\bar{\tau}_i^2}{d_i}\left(\frac{\theta_{i-1}+\phi_i}{\tau_{i-1}}-3\phi_i\right)=\frac{\tau_i^2}{d_{i+1}}\left(\frac{\theta_i+\phi_{i+1}}{\bar{\tau}_{i+1}}-3\theta_i\right). \qquad (4.14)$$

For non-periodic interpolation we have further constraints. If we have the first direction vector, θ_0 is determined, otherwise the curl γ_0 is used in the following equation

$$\tau_0^2\left(\frac{1}{\bar{\tau}_1}(\theta_0+\phi_1)-3\theta_0\right)=\gamma_0\bar{\tau}_1^2\left(\frac{1}{\tau_0}(\theta_0+\phi_1)-3\phi_1\right) \qquad (4.15)$$

and in a similar fashion, if the last direction vector is specified, then ϕ_n, otherwise we use the "curl" γ_n to get

$$\bar{\tau}_n^2\left(\frac{1}{\tau_{n-1}}(\theta_{n-1}+\phi_n)-3\phi_n\right)=\gamma_n\tau_{n-1}^2\left(\frac{1}{\bar{\tau}_{n-1}}(\theta_{n-1}+\phi_n)-3\theta_{n-1}\right). \qquad (4.16)$$

The equations 4.14 (and in the non-periodic case equations 4.15 and 4.16) are linear equations. If $\tau_i \geq 3/4$, $\bar{\tau}_i \geq 3/4$ and $\gamma_i \geq 0$, then there is a unique solution.

We now know how METAPOST draws its diagrams, we next proceed to look at a few examples. The examples used for interpolation using B-splines are duplicated for METAPOST in figures 4.15 and 4.16. B-splines and META-POST curves are both piecewise cubic polynomial curves (as we use them). The same is true of Catmull-Rom splines and many of the others we have discussed. Each curve can thus be represented exactly by one of the other curves. We simply have to find a set of control points that produces the desired curve. The key differences in the curves, especially in terms of interpolation, is how the control points are chosen, and what effect the control points have on the curve. The results produced by METAPOST are thus of relevance to the other cubic curves as well.

4.14.1   METAPOST Example

The following METAPOSTcode fragment was used to create figure 4.15.

```
u:=0.9cm;
beginfig(1);
```

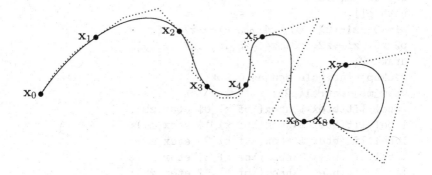

Figure 4.15: Interpolation using METAPOST.

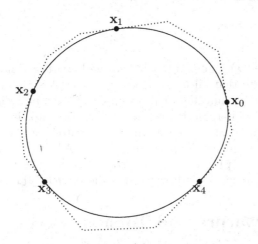

Figure 4.16: Periodic interpolation using METAPOST.

```
z0=(0u,0u); z1=(2u,2u); z2=(5u,2.2u); z3=(6u,0.25u);
z4=(7.4u,0.3u); z5=(8u,2u); z6=(9.5u,-1u); z7=(11u,1u);
z8=(10.5u,-1u);
path p[];
p1=z0--z1--z2--z3--z4--z5--z6--z7--z8;
p2=z0..z1..z2..z3..z4..z5..z6..z7..z8;
draw p2;
pickup pencircle scaled 0.9pt;
draw_mp_control(p2);
label.lft(btex $\hbox{\bf x}_0$ etex,z0);
label.lft(btex $\hbox{\bf x}_1$ etex,z1);
label.lft(btex $\hbox{\bf x}_2$ etex,z2);
label.lft(btex $\hbox{\bf x}_3$ etex,z3);
label.lft(btex $\hbox{\bf x}_4$ etex,z4);
label.lft(btex $\hbox{\bf x}_5$ etex,z5);
label.lft(btex $\hbox{\bf x}_6$ etex,z6);
label.lft(btex $\hbox{\bf x}_7$ etex,z7);
label.lft(btex $\hbox{\bf x}_8$ etex,z8);

pickup pencircle scaled 4pt;
draw z0; draw z1; draw z2; draw z3;
draw z4; draw z5; draw z6; draw z7;
draw z8;
endfig;
end;
```

A figure is started with **beginfig** and ends with **endfig**. The keyword **end** is used to indicate that all figures have been completed. Each statement is terminated by a semi-colon. This example uses the predefined variables $z_0, \ldots, z_8$ to store interpolation points. The **--** operator is used to create a path from straight lines whereas the **..** operator applies the algorithm above to create a smooth interpolating curve. A path is an ordered list of points, and **path p[];** declares an array of paths. METAPOST does not require brackets to specify indices so **p1** is the same as **p[1]**.

4.15   Curvature and Torsion

We consider the curvature of curves in $\mathbb{R}^2$ and $\mathbb{R}^3$. A *parameterized curve* in $\mathbb{R}^n$ is a smooth function $\mathbf{x} : I \to \mathbb{R}^n$, where I is some interval in $\mathbb{R}$. By smoothness of such a function we mean that $\mathbf{x}$ is of the form

$$\mathbf{x}(t) = (x_0(t) \ x_1(t) \ \ldots \ x_{n-1}(t))^T$$

where each x_i is a smooth real valued function on I. The *length* of the curve is given by $(t \in [a, b])$

$$\ell = \int_a^b \sqrt{\left(\frac{dx_0}{dt}\right)^2 + \left(\frac{dx_1}{dt}\right)^2 + \cdots + \left(\frac{dx_{n-1}}{dt}\right)^2} \, dt.$$

We can thus compute the arc length of the curve

$$\mathbf{x}(t') = (x_0(t') \ x_1(t') \ \cdots \ x_{n-1}(t'))^T$$

from an initial parameter value t_0 by

$$s(t) = \int_{t_0}^t \sqrt{\left(\frac{dx_0}{dt'}\right)^2 + \left(\frac{dx_1}{dt'}\right)^2 + \cdots + \left(\frac{dx_{n-1}}{dt'}\right)^2} \, dt'$$

for any value of t. The velocity vector at a time $t \in I$ of the parameterized curve $\mathbf{x} : I \to \mathbb{R}^n$ is defined as

$$\dot{\mathbf{x}} := \frac{d\mathbf{x}(t)}{dt} = \left(\frac{dx_0(t)}{dt} \ \frac{dx_1(t)}{dt} \ \cdots \ \frac{dx_{n-1}(t)}{dt}\right)^T.$$

We need to develop further tools to determine in some fashion if one smooth curve is better than another. *Curvature* is a measure that can be used to determine how quickly a curve changes direction. Curves that change direction slowly are preferable to curves that change direction quickly or discontinuously.

We begin by examining the curvature for curves in the plane $\mathbb{R}^2$. Let $\mathbf{t}(s)$ be the tangent vector to the curve $\mathbf{x}(s)$ at arc length s. We will thus be using arc length parameterization. The tangent vector $\mathbf{t}(s)$ is a unit vector by virtue of the arc length parameterization. We define $\psi(s)$ to be the angle between the tangent $\mathbf{t}(s)$ and the positive x-axis. The curvature measures the rate of curving, and is thus defined as

$$\kappa(s) = \frac{d\psi(s)}{ds}.$$

Now we can introduce the curvature plot in terms of a parametrically defined curve. A *curvature plot* displays curvature verse arc length, or the parameter of the curve. Curvature is nonnegative by definition, but we are primarily interested in signed curvature κ of a parametric curve $\mathbf{x}(t) = (x_0(t) \ x_1(t))^T$ defined as [32]

$$\kappa(t) = \frac{\dot{x}_0(t)\ddot{x}_1(t) - \dot{x}_1(t)\ddot{x}_0(t)}{[(\dot{x}_0(t))^2 + (\dot{x}_1(t))^2]^{3/2}}$$

where $\dot{x}_0(t) = \frac{dx_0(t)}{dt}$ and likewise for $\ddot{x}_0, \dot{x}_1$ and $\ddot{x}_1$. Using the arc length parameterization we obtain

$$\kappa(s) = \dot{x}_0(s)\ddot{x}_1(s) - \dot{x}_1(s)\ddot{x}_0(s)$$

where $\dot{x}_0(s) = \frac{dx_0(s)}{ds}$, $\ddot{x}_0(s) = \frac{d^2 x_0(s)}{ds^2}$ and so forth. The curvature plot shows points of inflection quite clearly by $\kappa = 0$. We can now define *fair* curves. A curve is *fair* if its curvature plot is continuous and consists of only a few monotone pieces [32]. Curvature plots will provide us with an additional measure of the quality of curves.

Example. We determine the curvature of the *catenary* curve given in parameter form

$$\mathbf{x}(t) = \begin{pmatrix} x_0(t) \\ x_1(t) \end{pmatrix} = \begin{pmatrix} t \\ \cosh t \end{pmatrix}.$$

Thus $x_1 = \cosh x_0$. We find the curvature $\kappa(t)$ using $\cosh t \equiv \frac{1}{2}(e^t + e^{-t})$,

$$\kappa(t) = \frac{\dot{x}_0(t)\ddot{x}_1(t) - \dot{x}_1(t)\ddot{x}_0(t)}{[(\dot{x}_0(t))^2 + (\dot{x}_1(t))^2]^{3/2}} = \frac{\frac{1}{2}(e^t + e^{-t})}{[1 + \frac{1}{4}(e^t - e^{-t})^2]^{3/2}}$$

$$= \frac{\frac{1}{2}(e^t + e^{-t})}{[1 + \frac{1}{4}(e^{2t} - 2 + e^{-2t})]^{3/2}} = \frac{\frac{1}{2}(e^t + e^{-t})}{[\frac{1}{4}(e^{2t} + 2 + e^{-2t})]^{3/2}}$$

$$= \frac{\frac{1}{2}(e^t + e^{-t})}{[\frac{1}{4}(e^t + e^{-t})^2]^{3/2}} = \frac{\frac{1}{2}(e^t + e^{-t})}{\frac{1}{8}(e^t + e^{-t})^3}$$

$$= \frac{1}{\frac{1}{4}(e^t + e^{-t})^2} = \frac{1}{\cosh^2 t}.$$

Figure 4.17(a) shows the catenary, and the tangent to the curve at parameter value $u = 0.25$. Figure 4.17(b) shows the curvature plot obtained using the curvature derived above for the parameter values $t \in [0, 1]$. $\square$

We now turn our attention to curvature of smooth curves defined in $\mathbb{R}^3$. A curve in $\mathbb{R}^3$ can be defined by (parametric form)

$$\mathbf{x}(t) = (x_0(t)\ x_1(t)\ x_2(t))^T.$$

For a curve in $\mathbb{R}^3$, the arc length for parameter value t is given by

$$s(t) = \int_{t_0}^{t} \sqrt{\left(\frac{dx_0}{dt'}\right)^2 + \left(\frac{dx_1}{dt'}\right)^2 + \left(\frac{dx_2}{dt'}\right)^2}\, dt' = \int_{t_0}^{t} \left\|\frac{d\mathbf{x}}{dt'}\right\|\, dt'.$$

When analyzing curvature, the arc length parameterization is often better. The tangent to a curve $\mathbf{x}(s)$ parameterized by arc length in $\mathbb{R}^3$ is defined

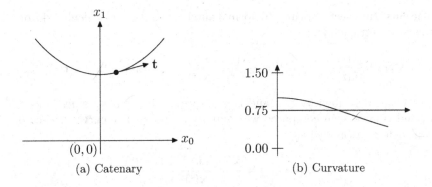

(a) Catenary   (b) Curvature

Figure 4.17: Catenary and its curvature.

as

$$\mathbf{t}(s) := \frac{d\mathbf{x}(s)}{ds}.$$

The tangent is a unit vector as a result of the arc length parameterization.
If we consider three points on the curve defined by parameter values $s-\epsilon$, s
and $s+\epsilon$, we can form a plane from these points. The plane obtained when
we take the limit $\epsilon \to 0$ is known as the *osculating plane*. The tangent
vector lies entirely in the osculating plane. There are an infinite number of
normals to the curve at arc length parameter value s. The *principal normal*
$\mathbf{n}$ is the line that is perpendicular to the tangent in the osculating plane.
We now define the *curvature vector* [32] as

$$\mathbf{k}(s) := \frac{d\mathbf{t}(s)}{ds} = \kappa \mathbf{n}(s).$$

The value κ is the curvature of the curve in $\mathbb{R}^3$. If we consider the prior
three points again ($s-\epsilon$, s and $s+\epsilon$) we can find a circle that passes through
these points. The circle obtained as we take the limit $\epsilon \to 0$ is known as
the *osculating circle*. The center of the osculating circle for a point $\mathbf{x}$ on
the curve is a distance $|\kappa|^{-1}$ in the direction of the principal normal from
the point $\mathbf{x}$. The value $|\kappa|^{-1}$ is known as the *radius of curvature*.

Curvature measures the rate of change of the tangent vector. *Torsion* measures the rate of change of the osculating plane. To define the rate of change
we need the *binormal*, the curve normal that is orthogonal to the osculating
plane. The torsion is then defined as the rate of change of the binormal
$\mathbf{b} := \mathbf{t} \times \mathbf{n}$ [32],

$$\frac{d\mathbf{b}}{ds} = -\tau \mathbf{n}.$$

The curvature vector, principal normal and binormal can be calculated from the parametric curve

$$\mathbf{t}(t) = \frac{\dot{\mathbf{x}}(t)}{\|\dot{\mathbf{x}}(t)\|}, \qquad \mathbf{b}(t) = \frac{\dot{\mathbf{x}}(t) \times \ddot{\mathbf{x}}(t)}{\|\dot{\mathbf{x}}(t) \times \ddot{\mathbf{x}}(t)\|}, \qquad \mathbf{n}(t) = \mathbf{b}(t) \times \mathbf{t}(t) \,.$$

The frame described by $\mathbf{t}$, $\mathbf{n}$ and $\mathbf{b}$ is known as the *Frenet frame*. Once $\mathbf{t}$, $\mathbf{n}$, and $\mathbf{b}$ have been computed we compute κ and τ. The curvature vector can then be expressed as

$$\mathbf{k}(t) = \kappa \mathbf{n}(t) = \frac{\ddot{\mathbf{x}}(t) - \mathbf{t}(t)(\ddot{\mathbf{x}}(t) \cdot \mathbf{t}(t))}{\dot{\mathbf{x}}(t) \cdot \dot{\mathbf{x}}(t)}$$

so that the curvature κ is given by

$$\kappa(t) = \frac{\ddot{\mathbf{x}}(t) \cdot \mathbf{n}(t)}{\dot{\mathbf{x}}(t) \cdot \dot{\mathbf{x}}(t)} = \frac{\|\dot{\mathbf{x}}(t) \times \ddot{\mathbf{x}}(t)\|}{\|\dot{\mathbf{x}}(t)\|^3} \,.$$

The torsion can be computed using

$$\tau(t) = \frac{(\dot{\mathbf{x}}(t) \times \ddot{\mathbf{x}}(t)) \cdot \dddot{\mathbf{x}}(t)}{\|\dot{\mathbf{x}}(t) \times \ddot{\mathbf{x}}(t)\|^2} \,.$$

Using the arc length parameterization we obtain

$$\|\mathbf{k}(s)\| = \kappa(s)\|\mathbf{n}(s)\| = \left\|\frac{d\mathbf{t}(s)}{ds}\right\| \,.$$

We thus have

$$\kappa(s) = \left\|\frac{d\mathbf{t}(s)}{ds}\right\| = \sqrt{\left(\frac{d^2 x_0}{ds^2}\right)^2 + \left(\frac{d^2 x_1}{ds^2}\right)^2 + \left(\frac{d^2 x_2}{ds^2}\right)^2} \,.$$

Likewise the torsion in terms of arc length parameterization is given by

$$\tau(s) = \frac{|\dot{\mathbf{x}}(s) \quad \ddot{\mathbf{x}}(s) \quad \dddot{\mathbf{x}}(s)|}{\ddot{\mathbf{x}}(s) \cdot \ddot{\mathbf{x}}(s)}$$

where $|\dot{\mathbf{x}}(s) \quad \ddot{\mathbf{x}}(s) \quad \dddot{\mathbf{x}}(s)|$ denotes the determinant of the matrix which is constructed from the three column vectors $\dot{\mathbf{x}}(s)$, $\ddot{\mathbf{x}}(s)$, and $\dddot{\mathbf{x}}(s)$.

Example. We examine the curvature of the spiral (illustrated in figure 4.18)

$$\mathbf{x}(t) = \begin{pmatrix} a\cos(t) \\ a\sin(t) \\ bt \end{pmatrix}$$

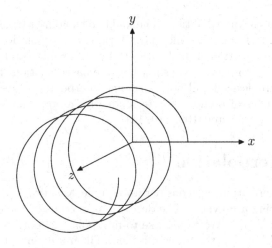

Figure 4.18: Spiral curve.

where $a > 0$ and $b < 0$ or $b > 0$. The arc length is then

$$s(t) = \int_0^t \sqrt{\left(\frac{dx_0}{dt'}\right)^2 + \left(\frac{dx_1}{dt'}\right)^2 + \left(\frac{dx_2}{dt'}\right)^2} \, dt' = t\sqrt{a^2 + b^2}.$$

The arc length parameterization of $\mathbf{x}$ is thus

$$x_0(s) = a\cos\left(\frac{s}{\sqrt{a^2 + b^2}}\right), \ x_1(s) = a\sin\left(\frac{s}{\sqrt{a^2 + b^2}}\right), \ x_2(s) = \frac{bs}{\sqrt{a^2 + b^2}}.$$

Consequently

$$\kappa(s) = \sqrt{\left(\frac{d^2x_0}{ds^2}\right)^2 + \left(\frac{d^2x_1}{ds^2}\right)^2 + \left(\frac{d^2x_2}{ds^2}\right)^2} = \frac{a}{a^2 + b^2}.$$

Thus the curvature is independent of s, i.e. constant. The torsion is given by

$$\tau(s) = \frac{|\dot{\mathbf{x}}(s) \ \ddot{\mathbf{x}}(s) \ \dddot{\mathbf{x}}(s)|}{\ddot{\mathbf{x}}(s) \cdot \ddot{\mathbf{x}}(s)} = \frac{b}{a^2 + b^2}$$

and is also constant.   □

4.16   Harmonic Interpolation

In this section we discuss a technique for producing periodic interpolating curves without numerical solution of systems of interpolation. To do so we introduce harmonic interpolation. The well known Fourier transform can be used for analysis of periodic functions. Harmonic interpolation is based on an interesting application of the Fourier transform, which produces periodic interpolation of data points. We show how the basis functions for harmonic interpolation are derived and how harmonic interpolation can be extended to an even number of points. The technique for an odd number of points was discussed by Schuster [109, 110, 111].

4.17   Interpolation

To begin the derivation, we consider an n-tuple $\mathbf{X} = (\mathbf{x}_0, \mathbf{x}_1, \ldots, \mathbf{x}_{n-1})$ of vectors describing a polygon. The derivation proceeds in the same way as that of Schuster [111]. We would like to interpolate smoothly between the points of the polygon in the order specified. The $n \times n$ permutation matrix

$$J = \begin{pmatrix} 0 & 1 & 0 & \cdots & 0 \\ 0 & 0 & 1 & \cdots & 0 \\ \vdots & \vdots & \vdots & \ddots & \vdots \\ 0 & 0 & 0 & \cdots & 1 \\ 1 & 0 & 0 & \cdots & 0 \end{pmatrix} \tag{4.17}$$

can be used to iterate through the vertices of the polygon. We note that the matrices J, J^2, ..., $J^n \equiv I_n$ form a commutative group under matrix multiplication. This is a subgroup of the $n \times n$ permutation matrices. Iteration is performed by $(J^k \mathbf{X})_0 = \mathbf{x}_k$. The eigenvalues of J are λ^j, $j = 0, \ldots, n-1$ where $\lambda = e^{(2\pi i)/n}$. The corresponding eigenvectors are

$$\mathbf{s}_j = \left(1 \ \ \lambda^j \ \ \lambda^{2j} \ \ \ldots \ \ \lambda^{(n-1)j} \right)^T.$$

Using the *spectral representation* [122] of J we get

$$J = \sum_{j=0}^{n-1} \lambda^j P_j \tag{4.18}$$

where P_j are projection matrices. We have $P_j P_k = 0$ for $j \neq k$ and $P_j^2 = P_j$, and thus also $P_j^k = P_j$ for $k = 1, \ldots, n$. We now consider

$$J^k = \sum_{j=0}^{n-1} \lambda^{jk} P_j, \quad k = 1, \ldots, n. \tag{4.19}$$

For $k = n$ we have $J^n = I$, so that

$$I = \sum_{j=0}^{n-1} P_j$$

where I is the identity matrix. We also have $J^0 = I$. Equation 4.19 forms a system of equations of the form $(J^k) = (\lambda^{jk})(P_j)$. Solving for P_j using the inverse of the matrix (λ^{jk}), given by $\frac{1}{n}(\lambda^{-jk})$ gives

$$P_j = \frac{1}{n} \sum_{k=0}^{n-1} \lambda^{-jk} J^k, \quad j = 0, \ldots, n-1. \tag{4.20}$$

We define $P_{-j} := P_{n-j}$ and note that P_{-j} can be determined using equation 4.20 because

$$P_{-j} = \frac{1}{n} \sum_{k=0}^{n-1} \lambda^{jk} J^k$$

$$= \frac{1}{n} \sum_{k=0}^{n-1} e^{(2\pi i)(jk)/n} J^k$$

$$= \frac{1}{n} \sum_{k=0}^{n-1} e^{(2\pi i)(jk)/n - k2\pi i} J^k$$

$$= \frac{1}{n} \sum_{k=0}^{n-1} e^{(2\pi i)(jk-kn)/n} J^k$$

$$= \frac{1}{n} \sum_{k=0}^{n-1} e^{(2\pi i)(-(n-j)k)/n} J^k$$

$$= P_{n-j}. \tag{4.21}$$

We can identify two possibilities, n is even $(n = 2m)$ and

$$J^k = P_0 + (-1)^k P_m + \sum_{j=1}^{m-1} \left(\lambda^{jk} P_j + \lambda^{-jk} P_{-j} \right), \tag{4.22}$$

with $\lambda^{(n-j)k} = \lambda^{-jk}$, or n is odd $(n = 2m + 1)$ and

$$J^k = P_0 + \sum_{j=1}^{m} \left(\lambda^{jk} P_j + \lambda^{-jk} P_{-j} \right). \tag{4.23}$$

We investigate what happens if the discrete iteration using $k \in \mathbb{Z}$ is replaced with continuous $t \in \mathbb{R}$. In the odd case, if $k \in \mathbb{Z}$ is replaced by $t \in \mathbb{R}$ then $J^t \in \mathbb{R}$. For the even case $(-1)^t \in \mathbb{C}$ so $J^t \in \mathbb{C}$. In the next section we look at each of these cases in turn and derive a simpler formula for $J^t \mathbf{X}$.

4.18   Odd Case

Once again we follow the derivation of Schuster [111]. When n is odd $(n = 2m + 1)$ we have

$$J^k = P_0 + \sum_{j=1}^{m} \left(\lambda^{jk} P_j + \lambda^{-jk} P_{-j} \right) \tag{4.24}$$

with $J^0 = J^n = I$. By replacing $k \in \mathbb{Z}$ with $u \in \mathbb{R}$ we have

$$J^u = P_0 + \sum_{j=1}^{m} \left(\lambda^{ju} P_j + \lambda^{-ju} P_{-j} \right)$$

$$J^u = P_0 + \sum_{j=1}^{m} \left(e^{(2\pi i(ju))/n} P_j + e^{(2\pi i(-ju))/n} P_{-j} \right). \tag{4.25}$$

We would prefer to work with a parameter in the range $[0, 1]$, so we perform the mapping $t = \frac{u}{n}$ (or $u = tn$) and define $\tilde{J}^t := J^{nt} = J^u$ with $\tilde{J}^0 = \tilde{J}^1 = I$. $\tilde{J}^t$ is thus 1 periodic so that $\tilde{J}^{t+1} = \tilde{J}^t$. Substituting the value for $u = nt$ into the equation we get

$$\tilde{J}^t = P_0 + \sum_{j=1}^{m} \left(e^{(2\pi i(jnt))/n} P_j + e^{(2\pi i(-jnt))/n} P_{-j} \right)$$

$$= P_0 + \sum_{j=1}^{m} \left(e^{2\pi ijt} P_j + e^{-2\pi ijt} P_{-j} \right). \tag{4.26}$$

We now substitute the values for the projection matrices given in equation 4.20 into the above equation to obtain

$$\tilde{J}^t = P_0 + \sum_{j=1}^{m} \left(e^{2\pi ijt} P_j + e^{-2\pi ijt} P_{-j} \right)$$

$$= \frac{1}{n} \sum_{k=0}^{n-1} J^k + \sum_{j=1}^{m} \left(e^{2\pi ijt} \frac{1}{n} \sum_{k=0}^{n-1} \lambda^{-jk} J^k + e^{-2\pi ijt} \frac{1}{n} \sum_{k=0}^{n-1} \lambda^{jk} J^k \right)$$

$$= \frac{1}{n} \sum_{k=0}^{n-1} J^k + \sum_{j=1}^{m} \left(e^{2\pi ijt} \frac{1}{n} \sum_{k=0}^{n-1} e^{-2\pi ijk/n} J^k + e^{-2\pi ijt} \frac{1}{n} \sum_{k=0}^{n-1} e^{2\pi ijk/n} J^k \right)$$

$$= \frac{1}{n} \sum_{k=0}^{n-1} \left(1 + \sum_{j=1}^{m} e^{2\pi ij(t-k/n)} + e^{-2\pi ij(t-k/n)} \right) J^k. \tag{4.27}$$

The inner sum has the form $\sigma = 1 + \sum_{j=1}^{m} \left(x^j + x^{-j} \right)$ with $x := e^{2\pi i(t-k/n)}$. We calculate the sum of the geometric series x^j and x^{-j} and add 1 to get

$$
\begin{aligned}
\sigma &= 1 + \sum_{j=1}^{m} \left(x^j + x^{-j} \right) \\
&= 1 + \frac{x^{m+1} - x}{x - 1} + \frac{x^{-1} - x^{-m-1}}{1 - x^{-1}} \cdot \frac{x}{x} \\
&= 1 + \frac{x^{m+1} - x}{x - 1} + \frac{1 - x^{-m}}{x - 1} \\
&= \frac{x^{m+1} - x^{-m}}{x - 1}, \quad \text{with } m = \tfrac{n-1}{2} \\
&= \frac{x^{\frac{n+1}{2}} - x^{-\frac{n-1}{2}}}{x - 1} \cdot \frac{x^{-\frac{1}{2}}}{x^{-\frac{1}{2}}} \\
&= \frac{x^{\frac{n}{2}} - x^{-\frac{n}{2}}}{x^{\frac{1}{2}} - x^{-\frac{1}{2}}} \\
&= \frac{e^{\pi i(t-k/n)n} - e^{\pi i(t-k/n)(-n)}}{e^{\pi i(t-k/n)} - e^{-\pi i(t-k/n)}} \\
&= \frac{\sin(n\pi(t - k/n))}{\sin(\pi(t - k/n))} .
\end{aligned}
\tag{4.28}
$$

We define

$$
\sigma(t) := \frac{\sin(n\pi t)}{n \sin(\pi t)} \quad \text{and} \quad \sigma_k(t) := \frac{\sin(n\pi(t - k/n))}{n \sin(\pi(t - k/n))}
\tag{4.29}
$$

and note that $\sigma_k(t) = \sigma(t - k/n)$. Equation 4.27 becomes

$$
\tilde{J}^t = \sum_{k=0}^{n-1} \sigma_k(t) J^k .
\tag{4.30}
$$

To permutate the polygon given by $\mathbf{X}$ we multiply by J^k. To interpolate the points of the polygon continuously we calculate

$$
\hat{\mathbf{X}}(t) = \tilde{J}^t \mathbf{X} = \sum_{k=0}^{n-1} \sigma_k(t) J^k \mathbf{X} .
\tag{4.31}
$$

We consider element ℓ of the polygon given by $\hat{\mathbf{X}}(t)$

$$
\hat{\mathbf{X}}_\ell(t) = \sum_{k=0}^{n-1} \sigma_k(t) \mathbf{x}_{k+\ell}
$$

$$= \sum_{k=0}^{n-1} \sigma(t - k/n)\mathbf{x}_{k+\ell}$$

$$= \sum_{k=0}^{n-1} \sigma(t + \ell/n - (k + \ell)/n)\mathbf{x}_{k+\ell}$$

$$= \sum_{k=0}^{n-1} \sigma_{k+\ell}(t + \ell/n)\mathbf{x}_{k+\ell}$$

$$= \hat{\mathbf{X}}_0(t + \ell/n) \tag{4.32}$$

where $k + \ell$ is calculated modulo n. Thus we get the same curve for any value of ℓ. We define the harmonic interpolation by $\mathbf{X}(t) := \hat{\mathbf{X}}_0(t)$. $\mathbf{X}(t)$ is known as the Lagrange trigonometric interpolation of $\mathbf{X}$ [68]. The $\sigma(t)$ function is known as the periodic *Dirichlet kernel*.

This is only the case for when n is odd, in the next section we see how a similar derivation can be applied for the even case.

4.19 Even Case

In the even case, equation 4.33 is continuous in the complex domain. The definition of continuity [78] implies that the real portion should also be continuous. We can thus derive a similar formula to equation 4.31 for the even case [54, 55]. Here we fill in the details and prove certain properties.

For the continuous case we replace $k \in \mathbb{Z}$ with $u \in \mathbb{R}$, $0 \le u \le n$. In the continuous even case $(n = 2m)$ we thus have

$$J^u = P_0 + (-1)^u P_m + \sum_{j=1}^{m-1} \left(\lambda^{ju} P_j + \lambda^{-ju} P_{-j} \right), \tag{4.33}$$

which is in the complex domain since $(-1)^u = e^{\pi i u}$. We derive the formulas for the complex domain, and then examine the real portion at the end of the derivation. We begin by substituting the values for the projection matrices P_j into equation 4.33

$$J^u = P_0 + (-1)^u P_m + \sum_{j=1}^{m-1} \left(\lambda^{ju} P_j + \lambda^{-ju} P_{-j} \right) \tag{4.34}$$

$$= \frac{1}{n} \sum_{k=0}^{n-1} J^k + (-1)^u \frac{1}{n} \sum_{k=0}^{n-1} \lambda^{-mk} J^k$$

$$+ \sum_{j=1}^{m-1} \left(\lambda^{ju} \frac{1}{n} \sum_{k=0}^{n-1} \lambda^{-jk} J^k + \lambda^{-ju} \frac{1}{n} \sum_{k=0}^{n-1} \lambda^{jk} J^k \right)$$

$$= \frac{1}{n} \left(1 + (-1)^u \sum_{k=0}^{n-1} \lambda^{-mk} \right.$$

$$\left. + \sum_{j=1}^{m-1} \left(\lambda^{ju} \sum_{k=0}^{n-1} \lambda^{-jk} + \lambda^{-ju} \sum_{k=0}^{n-1} \lambda^{jk} \right) \right) J^k$$

$$= \frac{1}{n} \left(1 + \sum_{k=0}^{n-1} \left(e^{\pi i u} e^{-2\pi i m k / n} \right) \right.$$

$$\left. + \sum_{k=0}^{n-1} \sum_{j=1}^{m-1} \left(e^{2\pi i j u / n} e^{-2\pi i j k / n} + e^{-2\pi i j u / n} e^{2\pi i j k / n} \right) \right) J^k .$$

Once again we replace u by $t \in [0,1]$ to get a 1-periodic function $\tilde{J}^t$ using the substitution $u = nt$ and $n = 2m$

$$\tilde{J}^t = \frac{1}{n} \left(1 + \sum_{k=0}^{n-1} \left(e^{\pi i n t} e^{-(2\pi i m k)/n} \right) \right.$$

$$\left. + \sum_{k=0}^{n-1} \sum_{j=1}^{m-1} \left(e^{2\pi i j t} e^{-(2\pi i j k)/n} + e^{-2\pi i j t} e^{(2\pi i j k)/n} \right) \right) J^k$$

$$= \frac{1}{n} \left(1 + \sum_{k=0}^{n-1} \left(\left(e^{\pi i (nt - k)} \right) + \sum_{j=1}^{m-1} \left(e^{2\pi i j (t - k/n)} + e^{-2\pi i j (t - k/n)} \right) \right) \right) J^k .$$

$$(4.35)$$

As in the odd case, the inner sum has the form $\phi = 1 + \sum_{j=1}^{m-1} \left(x^j + x^{-j} \right)$ with $x := e^{2\pi i (t - k/n)}$. We calculate the sum of the geometric series x^j and x^{-j} and add 1 to get

$$\phi = 1 + \sum_{j=1}^{m-1} \left(x^j + x^{-j} \right)$$

$$= 1 + \frac{x^m - x}{x - 1} + \frac{x^{-1} - x^{-m}}{1 - x^{-1}} \cdot \frac{x}{x}$$

$$= 1 + \frac{x^m - x}{x - 1} + \frac{1 - x^{-m+1}}{x - 1}$$

$$= \frac{x^m - x^{-m+1}}{x - 1}, \quad \text{with } m = \frac{n}{2}$$

$$= \frac{x^{\frac{n}{2}} - x^{-\frac{n-2}{2}}}{x-1} \cdot \frac{x^{-\frac{1}{2}}}{x^{-\frac{1}{2}}}$$

$$= \frac{x^{\frac{n-1}{2}} - x^{-\frac{n-1}{2}}}{x^{\frac{1}{2}} - x^{-\frac{1}{2}}}$$

$$= \frac{e^{\pi i(t-k/n)(n-1)} - e^{-\pi i(t-k/n)(n-1)}}{e^{\pi i(t-k/n)} - e^{-\pi i(t-k/n)}}$$

$$= \frac{\sin(\pi(t-k/n)(n-1))}{\sin(\pi(t-k/n))}. \tag{4.36}$$

We define

$$\phi(t) := \frac{\sin((n-1)\pi t)}{n\sin(\pi t)} \quad \text{and} \quad \phi_k(t) := \frac{\sin((n-1)\pi(t-k/n))}{n\sin(\pi(t-k/n))} \tag{4.37}$$

and note that $\phi_k(t) = \phi(t - k/n)$. At this point we can substitute $\phi_k(t)$ back into equation 4.35, so that

$$\tilde{J}^t = \sum_{k=0}^{n-1} \left(\frac{1}{n} e^{\pi i(nt-k)} + \phi_k(t) \right) J^k$$

$$= \sum_{k=0}^{n-1} \left(\frac{1}{n} \cos(\pi(nt-k)) + \frac{i}{n} \sin(\pi(nt-k)) + \phi_k(t) \right) J^k.$$

We can rewrite $\tilde{J}^t$ in terms of $\sigma_k(t)$ by noting the identity

$$\sin((n-1)\pi(t-k/n)) \equiv \sin(\pi(nt-k))\cos(\pi(t-k/n)) \\ - \cos(\pi(nt-k))\sin(\pi(t-k/n))$$

and

$$\frac{1}{n}\cos(\pi(nt-k)) + \phi_k(t) = \cos(\pi(t-k/n))\sigma_k(t).$$

To simplify further discussions we define $\varphi(t) := \cos(\pi t)\sigma(t)$. The definition $\varphi_k(t) := \varphi(t-k/n)$ follows naturally. We now have

$$\tilde{J}^t = \sum_{k=0}^{n-1} \left(\frac{i}{n} \sin(\pi(nt-k)) + \cos(\pi(t-k/n))\sigma_k(t) \right) J^k. \tag{4.38}$$

We are only interested in the real portion of $\tilde{J}^t$, so we define

$$\hat{J}^t := \sum_{k=0}^{n-1} \varphi_k(t) J^k.$$

To permutate the polygon given by $\mathbf{X}$ we multiply by J^k. To interpolate the points of the polygon continuously we calculate

$$\hat{\mathbf{X}}(t) = \hat{J}^t \mathbf{X} = \sum_{k=0}^{n-1} \varphi_k(t) J^k \mathbf{X}.$$

We consider element ℓ of the polygon given by $\hat{\mathbf{X}}(t)$

$$
\begin{aligned}
\hat{\mathbf{X}}_\ell(t) &= \sum_{k=0}^{n-1} \varphi_k(t) \mathbf{x}_{k+\ell} \\
&= \sum_{k=0}^{n-1} \varphi(t - k/n) \mathbf{x}_{k+\ell} \\
&= \sum_{k=0}^{n-1} \varphi(t + \ell/n - (k+\ell)/n) \mathbf{x}_{k+\ell} \\
&= \sum_{k=0}^{n-1} \varphi_{k+\ell}(t + \ell/n) \mathbf{x}_{k+\ell} \\
&= \hat{\mathbf{X}}_0(t + \ell/n)
\end{aligned}
\tag{4.39}
$$

where $k + \ell$ is calculated modulo n. Thus we get the same curve for any value of ℓ. We define the harmonic interpolation by $\mathbf{X}(t) := \hat{\mathbf{X}}_0(t)$.

We now have a formula for drawing a curve that interpolates the points of a polygon for both an even number and odd number of points. In the following section we look at some examples of harmonic interpolation.

4.20   Examples

From this point onwards, we use the σ function defined as

$$
\sigma(t) := \begin{cases} \dfrac{\sin(n\pi t)}{n\sin(\pi t)}, & \text{if } n \text{ is odd} \\[2ex] \cos(\pi t)\dfrac{\sin(n\pi t)}{n\sin(\pi t)}, & \text{if } n \text{ is even} \end{cases}
\tag{4.40}
$$

and $\sigma_k(t) := \sigma(t - k/n)$. Harmonic interpolation can now be applied in both even and odd cases as

$$\mathbf{X}(t) = \sum_{k=0}^{n-1} \sigma_k(t) \mathbf{x}_k.
\tag{4.41}$$

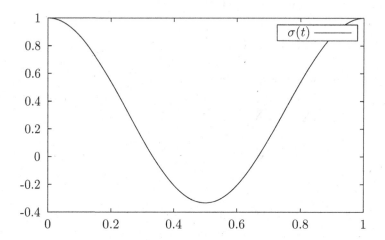

Figure 4.19: $\sigma(t)$ function for $n = 3$.

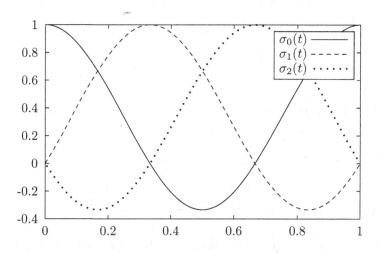

Figure 4.20: $\sigma_k(t)$ basis functions for $n = 3$.

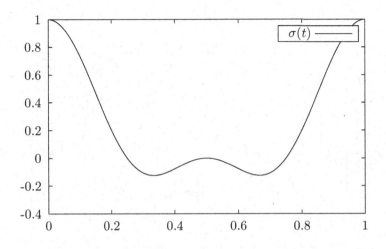

Figure 4.21: $\sigma(t)$ function for $n = 4$.

Harmonic interpolation can be applied to points of any dimension. In this section we examine some examples of harmonic interpolation and compare the examples to some of the techniques presented in chapter 1. First we graph the basis functions. Figure 4.19 and 4.21 show $\sigma(t)$ for $n = 3$ and $n = 4$. Figure 4.20 and 4.22 show all of the basis functions for $n = 3$ and $n = 4$. Of particular interest is the fact that $\sigma(t) = 1$ when $t \in \mathbb{Z}$. In particular, at the beginning of the curve $(t = 0)$ and at the end of the curve $(t = 1)$ $\sigma(t) = 1$. In addition, when one of the basis functions has value 1, all the other basis functions have value 0. Harmonic interpolation thus interpolates the points of the control polygon. Figures 4.23 and 4.24 show the behavior of $\sigma(t)$ for larger values of n. We now compare a few piecewise continuous curves produced by METAPOST [62], trigonometric interpolation, and harmonic interpolation. We chose METAPOST, since it interpolates a set of control points using cubic Bézier curves. Comparing directly to Bézier curves would be meaningless, since Bézier curves only interpolate the end control points. Figure 4.25 illustrates a circle drawn with Bézier curves in METAPOSTand harmonic interpolation. The dashed line indicates the control polygon. The feint line indicates the control polygon selected by METAPOST for piecewise continuity. Bézier curves cannot be used to draw a circle. Although there is no noticeable error in the circle drawn by METAPOST, it is not a circle. METAPOST uses several curves to draw the circle. Harmonic interpolation generates a circle precisely. Figure 4.27 illustrates the smooth curve generated by harmonic interpolation when seven control points are used. Figure 4.29 shows another comparison

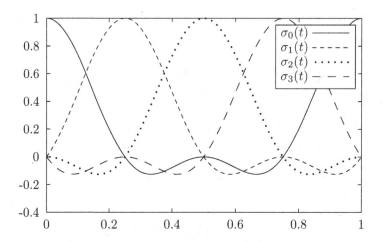

Figure 4.22: $\sigma_k(t)$ basis functions for $n = 4$.

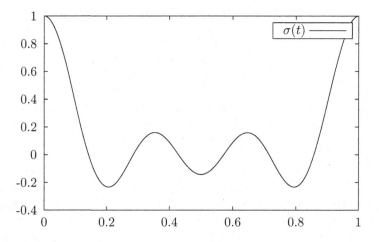

Figure 4.23: $\sigma(t)$ function for $n = 7$.

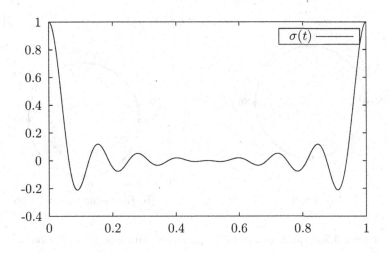

Figure 4.24: $\sigma(t)$ function for $n = 16$.

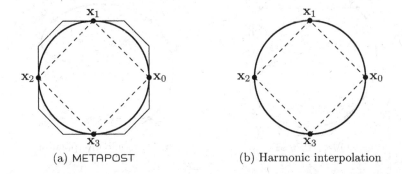

(a) METAPOST   (b) Harmonic interpolation

Figure 4.25: Circle drawn by METAPOST and harmonic interpolation.

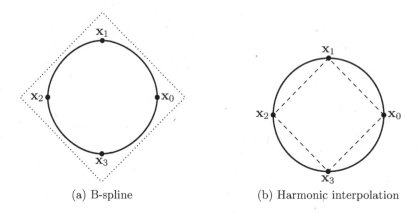

(a) B-spline   (b) Harmonic interpolation

Figure 4.26: Circle drawn by B-spline and harmonic interpolation.

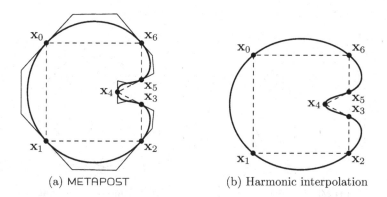

(a) METAPOST   (b) Harmonic interpolation

Figure 4.27: Seven sided polygon drawn by METAPOST and harmonic interpolation.

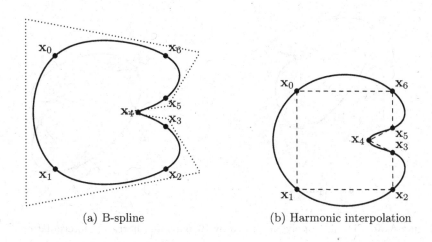

(a) B-spline   (b) Harmonic interpolation

Figure 4.28: Seven sided polygon drawn by B-spline and harmonic interpolation.

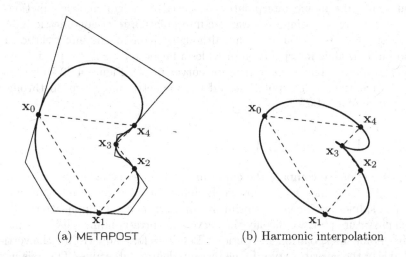

(a) METAPOST   (b) Harmonic interpolation

Figure 4.29: Five sided polygon drawn by METAPOST and harmonic interpolation.

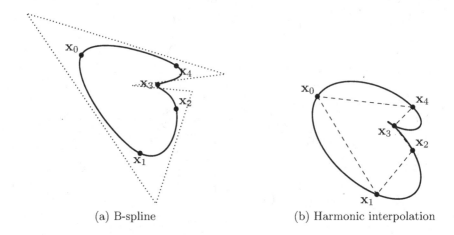

(a) B-spline   (b) Harmonic interpolation

Figure 4.30: Five sided polygon drawn by B-spline and harmonic interpolation.

with five control points. The curve produced by harmonic interpolation seems more representative of the polygon. However a cusp is produced, which is not desirable. Figures 4.26, 4.28 and 4.30 compare B-spline curves to harmonic interpolation. We discuss the results further in the next section. Since harmonic interpolation is based on trigonometric functions, it is instructive to compare harmonic interpolation to trigonometric interpolation. Figure 4.31 shows that, although trigonometric interpolation is smooth, harmonic interpolation provides a far better result for use in computer graphics. The same is true for curves in 3D. Figure 4.32 shows the result of harmonic interpolation and trigonometric interpolation through the points of a cube.

4.21   Curvature Plots

In this section we compare the curvature plots of some of the previous figures. We have chosen to compare B-splines and harmonic interpolation, since B-splines are a common primitive in most modeling applications. For each curvature plot, we display the curve and corresponding curvature plot of harmonic interpolation and periodic B-splines for comparison. The vertical axis of the curvature plot is the measured curvature value. The axis has been scaled to try to provide the most information possible. The vertical axis is labeled to indicate the minimum and maximum curvature values. The horizontal axis is unmarked, and represents the parameter value of the curve. The parameter values are not marked, since harmonic interpolation

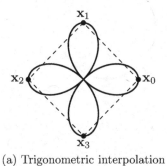
(a) Trigonometric interpolation

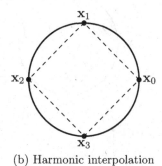
(b) Harmonic interpolation

Figure 4.31: Four point polygon drawn by trigonometric and harmonic interpolation.

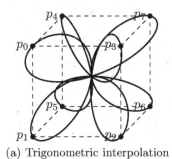
(a) Trigonometric interpolation

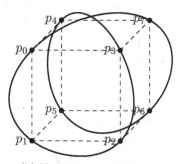
(b) Harmonic interpolation

Figure 4.32: 3D curves drawn with trigonometric and harmonic interpolation.

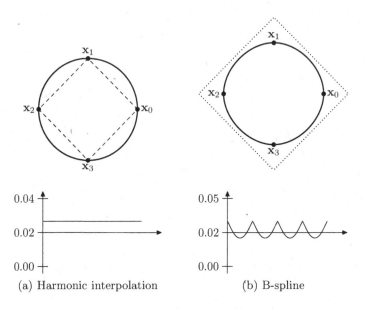

Figure 4.33: Curvature plot of figure 4.26.

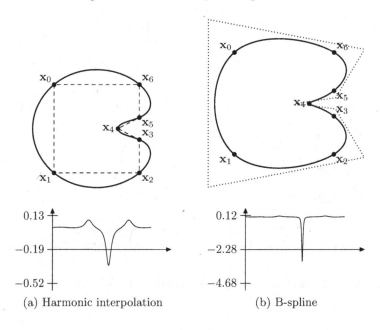

Figure 4.34: Curvature plot of figure 4.28.

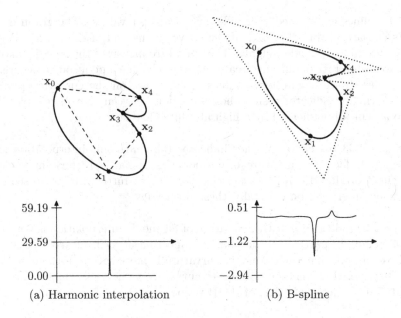

(a) Harmonic interpolation   (b) B-spline

Figure 4.35: Curvature plot of figure 4.30.

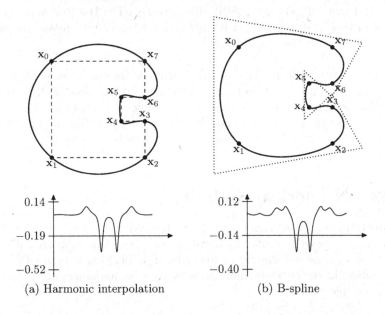

(a) Harmonic interpolation   (b) B-spline

Figure 4.36: Curvature plot of an eight sided figure.

and B-splines are defined over different parameter values. The graph depicts curvature from the start of the curve to the end of the curve. The curvature plots coincide roughly. The curvature measures the rate of curving, so a high rate of curving creates a relatively sharp point on the curve. We prefer to see low absolute values of curvature on the curvature plot. This normally indicates a smoother transition between control points. A cusp is typically indicated by a high absolute curvature value.

In figure 4.33 the curvature plot indicates that harmonic interpolation is superior. In fact, the curvature for harmonic interpolation is constant, since the curve produced is a perfect circle. We look at further curves to see if harmonic interpolation maintains these properties.

Figure 4.34 indicates that the curvature of harmonic interpolation is better in this case. In particular, the point of inflection at x_4 is clearly marked, and we can see that the change in curvature is more severe in the case of the B-spline. The maximum absolute curvature value for harmonic interpolation is far less than that of the B-spline.

Harmonic interpolation has some issues with cusps, as illustrated in figure 4.35. The cusp has a marked effect on the curvature plot. We see that the scale of figure 4.35(a) and 4.35(b) differ greatly. The B-spline appears to better in this case, although it is difficult to say how the curves compare further away from the cusp.

Finally in figure 4.36 it appears that harmonic interpolation produces a better curve in the sense that there are fewer monotone pieces in the curvature plot. This would indicate that the harmonic interpolation is *fairer* (as defined in section 4.15) in this case. It appears that harmonic interpolation produces curves with *fair* qualities, although there is a danger of oscillation and cusps.

4.22   Numerical Stability

Figure 4.37 shows how a small change in the points which are interpolated influence the curve generated by harmonic interpolation. In figure 4.37(b), the point x_0 is moved slightly to the right of its position in figure 4.37(a). The change in the curve is minimal, showing that harmonic interpolation is quite stable.

There is, however, potential numerical instability near $t = 0$ and $t = 1$. We

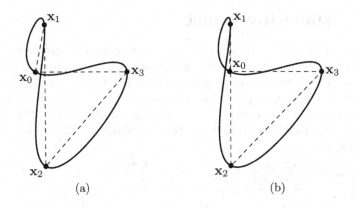

Figure 4.37: Stability of harmonic interpolation.

can compute the limit as $t \to 0$, but there is another alternative. We define

$$\varsigma_n(t) := \frac{\sin(n\pi t)}{\sin(\pi t)}.$$

We can now recursively expand $\varsigma_n(t)$ as follows

$$\varsigma_n(t) = \frac{\cos((n-1)\pi t)\sin(\pi t) + \sin((n-1)\pi t)\cos(\pi t)}{\sin(\pi t)}$$

$$= \cos((n-1)\pi t) + \cos(\pi t)\frac{\sin((n-1)\pi t)}{\sin(\pi t)}$$

$$= \cos((n-1)\pi t) + \cos(\pi t)\varsigma_{n-1}(t)$$

for $n = 2, 3, \ldots$ and note that $\varsigma_1(t) = 1$. We also note that the potential instability of dividing by a small real number is no longer an issue. This approach has the advantage that we don't have to have an accurate idea of exactly when numerical stability becomes a problem. The formula is always correct. Other approaches are only valid if t is small enough. For small values of t (or when t is near an integer value) we can use

$$\sigma(t) := \begin{cases} \frac{1}{n}\varsigma_n(t), & \text{if } n \text{ is odd} \\ \frac{1}{n}\cos(\pi t)\varsigma_n(t), & \text{if } n \text{ is even.} \end{cases} \qquad (4.42)$$

If we refer to equations 4.27 and 4.35 we see that an alternative is

$$\sigma(t) := \begin{cases} \frac{1}{n}\left(1 + 2\sum_{j=1}^{m}\cos(2\pi jt)\right), & \text{if } n \text{ is odd} \\ \frac{1}{n}\left(1 + \cos(\pi nt) + 2\sum_{j=1}^{m-1}\cos(2\pi jt)\right), & \text{if } n \text{ is even} \end{cases} \qquad (4.43)$$

with $n = 2m + 1$ in the odd case, and $n = 2m$ in the even case.

4.23   Affine Invariance

As shown in chapter 1, an important property of curves (and surfaces) is affine invariance. If a curve is affine invariant, then we can apply an affine transformation to the control points, and the curve that is produced will be identical to the curve produced by first generating the curve and then applying the affine transformation. A curve is affine invariant if the basis functions are a partition of unity as stated in theorem 4.1. Schuster [111] states that

$$\sum_{k=0}^{n-1} \sigma_k(t) = 1 \quad \text{and} \quad \sum_{k=0}^{n-1} \sigma_k^2(t) = 1$$

when n is odd. We show that this is indeed the case, and that $\sum_{k=0}^{n-1} \sigma_k(t) = 1$ when n is even.

Theorem 4.3. *The σ function (equation 4.40) is a partition of unity*

$$\sum_{k=0}^{n-1} \sigma_k(t) = 1 \,.$$

Proof. We split the proof into two parts. The first part examines the case where n is odd, and the second part examines the case where n is even.

First case: n odd ($n = 2m + 1$)   We refer back to equation 4.27 and compare the result to the σ function.

$$\tilde{J}^t = \frac{1}{n}\sum_{k=0}^{n-1}\left(1 + \sum_{j=1}^{m}\left(e^{2\pi ij(t-k/n)} + e^{-2\pi ij(t-k/n)}\right)\right)J^k,$$

$$\hat{\mathbf{X}}(t) = \tilde{J}^t\mathbf{X} = \sum_{k=0}^{n-1}\sigma_k(t)J^k\mathbf{X},$$

$$\sum_{k=0}^{n-1}\sigma_k(t) = \frac{1}{n}\sum_{k=0}^{n-1}\left(1 + \sum_{j=1}^{m}\left(e^{2\pi ij(t-k/n)} + e^{-2\pi ij(t-k/n)}\right)\right).$$

This form of the σ function will be useful to prove the desired result. We split the sum to find an alternative condition to prove, the sum then becomes

$$\sum_{k=0}^{n-1}\sigma_k(t) = \frac{1}{n}\sum_{k=0}^{n-1}\left(1 + \sum_{j=1}^{m}\left(e^{2\pi ij(t-k/n)} + e^{-2\pi ij(t-k/n)}\right)\right)$$

$$= \frac{1}{n} \sum_{k=0}^{n-1} \left(1 + 2 \sum_{j=1}^{m} \cos\left(2\pi j(t - k/n)\right) \right)$$

$$= \sum_{k=0}^{n-1} \left(\frac{1}{n} + \frac{2}{n} \sum_{j=1}^{m} \cos\left(2\pi j(t - k/n)\right) \right)$$

$$= 1 + \frac{2}{n} \sum_{k=0}^{n-1} \sum_{j=1}^{m} \cos\left(2\pi j(t - k/n)\right)$$

$$= 1 + \frac{2}{n} \sum_{j=1}^{m} \sum_{k=0}^{n-1} \cos\left(2\pi j(t - k/n)\right).$$

So it suffices to show that

$$\sum_{k=0}^{n-1} \cos(2\pi j(t - k/n)) = 0$$

for all $n > 2$, $0 < j < n$, $t \in \mathbb{R}$, $j \in \mathbb{Z}$, $n \in \mathbb{N}$, n odd. The proof follows.

$$\sum_{k=0}^{n-1} \cos(2\pi j(t - k/n)) = \frac{1}{2} \sum_{k=0}^{n-1} e^{i2\pi j(t - k/n)} + \frac{1}{2} \sum_{k=0}^{n-1} e^{-i2\pi j(t - k/n)}$$

$$= \frac{1}{2} e^{i2\pi jt} \sum_{k=0}^{n-1} e^{i2\pi j(-k/n)} + \frac{1}{2} e^{-i2\pi jt} \sum_{k=0}^{n-1} e^{i2\pi j(k/n)}.$$

At this point we note that $\sum_{k=0}^{n-1} e^{i2\pi j(-k/n)}$ and $\sum_{k=0}^{n-1} e^{i2\pi j(k/n)}$ are geometric series so that

$$\sum_{k=0}^{n-1} \cos(2\pi j(t - k/n)) = \frac{1}{2} e^{i2\pi jt} \left(\frac{1 - e^{-i2\pi j}}{1 - e^{-i2\pi j/n}} \right) + \frac{1}{2} e^{-i2\pi jt} \left(\frac{1 - e^{i2\pi j}}{1 - e^{i2\pi j/n}} \right)$$

$$= \frac{1}{2} e^{i2\pi jt} \left(\frac{1 - 1}{1 - e^{-i2\pi j/n}} \right) + \frac{1}{2} e^{-i2\pi jt} \left(\frac{1 - 1}{1 - e^{i2\pi j/n}} \right)$$

$$= 0 \hspace{6cm} (4.44)$$

as required.

Second case: n even $(n = 2m)$ Now we consider the even case. We refer back to equation 4.35 and compare the result to the σ function

$$\tilde{J}^t = \frac{1}{n} \left(1 + \sum_{k=0}^{n-1} \left(e^{\pi i(nt-k)} \right) + \sum_{j=1}^{m-1} \left(e^{2\pi ij(t-k/n)} + e^{-2\pi ij(t-k/n)} \right) \right) J^k$$

$$\hat{\mathbf{X}}(t) = \tilde{J}^t \mathbf{X} = \sigma_k(t) J^k \mathbf{X}$$

$$\sum_{k=0}^{n-1} \sigma_k(t) = \frac{1}{n} \left(1 + \sum_{k=0}^{n-1} \left(e^{\pi i (nt-k)} \right) + \sum_{j=1}^{m-1} \left(e^{2\pi i j(t-k/n)} + e^{-2\pi i j(t-k/n)} \right) \right).$$

We are only interested in the real part, however we show that the σ function including the imaginary part is still a partition of unity. The real part of $\sigma_k(t)$ is

$$Re(\sum_{k=0}^{n-1} \sigma_k(t)) = \frac{1}{n} \sum_{k=0}^{n-1} \left(1 + \cos(\pi(nt-k)) + 2 \sum_{j=1}^{m-1} \cos(2\pi j(t-k/n)) \right)$$

$$= \sum_{k=0}^{n-1} \left(\frac{1}{n} + \frac{2}{n} \sum_{j=1}^{m-1} \cos(2\pi j(t-k/n)) \right) + \frac{1}{n} \sum_{k=0}^{n-1} \cos(\pi(nt-k))$$

$$= 1 + \frac{2}{n} \sum_{k=0}^{n-1} \sum_{j=1}^{m-1} \cos(2\pi j(t-k/n)) + \frac{1}{n} \sum_{k=0}^{n-1} \cos(\pi(nt-k))$$

$$= 1 + \frac{2}{n} \sum_{j=1}^{m-1} \sum_{k=0}^{n-1} \cos(2\pi j(t-k/n)) + \frac{1}{n} \sum_{k=0}^{n-1} \cos(\pi(nt-k)).$$

Thus it suffices to show that

$$\sum_{k=0}^{n-1} \cos(2\pi j(t-k/n)) = 0$$

which we have already done in the odd case, and

$$\sum_{k=0}^{n-1} \cos(\pi(nt-k)) = 0$$

which is clearly the above sum with $j = \frac{n}{2}$. The imaginary part can also be shown to add to zero

$$\frac{i}{n} \sum_{k=0}^{n-1} \sin(\pi(nt-k)) = 0$$

by noting the identity

$$i \sum_{k=0}^{n-1} \sin(2\pi j(t-k/n)) \equiv \frac{1}{2} \sum_{k=0}^{n-1} e^{i 2\pi j(t-k/n)} - \frac{1}{2} \sum_{k=0}^{n-1} e^{-i 2\pi j(t-k/n)}.$$

This equation is almost identical to equation 4.44 (except for a change in sign), so we can simplify to get

$$i \sum_{k=0}^{n-1} \sin(2\pi j(t - k/n)) = 0 \, .$$

We note that

$$i \sum_{k=0}^{n-1} \sin(\pi(nt - k)) = 0$$

is simply the above sum with $j = \frac{n}{2}$. Thus, for both the even and the odd case

$$\sum_{k=0}^{n-1} \sigma_k(t) = 1 \, . \qquad \qquad \square$$

The theorem shows that harmonic curves (and later surfaces) are affine invariant according to theorem 4.1. We now examine other properties of curves produced by harmonic interpolation.

4.24 Convex Hull Property

After examining figures 4.19 to 4.24 we note that the function $\sigma_k(t)$ is sometimes less than zero. Points on the curve are thus not always a weighted average of the control points. As a result we encounter some difficulties when rendering harmonic surfaces in chapter 6. In chapter 6 we discuss techniques that enable efficient rendering of harmonic surfaces and address the problem of the convex hull.

4.25 C# Implementation of Harmonic Interpolation

```
//Harmonic.cs
using System;

public class Harmonic:Curve {
    public static double safe_sigma(int n,double t) {
        int m=n/2;
        double r=1.0;
        if(n%2==0) m--;
        for(int j=1;j<=m;j++) r+=2.0*Math.Cos(2.0*Math.PI*j*t);
        if(n%2==0) r+=Math.Cos(Math.PI*n*t);
```

```
      return r/n;
}

public static double sigma(int n,double t) {
   double num, den;
   num=Math.Sin(n*Math.PI*t);
   den=n*Math.Sin(Math.PI*t);
   if(Math.Abs(den)<1e-6) return safe_sigma(n,t);
   if(n%2==0) return Math.Cos(Math.PI*t)*num/den;
   else return num/den;
}

public static double sigma(int n,int k,double t)
{ return sigma(n,t-k/(double)n); }

public override Vector evaluate(Vector[] p,double t) {
   Vector r=new Vector();
   int n=p.GetLength(0);
   for(int i=0;i<n;i++) r+=sigma(n,i,t)*p[i];
   return r;
}
}
```

4.26   Chebyshev Polynomials

The *Chebyshev polynomial* [123] of degree n (of the first kind) is given by

$$T_n(x) := \cos(n \arccos(x)) \qquad (4.45)$$

where $n = 0, 1, 2, \ldots$. Although the functions T_n appear to be trigonometric, they are in fact polynomials. If we examine a few expansions of $T_n(x)$, using various trigonometric identities to simplify, we can verify the algebraic nature of T_n as follows

$$T_0(x) = 1$$
$$T_1(x) = x$$
$$T_2(x) = 2x^2 - 1$$
$$T_3(x) = 4x^3 - 3x$$
$$\vdots$$
$$T_{n+1}(x) = 2xT_n(x) - T_{n-1}(x), \quad n \geq 1.$$

The Chebyshev polynomial of degree n (of the second kind) is given by

$$U_n(x) := \frac{\sin\left((n+1)\arccos(x)\right)}{\sin\left(\arccos(x)\right)} \qquad (4.46)$$

where $n = 0, 1, 2, \ldots$. Once again we have polynomials

$$U_0(x) = 1$$
$$U_1(x) = 2x$$
$$U_2(x) = 4x^2 - 1$$
$$U_3(x) = 8x^3 - 4x$$

$$\vdots$$

$$U_{n+1}(x) = 2xU_n(x) - U_{n-1}(x), \quad n \geq 1 .$$

For details of these derivations we refer the reader to [69]. We now examine the relationship between Chebyshev polynomials and the basis functions for harmonic interpolation.

4.26.1 Odd Case

We follow a similar argument in the odd case as the one presented by Schuster [109]. In the odd case ($n = 2m + 1$), the curve produced by harmonic interpolation that interpolates the points $\mathbf{x}_k$ is given by

$$\mathbf{X}(t) = \sum_{k=0}^{n-1} \sigma_k(t)\mathbf{x}_k,$$

with

$$\sigma_k(t) = \frac{\sin(n\pi(t - k/n))}{n \sin(\pi(t - k/n))} .$$

The function $\sigma_k(t)$ can be represented by Chebyshev polynomials of the second kind by noting that

$$\frac{1}{n}U_{n-1}(\cos(\pi(t - k/n))) = \frac{\sin(n\pi(t - k/n)}{n \sin(\pi(t - k/n))} = \sigma_k(t) .$$

We thus make the substitution $s = \cos(\pi t)$. Then we have the identity

$$\cos(\pi(t - k/n)) \equiv s \cos(\pi k/n) + \sqrt{1 - s^2} \sin(\pi k/n) .$$

The curve $\mathbf{X}(t)$ can thus be written in terms of Chebyshev polynomials of the second kind. The curve $\mathbf{X}(t)$ is then

$$\mathbf{X}(s) = \frac{1}{n} \sum_{k=0}^{n-1} U_{n-1}(\phi(s))\mathbf{x}_k, \quad -1 \leq s \leq 1$$

with

$$\phi(s) = s \cos(\pi k/n) + \sqrt{1 - s^2} \sin(\pi k/n) .$$

4.26.2 Even Case

In the even case $(n = 2m)$, the curve produced by harmonic interpolation that interpolates the points $\mathbf{x}_k$ is given by

$$\mathbf{X}(t) = \sum_{k=0}^{n-1} \cos(\pi(t - k/n))\sigma_k(t)\mathbf{x}_k$$

with

$$\sigma_k(t) = \frac{\sin(n\pi(t - k/n))}{n \sin(\pi(t - k/n))}.$$

We can rewrite $\sigma_k(t)$ in terms of Chebyshev polynomials of the second kind as in the odd case. We note that

$$T_1(\cos(\pi(t - k/n))) = \cos(\pi(t - k/n)).$$

Once again we can use the substitution $s = \cos(\pi t)$ to rewrite harmonic interpolation in the even case in terms of Chebyshev polynomials of the first and second kind as

$$\mathbf{X}(s) = \frac{1}{n} \sum_{k=0}^{n-1} T_1(\phi(s))U_{n-1}(\phi(s))\mathbf{x}_k, \quad -1 \le s \le 1$$

with

$$\phi(s) = s \cos(\pi k/n) + \sqrt{1 - s^2} \sin(\pi k/n).$$

We thus find that harmonic interpolation, in both the even and odd cases, are algebraic curves. Furthermore, we can evaluate the Chebyshev polynomials quite quickly [76] $(O(\log n))$ in comparison to equations 4.42 and 4.43 $(O(n))$ without the numerical instability of $\sigma_k(t)$ as $t \to 0$ in equation 4.40.

4.27 Non-Uniform Harmonic Interpolation

In the uniform case we have equation 4.20,

$$P_j = \frac{1}{n} \sum_{k=0}^{n-1} \lambda^{-jk} J^k, \quad j = 0, \ldots, n-1$$

$$= \frac{1}{n} \sum_{k=0}^{n-1} e^{-2\pi ijk/n} J^k$$

which is the spectral projection or Fourier transform of J^k, $k = 0, \ldots, n-1$. The P_j's are the Fourier coefficients obtained from solving the system of equations 4.19

$$J^k = \sum_{j=0}^{n-1} e^{2\pi ijk/n} P_j, \quad k = 0, \ldots, n.$$

For the non-uniform case, points are not sampled with the uniform spacing $t_j = j/n$ but rather at arbitrary points t_j with $t_j < t_{j+1}$. We also require $0 \leq t_j \leq 1$. We thus need to solve the system of equations

$$J^k = \sum_{j=0}^{n-1} e^{2\pi ikt_j} P_j, \quad k = 0, \ldots, n-1. \tag{4.47}$$

We thus have n equations in n unknowns. With the assumption $t_j < t_{j+1}$, which implies that $t_j \neq t_k, k \neq j$, the system of linear equations takes the form

$$J^k = \sum_{j=0}^{n-1} a_j^k P_j, \quad k = 0, \ldots, n-1.$$

The inverse Fourier transform is then given by

$$\mathbf{J} = A\mathbf{P}$$

with

$$\mathbf{J} = \left(J^0 \ J^1 \ \ldots \ J^{n-1} \right)^T, \qquad \mathbf{P} = \left(P_0 \ P_1 \ \ldots \ P_{n-1} \right)^T$$

and

$$A_{k,j} = a_j^k = e^{2\pi ikt_j}.$$

The forward Fourier transform (non-uniform) is given by

$$\mathbf{P} = A^{-1}\mathbf{J}.$$

The matrix A has the form

$$A = \begin{pmatrix} 1 & 1 & 1 & 1 & \ldots & 1 \\ a_0 & a_1 & a_2 & a_3 & \ldots & a_{n-1} \\ a_0^2 & a_1^2 & a_2^2 & a_3^2 & \ldots & a_{n-1}^2 \\ a_0^3 & a_1^3 & a_2^3 & a_3^3 & \ldots & a_{n-1}^3 \\ \vdots & \vdots & \vdots & \vdots & \ldots & \vdots \\ a_0^{n-1} & a_1^{n-1} & a_2^{n-1} & a_3^{n-1} & \ldots & a_{n-1}^{n-1} \end{pmatrix}$$

with $a_j := e^{2\pi i t_j}$. This matrix is known as a *Vandermonde matrix* [101], and is related to the problem of moments. The inverse of the matrix is closely related to Lagrange interpolation. Let

$$p_k(x) := \prod_{\substack{j=0 \\ j \neq k}}^{n-1} \frac{x - a_j}{a_k - a_j} = \sum_{j=0}^{n-1} B_{k,j} x^j.$$

We thus have

$$p_k(a_\ell) = \prod_{\substack{j=0 \\ j \neq k}}^{n-1} \frac{a_\ell - a_j}{a_k - a_j} = \delta_{\ell,k} = \sum_{j=0}^{n-1} B_{k,j} a_\ell^j$$

so that $B = A^{-1}$. The coefficients of the polynomial produced by Lagrange interpolation are the elements of the inverse of A. We can compute the elements of A^{-1} efficiently by defining

$$p(x) := \prod_{j=0}^{n-1} (x - a_j).$$

Consequently

$$p_k(x) = \frac{p(x)}{(x - a_k) p'(a_k)}$$

where p' denotes the derivative of p with respect to x. We thus need only compute the coefficients of $p(x)$ and then for each $p_k(x)$, the coefficients are found by division by a simple polynomial and a constant. For each of the n polynomials a division calculation of order $O(n)$ is performed. The order of the calculation is thus $O(n^2)$. To calculate the coefficients of $p(x) = \sum_{j=0}^{n} c_j x^j$ we note that

$$c_j = f_j(0)$$

where

$$f_j(i) = -\sum_{\ell=i}^{j} a_\ell f_{j+1}(\ell + 1), \quad i \geq 0$$
$$f_j(i) = 0, \quad i > j$$
$$f_n(i) = 1 \quad 0 \leq i < n.$$

The function $f_j(i)$ uses a combinatorial approach to computing the coefficient of x^j. The parameter i determines which $(x - a_i)$ terms in the product are under consideration. For each term, we may either include the term, or exclude the term. If we include the term, then a_i forms part of the coefficient, otherwise x contributes to the factor x^j. If $i > j$ then there aren't enough factors left to construct x^j and thus this term must be 0. The formula $f_j(i) = -\sum_{\ell=i}^{j} a_\ell f_{j+1}(\ell + 1)$ considers the terms i up to j. The sum simply selects each term in the product (in turn) to be included and determines what the contribution this particular a_ℓ makes to the coefficient. Any further values must come from later terms in the product since we have elected not to include the previous terms' a_i values.

We have the recursive relationship

$$f_j(i) - f_j(i + 1) = -a_i f_{j+1}(i + 1)\,.$$
$$f_j(i) = f_j(i + 1) - a_i f_{j+1}(i + 1)\,.$$

Thus, if we have all f_{j+1} we can compute f_j starting with $f_j(n - 1)$ and working down to $f_j(0)$. We would thus have to store both f_j and f_{j+1}. We can avoid the extra storage requirements by starting with $f_{n-1}(n - 1)$, we have

$$f_{n-1}(i) = -\sum_{\ell=i}^{n-1} a_\ell f_n(\ell + 1)\,.$$

Since $f_n(i) = 1$ it follows that

$$f_{n-1}(i) = -\sum_{\ell=i}^{n-1} a_\ell\,.$$

Now we have

$$f_{n-1}(n - 1) = -\sum_{\ell=n-1}^{n-1} a_\ell = -a_{n-1}$$
$$f_{n-2}(n - 2) = f_{n-2}(n - 1) - a_{n-2} f_{n-1}(n - 1)$$
$$\vdots$$
$$f_0(n - 2) = f_0(n - 1) - a_{n-2} f_1(n - 1)\,.$$

In the next iteration we have

$$f_{n-1}(n - 2) = -\sum_{\ell=n-2}^{n-1} a_\ell = f_{n-1}(n - 1) - a_{n-2}$$
$$f_{n-2}(n - 3) = f_{n-2}(n - 2) - a_{n-3} f_{n-1}(n - 2)$$

$$\vdots$$

$$f_0(n-3) = f_0(n-2) - a_{n-3}f_1(n-2).$$

Since we only wish to calculate $f_j(0)$ it is unnecessary to store $f_j(i)$, $i > 0$. The calculation can thus proceed with the iterations, only storing $f_j(i)$ for successively decreasing values of i, until $i = 0$. We thus have n iterations computing n function values. The calculation of coefficients is thus $O(n^2)$. Now we can apply

$$\mathbf{P} = A^{-1}\mathbf{J}$$

to calculate

$$P_j = \sum_{k=0}^{n-1} A_{j,k}^{-1} J^k.$$

The continuous transform is then given by

$$J^u = \sum_{j=0}^{n-1} e^{2\pi i u t_j} P_j$$

$$J^u = \sum_{j=0}^{n-1} e^{2\pi i u t_j} \sum_{k=0}^{n-1} A_{j,k}^{-1} J^k$$

with $0 \le u \le n$. To interpolate we apply the substitution $nt = u$ to obtain

$$\mathbf{X}(t) = J^{nt}\mathbf{X} = \sum_{j=0}^{n-1} e^{2\pi i n t t_j} \sum_{k=0}^{n-1} A_{j,k}^{-1} J^k \mathbf{X}.$$

The first element is then given by

$$\mathbf{X}_0(t) = \sum_{j=0}^{n-1} e^{2\pi i n t t_j} \sum_{k=0}^{n-1} A_{j,k}^{-1} \mathbf{x}_k.$$

The set of equations 4.47 can be solved efficiently using the unequally spaced fast Fourier transform (USFFT [4]). Alternatives are discussed in [24] and [25]. Another technique suggested by Pohlman [7], represents the inverse Fourier transform (non-uniform) as

$$\mathbf{J} = A\hat{\mathbf{P}}$$

with

$$\mathbf{J} = \begin{pmatrix} J^0 & J^1 & \dots & J^{n-1} \end{pmatrix}^T$$

and $A_{k,j} = e^{2\pi i k t_j}$. The problem is thus to find $\hat{\mathbf{P}}$ to solve these equations. The forward Fourier transform (non-uniform) is given by

$$\mathbf{P} = \frac{1}{n} A^* \mathbf{J}$$

with

$$\mathbf{P} = \begin{pmatrix} P_0 & P_1 & \cdots & P_{n-1} \end{pmatrix}^T$$

and $A^* = \bar{A}^T$ where $\bar{x}$ is the complex conjugate of x. Although it is not (necessarily) true that $\mathbf{P} = \hat{\mathbf{P}}$, the transform is similar to the Fourier transform. We try to use this relationship to find a solution. We then have

$$A^* \mathbf{J} = A^* A \hat{\mathbf{P}}$$

with the matrix $A^* A$ Hermitian and Toeplitz, so we can solve for $\hat{\mathbf{P}}$ efficiently. The algorithm by Pohlman [7] and the USFFT are more efficient ($O(n \log n)$) and can usually be evaluated to a required degree of accuracy. A matrix A is Hermitian if $A = A^* \equiv \bar{A}^T$. An $n \times n$ *Toeplitz matrix* is specified by $2n - 1$ numbers R_k, $k = -n + 1, \ldots, n - 1$ and has the form

$$\begin{pmatrix} R_0 & R_{-1} & R_{-2} & \cdots & R_{-(n-2)} & R_{-(n-1)} \\ R_1 & R_0 & R_{-1} & \cdots & R_{-(n-3)} & R_{-(n-2)} \\ R_2 & R_1 & R_0 & \cdots & R_{-(n-4)} & R_{-(n-3)} \\ & & & \vdots & & \\ R_{n-2} & R_{n-3} & R_{n-4} & \cdots & R_0 & R_{-1} \\ R_{n-1} & R_{n-2} & R_{n-3} & \cdots & R_1 & R_0 \end{pmatrix}.$$

The non-uniform Fourier transform does not yield the same results as harmonic interpolation when applied to points with parametric values $t_j = \frac{i}{n}$. Harmonic interpolation was identified as Lagrange trigonometric interpolation, and we can see that it does not correspond to (Fourier) trigonometric interpolation, identified in section 4.13. This becomes obvious when we note that $\lambda^{(n-j)k} = \lambda^{-jk}$ in equation 4.23, but $\lambda^{(n-j)u} \neq \lambda^{-ju}$ in equation 4.25. A variation of the Fourier transform applied to an odd set of points ($n = 2m + 1$) is given by

$$P_j = \frac{1}{n} \sum_{k=0}^{n-1} e^{-2\pi i j k / n} J^k, \quad j = -m, \ldots, m$$

$$J^k = \sum_{j=-m}^{m} e^{2\pi i j k / n} P_j, \quad k = 0, \ldots, n. \tag{4.48}$$

We note that

$$J^k = \sum_{j=-m}^{m} e^{2\pi ijk/n} P_j, \quad k = 0, \ldots, n$$

$$= P_0 + \sum_{j=1}^{m} \left(e^{2\pi ijk/n} + e^{-2\pi ijk/n} \right) P_j$$

which is simply harmonic interpolation. We might then try non-uniform harmonic interpolation as

$$\mathbf{X}(t) = \sum_{j=-m}^{m} e^{2\pi intt_j} \sum_{k=0}^{n-1} A_{j+m,k}^{-1} \mathbf{x}_k .$$

However t_k, $k < 0$, has not been defined. And if we define t_k so that $0 \le t_k \le 1$ (for $k < 0$) then this does not differ from the non-uniform Fourier transform. Instead we rewrite 4.48 as

$$P_j = \frac{1}{n} \sum_{k=0}^{n-1} e^{-2\pi ijk/n} J^k, \quad j = -m, \ldots, m$$

$$J^k = \sum_{j=0}^{n-1} e^{2\pi ik(j-m)/n} P_j, \quad k = 0, \ldots, n$$

$$= \sum_{j=0}^{n-1} e^{2\pi ik(j/n - m/n)} P_j .$$

Taking

$$J^k = \sum_{j=0}^{n-1} e^{2\pi ik(j/n - m/n)} P_j$$

we then obtain

$$\mathbf{X}(t) = \sum_{j=0}^{n-1} e^{2\pi int(t_j - m/n)} \sum_{k=0}^{n-1} A_{j,k}^{-1} \mathbf{x}_k$$

$$= \sum_{j=0}^{n-1} e^{2\pi int(t_j - m/n)} \mathbf{f}_j$$

as the interpolation formula, where $\mathbf{f}_j = (f_0(0) \; f_1(0) \; f_2(0) \; \ldots \; f_{n-1}(0))^T$. The calculation of $A_{j,k}^{-1}$ should be adjusted accordingly. This equation corresponds with harmonic interpolation in the case where $t_k = k/n$. We

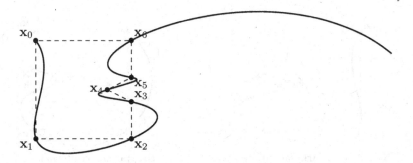

Figure 4.38: Non-uniform harmonic interpolation of seven points.

also note that non-uniform harmonic interpolation is not guaranteed to be periodic. The last segment is usually not very pleasing as illustrated in figure 4.38. We thus only interpolate up to the last point provided and the interpolation formula becomes

$$\mathbf{X}(t) = \sum_{j=0}^{n-1} e^{2\pi i(n-1)t(t_j - m/n)} \sum_{k=0}^{n-1} A_{j,k}^{-1} \mathbf{x}_k$$

$$= \sum_{j=0}^{n-1} e^{2\pi i(n-1)t(t_j - m/n)} \mathbf{f}_j \, .$$

We illustrate some of the previous figures using non-uniform harmonic interpolation. In each figure uniform harmonic interpolation is compared to the non-uniform case. Note that the non-uniform curve ends before the uniform curve does. For the non-uniform case, we have selected t_j as

$$t_j = \frac{1}{\ell} \sum_{k=0}^{j} \| \mathbf{x}_{k+1} - \mathbf{x}_k \|$$

where

$$\ell = \| \mathbf{x}_0 - \mathbf{x}_{n-1} \| + \sum_{k=0}^{n-2} \| \mathbf{x}_{k+1} - \mathbf{x}_k \| \, .$$

The previous diagrams with seven and five points are illustrated in figures 4.39 and 4.40. The non-uniform interpolation algorithm is applied for both the uniform and non-uniform interpolation. An example of the even case is illustrated in figure 4.41.

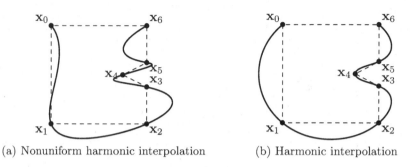

(a) Nonuniform harmonic interpolation   (b) Harmonic interpolation

Figure 4.39: Seven sided polygon drawn by non-uniform and uniform harmonic interpolation.

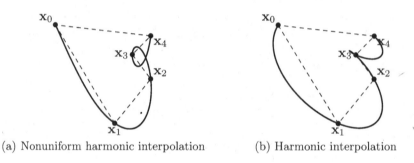

(a) Nonuniform harmonic interpolation   (b) Harmonic interpolation

Figure 4.40: Five sided polygon drawn by non-uniform and uniform harmonic interpolation.

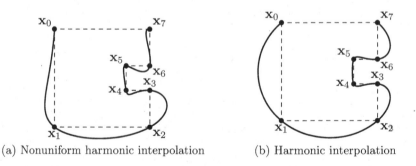

(a) Nonuniform harmonic interpolation   (b) Harmonic interpolation

Figure 4.41: Eight sided polygon drawn by non-uniform and uniform harmonic interpolation.

Chapter 5

Wavelets

5.1 Introduction

In the same way that we represented a function (data) in terms of a set of trigonometric basis functions, we may also try to represent the function (data) in another basis. The work of Daubechies [19] and many others has provided a solid theoretical basis for further work.

In most cases the discrete wavelet transform is an orthogonal function which can be applied to a finite group of data. The discrete wavelet transform is functionally very similar to the Fourier transform, in the sense that a signal that is transformed and then undergoes the inverse transform is left unchanged. Fourier transforms use sinusoidal basis functions whereas wavelet basis functions are defined by a recursive difference equation for a scaling function ϕ. The scaling function ϕ is also known as the *father wavelet* and satisfies

$$\phi(x) = \sum_{k=0}^{M} c_k \phi(2x - k)$$

where M is determined by the number of nonzero coefficients in the data, and k is a translation parameter. In general the area under the scaling function should be unity, that is

$$\int_{\mathbb{R}} \phi(x)\,dx = 1\,.$$

The scaling function ϕ is orthogonal to its translations in the Hilbert space

$L_2(\mathbb{R})$ with the scalar product

$$\langle f, g \rangle := \int_{\mathbb{R}} f(x)\overline{g}(x)\,dx\,.$$

Thus

$$\int_{\mathbb{R}} \phi(x)\phi(x - k)\,dx = 0 \qquad k \in \mathbb{Z}\backslash\{0\}\,.$$

A function is needed that is also orthogonal to its dilations or scales, that is

$$\int_{\mathbb{R}} \psi(x)\psi(2x - k)\,dx = 0\,.$$

The function $\psi(x)$ is known as the *mother wavelet* and is given by

$$\psi(x) = \sum_{k=1}^{M} (-1)^k c_{1-k}\phi(2x - k)\,.$$

Wavelet functions typically have compact support, i.e. they are zero outside of a small interval. This property makes wavelets useful for operation on a finite set of data. In the next section we examine a particular 1-dimensional wavelet, namely the Haar wavelet.

5.2 One-Dimensional Wavelets

In this section, we consider the wavelet transform for representing functions (data) in another basis, we concentrate on the application of wavelets in computer graphics. To begin, we describe the *Haar wavelet transform*. We follow a similar approach to Stollnitz et al. [128, 129].

Example. Consider a one-dimensional set of data given by

$$\mathbf{x} = (17\ 3\ 5\ 7)^T\,.$$

We compute a wavelet transform to represent the data in the *Haar basis*. To do so, we first calculate the average of adjacent values x_{2k} and x_{2k+1} to get

$$H_1\mathbf{x} = (10\ 6)^T$$

where

$$H_1 = \frac{1}{2}\begin{pmatrix} 1 & 1 & 0 & 0 \\ 0 & 0 & 1 & 1 \end{pmatrix}\,.$$

To fully reconstruct the signal we need more data. We thus add the detail coefficients

$$G_1\mathbf{x} = (7\ -1)^T$$

where

$$G_1 = \frac{1}{2}\begin{pmatrix} 1 & -1 & 0 & 0 \\ 0 & 0 & 1 & -1 \end{pmatrix}.$$

The detail coefficients allow us to reconstruct the original data since $10+7 = x_0$, $10-7 = x_1$, $6-(-1) = x_2$ and $6+(-1) = x_3$. We can apply this process repeatedly to the averages obtained, until only one average remains. The number of detail coefficients plus the one average coefficient is 4. We have not gained or lost anything, since the number of data is still 4 and the original signal can be reconstructed. We can then further apply the averaging process on the detail coefficients $G_1\mathbf{x}$. The final average, followed by the detail coefficients is known as the *wavelet transform* or *wavelet decomposition* of the original data. In our case the wavelet transform of the data is given by

$$(H_2H_1\mathbf{x} \quad G_2H_1\mathbf{x} \quad H_2G_1\mathbf{x} \quad G_2G_1\mathbf{x})^T = (8 \ 2 \ 3 \ 4)^T$$

with

$$H_2 = \frac{1}{2}(1 \ \ 1) \qquad G_2 = \frac{1}{2}(1 \ \ -1).$$

The process of averaging and filtering is known as a *filter bank*. To reconstruct the original data, we need to work out the inverse transforms. If we have the wavelet transform of the original data $\mathbf{x}$

$$(H_2H_1\mathbf{x} \quad G_2H_1\mathbf{x} \quad H_2G_1\mathbf{x} \quad G_2G_1\mathbf{x})^T = (8 \ 2 \ 3 \ 4)^T = \mathbf{w},$$

then we see that $w_0 = H_2H_1\mathbf{x}$ and $w_2 = H_2G_1\mathbf{x}$. We also have $w_1 = G_2H_1\mathbf{x}$ and $w_3 = G_2G_1\mathbf{x}$. Using the matrices

$$X_1 = \begin{pmatrix} 1 & 1 & 0 & 0 \\ 1 & -1 & 0 & 0 \end{pmatrix} \qquad Y_1 = \begin{pmatrix} 0 & 0 & 1 & 1 \\ 0 & 0 & 1 & -1 \end{pmatrix}$$

we obtain

$$X_1\mathbf{w} = (10 \ 6)^T \qquad Y_1\mathbf{w} = (7 \ \ -1)^T.$$

Next we apply the matrices

$$X_2 = \begin{pmatrix} 1 & 0 & 1 & 0 \\ 1 & 0 & -1 & 0 \end{pmatrix} \qquad Y_2 = \begin{pmatrix} 0 & 1 & 0 & 1 \\ 0 & 1 & 0 & -1 \end{pmatrix}$$

to the vector $(X_1\mathbf{w} \ Y_1\mathbf{w})^T$ to obtain

$$X_2(X_1\mathbf{w} \ Y_1\mathbf{w})^T = X_2(10 \ 6 \ 7 \ -1)^T = (17 \ 3)^T$$

and

$$Y_2(X_1\mathbf{w} \ Y_1\mathbf{w})^T = Y_2(10 \ 6 \ 7 \ -1)^T = (5 \ 7)^T$$

which yields the original data $(17 \ 3 \ 5 \ 7)^T$. If we multiply

$$\begin{pmatrix} X_2 \\ Y_2 \end{pmatrix} \begin{pmatrix} X_1 \\ Y_1 \end{pmatrix}$$

we obtain the single reconstruction matrix

$$M = \begin{pmatrix} 1 & 1 & 1 & 1 \\ 1 & 1 & -1 & -1 \\ 1 & -1 & 1 & -1 \\ 1 & -1 & -1 & 1 \end{pmatrix}$$

with $M^T = M$ and $M^T M = 4I$. Thus M is a *Hadamard matrix* [122]. $\square$

To determine the basis functions used for the transform, we need to determine the vector spaces which we work in. We can view the data as piecewise-constant functions on the half-open interval $[0, 1)$. A single value, c, is then a constant function over the interval $f(x) = c$. Let V^0 be the vector space of these functions. Two values, c_1 and c_2, can be described by a function with two constant portions

$$f(x) = \begin{cases} c_1, & 0 \le x < 0.5 \\ c_2, & 0.5 \le x < 1. \end{cases}$$

The vector space of functions based on two values will be referred to as V^1. Continuing in this manner, we obtain the vector space V^j of all functions defined on the interval $[0, 1)$ that are constant over each of the 2^j equal sub-intervals. By construction, if $\mathbf{x} \in V^j$, then $\mathbf{x} \in V^{j+1}$. The spaces V^j are nested,

$$V^0 \subset V^1 \subset V^2 \subset \cdots.$$

We now find a set of basis functions for V^j. These basis functions are known as *scaling functions*. A simple basis for V^j is the set of *box functions*

$$\phi_i^j(x) := \phi(2^j x - i), \qquad i = 0, \ldots, 2^j - 1,$$

with

$$\phi(x) := \begin{cases} 1, & 0 \le x < 1 \\ 0, & \text{otherwise.} \end{cases}$$

We note that the functions ϕ_i^j are translates and dilates of each other. We choose the standard inner product for functions

$$\langle f, g \rangle := \int_0^1 f(x)g(x)\, dx.$$

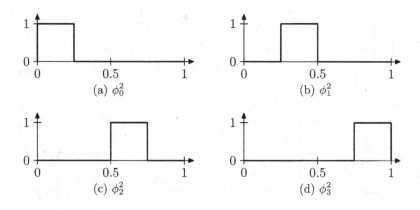

Figure 5.1: The box functions for V^2.

We now define W^j, the orthogonal complement of V^j in V^{j+1}. All functions in W^j must then be orthogonal to all functions in V^j, that is

$$\langle f, g \rangle = 0$$

for $f \in V^j$ and $g \in W^j$. A collection of linearly independent functions $\psi_i^j(x)$ that span W^j are known as *wavelets*. The basis functions for W^j (ψ_i^j) and V^j (ϕ_i^j) form a basis for V^{j+1}. We see that the detail coefficients are thus coefficients of the wavelet basis functions, since we reduce the data from V^j to V^{j-1}. The wavelets corresponding to the box basis are known as the *Haar wavelets*. The Haar wavelets are given by

$$\psi_i^j(x) := \psi(2^j x - i), \qquad i = 0, \ldots, 2^j - 1$$

with

$$\psi(x) := \begin{cases} 1, & 0 \le x < 0.5 \\ -1, & 0.5 \le x < 1 \\ 0, & \text{otherwise.} \end{cases}$$

If we examine figures 5.1 and 5.2, we can establish the relationship between the wavelet decomposition and the Haar wavelets. The original data set can be expressed in terms of ϕ_i^j and ψ_i^j by

$$\begin{aligned} f(x) &= 17\phi_0^2(x) + 3\phi_1^2(x) + 5\phi_2^2(x) + 7\phi_3^2(x) \\ &= 10\phi_0^1(x) + 6\phi_1^1(x) + 7\psi_0^1(x) - \psi_1^1(x) \\ &= 8\phi_0^0(x) + 2\psi_0^0(x) + 7\psi_0^1(x) - \psi_1^1(x). \end{aligned}$$

The functions $\phi_0^0(x)$, $\psi_0^0(x)$, $\psi_0^1(x)$ and $\psi_1^1(x)$ are known as the Haar basis for V^2. The Haar basis functions are orthogonal, although this is not a

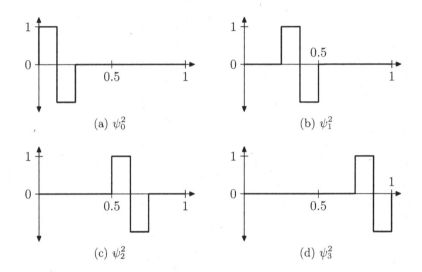

Figure 5.2: The Haar wavelets for W^2.

requirement for the wavelet basis. We can also normalize the basis functions so that $\langle u, u \rangle = 1$ for any basis function $u(x)$. The normalized Haar basis is obtained by using the definition

$$\phi_i^j(x) := 2^{j/2} \phi(2^j x - i)$$
$$\psi_i^j(x) := 2^{j/2} \psi(2^j x - i).$$

We can view the wavelet transform as consisting of two parts. First we have a predictor. In the case of the Haar basis, we assume that the function is constant. We then have a detail coefficient that corrects for the error in the prediction. The detail coefficients allow us to fully reconstruct the signal. If the error in the prediction is small, then we can omit or reduce the number of detail coefficients and thus compress the signal. Wavelets have been applied in many areas [130, 49] including image compression [128]. We can efficiently calculate the wavelet transform if we use a *lifting scheme* [132]. The lifting scheme simply describes the wavelet transform in such a way that it can be computed in place (without extra storage requirements) and gives an immediate form for the inverse transform.

5.3 Two-Dimensional Wavelets

The discussion so far has focused on wavelets on one-dimensional data. We can also apply wavelets to two-dimensional data such as images. The simplest way to build a basis for two-dimensional data is to use separable wavelets [124]. We use a tensor product of a one-dimensional wavelet ψ and scaling function ϕ. The two-dimensional scaling function is given by

$$\Phi(x_0, x_1) := \phi(x_0)\phi(x_1)$$

and the three wavelet functions are given by

$$\Psi^{(1)}(x_0, x_1) := \phi(x_0)\psi(x_1)$$
$$\Psi^{(2)}(x_0, x_1) := \psi(x_0)\phi(x_1)$$
$$\Psi^{(3)}(x_0, x_1) := \psi(x_0)\psi(x_1).$$

We define
$$\Psi_{\mathbf{i},j}^{(k)}(\mathbf{x}) := 2^j \Psi^{(k)}(2^j \mathbf{x} - \mathbf{i}), \qquad k = 1, 2, 3$$

where $j \in \mathbb{Z}$ and $\mathbf{i} \in \mathbb{Z}^2$ and $\mathbf{x} = (x_0 \ x_1)^T$. The factor 2^j ensures that we have an orthonormal basis. Let $L_2(\mathbb{R}^2)$ be the Hilbert space of square integrable functions with underlying domain $\mathbb{R}^2$. We can now express any function $f \in L_2(\mathbb{R}^2)$ in terms of the wavelet functions as

$$f(\mathbf{x}) = \alpha_\Phi \Phi(\mathbf{x}) + \sum_{\mathbf{i},j,k} \alpha_{\mathbf{i},j,\Psi} \Psi_{\mathbf{i},j}^{(k)}(\mathbf{x})$$

where $\alpha_\Phi = \langle f, \Phi \rangle$ and $\alpha_{\mathbf{i},j,\Psi} = \langle f, \Psi_{\mathbf{i},j}^{(k)} \rangle$. This is known as the *nonstandard construction* of basis functions. There is also the *standard construction* for which we refer the reader to Stollnitz et al. [128]. For the nonstandard construction, the process corresponds to transforming rows (one iteration only), and then transforming columns (one iteration only). The process is repeated until the full transform is completed. After the transform is completed the function f can be written as

$$f(\mathbf{x}) = \sum_{\mathbf{i},j,\Psi} \langle f, \Psi_{\mathbf{i},j} \rangle \Psi_{\mathbf{i},j}(\mathbf{x})$$

where Ψ ranges over all the wavelet functions.

Example. Suppose we have the image

$$A = \begin{pmatrix} 17 & 3 & 5 & 7 \\ 2 & 8 & 7 & 7 \\ 2 & 16 & 5 & 3 \\ 10 & 6 & 8 & 6 \end{pmatrix}.$$

We perform the nonstandard decomposition using the Haar basis. We first apply the transform AH_1^r with

$$H_1^r = \frac{1}{2}\begin{pmatrix} 1 & 0 \\ 1 & 0 \\ 0 & 1 \\ 0 & 1 \end{pmatrix}$$

to obtain the averages for each row. The averages are

$$AH_1^r = \begin{pmatrix} 17 & 3 & 5 & 7 \\ 2 & 8 & 7 & 7 \\ 2 & 16 & 5 & 3 \\ 10 & 6 & 8 & 6 \end{pmatrix}\frac{1}{2}\begin{pmatrix} 1 & 0 \\ 1 & 0 \\ 0 & 1 \\ 0 & 1 \end{pmatrix} = \begin{pmatrix} 10 & 6 \\ 5 & 7 \\ 9 & 4 \\ 8 & 7 \end{pmatrix}.$$

The detail coefficients are obtained using the transform AG_1^r with

$$G_1^r = \frac{1}{2}\begin{pmatrix} 1 & 0 \\ -1 & 0 \\ 0 & 1 \\ 0 & -1 \end{pmatrix}.$$

The detail coefficients are

$$AG_1^r = \begin{pmatrix} 17 & 3 & 5 & 7 \\ 2 & 8 & 7 & 7 \\ 2 & 16 & 5 & 3 \\ 10 & 6 & 8 & 6 \end{pmatrix}\frac{1}{2}\begin{pmatrix} 1 & 0 \\ -1 & 0 \\ 0 & 1 \\ 0 & -1 \end{pmatrix} = \begin{pmatrix} 7 & -1 \\ -3 & 0 \\ -7 & 1 \\ 2 & 1 \end{pmatrix}.$$

After applying the first iteration of the row transform we get

$$A_r^1 = \begin{pmatrix} 10 & 6 & 7 & -1 \\ 5 & 7 & -3 & 0 \\ 9 & 4 & -7 & 1 \\ 8 & 7 & 2 & 1 \end{pmatrix}.$$

Now we apply the column transform $H_1^c A_r^1$ where

$$H_1^c = (H_1^r)^T = \frac{1}{2}\begin{pmatrix} 1 & 1 & 0 & 0 \\ 0 & 0 & 1 & 1 \end{pmatrix}.$$

The result obtained is

$$H_1^c A_r^1 = \begin{pmatrix} 7.5 & 6.5 & 2 & -0.5 \\ 8.5 & 5.5 & -2.5 & 1 \end{pmatrix}.$$

Likewise the detail coefficients are calculated from $G_1^c A_r^1$ with

$$G_1^c = (G_1^r)^T = \frac{1}{2}\begin{pmatrix} 1 & -1 & 0 & 0 \\ 0 & 0 & 1 & -1 \end{pmatrix}.$$

The detail coefficients are

$$G_1^c A_r^1 = \begin{pmatrix} 2.5 & -0.5 & 5 & -0.5 \\ 0.5 & -1.5 & -4.5 & 0 \end{pmatrix}.$$

After the transform we obtain

$$A_c^1 = \begin{pmatrix} 7.5 & 6.5 & 2 & -0.5 \\ 8.5 & 5.5 & -2.5 & 1 \\ 2.5 & -0.5 & 5 & -0.5 \\ 0.5 & -1.5 & -4.5 & 0 \end{pmatrix}.$$

The averages are in the top left corner of the matrix A_c^1. For the next iteration we once again need to perform a series of transforms. We now use

$$H_2^r = \frac{1}{2}\begin{pmatrix} 1 \\ 1 \end{pmatrix} \qquad G_2^r = \frac{1}{2}\begin{pmatrix} 1 \\ -1 \end{pmatrix}$$

$$H_2^c = (H_2^r)^T \qquad G_2^c = (G_2^r)^T.$$

Applying these transforms in the same way as above, to each quadrant of the matrix, we obtain the wavelet decomposition

$$A' = \begin{pmatrix} H_2^c Q_1 H_2^r & H_2^c Q_1 G_2^r & H_2^c Q_2 H_2^r & H_2^c Q_2 G_2^r \\ G_2^c Q_1 H_2^r & G_2^c Q_1 G_2^r & G_2^c Q_2 H_2^r & G_2^c Q_2 G_2^r \\ H_2^c Q_3 H_2^r & H_2^c Q_3 G_2^r & H_2^c Q_4 H_2^r & H_2^c Q_4 G_2^r \\ G_2^c Q_3 H_2^r & G_2^c Q_3 G_2^r & G_2^c Q_4 H_2^r & G_2^c Q_4 G_2^r \end{pmatrix}$$

$$= \begin{pmatrix} 7 & 1 & 0 & -0.25 \\ 0 & -0.5 & 0.75 & 1.5 \\ 0.25 & 1.25 & 0 & 0.25 \\ 0.75 & 0.25 & 2.25 & 2.5 \end{pmatrix}$$

with

$$Q_1 = \begin{pmatrix} 7.5 & 6.5 \\ 8.5 & 5.5 \end{pmatrix} \qquad Q_2 = \begin{pmatrix} 2 & -0.5 \\ -2.5 & 1 \end{pmatrix}$$

$$Q_3 = \begin{pmatrix} 2.5 & -0.5 \\ 0.5 & -1.5 \end{pmatrix} \qquad Q_4 = \begin{pmatrix} 5 & -0.5 \\ -4.5 & 0 \end{pmatrix}.$$

Given the data after the wavelet transform

$$A' = \begin{pmatrix} 7 & 1 & 0 & -0.25 \\ 0 & -0.5 & 0.75 & 1.5 \\ 0.25 & 1.25 & 0 & 0.25 \\ 0.75 & 0.25 & 2.25 & 2.5 \end{pmatrix}$$

we can reconstruct the original matrix by applying the reverse procedure. To obtain A_c^1 we calculate the quadrants

$$Q_1 = \begin{pmatrix} 1 & 1 \\ 1 & -1 \end{pmatrix} \begin{pmatrix} 7 & 1 \\ 0 & -0.5 \end{pmatrix} \begin{pmatrix} 1 & 1 \\ 1 & -1 \end{pmatrix} = \begin{pmatrix} 7.5 & 6.5 \\ 8.5 & 5.5 \end{pmatrix}$$

$$Q_2 = \begin{pmatrix} 1 & 1 \\ 1 & -1 \end{pmatrix} \begin{pmatrix} 0 & -0.25 \\ 0.75 & 1.5 \end{pmatrix} \begin{pmatrix} 1 & 1 \\ 1 & -1 \end{pmatrix} = \begin{pmatrix} 2 & -0.5 \\ -2.5 & 1 \end{pmatrix}$$

$$Q_3 = \begin{pmatrix} 1 & 1 \\ 1 & -1 \end{pmatrix} \begin{pmatrix} 0.25 & 1.25 \\ 0.75 & 0.25 \end{pmatrix} \begin{pmatrix} 1 & 1 \\ 1 & -1 \end{pmatrix} = \begin{pmatrix} 2.5 & -0.5 \\ 0.5 & -1.5 \end{pmatrix}$$

$$Q_4 = \begin{pmatrix} 1 & 1 \\ 1 & -1 \end{pmatrix} \begin{pmatrix} 0 & 0.25 \\ 2.25 & 2.5 \end{pmatrix} \begin{pmatrix} 1 & 1 \\ 1 & -1 \end{pmatrix} = \begin{pmatrix} 5 & -0.5 \\ -4.5 & 0 \end{pmatrix}.$$

We now have A_c^1, to compute A, we do the inverse of the column transform by computing $Y A_c^1$, with

$$Y = \begin{pmatrix} 1 & 0 & 1 & 0 \\ 1 & 0 & -1 & 0 \\ 0 & 1 & 0 & 1 \\ 0 & 1 & 0 & -1 \end{pmatrix}.$$

We then compute the inverse of the row transform by computing $Y A_c^1 X$, with

$$X = \begin{pmatrix} 1 & 1 & 0 & 0 \\ 0 & 0 & 1 & 1 \\ 1 & -1 & 0 & 0 \\ 0 & 0 & 1 & -1 \end{pmatrix}$$

where $X = Y^T$ and $XY = 2I_4$. Performing the computation we find that

$$A = Y A_c^1 X = \begin{pmatrix} 17 & 3 & 5 & 7 \\ 2 & 8 & 7 & 7 \\ 2 & 16 & 5 & 3 \\ 10 & 6 & 8 & 6 \end{pmatrix}.$$

5.4   Curves

We now consider an application of the wavelet transform for curves as described by Finkelstein [34]. We begin with the cubic B-spline blending functions given by the Cox-de Boor formula

$$N_{i,1}(t) = \begin{cases} 1, & \text{if } t_i \leq t \leq t_{i+1} \\ 0, & \text{otherwise.} \end{cases}$$

$$N_{i,k}(t) = \frac{t - t_i}{t_{i+k-1} - t_i} N_{i,k-1}(t) + \frac{t_{i+k} - t}{t_{i+k} - t_{i+1}} N_{i+1,k-1}(t),$$

for $i = 0, \ldots, n$ and $k = 2, \ldots, d$, where $d = 4$ is one more than the degree of the curve. We will be working with uniform B-spline curves, that is $t_i = i$. The support of $N_{i,4}$ is (t_i, t_{i+4}) and so we define t_0 to t_{n+4} as in section 4.10. We thus have $n + 4 + 1$ knots in the knot vector, which we define to interpolate the end points. With the substitution $m = n + 4$ the Cox-de Boor is defined for $i = 0, \ldots, m - k$ and $k < m$. The cubic B-spline curve is defined by

$$\mathbf{q}(t) = \sum_{i=0}^{n} N_{i,4}(t)\mathbf{x}_i, \quad t \in [0, n-2].$$

The curve is thus a linear combination of the blending functions $N_{i,4}$. The coefficients are linear combinations of the control points $\mathbf{x}_i$. The blending functions are clearly translates of each other (see figure 4.10). We also note that the coefficients of $\mathbf{x}_i$ are linear combinations of the B-spline basis functions (see figure 4.9). The B-spline basis functions $B_{i,4}$ are used as scaling functions, and form the basis for the vector space V^j. We define 2^j equally spaced intervals $t_0, \ldots, t_k$, where $k = 2^j$. Using the subdivision relationship for knot insertion [32] we obtain

$$\mathbf{q}(t) = \sum_{i=0}^{n} N_i(t)\mathbf{x}_i = \sum_{i=0}^{2n} N_i(2t)\mathbf{x}_i^{(1)}, \quad t \in [0, n-2]$$

where $\mathbf{x}_{2i}^{(1)} = \frac{1}{8}(\mathbf{x}_{i-1} + 6\mathbf{x}_i + \mathbf{x}_{i+1})$ and $\mathbf{x}_{2i+1}^{(1)} = \frac{1}{2}(\mathbf{x}_i + \mathbf{x}_{i+1})$. We thus have the embedding

$$V^0 \subset V^1 \subset V^2 \subset \cdots$$

It appears that B-splines are suitable for a wavelet transform. We use the same inner product in the Hilbert space $L_2(\mathbb{R})$ as for the Haar wavelet, namely

$$\langle f, g \rangle := \int_0^1 f(x)\overline{g}(x)\, dx.$$

Since we only consider the real-valued functions we have $\overline{g}(x) = g(x)$. Now we need to determine the wavelet functions that form the basis of W^j. In the wavelet transform we replaced the functions ϕ_i^j by functions ϕ_i^{j-1} and ψ_i^{j-1}. In the case of B-splines, we remove knots. We thus change the intervals $t_0, \ldots, t_{2k}$ to the intervals $t_0, \ldots, t_k$. To ensure that $\mathbf{q}(t)$ is represented correctly we compensate using wavelet functions. We thus have the wavelet component defined so that the original curve is still produced, that is

$$\mathbf{q}_L(t) = \sum_{i=0}^{n} N_i(t)\mathbf{x}_i$$

$$\mathbf{q}_H(t) = \sum_{i=0}^{2n} N_i(2t)\mathbf{x}_i^{(1)} - \sum_{i=0}^{n} N_i(t)\mathbf{x}_i$$

where $\mathbf{q}(t) = \mathbf{q}_H(t) + \mathbf{q}_L(t)$. So we see that the sum of the wavelets introduced is a linear combination of the basis functions $B_{i,4}$. Using this relationship and a few extra constraints (described by Stollnitz et al. [129]) we can solve for the coefficients of the B-spline basis functions to obtain the wavelet functions. The solution is not readily written in a closed form, so we refer the reader to the work of Finkelstein [34] and Stollnitz et al. [129]. Once the wavelet transform has been computed, we have a representation of the curve that permits us to analyze the overall form and detail of the curve. Finkelstein [34] shows how the wavelet representation may be used to alter a curve, but not the 'character' of the curve. In a similar fashion, the 'character' of the curve, but not the shape, may be changed. The application of this work to surfaces is discussed by Stollnitz et al.[129]. Wavelets have also been applied to other areas of computer graphics. For an overview of this work we refer the reader to the discussion by Schröder [108].

5.5   C# Implementation

In this section we present a program that transforms an image in stages using an integer Haar wavelet transform [9]. The integer Haar wavelet transform is identical to the Haar transform except that the Haar transform is applied in such a way that the reconstruction is precise despite loss of precision during integer division. The program allows bitmap files to be opened and saved, and applies the integer Haar wavelet transform and the inverse transform. For photographic images the potential for compression is evident from the large number of gray pixels produced. To implement the lossless transform a signed 8-bit number is simulated and overflow is handled by the C# program.

The Haar transform is performed in two stages. First each row is transformed. Then each column is transformed. The coeffcients that store the "averages" are moved into the first portion of the image while the detail coefficients remain on the outer portion of the image. Since the averaged version is in the top left, further transforms can be applied directly to that quarter of the image. Hence the use of a scale variable to determine which portion of the image to transform. Note that the image stored in the Bitmap bmp should have dimensions that are a power of 2.

```
int x, y, w=bmp.Width/scale, h=bmp.Height/scale;
```

```
int r1, g1, b1, r2, g2, b2;
//samples from image
Color s1, s2;
Bitmap newbmp=new Bitmap(bmp);
//Apply the 2D haar wavelet transform: perform one horizontal pass
for(y=0;y<h;y++) {
    for(x=0;x<w;x+=2) {
        s1=bmp.GetPixel(x,y); s2=bmp.GetPixel(x+1,y);
        r2=(s2.R-s1.R); g2=(s2.G-s1.G); b2=(s2.B-s1.B);
        if(r2<-128) r2+=256; if(r2>127) r2-=256;
        if(g2<-128) g2+=256; if(g2>127) g2-=256;
        if(b2<-128) b2+=256; if(b2>127) b2-=256;
        r1=(s1.R-128+r2/2); g1=(s1.G-128+g2/2);
        b1=(s1.B-128+b2/2);
        if(r1<-128) r1+=256; if(r1>127) r1-=256;
        if(g1<-128) g1+=256; if(g1>127) g1-=256;
        if(b1<-128) b1+=256; if(b1>127) b1-=256;
        r1+=128; g1+=128; b1+=128;
        r2+=128; g2+=128; b2+=128;
        newbmp.SetPixel(x/2,y,Color.FromArgb(r1,g1,b1));
        newbmp.SetPixel(x/2+w/2,y,Color.FromArgb(r2,g2,b2));
    }
}
bmp=newbmp;
newbmp=new Bitmap(bmp);
//Perform one vertical pass
for(y=0;y<h;y+=2) {
    for(x=0;x<w;x++) {
        s1=bmp.GetPixel(x,y); s2=bmp.GetPixel(x,y+1);
        r2=(s2.R-s1.R); g2=(s2.G-s1.G); b2=(s2.B-s1.B);
        if(r2<-128) r2+=256; if(r2>127) r2-=256;
        if(g2<-128) g2+=256; if(g2>127) g2-=256;
        if(b2<-128) b2+=256; if(b2>127) b2-=256;
        r1=(s1.R-128+r2/2); g1=(s1.G-128+g2/2);
        b1=(s1.B-128+b2/2);
        if(r1<-128) r1+=256; if(r1>127) r1-=256;
        if(g1<-128) g1+=256; if(g1>127) g1-=256;
        if(b1<-128) b1+=256; if(b1>127) b1-=256;
        r1+=128; g1+=128; b1+=128;
        r2+=128; g2+=128; b2+=128;
        newbmp.SetPixel(x,y/2,Color.FromArgb(r1,g1,b1));
        newbmp.SetPixel(x,y/2+h/2,Color.FromArgb(r2,g2,b2));
    }
}
bmp=newbmp;
picture.BackgroundImage=bmp;
scale*=2;
```

The Inverse transform simply applies the operations in the reverse order.
Note how the data is unpacked into the original positions.

```
scale/=2;
int x, y, w=bmp.Width/scale, h=bmp.Height/scale;
int r1, g1, b1, r2, g2, b2;
//samples from image
Color s1, s2;
Bitmap newbmp=new Bitmap(bmp);
//Apply the 2D haar wavelet transform
//Perform one vertical pass
for(y=0;y<h;y+=2) {
    for(x=0;x<w;x++) {
        s1=bmp.GetPixel(x,y/2);
        s2=bmp.GetPixel(x,y/2+h/2);
        r1=s1.R-128; g1=s1.G-128; b1=s1.B-128;
        r2=s2.R-128; g2=s2.G-128; b2=s2.B-128;
        r1=(r1-r2/2); g1=(g1-g2/2); b1=(b1-b2/2);
        if(r1<-128) r1+=256; if(r1>127) r1-=256;
        if(g1<-128) g1+=256; if(g1>127) g1-=256;
        if(b1<-128) b1+=256; if(b1>127) b1-=256;
        r2=(r2+r1); g2=(g2+g1); b2=(b2+b1);
        if(r2<-128) r2+=256; if(r2>127) r2-=256;
        if(g2<-128) g2+=256; if(g2>127) g2-=256;
        if(b2<-128) b2+=256; if(b2>127) b2-=256;
        r1+=128; g1+=128; b1+=128;
        r2+=128; g2+=128; b2+=128;
        newbmp.SetPixel(x,y,Color.FromArgb(r1,g1,b1));
        newbmp.SetPixel(x,y+1,Color.FromArgb(r2,g2,b2));
    }
}
bmp=newbmp;
newbmp=new Bitmap(bmp);
//Perform one horizontal pass
for(y=0;y<h;y++) {
    for(x=0;x<w;x+=2) {
        s1=bmp.GetPixel(x/2,y);
        s2=bmp.GetPixel(x/2+w/2,y);
        r1=s1.R-128; g1=s1.G-128; b1=s1.B-128;
        r2=s2.R-128; g2=s2.G-128; b2=s2.B-128;
        r1=(r1-r2/2); g1=(g1-g2/2); b1=(b1-b2/2);
        if(r1<-128) r1+=256; if(r1>127) r1-=256;
        if(g1<-128) g1+=256; if(g1>127) g1-=256;
        if(b1<-128) b1+=256; if(b1>127) b1-=256;
        r2=(r2+r1); g2=(g2+g1); b2=(b2+b1);
        if(r2<-128) r2+=256; if(r2>127) r2-=256;
        if(g2<-128) g2+=256; if(g2>127) g2-=256;
        if(b2<-128) b2+=256; if(b2>127) b2-=256;
        r1+=128; g1+=128; b1+=128;
        r2+=128; g2+=128; b2+=128;
        newbmp.SetPixel(x,y,Color.FromArgb(r1,g1,b1));
        newbmp.SetPixel(x+1,y,Color.FromArgb(r2,g2,b2));
    }
}
bmp=newbmp;
picture.BackgroundImage=bmp;
```

Chapter 6

Surfaces

In chapter 4 we discussed existing curve drawing algorithms and harmonic interpolation for drawing curves. We now extend these algorithms to draw surfaces. The ability to interpolate surfaces is important for a variety of disciplines in computer graphics, models may be digitized so that they may be used and manipulated in digital form for animation purposes. In our discussions concerning surfaces, we try to show how the techniques may be used to interpolate such data points. As in chapter 4, we do not try to produce an exhaustive list of techniques, and instead discuss the techniques that we use later on. In so doing we try to discover a relationship between these surfaces and harmonic surfaces, although these relationships are not extensively analyzed. We begin in the next section with a description of surfaces in the form we work with, namely parametric surfaces.

6.1 Parametric Surfaces

A surface is a set of points (usually in $\mathbb{R}^3$), such that the surface can be described by a smooth function. A surface in $\mathbb{R}^2$ is called a *plane curve*. We refer to a surface in $\mathbb{R}^3$ simply as a surface. We call a surface in $\mathbb{R}^n$, $n > 3$, a *hypersurface*. The function that we use to describe surfaces in $\mathbb{R}^3$ is often of the form

$$\mathbf{f}(u, v) = \begin{pmatrix} x_0(u, v) \\ x_1(u, v) \\ x_2(u, v) \end{pmatrix}.$$

The surface is thus described by two parameters u and v. We thus call the surface a *parametric surface*. Other options are also possible, but parametric surfaces described by two parameters are quite common. An example

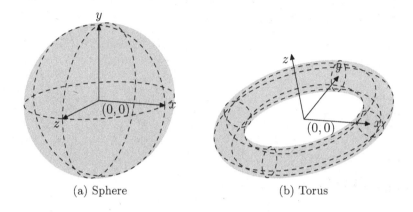

(a) Sphere   (b) Torus

Figure 6.1: Example parametric surfaces.

of such a parametric surface is the *sphere*

$$\mathbf{f}(u,v) = \begin{pmatrix} \sin u \cos v \\ \sin u \sin v \\ \cos u \end{pmatrix}, \tag{6.1}$$

with $0 \le u \le \pi$ and $0 \le v \le 2\pi$. Another example of a parametric surface is the *torus*

$$\mathbf{f}(u,v) = \begin{pmatrix} (r_1 + r_2 \cos v) \cos u \\ (r_1 + r_2 \cos v) \sin u \\ r_2 \sin v \end{pmatrix}, \tag{6.2}$$

with $0 \le u \le 2\pi$, $0 \le v \le 2\pi$ and $r_2 > r_1$. The sphere is shown in figure 6.1(a), and the torus in figure 6.1(b). Curves of constant u or v (*isocurves*) have been drawn as dashed lines to provide a better idea of the shape of the surface. Now that surfaces have been defined, we can introduce a specific form of parametric surfaces, namely tensor product surfaces.

6.2   Tensor Product Surfaces

Suppose we can define a curve with control (or interpolation) points $\mathbf{x}_k$ as

$$\mathbf{q}(v) := \sum_{k=0}^{n-1} f_k^n(v)\mathbf{x}_k$$

where $f_k^n(v)$ are the basis functions for the curve, and suppose further that we have defined m such curves $\mathbf{q}_j(v)$ so that curve $\mathbf{q}_j(v)$ is defined by the points $x_{j,k}$. Then each curve is defined as

$$q_j(v) := \sum_{k=0}^{n-1} f_k^n(v) x_{j,k} \, .$$

If we choose a particular value for v on each of these curves, we then have m points which we can use to create another curve $\mathbf{p}$. The curve $\mathbf{p}$ is then defined by

$$\mathbf{p}(u,v) := \sum_{j=0}^{m-1} f_j^m(u) q_j(v) = \sum_{j=0}^{m-1} f_j^m(u) \sum_{k=0}^{n-1} f_k^n(v) x_{j,k} \, .$$

The surface defined by all such curves is known as a *tensor product surface* and the curve of constant v is known as an *isocurve*. We can also choose to define n curves of m points each from the points $x_{j,k}$. Defining a curve from points (defined by parameter u) on each of these curves will define precisely the same surface. So we can simply write the surface as

$$\mathbf{p}(u,v) = \sum_{j=0}^{m-1} \sum_{k=0}^{n-1} f_j^m(u) f_k^n(v) x_{j,k} \, .$$

In most cases we choose $n = m$, but this is not required. If the functions f_k^n are such that the curves are affine invariant, then so is the surface. Likewise, if the curves produced using f_k^n have the convex hull property, then so does the surface. If the curve is affine invariant then

$$\sum_{k=0}^{n-1} f_k^n(t) = 1 \, .$$

For a surface we have

$$\sum_{j=0}^{m-1} \left(\sum_{k=0}^{n-1} f_k^n(v) \right) f_j^m(u) = \sum_{j=0}^{m-1} 1 \cdot f_j^m(u) = 1$$

so that the surface is affine invariant. This is only one way to define a surface, in the next section we examine a few examples of Bézier tensor product surfaces. Thereafter we discuss some surfaces not produced by tensor products.

6.3 Bézier Surfaces

Since all the polynomial curves presented in chapter 4 can be represented as Bézier curves, it is sufficient to discuss Bézier surfaces. Algorithms to obtain control points so that the surfaces interpolate a data set is another problem that will be discussed separately.

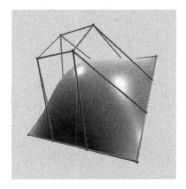 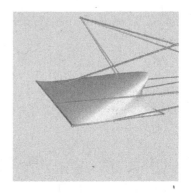

Figure 6.2: Example Bézier surface patches.

6.3.1   Tensor Product Bézier Surfaces

The *tensor product Bézier surface* is given by

$$\mathbf{p}(u,v) = \sum_{j=0}^{m} \sum_{k=0}^{n} B_j^m(u) B_k^n(v) \mathbf{x}_{j,k}$$

where B_k^n are the Bernstein polynomials introduced in chapter 4 in equation 4.2. The Bézier surface produced is known as a *Bézier patch*. Owing to the properties of the Bernstein polynomials the surface is affine invariant and lies within the convex hull of the control points. An example of a Bézier surface is illustrated in figure 6.2. Both the surface and the control polygon are visible. Bézier patches interpolate the corner points, but not necessarily the other points. We note that each boundary of the Bézier patch is a Bézier curve. The derivatives of $\mathbf{p}$ are given by

$$\frac{\partial \mathbf{p}(u,v)}{\partial u} = m \sum_{j=0}^{m-1} \sum_{k=0}^{n} B_j^{m-1}(u) B_k^n(v) (\mathbf{x}_{j+1,k} - \mathbf{x}_{j,k})$$

$$\frac{\partial \mathbf{p}(u,v)}{\partial v} = n \sum_{j=0}^{m} \sum_{k=0}^{n-1} B_j^m(u) B_k^{n-1}(v) (\mathbf{x}_{j,k+1} - \mathbf{x}_{j,k}).$$

Once the partial derivatives have been calculated the *normal to the surface* is given by

$$\mathbf{n}(u,v) := \frac{\partial \mathbf{p}(u,v)}{\partial u} \times \frac{\partial \mathbf{p}(u,v)}{\partial v}$$

where $\times$ denotes the cross product. Using the normals, we can define piecewise continuous Bézier surfaces. An example of such a surface is illustrated

Figure 6.3: Surface constructed from piecewise continuous Bézier patches [18].

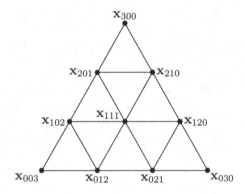

Figure 6.4: A Bézier triangle control mesh.

in figure 6.3. The surface consists of 32 Bézier patches [18]. de Casteljau's algorithm can be applied to efficiently render these surfaces.

Tensor product Bézier surfaces are not the only possibility, next we consider a triangular Bézier surface.

6.3.2   Triangular Bézier Surfaces

Instead of arranging the initial configuration of the control points in a rectangular fashion as with tensor product Bézier surfaces, we can arrange the control points in a triangle [1] as in figure 6.4. If the degree of the Bézier surface is n, then there are $n + 1$ control points on each side. The control points are $\mathbf{x}_{ijk}$, with $i + j + k = n$ and $i, j, k \geq 0$. The total number of control points is then

$$\sum_{k=1}^{n+1} k = \frac{(n+1)(n+2)}{2}.$$

Bézier triangles can be efficiently rendered using a variation of de Casteljau's method [1]. However, instead of the usual parameters, we must use *barycentric coordinates*. A triangle in $\mathbb{R}^3$ with vertices $\mathbf{x}_0$, $\mathbf{x}_1$ and $\mathbf{x}_2$ can be described with barycentric coordinates as

$$\begin{aligned}
\mathbf{p}(u, v) &= \mathbf{x}_0 + u(\mathbf{x}_1 - \mathbf{x}_0) + v(\mathbf{x}_2 - \mathbf{x}_0) \\
&= (1 - u - v)\mathbf{x}_0 + u\mathbf{x}_1 + v\mathbf{x}_2
\end{aligned}$$

where $u, v \geq 0$ and $u + v \leq 1$.

In terms of Bernstein polynomials the Bézier triangle is written as

$$\mathbf{p}(u, v) = \sum_{\substack{i,j,k=0 \\ i+j+k=n}}^{n} B_{ijk}^n(u, v)\mathbf{p}_{ijk}$$

with the *Bernstein polynomials* defined by

$$B_{ijk}^n(u, v) := \frac{n!}{i!j!k!} u^i v^j (1 - u - v)^k, \quad i + j + k = n.$$

The partial derivatives of $\mathbf{p}$ are given by

$$\frac{\partial \mathbf{p}(u, v)}{\partial u} = \sum_{i+j+k=n-1} B_{ijk}^{n-1}(u, v)\mathbf{p}_{i+1,j,k}$$

$$\frac{\partial \mathbf{p}(u, v)}{\partial v} = \sum_{i+j+k=n-1} B_{ijk}^{n-1}(u, v)\mathbf{p}_{i,j+1,k}.$$

The Bézier triangle has many of the same properties as Bézier patches. Bézier triangles are affine invariant, the surface interpolates the three corner control points and the surface lies within the convex hull of the control points. Bézier surfaces have been used effectively in N-patches or PN triangles [135]. The Bézier surfaces can be generalized to form so called S-patches. Details can be found in [86].

6.3.3   Rational Bézier Surfaces

In the same way that Bézier curves can be extended to rational Bézier curves, we can extend Bézier surfaces to rational Bézier surfaces to obtain further control of the surface. The surface is then given by (tensor product surface)

$$\mathbf{p}(u,v) = \frac{\sum_{j=0}^{m} \sum_{k=0}^{n} B_j^m(u) B_k^n(v) w_{j,k} \mathbf{x}_{j,k}}{\sum_{j=0}^{m} \sum_{k=0}^{n} B_j^m(u) B_k^n(v) w_{j,k}}$$

where the control points are specified in homogeneous form $(w_{j,k}\mathbf{x}_{j,k} \; w_{j,k})^T$. The $w_{j,k}$ weights thus determine a degree of importance of each control point. The resulting curve is clearly a rational polynomial.

6.3.4   Bézier Surface Interpolation

Bézier surfaces are relatively easy to work with when designing an object. However, we often want to fit a Bézier surface to a set of points. To do so the Bézier surface must interpolate those points. This problem is addressed by Shirman in [117] and [118]. In the next section we see an example of how B-splines can be used to interpolate data points. The B-splines are then used to produce Bézier patches that interpolate the data points.

6.4   B-Spline Tensor Product Surfaces

With tensor products we can express the surface generated with B-splines as

$$\mathbf{p}(u,v) = \sum_{j=0}^{m} \sum_{k=0}^{n} N_j(u) N_k(v) \mathbf{x}_{j,k}, \quad u \in [0, m-2], v \in [0, n-2].$$

B-spline surfaces are slightly easier to work with than Bézier surfaces, since continuity is automatically maintained. The question once again is how to interpolate with B-spline surfaces. We examine the answer to this question in the next section.

As in the case of rational Bézier curves, NURBS surfaces can also be constructed as a tensor product surface. To interpolate a surface with NURBS, we have the problem of finding the control points, the weights associated with each point and the knot vector to use. We omit the details of such an algorithm here and refer the reader to [89] and [99]. In the next section we examine a simple algorithm by Watt & Watt [138] for B-spline surface fitting.

6.4.1   B-Spline Surface Interpolation

Fitting a B-spline tensor product surface to a set of data points is a non-trivial task. The literature has a few pointers to how this can be done. Cheng [16] discusses a parallel implementation of surface fitting. In their algorithm, they fit a B-spline tensor product surface to points on a regular grid. To do so, a system of equations must be satisfied. These equations are solved in parallel to improve performance.

Greiner et al. [50] and [81] discuss hierarchical B-spline fitting. In the case of [50] the data set is assumed to be homeomorphic to a plane. This places some restrictions on the data which can be reconstructed. Under these assumptions the surface to be fit can be expressed by $f(u_i, v_i) = z_i$. First a spring model is used to determine the values u_i and v_i for each point. Once the parameterization has been determined a system of equations is produced and solved to obtain the interpolating surface. Lee et al. [81] also create an initial parameterization that is used to produce the B-spline surface. Hierarchies are created to improve performance of evaluating the B-spline approximation of the data. Optimization is performed to find a surface that interpolates or approximates the data points at each level of the hierarchy.

Wiley et al. [139] discuss hierarchical B-splines for approximation. In their approach, an initial course triangulation is generated, and a corresponding set of B-splines for the triangulation. An error metric is measured, and the triangle with highest error is subdivided. This approach builds a hierarchical set of B-splines that approximate the surface with different levels of detail. At each subdivision step the spline surface must be refitted. This involves solving a system of equations.

Eck [28] discusses another approach based on the work of Hoppe [63]. The construction of the surface follows several steps

- Construct an initial surface approximation using the algorithm of Hoppe [63]. This yields a dense mesh.

- Reparameterize over a simple triangular mesh, using harmonic maps.

- Merge triangles to produce a quadrilateral mesh.

- Fit a B-spline patch to each quadrilateral using the scheme of Peters [98]. This step involves optimization of the control points.

- Adaptively refine the faces (B-spline patches) until a user specified tolerance is met.

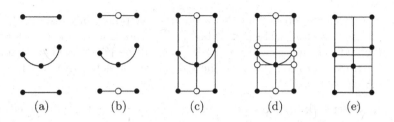

Figure 6.5: B-spline surface fitting: Curve network (after [138]).

In all of the above algorithms, a set of equations must be solved or some optimization must be performed. In the next example, we must also solve a system of equations. Here we discuss the algorithm of Watt & Watt [138]. The algorithm consists of several steps, enumerated here.

1. The data points are separated into groups. Each group may have a different number of data points and a different knot vector. Taking slices of the data may be one option. A curve is interpolated through each separate group, using the techniques listed in chapter 4. Each curve is parameterized using chord length parameterization. Chord length parameterization uses a heuristic to approximate arc length parameterization, so that the parameter spacing coincides roughly with arc length. The *Chord length* [32] is given by

$$S = \sum_i \|\Delta\mathbf{x}_i\| \equiv \sum_i \left\|\frac{\Delta\mathbf{x}_i}{\Delta t}\right\| \Delta t$$

   where $\Delta\mathbf{x}_i := \mathbf{x}_{i+1} - \mathbf{x}_i$. These curves will be known as the U-curves. This first stage is illustrated in figure 6.5(a).

2. A single knot vector must now be chosen for all the curves. The union of the distinct knot vectors produces the desired knot vector – the U-knot vector.

3. Each of the U-curves is updated so that the knot vector coincides with the U-knot vector as in figure 6.5(b).

4. The V-curves are obtained by selecting a knot from the U-knot vector and constructing a curve that interpolates the data points of each of the U-curves. Once again, chord length parameterization is used. The V-curves thus intersect the U curves at points of constant u. The V-curves are illustrated in figure 6.5(c).

5. The V-curves do not intersect U-curves at points of constant v, so the knot vectors will differ. The knot vectors from the V-curves are merged to form the V-knot vector. Each of the V-curves knot vectors are updated to coincide with the V-knot vector as illustrated in figure 6.5(d).

The curve network has now been set up, the final result is illustrated in figure 6.5(e). The figure only illustrates curves of constant u or v. The network thus represents a B-spline tensor product surface. Watt & Watt [138] proceed to create Bézier patches from these curves as follows

1. Each curve in the curve network is converted to cubic Bézier curves by multiple knot insertion. We thus have a series of parametrically discontinuous Bézier curve segments. The control points of the Bézier curves are uniquely determined by this process (since every cubic curve can be represented as a cubic Bézier curve).

2. Each rectangular region bounded by (u_i, v_j), (u_{i+1}, v_{j+1}) is bounded by four Bézier curves from the previous step. These four curves are then converted into a Bézier patch.

Once the Bézier boundary curves for each patch have been obtained, the interior control points must be determined. The Bézier patch is a tensor product surface given by

$$\mathbf{p}(u, v) = \sum_{j=0}^{3} \sum_{k=0}^{3} B_j^3(u) B_k^3(v) \mathbf{x}_{j,k}$$

where $\mathbf{x}_{0,k}$, $\mathbf{x}_{3,k}$, $\mathbf{x}_{j,0}$, and $\mathbf{x}_{j,3}$ have already been determined. The remaining interior points depend on the partial derivatives in both u and v of $\mathbf{p}(u, v)$, denoted by $\mathbf{p}_{uv}(u, v)$. The vector $\mathbf{p}_{uv}(u, v)$ is known as the *twist vector*. In the following we set

$$\mathbf{p}_u = \frac{\partial \mathbf{p}}{\partial u}, \qquad \mathbf{p}_v = \frac{\partial \mathbf{p}}{\partial v}, \qquad \mathbf{p}_{uv} = \frac{\partial^2 \mathbf{p}}{\partial u \partial v}.$$

The derivative vectors of the Bézier patch at $u = 0, v = 0$ are given by [138]

$$\mathbf{p}_u(0, 0) = 3(\mathbf{x}_{1,0} - \mathbf{x}_{0,0}),$$
$$\mathbf{p}_v(0, 0) = 3(\mathbf{x}_{0,1} - \mathbf{x}_{0,0}),$$
$$\mathbf{p}_{uv}(0, 0) = 9(\mathbf{x}_{0,0} - \mathbf{x}_{0,1} - \mathbf{x}_{1,0} + \mathbf{x}_{1,1}).$$

We can compute some of the points $\mathbf{x}_{j,k}$ from these equations to get

$$\mathbf{x}_{0,0} = \mathbf{p}(0, 0)$$

$$\mathbf{x}_{0,1} = \frac{\mathbf{p}_v(0,0)}{3} + \mathbf{p}(0,0)$$

$$\mathbf{x}_{1,0} = \frac{\mathbf{p}_u(0,0)}{3} + \mathbf{p}(0,0)$$

$$\mathbf{x}_{1,1} = \frac{\mathbf{p}_{uv}(0,0)}{9} + \frac{\mathbf{p}_u(0,0) + \mathbf{p}_v(0,0)}{3} + \mathbf{p}(0,0) .$$

Let $\mathbf{x}$ be the point that makes $\mathbf{x}_{0,0}$, $\mathbf{x}_{0,1}$, $\mathbf{x}_{1,0}$ and $\mathbf{x}$ a parallelogram in $\mathbb{R}^3$. Then

$$\mathbf{x} = \mathbf{x}_{1,0} + \mathbf{x}_{0,1} - \mathbf{x}_{0,0} .$$

We thus have

$$\mathbf{x}_{1,1} - \mathbf{x} = (\mathbf{x}_{1,1} - \mathbf{x}_{1,0}) - (\mathbf{x}_{0,1} - \mathbf{x}_{0,0}) = \frac{1}{9}\mathbf{p}_{uv} .$$

The vector $\mathbf{x}_{1,1} - \mathbf{x}$ measures the deviation of the patch from the quadrilateral. If $\mathbf{p}_{uv}(u,v) = \mathbf{0}$ then there is no deviation and the Bézier patch is a planar surface. If we set $\mathbf{p}_{uv}(u,v) = \mathbf{0}$ at the patch corners then the patch is locally flat and produces 'pseudo-flats'. To avoid these 'pseudo-flats' Watt & Watt [138] suggest the use of *Adini's method* which considers the patch as part of a larger surface and computes the twist vector accordingly. The twist vector at a corner is computed from the four patches adjacent to this corner. The complete surface has a well defined twist given by

$$\mathbf{p}_{UV}(U_i, V_j) = \frac{\mathbf{p}_V(U_{i+1}, V_j) - \mathbf{p}_V(U_{i-1}, V_j)}{U_{i+1} - U_{i-1}} + \frac{\mathbf{p}_U(U_i, V_{j+1}) - \mathbf{p}_U(U_i, V_{j-1})}{V_{j+1} - V_{j-1}}$$
$$- \frac{\mathbf{p}(U_{i+1}, V_{j+1}) - \mathbf{p}(U_{i-1}, V_{j+1}) - \mathbf{p}(U_{i+1}, V_{j-1}) + \mathbf{p}(U_{i-1}, V_{j-1})}{(U_{i+1} - U_{i-1})(V_{j+1} - V_{j-1})}$$

where U_i and V_j are surface level parameters and u and v are patch level parameters. The patch parameters u, v and surface level parameters U_i, V_j are related by

$$u := \frac{U - U_i}{U_{i+1} - U_i}, \qquad v := \frac{V - V_j}{V_{j+1} - V_j} .$$

Using the chain rule for differentiation we get

$$\mathbf{p}_{uv} = (U_{i+1} - U_i)(V_{j+1} - V_j)\mathbf{p}_{UV} .$$

6.5 Subdivision Surfaces

In section 4.5.5 we saw how to subdivide a Bézier curve using de Casteljau's method. With sufficient subdivision, the Bézier curve segments can be

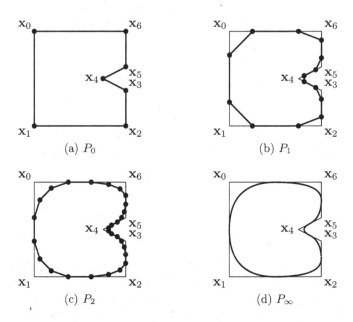

Figure 6.6: Stages in subdivision using Chaikin's scheme.

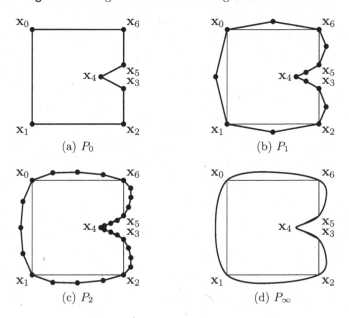

Figure 6.7: Stages in interpolatory subdivision using the 4-point scheme.

approximated by lines. If we proceed to subdivide an infinite number of times, the limit curve is the Bézier curve. Naturally we could then ask, are there other subdivision methods that can be used? Two such schemes are illustrated in figures 6.6 and 6.7. In figure 6.6 we use the initial control points for a seven sided polygon that has been used in the examples through out. We begin with the points

$$\mathbf{x}_i^0 = \mathbf{x}_i$$

and proceed to subdivide the line segments using the formula

$$\mathbf{x}_{2i}^{k+1} = \frac{3}{4}\mathbf{x}_i^k + \frac{1}{4}\mathbf{x}_{i+1}^k$$

$$\mathbf{x}_{2i+1}^{k+1} = \frac{1}{4}\mathbf{x}_i^k + \frac{3}{4}\mathbf{x}_{i+1}^k .$$

At each stage we have a polygon P_k defined by the points $\mathbf{x}_i^k$. In the limit we have a curve P_∞. The scheme presented here is known as *Chaikin's scheme* [15]. Chaikin's scheme is an approximating curve. An alternative that interpolates the points of the curve is given by the 4-point scheme [26]

$$\mathbf{x}_{2i}^{k+1} = \mathbf{x}_i^k$$

$$\mathbf{x}_{2i+1}^{k+1} = (\frac{1}{2} + w)(\mathbf{x}_i^k + \mathbf{x}_{i+1}^k) + w(\mathbf{x}_{i-1}^k + \mathbf{x}_{i+2}^k)$$

where $w \in \mathbb{R}$. The weight w is known as the tension parameter. When $w = 0$, we have linear interpolation. If $0 < w < 1/8$, then the curve has C^1 continuity. Since we are examining periodic curves, the points $\mathbf{x}_i^k$ are calculated modulo $(k + 1)n$ where n is the number of control or interpolation points. This scheme is illustrated in figure 6.7.

In the same way that curves can be recursively subdivided, we can subdivide a surface control mesh. The tensor product Bézier surfaces can be modeled in this fashion, but subdivision is not limited to rectangular meshes. Subdivision curves and surfaces can be thought of as a two phase process [74]. The refinement phase creates new vertices and new polygons from the control mesh, and the smoothing phase computes new positions for some or all of the vertices in the new control mesh. A subdivision scheme can be categorized as *stationary* if the same subdivision rules are used at every subdivision step. A non-stationary scheme changes the rules according to the subdivision step. A *uniform* scheme uses the same rules for every vertex or edge, while non-uniform may use different rules for each vertex or edge. Often, the rule selected may depend on the *valence* of the vertex. The *valence* of a vertex $\mathbf{x}$ on the subdivision surface is the number of neighboring

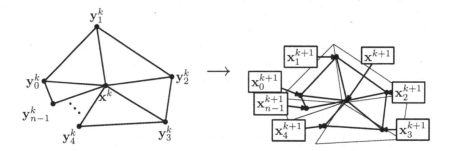

Figure 6.8: Notation for Loop subdivision.

vertices, that is the number of vertices connected to $\mathbf{x}$ by an edge.

In the next sections we discuss some of the subdivision algorithms described in the literature [1]. For a more comprehensive treatment refer to the SIGGRAPH 2000 course notes [143].

6.5.1   Loop Subdivision

Loop's [85] subdivision scheme works on triangles. The surface is an approximating surface. A new vertex is added for each edge, at each subdivision step. A vertex with valence 6 is known as *regular* or *ordinary*, otherwise it is known as *irregular* or *extraordinary*. At each subdivision step, the existing point $\mathbf{x}^k$ is updated with the scheme

$$\mathbf{x}^{k+1} = (1 - n\beta)\mathbf{x}^k + \beta \sum_{i=0}^{n-1} \mathbf{y}_i^k$$

where $\mathbf{y}_i^k$ are the n neighboring vertices, and β is a constant determined by $\mathbf{x}^k$ (shown later). For each edge connecting $\mathbf{x}^k$ to a neighbor, a new vertex is created via

$$\mathbf{x}_i^{k+1} = \frac{3\mathbf{x}^k + 3\mathbf{y}_i^k + \mathbf{y}_{i-1}^k + \mathbf{y}_{i+1}^k}{8}, \quad i = 0, \ldots, n-1.$$

The subscripts i are calculated modulo n. The arrangement of the neighboring vertices and notation is illustrated in figure 6.8. Once the new vertices have been determined, each triangle is subdivided into four triangles as in figure 6.9. Figure 6.9(a) shows the original mesh, 6.9(b) adds the new points and 6.9(c) illustrates the mesh after triangle subdivision. Often a mask or stencil is used to visualize the subdivision. The entries in the mask

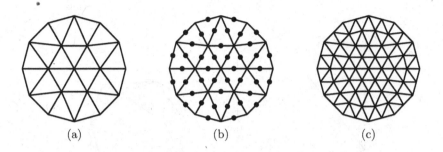

Figure 6.9: Triangle subdivision for Loop subdivision (after [74]).

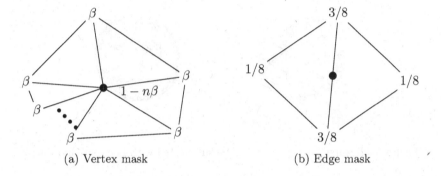

(a) Vertex mask   (b) Edge mask

Figure 6.10: Masks for Loop subdivision.

are the weights for the contributing points. The masks for Loop subdivision are illustrated in figure 6.10. We note that the sum of the weights is 1 for both the vertex and edge mask. The mask consists of edges and vertices. The vertices are connected by lines (edges). The entry at the vertex is the weight which is multiplied by the vertex to obtain the contribution of that vertex. The edges are not arbitrary, if three edges form a triangle, then that triangle must be a face of the object.

The constant β is actually a function of n, the number of neighboring vertices. Loop [85] suggests the function

$$\beta(n) = \frac{1}{n}\left(\frac{5}{8} - \frac{(3 + 2\cos(2\pi/n))^2}{64}\right).$$

Möller and Haines [1] suggest the alternative by Warren and Weimer [137]

$$\beta(n) = \frac{3}{n(n+2)}.$$

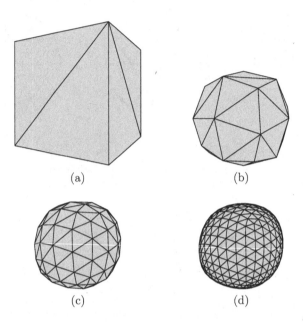

Figure 6.11: First four steps of a cube subdivided with Loop subdivision.

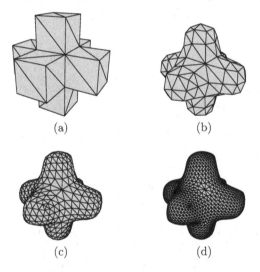

Figure 6.12: First four steps of a star shape subdivided with Loop subdivision.

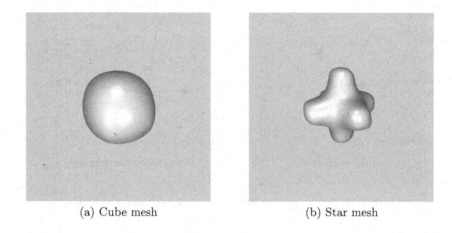

(a) Cube mesh   (b) Star mesh

Figure 6.13: Limit surfaces (Loop subdivision).

In both cases the surface is C^2 at vertices of regular valence, and C^1 otherwise. The scheme listed so far can only work on closed surfaces. The scheme needs to be adjusted for open surfaces. We refer the reader to Loop [85] for a discussion of these boundary problems.

The surface generated is affine invariant and lies entirely in the convex hull of its control points (see section 4.5.2 for the definition of the complex hull). Two limit tangents can be computed by a weighted sum of the immediate control points or 1-*ring*, or 1-*neighborhood* of a point $\mathbf{x}^k$. The tangents are

$$\mathbf{t}_u = \sum_{i=0}^{n-1} \cos(2\pi i/n)\mathbf{y}_i^k, \quad \mathbf{t}_v = \sum_{i=0}^{n-1} \sin(2\pi i/n)\mathbf{y}_i^k .$$

The normal vector is then given by $\mathbf{n} = \mathbf{t}_u \times \mathbf{t}_v$. The resulting surface is quite *fair* [94]. Informally that means the surface bends quite smoothly. Figure 6.13 illustrates the limit surfaces of the examples provided in this section.

6.5.2 Modified Butterfly Subdivision

The modified butterfly scheme [144] is an interpolating scheme which operates on triangles. Since the surface is interpolated, none of the existing vertices are modified. The scheme is non-uniform in the sense that different rules are used according to the valence of the vertices (and for boundaries). New vertices are created for each edge, and faces are created in the same

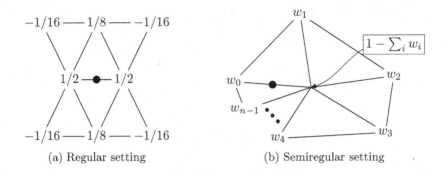

(a) Regular setting   (b) Semiregular setting

Figure 6.14: Masks for modified butterfly subdivision (after [1]).

way as the loop subdivision scheme (figure 6.9). The rules selected for new vertices, depending on the valence, are as follows

- **Regular:** When two vertices $\mathbf{x}_i$ and $\mathbf{x}_j$ are connected by an edge and both $\mathbf{x}_i$ and $\mathbf{x}_j$ have regular valence (6 neighbors), then we call this setting regular. The mask used to construct the new edge point is illustrated in figure 6.14(a).

- **Semiregular:** We have a semiregular setting if one of the vertices of the edge is regular (6 neighbors), and the other is irregular (valence $\neq 6$). In this case we compute the new vertex using a set of weights calculated from the valence n of the irregular vertex. The weights are given by

$$n = 3: \quad w_0 = 5/12, \quad w_1 = -1/12, \quad w_2 = -1/12.$$
$$n = 4: \quad w_0 = 3/8, \quad w_1 = 0, \quad w_2 = -1/8, \quad w_3 = 0.$$
$$n \geq 5: \quad w_j = \frac{0.25 + \cos(2\pi j/n) + 0.5\cos(4\pi j/n)}{n},$$

where $j = 0, 1, \ldots, n - 1$. The calculation of the new vertex is illustrated in figure 6.14(b).

- **Irregular:** If both vertices of an edge are irregular (valence $\neq 6$), then the semiregular approach is used with each vertex taking the role of the regular vertex in turn. The two points created are then averaged to provide the final new edge point.

From figure 6.14(a) we can see that the modified butterfly scheme uses the *2-ring* or *2-neighborhood* of the vertex to be created. For boundary cases we refer the reader to [143]. Examples of the modified butterfly scheme

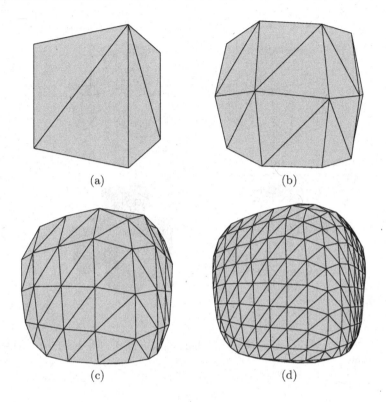

(a)   (b)

(c)   (d)

Figure 6.15: First four steps of a cube subdivided with modified butterfly subdivision.

are illustrated in figures 6.15 and 6.16. The limit surfaces are illustrated in figure 6.17.

6.5.3 $\sqrt{3}$ Subdivision

The previous subdivision schemes split each triangle into four new triangles. Kobbelt's $\sqrt{3}$ subdivision scheme creates only three new triangles for each triangle. The scheme thus has a lower triangle growth rate than the previous schemes. The lower growth rate implies that more levels of detail are available when applying the subdivision algorithm. In this scheme a new vertex is created in the middle of each triangle, instead of each edge. New points are added for each face by

$$\mathbf{x}_m^{k+1} = \frac{1}{3}(\mathbf{x}_a^k + \mathbf{x}_b^k + \mathbf{x}_c^k)$$

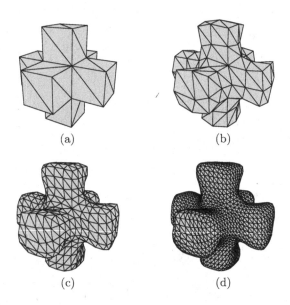

(a)   (b)

(c)   (d)

Figure 6.16: First four steps of a star shape subdivided with modified butterfly subdivision.

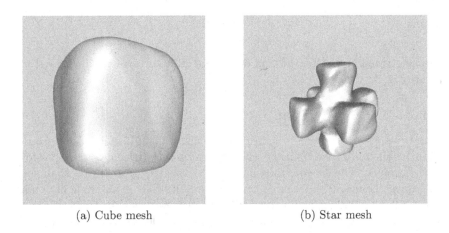

(a) Cube mesh   (b) Star mesh

Figure 6.17: Limit surfaces (modified butterfly subdivision).

where $\mathbf{x}_m^{k+1}$ is the new point and $\mathbf{x}_a^k$, $\mathbf{x}_b^k$ and $\mathbf{x}_c^k$ are the vertices of the triangle for which the new point is created. Existing points are updated with the rule

$$\mathbf{x}^{k+1} = (1 - n\beta)\mathbf{x}^k + \beta \sum_{i=0}^{n-1} \mathbf{y}_i^k$$

where β is a positive constant determined by $\mathbf{x}^k$. β is a function of the valence n of the point $\mathbf{x}^k$. This subdivision scheme is thus an approximating scheme. Kobbelt [74] suggests the following choice for $\beta(n)$

$$\beta(n) = \frac{4 - 2\cos(2\pi/n)}{9n}.$$

This choice generates a surface that is C^2 continuous except at irregular vertices ($n \neq 6$). At the irregular vertices the continuity is at least C^1. Masks for the update of vertices and addition of new vertices are shown in figure 6.18. One final detail of the subdivision scheme must be mentioned. After new triangles are created, the old edges are "flipped" so that the subdivision is similar to the original triangle mesh. The process is illustrated in figure 6.19. Figure 6.19(a) shows the initial triangle mesh, figure 6.19(b) illustrates the addition of new vertices, figure 6.19(c) performs the subdivision step (creating new triangles) and figure 6.19(d) illustrates the mesh after the old edges are "flipped". After two subdivision steps, a triangle is divided into 9 triangles, and an edge is split into 3 edges. Hence the name $\sqrt{3}$ subdivision. The surface produced has the convex hull property, and is affine invariant. Open surfaces must be dealt with differently. We refer the reader to Kobbelt [74] for a discussion of the algorithm dealing with boundaries. Figure 6.22 illustrates the limit surfaces for the examples given in this section.

6.5.4   Interpolating $\sqrt{3}$ Subdivision

Labsik and Greiner [79] have applied the $\sqrt{3}$ subdivision approach to interpolation. The resulting interpolating $\sqrt{3}$ subdivision uses the same triangle subdivision as illustrated in figure 6.19. Since the scheme interpolates, all existing vertices are left unchanged. A new vertex is created for each triangle. It is clear from the mask for a new point (illustrated in figure 6.23(a)) that we need the 2-ring or 2-neighborhood to compute the new vertex. As in the previous cases, we only consider closed surfaces. Boundaries are discussed by Labsik and Greiner [79]. The mask illustrated is only applicable for vertices of valence 6. Thus, as in the modified butterfly scheme, several different rules are necessary. The rules determine weights that are used as in figure 6.23 when irregular vertices are present in the triangle considered.

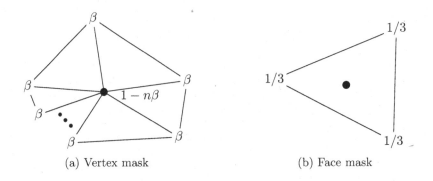

(a) Vertex mask   (b) Face mask

Figure 6.18: Masks for $\sqrt{3}$ subdivision (after [1]).

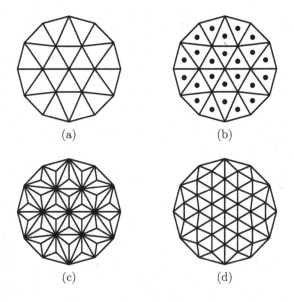

(a)   (b)

(c)   (d)

Figure 6.19: Triangle subdivision for $\sqrt{3}$ subdivision (after [74]).

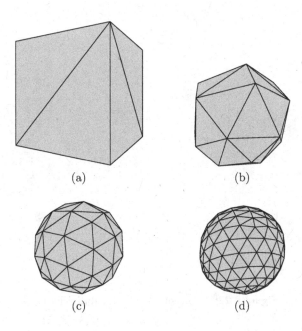

Figure 6.20: First four steps of a cube subdivided with $\sqrt{3}$ subdivision.

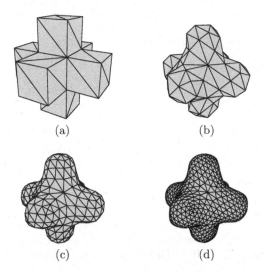

Figure 6.21: First four steps of a star shape subdivided with $\sqrt{3}$ subdivision.

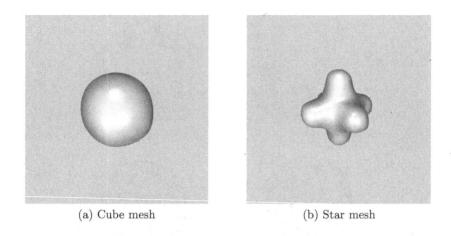

(a) Cube mesh   (b) Star mesh

Figure 6.22: Limit surfaces ($\sqrt{3}$ subdivision).

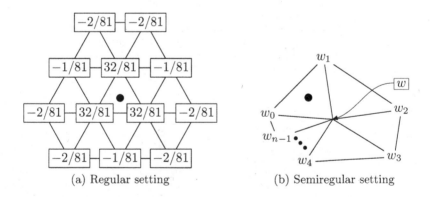

(a) Regular setting   (b) Semiregular setting

Figure 6.23: Masks for interpolating $\sqrt{3}$ subdivision.

We will not discuss the weights further here, as they are not trivially obtained. A brief description of the procedure is provided in section 6.10.4. We thus have three cases

- **Regular:** If all vertices have regular valence, the mask in figure 6.23(a) is applied.

- **Semiregular:** If one vertex is irregular, then the mask in figure 6.23(b) is used for the irregular vertex.

- **Irregular:** If two or more vertices are irregular, then the mask in figure 6.23(b) is applied for each irregular vertex and the average of these points is taken as the new vertex.

6.5.5 Catmull-Clark Subdivision

Catmull-Clark subdivision [12] is not restricted to triangle meshes but can divide polygonal meshes too. DeRose [21] has shown how Catmull-Clark subdivision surfaces have been used effectively in the making of animated films, and how sharp edges may be produced with Catmull-Clark surfaces, as illustrated by Hoppe [64]. Catmull-Clark surfaces are also affine invariant and lie within the complex hull of the control mesh that generates the surface. Also, since we are no longer restricted to triangles, many of the surfaces generated are more symmetrical. Compare figure 6.25 to figure 6.26, simply using quadrilaterals for the cube faces causes a definite improvement in the symmetry. For Catmull-Clark surfaces new points are created on the edges and faces. Our previous notation is no longer entirely adequate for the algorithm so we vary the notation slightly so that it corresponds to that of Halstead [53]. New face points are created with the rule

$$\mathbf{f}_j^{k+1} = \frac{1}{n} \sum_{i=0}^{n-1} \mathbf{v}_i^k$$

where $\mathbf{v}_i$ are the vertices of the jth face, and n is the number of vertices for that face. The level of subdivision is indicated by k. Existing vertices are updated with the rule

$$\mathbf{v}^{k+1} = \frac{n-2}{n} \mathbf{v}^k + \frac{1}{n^2} \sum_{i=0}^{n-1} \mathbf{e}_i^k + \frac{1}{n^2} \sum_{i=0}^{n-1} \mathbf{f}_i^{k+1}$$

where n is the valence of this vertex, $\mathbf{e}_i^k$ are the neighbors (vertices in the 1-ring) of $\mathbf{v}^k$, and $\mathbf{f}_i^{k+1}$ are the new face points created. In this case only

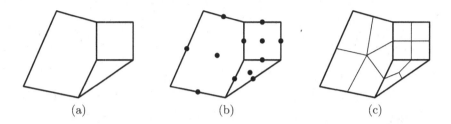

Figure 6.24: Subdivision for the Catmull-Clark scheme (after [1]).

the new face points of the faces to which this vertex belongs is considered.
New edge points are created with the rule

$$\mathbf{e}_i^{k+1} = \frac{1}{4}(\mathbf{v}^k + \mathbf{e}_i^k + \mathbf{f}_{i-1}^{k+1} + \mathbf{f}_j^{k+1})$$

where $\mathbf{v}^k$ and $\mathbf{e}_i^k$ are the endpoints of the considered edge, $\mathbf{f}_{i-1}^{k+1}$ and $\mathbf{f}_j^{k+1}$ are
the new face points of the faces adjacent to the considered edge (of which the
edge is a part). Once these vertices are created, new polygons are created as
in figure 6.24. Figure 6.24(a) shows the original mesh, figure 6.24(b) shows
the addition of new points and figure 6.24(c) illustrates how the points are
connected to form new polygons. After the first subdivision, all polygons
are quadrilaterals. Catmull-Clark surfaces are important because of their
modeling capabilities and the existence of an efficient evaluation algorithm
(by Bolz and Schröder [6]). Figures 6.25, 6.26, 6.27 and 6.28 illustrate the
application of the Catmull-Clark scheme for triangular and quadrilateral
meshes. The limit surfaces are shown in figure 6.29.

6.5.6   Doo-Sabin Subdivision

Doo-Sabin subdivision surfaces [23] are also not restricted to triangles. The
resulting surface is affine invariant and lies within the convex hull of the
control polygon. For each face f we create new vertices

$$\mathbf{x}_i^f = \sum_{j=0}^{n-1} \alpha_{ij} \mathbf{x}_j$$

where $\mathbf{x}_j$ are the vertices of the face. The constants α_{ij} are given by

$$\alpha_{ii} = \frac{n+5}{4n}$$
$$\alpha_{ij} = \frac{3 + 2\cos(2\pi(i-j)/n)}{4n}, \qquad j \neq i.$$

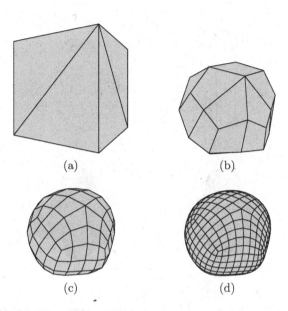

Figure 6.25: First four steps of a triangulated cube subdivided with Catmull-Clark subdivision.

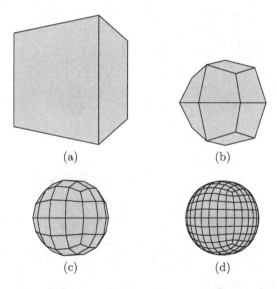

Figure 6.26: First four steps of a cube subdivided with Catmull-Clark subdivision.

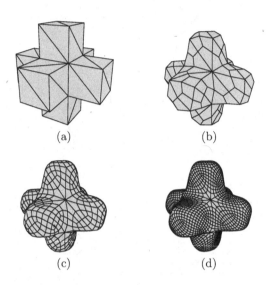

Figure 6.27: First four steps of a triangulated star shape subdivided with Catmull-Clark subdivision.

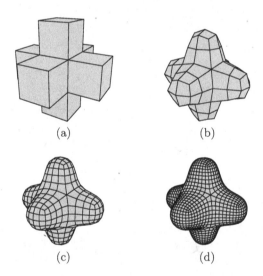

Figure 6.28: First four steps of a star shape subdivided with Catmull-Clark subdivision.

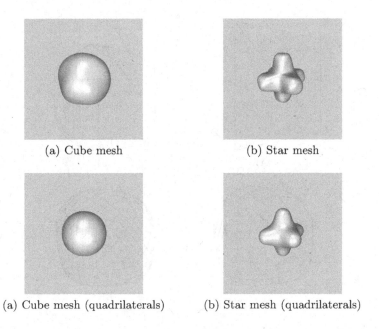

(a) Cube mesh   (b) Star mesh

(a) Cube mesh (quadrilaterals)   (b) Star mesh (quadrilaterals)

Figure 6.29: Limit surfaces (Catmull-Clark subdivision).

Once the new vertices are created the faces for the next step of the subdivision surface can be determined. Faces are obtained in three different ways.

1. By creating a polygon from the vertices $\mathbf{x}_0^f$, $\mathbf{x}_1^f$, ..., for a face f.

2. If $\mathbf{x}_i$ and $\mathbf{x}_j$ form an edge of the original surface, then a polygon is created from the vertices $\mathbf{x}_i^f$, $\mathbf{x}_i^g$, $\mathbf{x}_j^f$ and $\mathbf{x}_j^g$, where f and g are the faces sharing the edge.

3. By creating a polygon from the vertices $\mathbf{x}_m^f$, $\mathbf{x}_m^g$, ..., for a vertex $\mathbf{x}_m$.

Examples of the Doo-Sabin algorithm are illustrated in figures 6.30, 6.31, 6.32 and 6.33. As is the case with Catmull-Clark surfaces, we find that Doo-Sabin surfaces are more symmetrical if quadrilaterals are used. The limit surfaces are illustrated in figure 6.34.

6.5.7 Comparison

The subdivision schemes do not interpolate the control points (except the modified butterfly scheme and interpolating $\sqrt{3}$ scheme), however, when

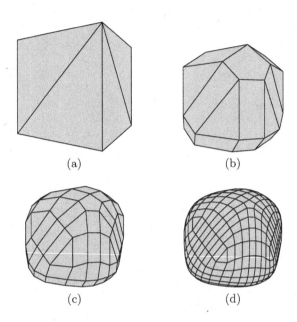

Figure 6.30: First four steps of a triangulated cube subdivided with Doo-Sabin subdivision.

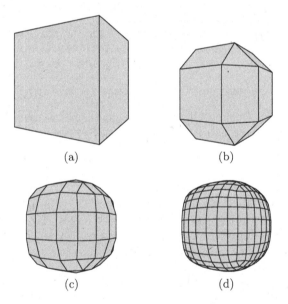

Figure 6.31: First four steps of a cube subdivided with Doo-Sabin subdivision.

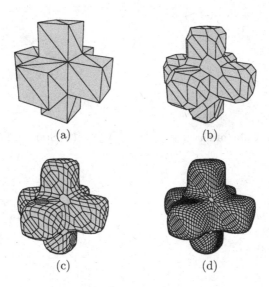

Figure 6.32: First four steps of a triangulated star shape subdivided with Doo-Sabin subdivision.

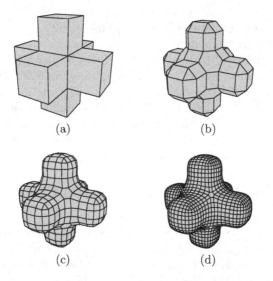

Figure 6.33: First four steps of a star shape subdivided with Doo-Sabin subdivision.

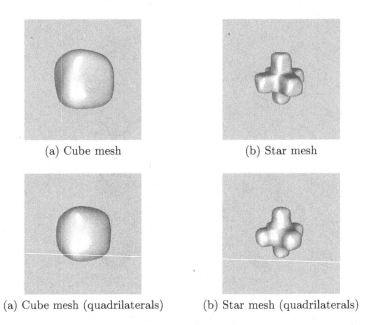

(a) Cube mesh   (b) Star mesh

(a) Cube mesh (quadrilaterals)   (b) Star mesh (quadrilaterals)

Figure 6.34: Limit surfaces (Doo-Sabin subdivision).

the mesh has sufficient detail the limit surface is quite close to the original shape. To compare the subdivision surfaces we have rendered the mannequin head introduced in Hoppe's PhD thesis [63] with the various subdivision schemes. The results are illustrated in figure 6.35. Triangles were used for all the subdivision schemes. We note that the modified butterfly scheme seems more erratic at the edges, but maintains more of the original mesh character. Table 6.1 compares the subdivision scheme in terms of the primitives supported for subdivision, whether the scheme is interpolating and the smoothness of the limit surfaces for regular meshes.

6.5.8   Interpolation with Subdivision Surfaces

In this section we mention a few techniques that have been employed to obtain interpolating surfaces from subdivision surfaces that do not naturally interpolate. Hoppe et al. [64] discuss how to construct an interpolating Loop subdivision surface. The surface is constructed through a number of phases, most described in Hoppe's PhD thesis [63], and finally involves the minimization of an energy function. Halstead [53] describes a technique for forming interpolating Catmull-Clark surfaces. To interpolate, a system

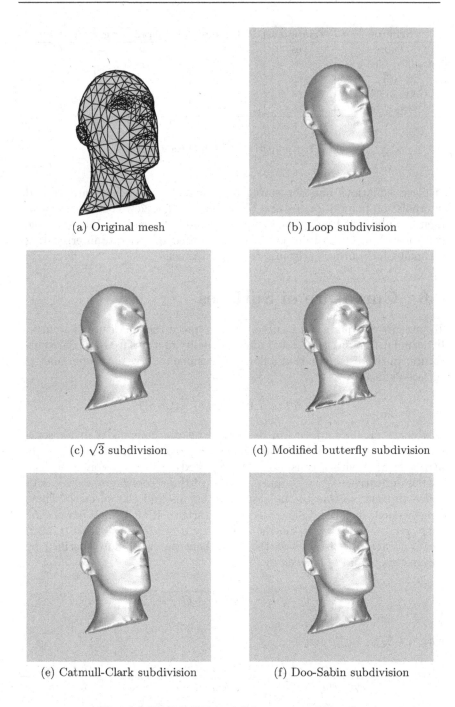

(a) Original mesh   (b) Loop subdivision

(c) $\sqrt{3}$ subdivision   (d) Modified butterfly subdivision

(e) Catmull-Clark subdivision   (f) Doo-Sabin subdivision

Figure 6.35: Subdivision of the mannequin head.

Scheme	Triangles	Polygonal	Interpolating	Continuity
Loop	yes	no	no	C^2
Modified butterfly	yes	no	yes	C^1
$\sqrt{3}$	yes	no	no	C^2
Catmull-Clark	yes	yes	no	C^2
Doo-Sabin	yes	yes	no	C^1

Table 6.1: Comparison of subdivision schemes.

of linear equations must be solved (determined by the limit surface and interpolation points) for the new control mesh. The new control mesh can then be subdivided using the usual Catmull-Clark scheme. Finally, Litke [84] shows how Quasi-Interpolation can be used to generate interpolating Catmull-Clark surfaces within a certain tolerance.

6.6   Curvature of Surfaces

To measure the quality of a curve, we introduced the curvature of a curve. In a similar fashion, we can describe the quality of a surface by surface curvature. In the discussion that follows, we assume that we have a parametric surface defined by

$$\mathbf{x}(u, v) = (x_0(u, v)\ \ x_1(u, v)\ \ x_2(u, v))^T .$$

Any curve on the surface can be defined by the points $\mathbf{x}(u, v)$ for some relation $\psi(u, v) = 0$. We are primarily interested in two such curves, namely $\mathbf{a}(u) = \mathbf{x}(u, v)$ with v constant and $\mathbf{b}(v) = \mathbf{x}(u, v)$ with u constant. The partial derivatives $\frac{d\mathbf{a}}{du} = \frac{\partial \mathbf{x}}{\partial u}$ and $\frac{d\mathbf{b}}{dv} = \frac{\partial \mathbf{x}}{\partial v}$ of these *coordinate curves* both define tangent vectors to the respective curves and the surface. These tangents are called the *basic vectors* of the surface. If we define a parametric curve $\mathbf{r}(t) := \mathbf{x}(u(t), v(t))$ on the surface by $u = u(t)$ and $v = v(t)$, then the *arc length* or distance on the curve between two points specified by parameters t_1 and t_2 is given by [32]

$$\int_{t_1}^{t_2} \sqrt{E\dot{u}^2 + 2F\dot{u}\dot{v} + G\dot{v}^2}\, dt$$

with $\dot{u} = \frac{du}{dt}$, $\dot{v} = \frac{dv}{dt}$ and

$$E(u, v) := \frac{\partial \mathbf{x}}{\partial u} \cdot \frac{\partial \mathbf{x}}{\partial u}, \qquad F(u, v) := \frac{\partial \mathbf{x}}{\partial u} \cdot \frac{\partial \mathbf{x}}{\partial v}, \qquad G(u, v) := \frac{\partial \mathbf{x}}{\partial v} \cdot \frac{\partial \mathbf{x}}{\partial v}$$

where · denotes the scalar product. The equation (square of arc length)

$$ds^2 = E(du)^2 + 2F\,du\,dv + G(dv)^2$$

is known as the *first fundamental form*. The normal to the surface is given
by

$$\mathbf{n}(u,v) = \frac{\mathbf{x}_u \times \mathbf{x}_v}{\|\mathbf{x}_u \times \mathbf{x}_v\|}$$

with $\mathbf{x}_u = \frac{\partial \mathbf{x}}{\partial u}$ and $\mathbf{x}_v = \frac{\partial \mathbf{x}}{\partial v}$ and $\times$ denotes the vector product. The angle θ
at which two curves, $\mathbf{a}(t)$ and $\mathbf{b}(t)$, on the surface intersect is given by [22]

$$\cos\theta = \frac{\dot{\mathbf{a}}(t_0) \cdot \dot{\mathbf{b}}(t_0)}{\|\dot{\mathbf{a}}(t_0)\|\|\dot{\mathbf{b}}(t_0)\|}$$

where the curves intersect at $t = t_0$. The angle ψ between the coordinate
curves of the parameterized surface $\mathbf{x}(u,v)$ is thus given by [22]

$$\cos\psi = \frac{\mathbf{x}_u \cdot \mathbf{x}_v}{\|\mathbf{x}_u\|\|\mathbf{x}_v\|} = \frac{F}{\sqrt{EG}}.$$

If $F(u,v) = 0$ for all u and v the curves are *orthogonal* and we have an
orthogonal parameterization of the surface. Now suppose we have the arc
length parameterization of the curve $\mathbf{r}$ on the surface, $u = u(s)$ and $v = v(s)$. The tangent of the curve is then given by

$$\mathbf{t} = \frac{d\mathbf{r}}{ds} = \frac{\partial \mathbf{x}}{\partial u}\frac{du}{ds} + \frac{\partial \mathbf{x}}{\partial v}\frac{dv}{ds},$$

by application of the chain rule. If we differentiate $\mathbf{t}$ with respect to the
arc length s we obtain

$$\frac{d\mathbf{t}}{ds} = \frac{\partial \mathbf{x}}{\partial u}\frac{d^2 u}{ds^2} + \frac{\partial \mathbf{x}}{\partial v}\frac{d^2 v}{ds^2} + \frac{\partial^2 \mathbf{x}}{\partial u^2}\left(\frac{du}{ds}\right)^2 + 2\frac{\partial^2 \mathbf{x}}{\partial u\,\partial v}\left(\frac{du}{ds}\right)\left(\frac{dv}{ds}\right) + \frac{\partial^2 \mathbf{x}}{\partial v^2}\left(\frac{dv}{ds}\right)^2.$$

Taking the dot product (scalar product) with the normal vector $\mathbf{n}$ on both
sides yields

$$\frac{d\mathbf{t}}{ds} \cdot \mathbf{n} = L\left(\frac{du}{ds}\right)^2 + 2M\left(\frac{du}{ds}\right)\left(\frac{dv}{ds}\right) + N\left(\frac{dv}{ds}\right)^2$$

with

$$L := \mathbf{n} \cdot \frac{\partial^2 \mathbf{x}}{\partial u^2} \qquad M := \mathbf{n} \cdot \frac{\partial^2 \mathbf{x}}{\partial u\,\partial v} \qquad N := \mathbf{n} \cdot \frac{\partial^2 \mathbf{x}}{\partial v^2}.$$

L, M and N are coefficients of the *second fundamental form*. Now the curvature vector of the curve at the point determined by u and v is given by

$$\mathbf{k} = \frac{d\mathbf{t}}{ds} = \kappa\mathbf{m}$$

where $\mathbf{m}$ is the main normal (or principal normal) of the curve. If we take the dot product with $\mathbf{n}$, the normal of the surface, we obtain

$$\frac{d\mathbf{t}}{ds} \cdot \mathbf{n} = \kappa\cos\phi$$

where ϕ is the angle between $\mathbf{n}$ and $\mathbf{m}$. From the above we obtain the equation for the second fundamental form [32]

$$\kappa\cos\phi\,ds^2 = L\,du^2 + 2M\,du\,dv + N\,dv^2\,.$$

If we divide the second fundamental form by the first, and consider the case when $\phi = 0$ we obtain

$$\kappa_0 = \frac{1}{\rho_0} = \frac{L + 2M\lambda + N\lambda^2}{E + 2F\lambda + G\lambda^2}$$

with $\lambda = \frac{dv}{ds} \div \frac{du}{ds} = \frac{dv}{du}$. The radius of the osculating circle is ρ_0 at the point determined by u and v. We have the following relationship for curves on the surface

$$\rho = \rho_0\cos\phi\,.$$

Meusnier's theorem [32] states that all osculating circles of all the curves on the surface that pass through the point under consideration, and have the same tangent $\mathbf{t}$, form a sphere. The radius of the sphere is ρ_0. We thus need only consider curves for which the main normal $\mathbf{m}$ is equal to $\mathbf{n}$. If $L = E$, $M = F$ and $N = G$, then the curvature is independent of λ and the point under consideration is known as an *umbilical point*. Otherwise the curvature is a function of λ. The extreme values of the curvature $\kappa(\lambda)$ occur at the roots λ_1 and λ_2 of [32]

$$\det\begin{pmatrix} \lambda^2 & -\lambda & 1 \\ E & F & G \\ L & M & N \end{pmatrix} = 0\,.$$

The solutions λ_1 and λ_2 correspond to directions on the $u - v$ plane. The corresponding directions in the tangent plane are known as *principal directions* and the values $\kappa_1 = \kappa(\lambda_1)$ and $\kappa_2 = \kappa(\lambda_2)$ are known as *principal curvatures*. The values of κ_1 and κ_2 are the roots of [32]

$$\det\begin{pmatrix} \kappa E - L & \kappa F - M \\ \kappa F - M & \kappa G - N \end{pmatrix} = 0\,.$$

Suppose κ is a polynomial of degree 2, then

$$(\kappa - \kappa_1)(\kappa - \kappa_2) = 0$$

can be used to compute the values κ_1 and κ_2. If we compare this answer to the determinant above we obtain the *Gaussian curvature*

$$\kappa_1 \kappa_2 = \frac{LN - M^2}{EG - F^2}$$

and the *mean curvature*

$$\kappa_1 + \kappa_2 = \frac{NE - 2MF + LG}{EG - F^2}.$$

The mean curvature measures the average curvature of perpendicular curves in the surface. The Gaussian curvature is often used to measure the quality of a surface. For a further discussion of surface curvature, we refer the reader to the text by Farin [32].

Example 1. We consider the *helicoid*, constructed from a helix (spiral) by drawing a line from every point on the helix to the x_2 axis, parallel to the plane formed from the x_0 and x_1 axes. The helicoid is parameterized by

$$\mathbf{x}(u, v) = (v \cos u, v \sin u, au), \qquad a > 0.$$

The partial derivatives are

$$\frac{\partial \mathbf{x}}{\partial u} = \begin{pmatrix} -v \sin u \\ v \cos u \\ a \end{pmatrix}, \qquad \frac{\partial \mathbf{x}}{\partial v} = \begin{pmatrix} \cos u \\ \sin u \\ 0 \end{pmatrix}$$

$$\frac{\partial^2 \mathbf{x}}{\partial u^2} = \begin{pmatrix} -v \cos u \\ -v \sin u \\ 0 \end{pmatrix}, \qquad \frac{\partial^2 \mathbf{x}}{\partial v^2} = \begin{pmatrix} 0 \\ 0 \\ 0 \end{pmatrix}$$

$$\frac{\partial^2 \mathbf{x}}{\partial u \, \partial v} = \begin{pmatrix} -\sin u \\ \cos u \\ 0 \end{pmatrix}.$$

Thus the coefficients of the first fundamental form are given by

$$E(u, v) = v^2 \sin^2 u + v^2 \cos^2 u + a^2 = v^2 + a^2$$
$$F(u, v) = -v \sin u \cos u + v \sin u \cos u + 0 = 0$$
$$G(u, v) = \cos^2 u + \sin^2 u + 0 = 1.$$

Since $F(u, v) = 0$ we have an orthogonal parameterization. The normal to the surface is given by

$$\frac{\partial \mathbf{x}}{\partial u} \times \frac{\partial \mathbf{x}}{\partial v} = \begin{pmatrix} -a \sin u \\ a \cos u \\ -v \end{pmatrix}$$

and after normalizing we obtain

$$\mathbf{n}(u, v) = \frac{1}{\sqrt{a^2 + v^2}} \begin{pmatrix} -a \sin u \\ a \cos u \\ -v \end{pmatrix}.$$

Now we can compute the coefficients of the second fundamental form to obtain

$$L = \frac{1}{\sqrt{a^2 + v^2}} (av \sin u \cos u - av \sin u \cos u + 0) = 0$$

$$M = \frac{1}{\sqrt{a^2 + v^2}} (a \sin^2 u + a \cos^2 u + 0) = \frac{a}{\sqrt{a^2 + v^2}}$$

$$N = \frac{1}{\sqrt{a^2 + v^2}} 0 = 0.$$

We find that the Gaussian curvature is

$$\kappa_1 \kappa_2 = \frac{LN - M^2}{EG - F^2} = -\frac{a^2}{(a^2 + v^2)^2}.$$

The mean curvature is given by

$$\kappa_1 + \kappa_2 = \frac{NE - 2MF + LG}{EG - F^2} = 0. \qquad \square$$

Example 2. We consider the sphere of radius r parameterized by

$$\mathbf{x}(u, v) = \begin{pmatrix} r \sin u \cos v \\ r \sin u \sin v \\ r \cos u \end{pmatrix}.$$

The partial derivatives are

$$\frac{\partial \mathbf{x}}{\partial u} = \begin{pmatrix} r\cos u \cos v \\ r\cos u \sin v \\ -r\sin u \end{pmatrix}, \qquad \frac{\partial \mathbf{x}}{\partial v} = \begin{pmatrix} -r\sin u \sin v \\ r\sin u \cos v \\ 0 \end{pmatrix}$$

$$\frac{\partial^2 \mathbf{x}}{\partial u^2} = \begin{pmatrix} -r\sin u \cos v \\ -r\sin u \sin v \\ -r\cos u \end{pmatrix}, \qquad \frac{\partial^2 \mathbf{x}}{\partial v^2} = \begin{pmatrix} -r\sin u \cos v \\ -r\sin u \sin v \\ 0 \end{pmatrix}$$

$$\frac{\partial^2 \mathbf{x}}{\partial u \, \partial v} = \begin{pmatrix} -r\cos u \sin v \\ r\cos u \cos v \\ 0 \end{pmatrix}.$$

The coefficients of the first fundamental form are given by

$$E(u,v) = r^2 \cos^2 u \cos^2 v + r^2 \cos^2 u \sin^2 v + r^2 \sin^2 u = r^2$$
$$F(u,v) = -r^2 \cos u \sin u \cos v \sin v + r^2 \cos u \sin u \cos v \sin v = 0$$
$$G(u,v) = r^2 \sin^2 u \sin^2 v + r^2 \sin^2 u \cos^2 v = r^2 \sin^2 u \,.$$

Since $F(u,v) = 0$ we have an orthogonal parameterization. The normal to the surface is given by

$$\frac{\partial \mathbf{x}}{\partial u} \times \frac{\partial \mathbf{x}}{\partial v} = r^2 \sin u \begin{pmatrix} \sin u \cos v \\ \sin u \sin v \\ \cos u \end{pmatrix}$$

so that

$$\mathbf{n}(u,v) = \begin{pmatrix} \sin u \cos v \\ \sin u \sin v \\ \cos u \end{pmatrix}.$$

The coefficients of the second fundamental form are

$$L = -r\sin^2 u \cos^2 v - r\sin^2 u \sin^2 v - r\cos^2 u = -r$$
$$M = -r\sin u \cos v \cos u \sin v + r\cos u \cos v \sin u \sin v + 0 = 0$$
$$N = -r\sin^2 u \cos^2 v - r\sin^2 u \sin^2 v + 0 = -r\sin^2 u \,.$$

We find that the Gaussian curvature

$$\kappa_1 \kappa_2 = \frac{LN - M^2}{EG - F^2} = \frac{1}{r^2}$$

is constant. The mean curvature

$$\kappa_1 + \kappa_2 = \frac{NE - 2MF + LG}{EG - F^2} = -\frac{2}{r}$$

is also constant. $\qquad\square$

6.7   Harmonic Surfaces

In this section we see how harmonic surfaces can be created. We begin
with the tensor product surface followed by a discussion of the potential
of applying a subdivision algorithm to produce subdivision curves. In the
process we prove some useful theorems allowing us to find alternative representations of a curve created using harmonic interpolation. One of the
theorems allows us to add interpolation points to curves produced by harmonic interpolation. We end off this chapter by discussing how harmonic
surfaces can be represented by Bézier patches.

6.8   Tensor Product Surface

The *tensor product harmonic surface* is given by

$$\mathbf{p}(u,v) = \sum_{j=0}^{m} \sum_{k=0}^{n} \sigma_j^m(u)\sigma_k^n(v)\mathbf{x}_{j,k}$$

where we define $\sigma_k^n(t) := \sigma^n(t - k/n)$,

$$\sigma^n(t) := \begin{cases} \dfrac{\sin(n\pi t)}{n\sin(\pi t)}, & \text{if } n \text{ is odd} \\[2ex] \cos(\pi t)\dfrac{\sin(n\pi t)}{n\sin(\pi t)}, & \text{if } n \text{ is even.} \end{cases}$$

Unlike Bézier patches, harmonic surface parameter values must be chosen
carefully. Since harmonic interpolation is periodic, we may duplicate the
surface at certain points. We illustrate two simple examples, the sphere
and torus. For a sphere, we can use four points arranged in a diamond
shape, and rotate the points 90°. By duplicating control points at the
poles we have 16 control points. There are thus four control points at
each pole. Each set of 4 horizontal or vertical control points describes a
circle. Creating a harmonic surface with parameter values $0 \leq u \leq 1$ and
$0 \leq v \leq 1$ will duplicate the surface. Instead we stop halfway with one
of the parameters, say $0 \leq u \leq 0.5$. A torus is simply created by taking
the same initial diamond shape, translating to the radius of the torus and
rotating through 90° three times to obtain 16 control points. A simplified
polygonal version of the sphere and torus were obtained by sampling the
harmonic surface at equally spaced parametric values. The results obtained
are illustrated in figure 6.36. The interpolation points are overlaid, ignoring
visibility so that the simple structure used can be seen.

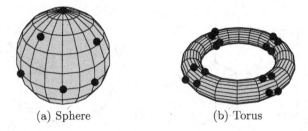

(a) Sphere   (b) Torus

Figure 6.36: Tensor product harmonic surfaces.

6.9 Harmonic Subdivision

To see that harmonic subdivision surfaces are a possibility, we rewrite harmonic interpolation into a subdivision form. We have (shown later in theorem 6.3)

$$\sum_{k=0}^{n-1} \sigma_k^n(t)\mathbf{x}_k = \sum_{j=0}^{2n-1} \sigma_j^{2n}(t)\mathbf{y}_j$$

where

$$\mathbf{y}_j = \sum_{k=0}^{n-1} \sigma_k^n\left(\frac{j}{2n}\right)\mathbf{x}_k\,.$$

We can thus add n points to the existing n and still have the same curve. If we repetitively iterate this process, the limit curve is the same as that produced by harmonic interpolation. We note that $\mathbf{y}_{2j} = \mathbf{x}_j$. We thus have the following subdivision scheme

$$\mathbf{x}_{2i}^{k+1} = \mathbf{x}_i^k,$$

$$\mathbf{x}_{2i+1}^{k+1} = \sum_{j=0}^{n-1} \sigma_j^n\left(\frac{2i+1}{2n}\right)\mathbf{x}_j^k\,. \tag{6.3}$$

The steps in repeated subdivision are shown in figure 6.37. The harmonic subdivision scheme is significantly slower than the other subdivision schemes. Both the use of trigonometric functions as opposed to polynomials and the fact that the σ_k basis functions for harmonic interpolation do not have local support contribute to the decreased performance of the method. Thus to get an accurate calculation of one surface point, all the points in the mesh have to be used. This becomes particularly difficult when trying to determine what masks can be used for an arbitrary mesh. The mask would have to be large enough to cover all points in the polygon. In addition, the requirement for periodicity must be met by the mask used. In the

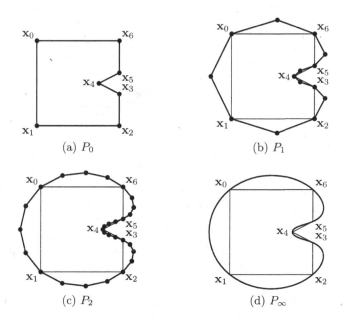

Figure 6.37: Stages in harmonic subdivision.

case where the interpolation points can be arranged to produce a tensor product surface, the task is somewhat simpler. To illustrate, we subdivide the control points of the torus. The process is illustrated in figure 6.38. Since we have a tensor product surface, we subdivide on parameter u and then parameter v for each subdivision step. The same process has been applied in figure 6.39 to a deformed torus.

6.10   Local Harmonic Subdivision

In this section we present an interpolating $\sqrt{3}$ subdivision scheme based on harmonic interpolation. We present subdivision curves based on harmonic interpolation and consider harmonic interpolation with a restricted basis. We then generalize the approach to triangle meshes of regular valence (valence = 6) and consider simplifications of a few existing rules for vertices of irregular valence (valence $\neq$ 6) as a result of harmonic interpolation.

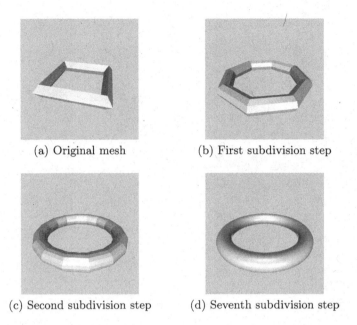

(a) Original mesh   (b) First subdivision step

(c) Second subdivision step   (d) Seventh subdivision step

Figure 6.38: Stages in subdivision to produce a torus.

6.10.1   Local Harmonic Interpolation for Curves

In previous sections we have seen that curves produced by harmonic interpolation can be subdivided with the rule

$$\mathbf{x}_{2i}^{k+1} = \mathbf{x}_i^k,$$

$$\mathbf{x}_{2i+1}^{k+1} = \sum_{j=0}^{n-1} \sigma_j \left(\frac{2i+1}{2n} \right) \mathbf{x}_j^k. \tag{6.4}$$

An important property is lacking in this subdivision scheme: limited support. The support of the basis function includes all points in the data set
(which doubles with each iteration) and is thus very expensive to evaluate.

In this section we modify harmonic interpolation so that only local support
is needed. The resulting curve differs significantly from the original curve
produced by harmonic interpolation, but can be applied to triangle meshes
in a simple fashion.

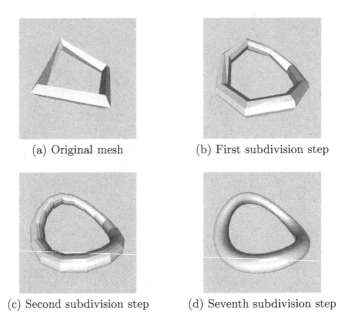

(a) Original mesh   (b) First subdivision step

(c) Second subdivision step   (d) Seventh subdivision step

Figure 6.39: Stages in subdivision to produce a deformed torus.

6.10.2 Parametric Distance

Examination of the $\sigma(t)$ basis function for $n = 4$ (similar arguments hold
for $n \neq 4$) illustrated in figure 4.20 yields two important properties:

- $\sigma(t)$ is symmetric around 0.

- $\sigma(t)$ is symmetric around 0.5.

Any parameter value t greater than 0.5 can be regarded as $-(t-0.5)+0.5 = 1.0 - t < 0.5$ due to symmetry around 0.5. And $t < 0.0$ can be regarded as
$-t$ due to symmetry around 0.

The previous subdivision rules can now be rewritten as

$$\mathbf{x}_{2i}^{k+1} = \mathbf{x}_i^k,$$

$$\mathbf{x}_{2i+1}^{k+1} = \sum_{j=0}^{n-1} \sigma\left(d_i(j)/n\right) \mathbf{x}_j^k,$$

where $d_i(j) = |i + 0.5 - j|$ is the "parametric distance" of point j from the
new point. Instead of using all the data points for a subdivision step, we

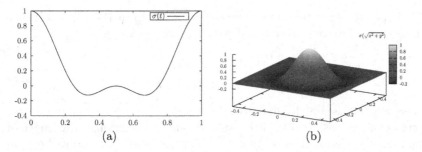

Figure 6.40: Basis functions for the 2D and 3D harmonic interpolation.

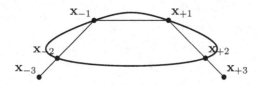

Figure 6.41: Harmonic interpolation of nearest 4 points.

limit the support to the nearest 4 points (in a "parametric distance" sense) to obtain local support. In this case $\sigma(t)$ is defined by $n = 4$. Analysis of the subdivision matrix indicates that the curve satisfies the necessary conditions for C^1 continuity [105, 142] (eigenvalues $\lambda_1 = 1$, $\lambda_2 = \frac{1}{2}$ and $|\lambda_j| < \lambda_2, j > 2$).

However, the resulting curve is less than pleasing (see figure 6.42(a)). The undesirable aspects are due to incorrect curvature estimation at the points farthest from the new point. The curve is assumed to be periodic and bends

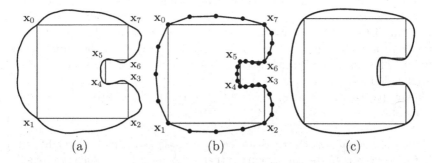

Figure 6.42: Harmonic subdivision with local support.

in sharply to reach the other farthest point (figure 6.41). To encourage flatter curves, we introduce two new virtual interpolation points

$$\mathbf{x}_{-3} := c(\mathbf{x}_{-2} - \mathbf{x}_{-1}) + \mathbf{x}_{-2}$$
$$\mathbf{x}_{+3} := c(\mathbf{x}_{+2} - \mathbf{x}_{+1}) + \mathbf{x}_{+2} \qquad (6.5)$$

where c is a constant that controls the shape of the curve. The parameter c creates an extension of the line segment, where c determines the length of the extension. With these virtual interpolation points the weights for each vertex are

$$w_{-1} = \sigma(0.5/6) - c\sigma(2.5/6)$$
$$w_{+1} = \sigma(0.5/6) - c\sigma(2.5/6)$$
$$w_{-2} = \sigma(1.5/6) + (1 + c)\sigma(2.5/6)$$
$$w_{+2} = \sigma(1.5/6) + (1 + c)\sigma(2.5/6)$$

with $n = 6$. Clearly $\sum_{i=0}^{n-1} w_i = 1$ and the weights are still a partition of unity. We have chosen $c = 1.3$ to create a visually pleasing curve. No further analysis as to suitable values for c have been performed. The interpolating curve still satisfies the necessary conditions for C^1 continuity ($\lambda_1 = 1$, $\lambda_2 = \frac{1}{2}$ and $|\lambda_j| < \lambda_2$, $j > 2$) and appears to be very similar to the 4-point interpolatory subdivision scheme [26] with $w = 1/16$. The new subdivision points and curve are displayed in figure 6.7(b) and (c).

In the next section we use the "parametric distance" to define a subdivision rule for regular vertices of a triangle mesh.

6.10.3   Subdivision Rules

In the previous section σ was redefined according to some distance measure. The two closest points during subdivision ($\mathbf{x}_{-1}$ and $\mathbf{x}_{+1}$) are regarded as being a distance of 0.5 away from the subdivision point. The points $\mathbf{x}_{-2}$ and $\mathbf{x}_{+2}$ are regarded as being a distance 1.5 away from the subdivision point. This notion of "parametric distance" is useful for the subdivision of a triangle mesh. The σ function can be redefined in terms of distance in a planar space. The resulting basis function for $n = 4$ is displayed in figure 6.40(b).

Vertices at equal parametric distance d_i are assigned the same weight during subdivision. In the case of curves there are precisely two such points and each point was given the weight $\sigma(d_i)$. Thus the total weight distributed between the points at a parametric distance of d_i is $2\sigma(d_i)$. In the same

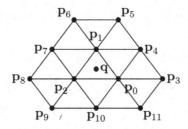

Figure 6.43: Stencil for regular vertices.

way, if there are m points at parametric distance d_i from the subdivision point, the weight of each is chosen to be $2\sigma(d_i)/m$. The weights will thus remain a partition of unity.

For subdivision we use the $\sqrt{3}$ subdivision scheme [74]. A new vertex is created in the center of each triangle. This vertex is then connected with the vertices of the triangle to create three new triangles. Existing vertices are not altered in any way, and so the scheme is an interpolating subdivision scheme. If only these steps are followed, then the triangles created become very thin and not all parts of the mesh are refined. To solve this problem, triangle edges are flipped after each subdivision step. The process is illustrated in figure 6.19.

We use the 12-neighborhood of the new subdivision vertex [79] to create the interpolatory scheme as illustrated in figure 6.43. Ring-1 of the subdivision point $\mathbf{q}$ is simply the triangle under consideration, that is $\mathbf{p}_0$, $\mathbf{p}_1$ and $\mathbf{p}_2$. Ring-2 is defined as the remaining points in the 12-neighborhood.

The weight for the 1-ring is $(2\sigma(0.5/6) - 2c\sigma(2.5/6))/3$. The weights for the 2-ring are $(2\sigma(1.5/6) + 2(1 + c)\sigma(2.5/6))/m$, where m is the number of vertices in the 2-ring. Note that points in the 1-ring are regarded as being a "parametric distance" of 0.5 from the new vertex, and points in the 2-ring have a "parametric distance" of 1.5. The points in the 1-ring and 2-ring are then used to create "virtual" interpolation points at distance 2.5. We do not compute the virtual interpolation points explicitly, instead the contribution of the virtual points is incorporated with the coefficients of the existing points. We have chosen $c = 0.45$ for surfaces and this seems to produce good results. Smaller values tend to produce surfaces with greater volume. The value for c must be chosen carfeully so that the surface still satisfies the necessary conditions for continuity. Since the weights for all vertices in the 1-ring are identical, and the same holds for the 2-ring, The average of the 1-ring and 2-ring can be computed, and the subdivision point is then given by

$$\mathbf{q} = (2\sigma(0.5/6) - 2c\sigma(2.5/6))\mathbf{a}_1 + (2\sigma(1.5/6) + 2(1+c)\sigma(2.5/6))\mathbf{a}_2$$

where $\mathbf{a}_1$ is the average of the vertices in ring-1 and $\mathbf{a}_2$ is the average of the vertices in ring-2.

To examine the continuity of the subdivision scheme we need to consider a subdivision matrix that maps from the neighborhood of a point to a similar neighborhood of a new point. The topology of this new neighborhood should be identical to the topology of the original neighborhood. If the subdivision matrix is to produce a 12-neighborhood for each vertex in the neighborhood then 37 vertices are required to define the subdivision matrix [79]. The subdivision matrix is thus a 37×37 matrix for regular vertices.

However, the topology at each subdivision step of $\sqrt{3}$ subdivision changes. The topology is restored every second step, thus two iterations of subdivision are required to obtain a neighborhood of identical topology (but smaller). This new neighborhood is rotated by the subdivision scheme [74] and so a further permutation matrix is required to match vertices from the original neighborhood to the new neighborhood. To analyse continuity of the surface, the eigenvalues of RSS must be computed, where R is the permutation matrix, and S describes one subdivision step.

For the scheme presented here the eigenvalues for a vertex of valence 6 are

$$\lambda_1 = 1, \quad \lambda_2 = \lambda_3 = \frac{1}{3}, \quad |\lambda_j| < \lambda_3, \quad j > 3.$$

The surface thus satisfies the necessary conditions for C^1 continuity [105] at regular vertices. However, the surface does not satisfy these constraints at irregular vertices. In the next section we present the approach of Labsik and Greiner [79] to solve this problem and present a few simplifications of their subdivision rules.

6.10.4   Irregular Vertices

The given scheme does not produce C^1 surfaces for irregular vertices. For irregular vertices we follow the same approach as Labsik and Greiner [79], that is only the vertices in the 1-ring of the irregular vertices are used to determine new vertices adjacent to the irregular vertex. If a triangle has two or more irregular vertices then we take the average of the point produced by each irregular vertex. The rest of this section is adapted from

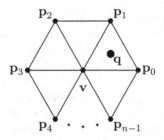

Figure 6.44: Stencil for irregular vertices.

Labsik and Greiner [79] with a few special cases that can be solved directly using harmonic interpolation.

After two steps of subdivision no triangles remain that have more than one vertex of irregular valence. To solve the irregular case, consider the one ring of an irregular vertex illustrated in figure 6.44. To create the subdivision vertex **q** we compute

$$\mathbf{q} = \alpha\mathbf{v} + \sum_{i=0}^{n-1} \alpha_i \mathbf{p}_i.$$

The new points are described by a $(n+1) \times (n+1)$ subdivision matrix. The subdivision matrix for valence 5 is given by [79]

$$S = \begin{pmatrix} 1 & 0 & 0 & 0 & 0 & 0 \\ \alpha & \alpha_0 & \alpha_1 & \alpha_2 & \alpha_3 & \alpha_4 \\ \alpha & \alpha_4 & \alpha_0 & \alpha_1 & \alpha_2 & \alpha_3 \\ \alpha & \alpha_3 & \alpha_4 & \alpha_0 & \alpha_1 & \alpha_2 \\ \alpha & \alpha_2 & \alpha_3 & \alpha_4 & \alpha_0 & \alpha_1 \\ \alpha & \alpha_1 & \alpha_2 & \alpha_3 & \alpha_4 & \alpha_0 \end{pmatrix}.$$

Due to the $\sqrt{3}$ subdivision algorithm it is once again necessary to consider two steps in the algorithm, which produces the subdivision matrix $\hat{S} = RSS$, where R is a permutation matrix. $\hat{S}$ has a similar structure to S and Labsik and Greiner [79] have determined the entries $\hat{\alpha}$ and $\hat{\alpha}_i$ such that the eigenvalues of $\hat{S}$ are

$$\lambda_1 = 1, \ \lambda_2 = \lambda_3 = 1/3, \ \lambda_4 = \lambda_5 = \lambda_6 = 1/9$$

which satisfies the necessary conditions for C^1 continuity. The coefficients for $v \geq 5$ is given by

$$\hat{\alpha} = 8/9, \quad \hat{\alpha}_i = \frac{1/9 + 2/3\cos\left(2\pi i/v\right) + 2/9\cos\left(4\pi i/v\right)}{v}.$$

For valence $v = 3$ the coefficients are $\hat{\alpha} = 8/9$, $\hat{\alpha}_0 = 7/27$, $\hat{\alpha}_1 = \hat{\alpha}_2 = -2/27$, and for $v = 4$ we have $\hat{\alpha} = 8/9$, $\hat{\alpha}_0 = 7/36$, $\hat{\alpha}_1 = \hat{\alpha}_3 = 1/36$, $\hat{\alpha}_2 = -5/36$. It is thus necessary to obtain a square root of $\hat{S}$ to be able to perform the subdivision.

Harmonic interpolation provides a direct method for obtaining a square root for valence 3 and 4. If we consider the new subdivision points to have distance 0.5 from the irregular vertex, and harmonic interpolation requires a minimum of 3 vertices, then $\alpha = \sigma(0.5/3) = 2/3$ with $n = 3$. The vertices from the 1-ring must thus have a total weight of $1/3$. Next harmonic interpolation is used to determine weights within the 1-ring. Each vertex thus has weight $\sigma_k/3$ according to the "parametric distance" from the subdivision point. The subdivision matrix RSS then has eigenvalue $\lambda_2 = 1/9$. The weights produced must be altered to provide the desired eigenvalues. We have determined experimentally that $1/3(\sqrt{3}\sigma_k + (1 - \sqrt{3})/v)$ provides the desired eigenvalues where v is the valence, $\sqrt{3}$ is used to scale the value of σ and the latter term ensures that the weights of the 1-ring sum to $1/3$. The resulting eigenvalues and subdivision matrix RSS are identical to the matrix proposed by Labsik and Greiner [79] for valence 3 and 4.

For valence 5 and higher we compute a square root of the matrix in a precomputation step [79] using a Newton iteration. Standard matrix square root iteration techniques such as [60] $(k = 0, 1, 2, \ldots)$

$$Y_0 = A, \quad Z_0 = I$$

$$Y_{k+1} = \frac{1}{2}(Y_k + Z_k^{-1})$$

$$Z_{k+1} = \frac{1}{2}(Z_k + Y_k^{-1})$$

or

$$Y_0 = A, \quad Z_0 = I$$

$$Y_{k+1} = \frac{1}{2}Y_k(3I - Z_kY_k)$$

$$Z_{k+1} = \frac{1}{2}(3I - Z_kY_k)Z_k$$

fail to yield the desired structure for the matrix (symmetry of weights for subdivision). However, restricting the matrix to be in the correct form and applying Newton iteration provides results fairly quickly. Newton iteration is quite sensitive to the starting point which often determines whether Newton iteration will converge to a solution or not. We have used the coefficients from harmonic interpolation $\alpha = 2/3$ and $\alpha_i = \sigma((i - 0.5)/n)/3$ as the starting point with great success.

(a)   (b)   (c)

Figure 6.45: Subdivision of a simple chess piece. (a) Base mesh. (b) Subdivision of Labsik and Greiner. (c) New subdivision scheme.

6.10.5   Boundaries

Boundary triangles are only subdivided every second subdivision step [74]. The edge on the boundary must be subdivided into 3 segments and so 2 new vertices must be created. There is no need to derive specific rules, since the harmonic interpolation using virtual points (equation 6.5) provides a parametric description of the curve. If the two vertices that define the edge are the first two vertices to be interpolated, then the parameter values $t_1 = 1/18$ and $t_2 = 2/18$ describe the two new interpolation points based on equation 6.3.

The subdivision point created in the centre of the triangle on a boundary will not have all vertices available. Labsik and Greiner [79] define virtual points to fill in the stencil required for subdivision. The chosen algorithm assumes that the surface is planar toward the boundary. We have attempted to incorporate the curvature of the mesh to determine these virtual points. That is, instead of reflecting vertices of the 1-ring triangle across the boundary, we reflect vertices of the 2-ring across the triangle centre. Since the new vertices are produced by interpolating averages, we simply reflect all points in the 2-ring that are adjacent to a vertex in the 1-ring that is not on the boundary. In this way we do not have to determine the connectivity of the vertices to see which stencil positions need to be filled. The obvious problem with this technique is that vertices adjacent to the boundary might contribute more to the average than they should. Nonetheless the results seem to be reasonable.

We have rendered a few subdivision surfaces using our algorithm, and the algorithm of Labsik and Greiner. For the implementation of Labsik and Greiner we have used our boundary algorithm. The algorithm for irregular

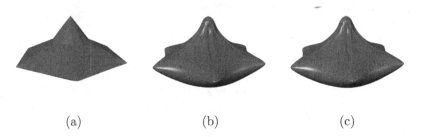

(a)   (b)   (c)

Figure 6.46: Subdivision of a simple diamond model with a valence 12 vertex. (a) Base mesh. (b) Subdivision of Labsik and Greiner. (c) Local harmonic subdivision.

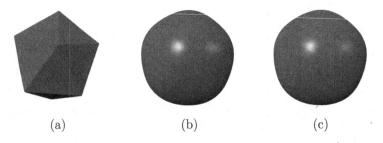

(a)   (b)   (c)

Figure 6.47: Subdivision for refining an icosahedron. (a) Base mesh. (b) Subdivision of Labsik and Greiner. (c) Local harmonic subdivision.

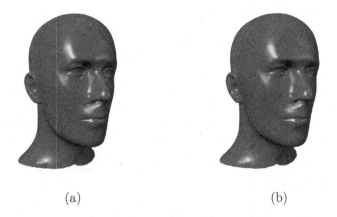

(a)   (b)

Figure 6.48: Subdivision for refining the mannequin head. (a) Subdivision of Labsik and Greiner.(b) Local harmonic subdivision.

vertices are also the same.

A rook model is displayed in figure 6.45, and the mannequin head model is displayed in figure 6.48.

Since this algorithm is simply a variation of the weights used in the algorithm of Labsik and Greiner, no significant difference in the quality of the interpolation is expected. The figures confirm this observation. Figures 6.46 and 6.47 are clear examples of the similarity of the algorithms, even though our algorithm is slightly simpler to implement.

6.11   Geometry Images and Parameterization

This section discusses the creation of a *geometry image* which can simply be regarded as a two-dimensional array of points. Geometry images are not restricted to rectangular images, but we focus on rectangular images. A disk [35], geometry atlas [116], or sphere [48, 100, 42, 114] could be used as well. The creation of geometry images is related to *mesh parameterization*. Mesh parameterization automatically assigns texture coordinates (usually in $\mathbb{R}^2$) to each vertex of the polygon mesh, in such a way that if a texture is applied to the mesh, there should be a minimum of distortion. In our case the texture coordinates are assigned so that the mesh lies in a rectangle in $\mathbb{R}^2$. To do so, the mesh must first be cut so that it is topologically equivalent to a disk (assuming this is possible). The parameterization algorithm assigns the texture coordinates which can then be used to define surface attributes, such as the color or normal at each surface position stored in the texture map. For a geometry image the position of the surface, instead of color, is stored in a two-dimensional array. The geometry can then be reconstructed by creating quadrilaterals (or triangles) from adjacent vertices in the geometry image. The geometry image is useful since it provides a regular tensor product surface for interpolation, and no connectivity information need be stored.

6.11.1   Cutting a Mesh into a Disk

A few techniques exist to cut a mesh into a disk in some optimal fashion. These include visibility critera [115] or determining the shortest required cuts [31]. In this section we discuss the algorithm due to Gu [51].

Any closed surface can be cut open into a topological disk [51]. Let the boundary edges of the initial mesh be denoted by B. Boundary edges are

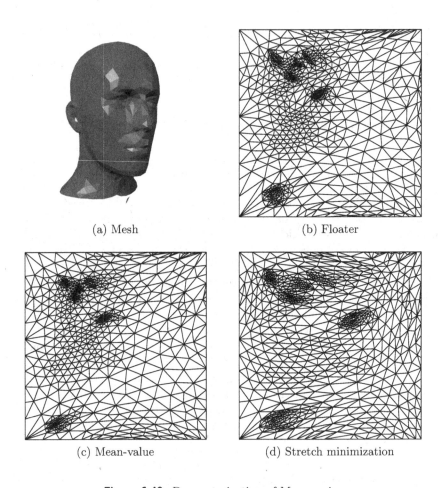

(a) Mesh   (b) Floater

(c) Mean-value   (d) Stretch minimization

Figure 6.49: Parameterization of Mannequin.

edges adjacent to only one triangle. To find such a cut a seed triangle is removed from the mesh. This triangle can be chosen a random or according to some fixed algorithm. After the seed triangle is removed, we search for an edge e that is adjacent to only one triangle but is not one of the original boundary edges B. Both the edge and the triangle adjacent to it are removed from the mesh. The process is repeated until no triangles remain. To attempt to produce a cut of minimum length triangles are removed according to geodesic distance. To compute the shortest distance between two vertices in the mesh we use Dijkstra's algorithm [17, 127] (which is an upper bound for geodesic distance). The shortest path between any two vertices can be computed before cutting the mesh. The triangles that have been removed form a topological disk. The edges that remain form a cut path that can be used to cut the mesh into a topological disk. However, several unnecessary cuts remain that can be pruned. Only the connected loops need to be kept. To prune these unnecessary cuts, we repeatedly identify a vertex adjacent to exactly one edge and remove the vertex and the edge. After all such vertices are removed the remaining vertices have valence of at least 2. Now only the connected loops remain. The connected loops may not be the shortest cut to obtain a topological disk. To attempt to smooth the cut, and reduce the length of the cut, we examine each original triangle of the mesh that has two edges that belong to the cut. If the length of the remaining edge is shorter than the sum of the lengths of the two cut edges, then we replace these two edges by the remaining edge in the triangle. This process is repeated until no more changes can be made to the cutpath. We only consider edges whose vertices are of valence 2 for this process, to prevent the intersection of two connected loops repeatedly being changed, resulting in an endless loop.

The cut may be augmented to assist the parameterization by adding cutpaths to locations of large stretch in the parameterized mesh. The stretch is a measure of how much a triangle in the mesh differs from the parameterized triangle in $\mathbb{R}^2$ [107]. To do so the mesh should be parameterized onto a disk using shape-preserving parameterization [35] (discussed shortly) so that stretch can be accurately determined. If the stretch is reduced by the parameterization method, then it is difficult to determine which cut path would assist in the reduction of stretch. The cut may be augmented several times until no improvement in stretch can be obtained.

If the cut contains no edges, then the mesh is of genus 0 (topologically equivalent to a sphere). In this case spherical parameterization is probably better [114, 42, 100, 48]. However, it is still possible to cut the mesh by creating a short cut path and using cut augmentation to assist in the parameterization.

We do not actually remove triangles, edges or vertices during the cut path identification process. Instead each edge, vertex and triangle is labelled so that we can determine if it has been removed for cutting purposes or remains in the cut path. These labels are cleared once the cut path has been computed. To cut along the cutpath we need to create new vertices for each vertex in the cutpath. If the valence of the vertex in the cutpath is n, then $n-1$ new vertices must be created. Each edge is spit into two edges, where new edges make use of the new vertices. Next the triangles must be modified to refer to the correct vertices and edges. To correctly assign vertices and edges to triangles, we consider each cut vertex independently. Each triangle around the cut vertex is assigned a label. The label of two adjacent triangles, where the edge shared by the triangles is a cut edge, must differ. The label of two triangles, where the edge shared by the triangles is not a cut edge, must be identical. The labels are simply the number of the vertex to use for each face. Once these labels have been allocated the new edges can be created and the face are modified accordingly. Although the process seems relatively simple, it is important to ensure that all the data structures remain consistent during this alteration of the mesh.

6.11.2 Parameterization

The goal of parameterization is to determine a planar embedding of some graph (mesh) [35]. Some terminology is required before a discussion on parameterization can begin. Let the vertices of the *graph* $G = G(V, E)$ be $V = \{x \mid x = 1, \ldots, n\}$. The edges E is a subset of ordered pairs (i, j) with $i \neq j$ such that if $(i, j) \in E$ then $(j, i) \in E$. Vertex i has vertex j as neighbor if $(i, j) \in E$. The degree (or valence) of a vertex is the number of neighbors it has. A graph G is *planar* if the following conditions hold

- Each vertex i is mapped to a point in $\mathbb{R}^2$.

- Each edge (i, j) is mapped to a curve whose endpoints are i and j.

- The only intersection between curves occurs at vertices of the graph.

Such a graph G is known as a plane graph. A triangulated plane graph whose edges are straight lines is a planar triangulation. A planar triangulation of G is thus isomorphic to G. Next we discuss three different parameterization techniques.

Shape-Preserving Parameterization

We briefly discuss the shape-preserving method of Floater [35], followed by a few alternatives. First the boundary is mapped to some convex polygon. A circle or rectangle can be used, although we generally use a rectangle for rasterization purposes. The vertices on the boundary can be equally spaced, but this approach does not take into account the relative size of triangles. To reduce distortion a chord length parameterization of the boundary can be performed. In this case we compute the sum of all the lengths of the edges on the boundary and allocate a proportion of the boundary of the rectangle (or circle) to the edge based on the length of the edge relative to the total length of all boundary edges. If the original mesh has been cut, then it may be necessary to ensure that cut vertices on the boundary correspond to locations in the final rasterized geometry image. This is necessary to allow the cut to be removed when the mesh is created from the geometry image.

Once the boundary has been fixed internal vertices are placed by ensuring that each interior vertex (a non boundary vertex) is a weighted average of its neighbors. If each neighbor is assigned an equal weight ($1/v$ where v is the valence of the vertex), then this is known as a *barycentric mapping*. The barycentric mapping does not take into account the shape of the triangles adjacent to the vertex so better weights should be selected. We postpone the discussion concerning the choices of these weights so that we can discuss parameterization given these weights.

Consider a vertex i. Let the weights for each neighbor j be denoted by $w_{i,j}$. The weights $w_{i,j}$ are chosen to be a weighted average (they form a partition of unity). We thus have

$$w_{i,j} = 0, \quad (i,j) \notin E, \quad w_{i,j} > 0, \quad (i,j) \in E, \quad \sum_{j=0}^{N-1} w_{i,j} = 1$$

where N is the number of vertices in the mesh. Let the texture coordinates of the vertices of the mesh be denoted by $\mathbf{u}_i$, where there are n vertices not on the boundary and $N - n$ vertices on the boundary. Each texture coordinate $\mathbf{u}_i$ is defined to be a weighted average of its neighbors so that

$$\mathbf{u}_i = \sum_{j=0}^{N-1} w_{i,j} \mathbf{u}_j, \quad i = 0, \dots, n-1.$$

The texture coordinates of the boundary vertices have already been determined so only n unknowns remain. The equations can thus be rewritten as

$$\mathbf{u}_i - \sum_{j=0}^{n-1} w_{i,j}\mathbf{u}_j = \sum_{j=n}^{N-1} w_{i,j}\mathbf{u}_j, \quad i = 0, \ldots, n-1.$$

If $\mathbf{u}_i = (s_i \ t_i)^T$ then this is equivalent to the two matrix equations

$$A\mathbf{s} = \mathbf{b}_0, \quad A\mathbf{t} = \mathbf{b}_1$$

where $\mathbf{s} = (s_0 \ldots s_{n-1})^T$, $\mathbf{t} = (t_0 \ldots t_{n-1})^T$ and A is an $n \times n$ matrix with elements

$$a_{i,i} = 0, \quad a_{i,j} = -w_{i,j}, \quad j \neq i.$$

The matrix A is invertible [35]. Gauss-Seidel iteration or more advanced techniques can be used to determine the solution to these equations. The only nonzero entries in each row of the matrix correspond to the vertex under consideration and the neighbors of this vertex. The matrix is thus sparse, and performance can be improved by applying Gauss-Seidel iteration to an implementation of a sparse matrix.

Floater's shape-preserving parameterization [35] begins by computing a local parameterization for each vertex. The vertex $\mathbf{v}$ and neighboring vertices $\mathbf{v}_k$ are mapped to $\mathbb{R}^2$ in such a way that arc length in the radial direction is preserved. Thus the neighboring vertices remain that same distance from the vertex $\mathbf{v}$. Let $\text{ang}(\mathbf{a}, \mathbf{b}, \mathbf{c})$ denote the angle between the vectors $\mathbf{a} - \mathbf{b}$ and $\mathbf{c} - \mathbf{b}$. This is a signed angle if it is computed in $\mathbb{R}^2$ so that a clockwise and anticlockwise rotation have opposite signs. Suppose the neighboring vertices are ordered so that $\mathbf{v}, \mathbf{v}_j$ and $\mathbf{v}_{j+1}$ are the vertices of one of the triangles adjacent to $\mathbf{v}$. The vertex $\mathbf{v}$ is mapped to $\mathbf{u} = \mathbf{0}$, and the first neighboring vertex is mapped to $\mathbf{u}_0 = (\|\mathbf{v}_0 - \mathbf{v}\| \ 0)^T$. The remaining vertices are mapped in such a way that

$$\|\mathbf{v}_k - \mathbf{v}\| = \|\mathbf{u}_k - \mathbf{u}\|, \quad \text{ang}(\mathbf{u}_k, \mathbf{u}, \mathbf{u}_{k+1}) = 2\pi\text{ang}(\mathbf{v}_k, \mathbf{v}, \mathbf{v}_{k+1})/\theta$$

where $\theta = \sum_{k=0}^{d-1} \text{ang}(\mathbf{v}_k, \mathbf{v}, \mathbf{v}_{k+1})$ and d is the valence of the vertex $\mathbf{v}$. If there are only three neighboring vertices, then $\mathbf{u}$ can be described by the barycentric coordinates

$$\mathbf{u} = \alpha\mathbf{u}_0 + \beta\mathbf{u}_1 + \gamma\mathbf{u}_2$$

where $\alpha + \beta + \gamma = 1$. These coefficients are computed with

$$\alpha = \frac{\text{area}(\mathbf{u}, \mathbf{u}_1, \mathbf{u}_2)}{\text{area}(\mathbf{u}_0, \mathbf{u}_1, \mathbf{u}_2)}, \quad \beta = \frac{\text{area}(\mathbf{u}_0, \mathbf{u}, \mathbf{u}_2)}{\text{area}(\mathbf{u}_0, \mathbf{u}_1, \mathbf{u}_2)}, \quad \gamma = \frac{\text{area}(\mathbf{u}_0, \mathbf{u}_1, \mathbf{u})}{\text{area}(\mathbf{u}_0, \mathbf{u}_1, \mathbf{u}_2)}.$$

In this case the barycentric coordinates are used as the weights $w_{i,j}$. If there

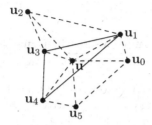

Figure 6.50: Shape-preserving parameterization: Computation of weights.

are more than three neighboring vertices, then we consider each neighboring vertex in turn. For each neighboring vertex $\mathbf{u}_j$ we construct a line through the vertex $\mathbf{u}$ and the neighboring vertex. This line will intersect one line segment between two vertices $\mathbf{u}_k$ and $\mathbf{u}_{k+1}$ or it will intersect at a vertex. This situation is illustrated in figure 6.50. If a line segment is intersected then we compute the barycentric coordinates α_j, β_j and γ_j of $\mathbf{u}$ for the triangle given by $\mathbf{u}_j$, $\mathbf{u}_k$ and $\mathbf{u}_{k+1}$. Let $m_{j,j} = \alpha_j$, $m_{j,k} = \beta_j$ and $m_{j,k+1} = \gamma_j$, so that

$$\mathbf{u} = m_{j,j}\mathbf{u}_j + m_{j,k}\mathbf{u}_k + m_{j,k+1}\mathbf{u}_{k+1}\,.$$

To obtain a weighted average over all vertices we compute

$$w_{i,j} = \frac{1}{d}\sum_{k=0}^{d-1} m_{k,j}\,.$$

As a result the weights satisfy $\sum_{j=0}^{d-1} w_{i,j} = 1$ for every i and $\mathbf{u} = \sum_{j=0}^{d-1} w_{i,j}\mathbf{u}_j$. With these weights, the system of equations for parameterization can be constructed and the unknown values $\mathbf{u}_i$ can be determined. An example of the results of such a parameterization are shown in figure 6.49. Figure 6.49(a) shows the original mesh that is to be parameterized. The mannequin head is already topologically a disk, but the mesh is cut further to reduce stretch in the parameterization. The shape-preserving parameterization is illustrated in figure 6.49(b).

Stretch Minimization

The shape-preserving parameterization does not always yield desirable results. To improve on the existing parameterization, it is necessary to quantify desirable parameterizations in some way. To do so Sander et al. [107] define *stretch*. Stretch measures how much a parameter space triangle differs from the original mesh triangle. To measure stretch we define the affine mapping from $\mathbb{R}^2$ to $\mathbb{R}^3$

$$S(\mathbf{u}) := \frac{\mathbf{v}_0 \text{area}(\mathbf{u}, \mathbf{u}_1, \mathbf{u}_2) + \mathbf{v}_1 \text{area}(\mathbf{u}, \mathbf{u}_2, \mathbf{u}_0) + \mathbf{v}_2 \text{area}(\mathbf{u}, \mathbf{u}_0, \mathbf{u}_2)}{\text{area}(\mathbf{u}_0, \mathbf{u}_1, \mathbf{u}_2)}$$

which corresponds to creating a weighted average from barycentric coordinates. Let $\mathbf{u} = (s\ t)^T$. The partial derivatives of S are constant over s and t since the mapping is affine. The signed area of a triangle in $\mathbb{R}^2$ is given by

$$\text{area}(\mathbf{u}_0, \mathbf{u}_1, \mathbf{u}_2) := ((s_1 - s_0)(t_2 - t_0) - (s_2 - s_0)(t_1 - t_0))/2$$

so that the partial derivatives of S are

$$\frac{\partial S}{\partial s} = (\mathbf{v}_0(t_1 - t_2) + \mathbf{v}_1(t_2 - t_0) + \mathbf{v}_2(t_0 - t_1))/(2A)$$

$$\frac{\partial S}{\partial t} = (\mathbf{v}_0(s_2 - t_1) + \mathbf{v}_1(s_0 - s_2) + \mathbf{v}_2(s_1 - s_0))/(2A)$$

where $A := \text{area}(\mathbf{u}_0, \mathbf{u}_1, \mathbf{u}_2)$. Let Γ and γ be the maximum and minimum singular value respectively of the Jacobian $J = (\frac{\partial S}{\partial s}\ \frac{\partial S}{\partial t})$. The singular values are the square root of the eigenvalues of the matrix $J^T J$. The singular values are given by [107]

$$\Gamma = \sqrt{\frac{1}{2}\left((a+c) + \sqrt{(a-c)^2 + 4b^2}\right)}$$

$$\gamma = \sqrt{\frac{1}{2}\left((a+c) - \sqrt{(a-c)^2 + 4b^2}\right)}$$

where $a := \frac{\partial S}{\partial s} \cdot \frac{\partial S}{\partial s}$, $b := \frac{\partial S}{\partial s} \cdot \frac{\partial S}{\partial t}$ and $c := \frac{\partial S}{\partial t} \cdot \frac{\partial S}{\partial t}$. The singular values represent the largest and smallest lengths obtained when mapping a unit vector from the parameter domain to the surface. Two measures of stretch can be defined, namely the worst-case stretch of a triangle T, $L^\infty(T) = \Gamma$, and the root-mean-square stretch

$$L^2(T) = \sqrt{(\Gamma^2 + \gamma^2)/2} = \sqrt{(a+c)/2}.$$

For stretch minimization we use the root-mean-quare stretch metric. If $\Gamma = \gamma$, then the parameterization is a *conformal mapping* and the mapping preserves angles.

The stretch for each triangle can now be computed. To increase the quality of parameterizations Yoshizawa et al.[140] developed an algorithm to systematically reduce stretch for the shape-preserving parameterization. To do so, they define the stretch per vertex as

$$\sigma(\mathbf{u}_i) := \sqrt{\sum_{j=0}^{n-1} \text{area}(T_j)\sigma^2(U_j) / \sum_{j=0}^{n-1} \text{area}(T_j)}$$

where n is the number of triangles adjacent to vertex i, T_j is the mesh triangle in $\mathbb{R}^3$ and U_j is the mapped triangle in the parameter space $\mathbb{R}^2$.

Shape-preserving parameterization is performed before the algorithm begins execution. Thereafter the stretch is redistributed between vertices to reduce stretch. To justify the redistribution of stretch we observe that the system of equations that define the parameterization correspond to the minimization of the local quadratic energy function [140]

$$E(\mathbf{u}_i) = \sum_{j=0}^{d-1} w_{i,j}(\mathbf{u}_j - \mathbf{u}_i)^2$$

where d is the valence of vertex i. The optimal positions are found by solving the linear equations

$$\sum_{j=0}^{d-1} w_{i,j}(\mathbf{u}_j - \mathbf{u}_i) = 0\,.$$

This can be interpreted as a mass spring system where the weights $w_{i,j}$ determine how strong each spring is. To decrease stretch we change the spring constants to relax or strengthen each spring by using the new weights

$$w_{i,j}^{new} = w_{i,j}^{old}/\sigma^{\eta}(\mathbf{u}_j)$$

where $\eta < 1$ determines how quickly the stretch is distributed. The value η can be used to control the quality of the parameterization and speed. The mesh is reparameterized with the new weights and the process is repeated until there is no more improvement in the overall stretch of the mesh. Stretch minimization applied to the mannequin head yields the parameterization in figure 6.49(d).

Mean Value Coordinates

Another alternative proposed by Floater [36] are *mean value coordinates*, so called because the weights are derived from an application of the mean value theorem for harmonic functions. The derivation of the weights is omitted. Figure 6.51 illustrates the information required to compute the

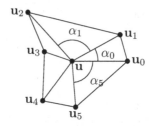

Figure 6.51: Mean value coordinates: Computation of weights.

weights for parameterization. The weights for a vertex i of valence d and neighbors $j = 1, \ldots, d-1$ are given by

$$w_{i,j} = \frac{\lambda_j}{\sum_{k=0}^{d-1} \lambda_k}$$

where

$$\lambda_j = \frac{\tan(\alpha_{j-1}/2) + \tan(\alpha_j/2)}{\|\mathbf{v}_j - \mathbf{v}\|} \, .$$

The mean value coordinates $w_{i,j}$ form a partition of unity and are all positive. After parameterization of the mannequin we obtain the parameterization in figure 6.49(c).

Several other parameterizations are available including angle based flattening [116] and periodic global parameterization [103]. A survey of some techniques can be found in [37].

6.11.3 Rasterization of the Geometry Image

The geometry image is created by considering a discrete regular sampling of the rectangle in $\mathbb{R}^2$. At each of these discrete sample points, the triangle that covers the point is determined which can be determined by computing the barycentric coordinates of the sample point for each triangle. The texture coordinates are used for this computation, not the vertices of the triangle. No more than two triangles should have valid barycentric coordinates (there will only be two such triangles if the sample point lies on an edge). The barycentric coordinates are then used to compute a weighted average of the vertices of the triangle and the resulting vertex is written to the geometry image. There are many ways to increase the speed of rasterization, including writing a conventional rasterizer which renders each of the triangles onto the geometry image and spatial partitioning. We have selected to follow a simpler approach and determine for each line of the geometry image which triangles intersect that line. The number of triangles to test for each sample is reduced significantly by this simple optimization.

To ensure that the original mesh is reproduced to some degree of accuracy, a topological sideband must be stored. This topological sideband stores information about the cut used. If the vertices of the cut are stored in the geometry image, and are equally spaced for both the edges created from each cut edge, the the topological sideband can be used to stitch together the mesh created from the geometry image.

This approach will create a geometry image that matches the polygonal nature of the mesh. It may be more desirable to compute points for the geometry image based on a smooth surface that interpolates the mesh. In this case the triangle can be subdivided repeatedly using an interpolating subdivision scheme until a point on the subdivision surface that corresponds to the sample point is found.

6.12 Interpolation of Geometry Images

In this section we apply harmonic interpolation to interpolate surfaces. Our goal is not to produce a robust or accurate surface fitting algorithm, but to instead try to determine what quality of surface is produced by harmonic interpolation. To provide a variety of interesting surfaces, we create a geometry image [52] from a triangle mesh. The resulting geometry image allows a tensor product surface to be used to interpolate the data [88]. We thus try to develop surface fitting algorithms that use harmonic interpolation for the surface, rather than other (perhaps more effective) techniques. We need two important results for the surface fitting algorithm. The first one involves "rotation" of the control points. We call the procedure "rotation" because we evaluate new control points that are parametrically further along the curve than the original control points, and the curve is periodic. The uniform harmonic curve interpolates the control points at $t = \frac{j}{n}$, $j \in \mathbb{Z}$. That is

$$\sum_{k=0}^{n-1} \sigma_k \left(\frac{j}{n} \right) \mathbf{x}_k = \mathbf{x}_j .$$

Since the curve is periodic we have

$$\sum_{k=0}^{n-1} \sigma_k \left(\frac{j}{n} + 1 \right) \mathbf{x}_k = \mathbf{x}_j .$$

So we could define the harmonic interpolation as

$$\sum_{k=0}^{n-1} \sigma_k(t+1)\mathbf{y}_k$$

where

$$\mathbf{y}_j = \sum_{k=0}^{n-1} \sigma_k\left(\frac{j}{n}+1\right)\mathbf{x}_k.$$

The generalization follows in the following theorem.

Definition 6.1. *"Rotation" by a parameter value o will be written as*

$$\sum_{k=0}^{n-1} \sigma_k(t)\mathbf{y}_k$$

where

$$\mathbf{y}_j = \sum_{k=0}^{n-1} \sigma_k\left(\frac{j}{n}+o\right)\mathbf{x}_k.$$

Theorem 6.1. *We have*

$$\sum_{k=0}^{n-1} \sigma_k(t+o)\mathbf{x}_k = \sum_{k=0}^{n-1} \sigma_k(t)\mathbf{y}_k.$$

Proof. We consider the even and odd cases separately.

Odd case $(n = 2m + 1)$ From equation 4.25 we see that

$$J^u = P_0 + \sum_{j=1}^{m}\left(\lambda^{ju}P_j + \lambda^{-ju}P_{-j}\right).$$

To permutate the control points of polygon $\mathbf{X}$ we evaluate $J^u\mathbf{X}$. To apply two permutations in sequence, J^u and J^s, we evaluate

$$J^u J^s \mathbf{X}.$$

We thus need to calculate

$$J^u J^s = \left(P_0 + \sum_{j=1}^{m}\left(\lambda^{ju}P_j + \lambda^{-ju}P_{-j}\right)\right)\left(P_0 + \sum_{j=1}^{m}\left(\lambda^{js}P_j + \lambda^{-js}P_{-j}\right)\right).$$

From section 4.17 we know that $P_j P_k = 0$ for $j \neq k$ and $P_j^2 = P_j$ so that

$$J^u J^s = P_0 + \sum_{j=1}^{m} \left(\lambda^{j(u+s)} P_j + \lambda^{-j(u+s)} P_{-j} \right) = J^{u+s} .$$

Let $s = on$, and $u = nt$. We also know how to calculate the entries of $J^s \mathbf{X}$ from equation 4.32. The entries are

$$J^{on} \mathbf{X} = \begin{pmatrix} \sum_{k=0}^{n-1} \sigma_k(o) \mathbf{x}_k \\ \sum_{k=0}^{n-1} \sigma_k(o + \frac{1}{n}) \mathbf{x}_k \\ \sum_{k=0}^{n-1} \sigma_k(o + \frac{2}{n}) \mathbf{x}_k \\ \vdots \\ \sum_{k=0}^{n-1} \sigma_k(o + \frac{n-1}{n}) \mathbf{x}_k \end{pmatrix} .$$

The harmonic interpolation of the polygon $J^s \mathbf{X}$ is given by $J^u J^s \mathbf{X} = J^{u+s} \mathbf{X}$. If we only consider the first entry of $J^u J^s \mathbf{X}$ we have

$$\sum_{k=0}^{n-1} \sigma_k(t+o) \mathbf{x}_k = \sum_{k=0}^{n-1} \sigma_k(t) \mathbf{y}_k$$

with

$$\mathbf{y}_j = \sum_{k=0}^{n-1} \sigma_k \left(\frac{j}{n} + o \right) \mathbf{x}_k .$$

Even case ($n = 2m$)   The proof in the even case is similar. From equation 4.34 we see that

$$J^u = P_0 + (-1)^u P_m + \sum_{j=1}^{m-1} \left(\lambda^{ju} P_j + \lambda^{-ju} P_{-j} \right) .$$

To permutate the control points of polygon $\mathbf{X}$ we evaluate $J^u \mathbf{X}$. To apply two permutations in sequence, J^u and J^s, we evaluate $J^u J^s \mathbf{X}$. We thus need to calculate $J^u J^s$. Once again we use $P_j P_k = 0$ for $j \neq k$ and $P_j^2 = P_j$ so that

$$J^u J^s = P_0 + (-1)^{(u+s)} P_m + \sum_{j=1}^{m-1} \left(\lambda^{j(u+s)} P_j + \lambda^{-j(u+s)} P_{-j} \right) = J^{u+s} .$$

Let $s = on$, and $u = nt$. We also know how to calculate the entries of $J^s\mathbf{X}$ from equation 4.39. The entries are

$$J^{on}\mathbf{X} = \begin{pmatrix} \sum_{k=0}^{n-1} \sigma_k(o)\mathbf{x}_k \\ \sum_{k=0}^{n-1} \sigma_k(o + \frac{1}{n})\mathbf{x}_k \\ \sum_{k=0}^{n-1} \sigma_k(o + \frac{2}{n})\mathbf{x}_k \\ \vdots \\ \sum_{k=0}^{n-1} \sigma_k(o + \frac{n-1}{n})\mathbf{x}_k \end{pmatrix}$$

where σ_k has been defined in equation 4.40. The harmonic interpolation of the polygon $J^s\mathbf{X}$ is given by $J^u J^s\mathbf{X} = J^{u+s}\mathbf{X}$. If we only consider the first entry of $J^u J^s\mathbf{X}$ we have

$$\sum_{k=0}^{n-1} \sigma_k(t + o)\mathbf{x}_k = \sum_{k=0}^{n-1} \sigma_k(t)\mathbf{y}_k$$

with

$$\mathbf{y}_j = \sum_{k=0}^{n-1} \sigma_k\left(\frac{j}{n} + o\right)\mathbf{x}_k. \qquad \square$$

This theorem allows us to place the control points in a more convenient arrangement in certain situations. In the next theorem, we show that we can replace the existing n control points by $n + m$ new control points and still have the same curve.

Theorem 6.2. *For every curve* $\mathbf{q}(t)$ *produced by harmonic interpolation of* n *points, the same curve can be produced by harmonic interpolation of* $n + m$ *(possibly different) points determined by* $\mathbf{q}(t)$. *Given* $\mathbf{x}_k$, *there exists* $\mathbf{y}_k$ *so that*

$$\sum_{k=0}^{n-1} \sigma_k^n(t)\mathbf{x}_k = \sum_{k=0}^{n+m-1} \sigma_k^{n+m}(t)\mathbf{y}_k.$$

Proof. In section 4.13 we introduced Lagrange interpolation by solving the system of equations $\mathbf{q}(t_j) = \mathbf{x}_j$, $t_j = 2\pi j/n$, with

$$\mathbf{q}(t) = \mathbf{a}_0 + \sum_{k=1}^{m} (\mathbf{a}_k \cos kt + \mathbf{b}_k \sin kt)$$

for $\mathbf{a}_k$ and $\mathbf{b}_k$. This was only applied to the case where n is odd. In section 4.18 we saw that this corresponds precisely to harmonic interpolation with n odd. In particular we note the similarity between equations 4.27 and

4.13. Likewise, when n is even $(n = 2m)$, we find harmonic interpolation corresponds to the solution of

$$\mathbf{q}(t) = \mathbf{a}_0 + \mathbf{a}_m \cos(mt) + \sum_{k=1}^{m-1} (\mathbf{a}_k \cos(kt) + \mathbf{b}_k \sin(kt))$$

which is simply

$$\mathbf{q}(t) = \mathbf{a}_0 + \sum_{k=1}^{m} (\mathbf{a}_k \cos(kt) + \mathbf{b}_k \sin(kt))$$

with the added restriction that $\mathbf{b}_m = \mathbf{0}$. The solution to the system of equations $\mathbf{q}(t_k) = \mathbf{x}_k$ is given by

$$\mathbf{a}_0 = \frac{1}{2m} \sum_{j=0}^{2m-1} \mathbf{x}_j$$

$$\mathbf{a}_m = \frac{1}{2m} \sum_{j=0}^{2m-1} \mathbf{x}_j \cos(mt_j)$$

$$\mathbf{b}_m = \frac{1}{2m} \sum_{j=0}^{2m-1} \mathbf{x}_j \sin(mt_j) = \mathbf{0}$$

$$\mathbf{a}_k = \frac{2}{2m} \sum_{j=0}^{2m-1} \mathbf{x}_j \cos(kt_j)$$

$$\mathbf{b}_k = \frac{2}{2m} \sum_{j=0}^{2m-1} \mathbf{x}_j \sin(kt_j) \tag{6.6}$$

since $\sin(mt_j) = 0$ given that $n = 2m$. If we substitute these values into the formula for $\mathbf{q}(t)$ as done in the odd case (equation 4.13) we note that the result corresponds to equation 4.35 and that the data points are interpolated. The above formulation is thus an alternative to the harmonic interpolation described previously. We rewrite $\mathbf{q}(t)$ using the identities

$$\cos(kt) \equiv \frac{1}{2} \left(e^{ikt} + e^{-ikt} \right) \qquad \sin(kt) \equiv -\frac{i}{2} \left(e^{ikt} - e^{-ikt} \right)$$

to get

$$\mathbf{q}(t) = \mathbf{a}_0 + \frac{1}{2} \sum_{k=1}^{m} \left((\mathbf{a}_k - i\mathbf{b}_k) e^{ikt} + (\mathbf{a}_k + i\mathbf{b}_k) e^{-ikt} \right) .$$

The system of equations $\mathbf{q}(t_j) = \mathbf{x}_j$, with $t_j = 2\pi j/n$, can be written in matrix form by noting that $e^{-ikt_j} = e^{-ik2\pi j/n} = e^{ik2\pi(n-j)/n}$. By defining the $n \times n$ matrix

$$
F := \begin{pmatrix}
1 & 1 & 1 & \cdots & 1 \\
1 & w & w^2 & \cdots & w^{n-1} \\
1 & w^2 & w^4 & \cdots & w^{2(n-1)} \\
\vdots & \vdots & \vdots & \ddots & \vdots \\
1 & w^{n-1} & w^{2(n-1)} & \cdots & w^{(n-1)^2}
\end{pmatrix}
$$

with $w^j := e^{it_j}$ we can write the linear system of equations as

$$
FP \begin{pmatrix} \mathbf{c}_0 \\ \mathbf{c}_1 \\ \mathbf{c}_2 \\ \vdots \\ \mathbf{c}_{n-1} \end{pmatrix} = \begin{pmatrix} \mathbf{x}_0 \\ \mathbf{x}_1 \\ \mathbf{x}_2 \\ \vdots \\ \mathbf{x}_{n-1} \end{pmatrix}
$$

where P is an appropriate permutation matrix. A permutation matrix is a matrix that contains exactly one 1 in each row and column. The coefficients $\mathbf{c}_j$ are given by

$$
\mathbf{c}_0 = \mathbf{a}_0
$$
$$
\mathbf{c}_k = \frac{1}{2}\left(\mathbf{a}_k - i\mathbf{b}_k\right), \quad k = 1, 2, \ldots, m-1
$$
$$
\mathbf{c}_k = \frac{1}{2}\left(\mathbf{a}_k + i\mathbf{b}_k\right), \quad k = m, m+1, \ldots, n-1.
$$

The matrix FP is thus unitary and invertible, and only one solution exists, namely equation 4.12 for n odd and equation 6.6 for n even. Now suppose we have n points, and that we have found the solution for $\mathbf{a}_k$ and $\mathbf{b}_k$ using equation 4.12 or equation 6.6. If we want the same curve, but with $n + p$ coefficients, we simply define

$$
\mathbf{a}_k := \mathbf{0}, \quad \mathbf{b}_k := \mathbf{0}, \quad k > m.
$$

These definitions ensure that $\mathbf{q}(t)$ remains the same, even though more coefficients are used in the definition. Now we consider the curve

$$
\mathbf{p}(t) = \mathbf{a}_0 + \sum_{k=1}^{r}\left(\mathbf{a}_k \cos(kt) + \mathbf{b}_k \sin(kt)\right)
$$

with $n + p = 2r$ if $n + p$ is even, and $n + p = 2r + 1$ if $n + p$ is odd. To solve for the coefficients we require $\mathbf{p}(t_j) = \mathbf{q}(t_j)$ with $t_j = 2\pi j/(n + p)$

and $j = 0, 1, \ldots, n + p - 1$. We thus have $n + p$ unknowns and $n + p$ equations. We know that equation 4.12 provides a solution in the odd case, and that equation 6.6 provides a solution in the even case. We also know that $\mathbf{q}(t)$ extended to have $n + p$ coefficients is a solution. As we have shown earlier, there is only one solution, namely the coefficients of the extended $\mathbf{q}(t)$. The solution provided by equation 4.12 or 6.6 is identical to the solution provided by extending $\mathbf{q}(t)$. The solution provided by extending $\mathbf{q}(t)$ is then the only solution, and the solution has a harmonic interpolation representation. We thus see that any curve described by n coefficients can also be described by $n + p$ coefficients.   □

We have verified the existence of a curve defined by more control points, that still interpolates the original control points. In the next theorem we determine the control points of this curve for harmonic interpolation.

Theorem 6.3. *To insert extra control points into the curve produced by harmonic interpolation we replace the existing n points $\mathbf{x}_k$ by $n + m$ new points $\mathbf{y}_k$ so that*

$$\sum_{k=0}^{n-1} \sigma_k^n(t)\mathbf{x}_k = \sum_{k=0}^{n+m-1} \sigma_k^{n+m}(t)\mathbf{y}_k,$$

with

$$\sigma_k^n(t) := \sigma^n(t - k/n), \quad \sigma^n(t) := \begin{cases} \dfrac{\sin(n\pi t)}{n\sin(\pi t)}, & \text{if } n \text{ is odd} \\[2ex] \cos(\pi t)\dfrac{\sin(n\pi t)}{n\sin(\pi t)}, & \text{if } n \text{ is even} \end{cases}$$

We find that

$$\mathbf{y}_j = \sum_{k=0}^{n-1} \sigma_k^n\left(\frac{j}{n+m}\right)\mathbf{x}_k$$

is a solution.

Proof. We want to find $n + m$ vectors $\mathbf{y}_k$ so that

$$\sum_{k=0}^{n-1} \sigma_k^n(t)\mathbf{x}_k = \sum_{k=0}^{n+m-1} \sigma_k^{n+m}(t)\mathbf{y}_k.$$

We thus need $n + m$ equations to solve. We choose the equations

$$\sum_{k=0}^{n-1} \sigma_k^n\left(\frac{j}{n+m}\right)\mathbf{x}_k = \sum_{k=0}^{n+m-1} \sigma_k^{n+m}\left(\frac{j}{n+m}\right)\mathbf{y}_k, \quad j = 0, \ldots, n+m-1.$$

$$(6.7)$$

From harmonic interpolation we have

$$\sum_{k=0}^{n+m-1} \sigma_k^{n+m}\left(\frac{j}{n+m}\right)\mathbf{y}_k = \mathbf{y}_j \,.$$

We thus obtain the solution

$$\mathbf{y}_j = \sum_{k=0}^{n-1} \sigma_k^n\left(\frac{j}{n+m}\right)\mathbf{x}_k \,.$$

All that remains is to prove that

$$\sum_{k=0}^{n-1} \sigma_k^n(t)\mathbf{x}_k = \sum_{k=0}^{n+m-1} \sigma_k^{n+m}(t)\mathbf{y}_k \,.$$

Now, suppose we solved the equations

$$\sum_{k=0}^{n-1} \sigma_k^n\left(t+\frac{j}{n+m}\right)\mathbf{x}_k = \sum_{k=0}^{n+m-1} \sigma_k^{n+m}\left(t+\frac{j}{n+m}\right)\mathbf{z}_k \qquad (6.8)$$

for a given $t \in \mathbb{R}$ and $j = 0,\ldots,n+m-1$, and assume that the curve produced is identical to the original curve. Then these equations hold for all $t \in \mathbb{R}$ including $t = 0$. We then have

$$\sum_{k=0}^{n-1} \sigma_k^n\left(\frac{j}{n+m}\right)\mathbf{x}_k = \sum_{k=0}^{n+m-1} \sigma_k^{n+m}\left(\frac{j}{n+m}\right)\mathbf{y}_k = \mathbf{y}_j, \quad j = 0,\ldots,n+m-1$$

and

$$\sum_{k=0}^{n-1} \sigma_k^n\left(\frac{j}{n+m}\right)\mathbf{x}_k = \sum_{k=0}^{n+m-1} \sigma_k^{n+m}\left(\frac{j}{n+m}\right)\mathbf{z}_k = \mathbf{z}_k, \quad j = 0,\ldots,n+m-1$$

and thus $\mathbf{z}_k = \mathbf{y}_k$. Thus the solution $\mathbf{y}_k$ produces the desired curve, and theorem 6.2 guarantees that the curve exists. $\qquad\qquad\qquad\qquad\qquad\square$

An interesting consequence of theorem 6.3, is that the σ_k^n functions can be written in terms of σ_ℓ^{n+m} functions as

$$\sigma_k^n(t) = \sum_{\ell=0}^{n+m-1} \sigma_\ell^{n+m}(t)\sigma_k^n\left(\frac{\ell}{n+m}\right)$$

with $m \geq 0$. To illustrate theorem 6.1 and 6.3, we apply the theorems to figure 4.27(b). Figure 6.52(a) shows the effect of theorem 6.1 and figure 6.52(b) illustrates theorem 6.3 applied to figure 6.52(a).

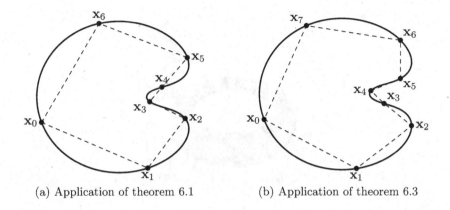

(a) Application of theorem 6.1   (b) Application of theorem 6.3

Figure 6.52: Application of theorems 6.1 and 6.3 (with $m = 1$).

6.13   Geometry Images — Approximation

Data provided in a triangle mesh or geometry image may contain noise. The surface produced may thus have unnecessary undulations to fit the data. This is a considerable problem for harmonic interpolation since cusps are easily produced. We do however have a useful result from the previous section in theorem 6.3. Theorem 6.3 states that

$$\sum_{k=0}^{n-1} \sigma_k^n(t)\mathbf{x}_k = \sum_{k=0}^{n+m-1} \sigma_k^{n+m}(t)\mathbf{y}_k$$

where

$$\mathbf{y}_j = \sum_{k=0}^{n-1} \sigma_k^n \left(\frac{j}{n+m}\right) \mathbf{x}_k \, .$$

If we have redundant data, say $n + m$ points where only n are needed, and we assume equally spaced data, then theorem 6.3 provides a technique for removing the redundant m points. We know that

$$\sum_{k=0}^{n-1} \sigma_k^n(j/n)\mathbf{x}_k = \mathbf{x}_j$$

and the same is true for the new curve. We can thus sample n equally spaced points and use harmonic interpolation on these n points. To determine if removing the m points yields an acceptable surface, we can simply evaluate an error metric for the interpolated data points. If the error metric is below a certain threshold then we can assume the error is due to noise.

Figure 6.53: Scanline-rendered harmonic surface (torus).

6.14 Rendering

We begin by discussing rendering techniques for polynomial tensor product surfaces. One technique that can be applied to obtain polygons, is to evaluate the parametric surface at discrete parametric values. The torus in figure 6.53 was rendered by a scanline renderer in this way. The control points used are the same as those used in figure 6.36(b). Schweitzer [112] discussed a way to perform scanline rendering of parametric surfaces. These techniques are more readily applied to polynomial surfaces such as Bézier patches where the convex hull property applies. To efficiently calculate the surface at parameter values, we can use *differencing*. Forward differencing [1] for polynomial surfaces (such as Bézier patches) are easily calculated. We first illustrate the process for a simple polynomial $f(x) = a + bx + cx^2$, and then we provide the general algorithm. If we wish to evaluate f at parameter values sk denoted by $f(sk) = f_k$, then we may try to use the difference between successive f_k to simplify calculations. The step size s is constant and $k \in \mathbb{Z}$. We have

$$f(sk) = a + bsk + cs^2k^2$$

and

$$f(s(k+1)) = a + bs(k+1) + cs^2(k+1)^2$$
$$= a + bsk + cs^2k^2 + bs + 2cks^2 + cs^2$$

so that

$$\delta_k^1 := f_{k+1} - f_k = bs + 2cks^2 + cs^2.$$

If we view $f(sk)$ as a polynomial in k, then we note that the difference is of lower degree than the original function. In the same way we note that

$$\delta_{k+1}^1 = bs + 2c(k+1)s^2 + cs^2$$
$$= bs + 2cks^2 + 3cs^2 .$$

The difference is then given by

$$\delta_k^2 := \delta_{k+1}^1 - \delta_k^1 = 2cs^2$$

which is constant. If we compute differences again, we see that $\delta_k^j = 0$, $j > 2$. We have thus obtained a series of differences that can be used to calculate the function f at the parameter values sk. The value of $f(sk)$ is calculated from

$$f_{k+1} = f_k + \delta_k^1$$
$$\delta_{k+1}^1 = \delta_k^1 + \delta_k^2$$
$$\delta_k^2 = 2cs^2 .$$

At each step we calculate the next value of the function f, and then we calculate the δ_k^1 and δ_k^2 values required for the next step. We can now apply the same algorithm to an arbitrary polynomial. Assume that we want to calculate the value of a polynomial function f (of degree n) at parameter values sk, denoted by $f(sk) = f_k$. The forward differences are given by

$$\delta_k^1 = f_{k+1} - f_k$$
$$\delta_k^2 = \delta_{k+1}^1 - \delta_k^1$$
$$\delta_k^3 = \delta_{k+1}^2 - \delta_k^2$$
$$\vdots$$
$$\delta_k^n = \delta_{k+1}^{n-1} - \delta_k^{n-1} .$$

The forward differences δ^{n+1} are all zero. With a few calculations the forward difference δ_0^k can be calculated (using the above formulas). We need the function values $f_0, f_1, \ldots f_{n+1}$ to do so. We can then calculate f_k as follows

$$f_k = f_{k-1} + \delta_{k-1}^1$$
$$\delta_k^1 = \delta_{k-1}^1 + \delta_{k-1}^2$$
$$\delta_k^2 = \delta_{k-1}^2 + \delta_{k-1}^3$$
$$\vdots$$
$$\delta_k^{n-1} = \delta_{k-1}^{n-1} + \delta_{k-1}^n .$$

Central differencing [1] may also be used. In some applications we may wish to vary the stepsize s, if so, we must apply an adaptive differencing algorithm [82]. Differencing may be used to produce polygons efficiently for display. Using the formulation of harmonic interpolation as Chebyshev polynomials (section 4.26) we obtain an algebraic function. The function $\phi(s)$ makes application of forward differencing difficult. However, the Chebyshev form can be evaluated quickly due to the lack of trigonometric functions. We have considered how to convert parametric surfaces to polygonal models that can be rasterized. We postpone a discussion on raytracing parametric surfaces to chapter 7. Next we consider approximation of surfaces produced by harmonic interpolation.

6.15   Approximating Basis Functions

The harmonic surfaces are difficult to ray trace, even using interval analysis. Much of the literature on ray tracing parametric patches exploit the convex hull property of Bézier patches. We have no similar result for harmonic surfaces. Although the techniques of interval analysis do provide a solution for rendering harmonic surfaces, the process is time consuming. We choose to approximate the harmonic surface by several Bézier patches. To do so, we approximate the σ function by a polynomial, in the form of a Bézier curve.

To approximate the σ function, we must decide on the degree of the polynomial to use, and how many to use. By combining several polynomials and ensuring piecewise continuity, we increase the possibility of modeling the σ function for larger n without using polynomials of excessively high degree. We can thus also reduce the time taken to solve for the coefficients of the polynomial.

We choose to approximate the σ function over separate intervals $[a, b]$ with $\sigma'(a) = \sigma'(b) = 0$, where $'$ denotes the derivative. This is a root finding problem. We choose to use interval analysis, since we want to find all roots of $\sigma'(t)$. The structure of a function can influence the results for interval analysis. By choosing functions that produce tighter bounds under the interval operators we obtain a solution far more quickly. We found that using

$$
\sigma(t) := \begin{cases} \dfrac{1}{n}\left(1 + 2\displaystyle\sum_{j=1}^{m}\cos(2\pi jt)\right), & \text{if } n \text{ is odd} \\[2em] \dfrac{1}{n}\left(1 + \cos(\pi nt) + 2\displaystyle\sum_{j=1}^{m-1}\cos(2\pi jt)\right), & \text{if } n \text{ is even} \end{cases}
$$

and the derivative

$$
\sigma'(t) = \begin{cases} \dfrac{1}{n}\left(-4\pi\displaystyle\sum_{j=1}^{m} j\sin(2\pi jt)\right), & \text{if } n \text{ is odd} \\[2em] \dfrac{1}{n}\left(-\pi n\sin(\pi nt) - 4\pi\displaystyle\sum_{j=1}^{m-1} j\sin(2\pi jt)\right), & \text{if } n \text{ is even} \end{cases}
$$

$$(6.9)$$

from equations 4.27 and 4.35 gave the best results. The root finding of $\sigma(t)$ proceeds without difficulty. We found (experimentally) that using two Bézier curves of degree 5 to approximate each interval between two roots of the σ function provided sufficient accuracy for rendering harmonic curves. We introduce an alternative to this approximation that has more desirable qualities a little later on. As a result, we do not give a rigorous analysis of the approximation quality here. After studying the $\sigma_k(t)$ functions for different values of n, it becomes clear that we need $2(n-1)$ Bézier curves to model the odd case and $2n$ Bézier curves to model the even case.

Once the basis functions have been approximated, the curve can be converted to several Bézier patches. We begin with the equation

$$
\sum_{k=0}^{n-1} \sigma_k(t)\mathbf{x}_k
$$

with $\sigma_k(t)$ approximated by Bézier curves

$$
\sigma_k(t) \approx \sum_{j=0}^{5} B_j^5(t'(t))p_{k,j}
$$

where $p_{k,j}$ is the jth coefficient of the Bézier curve that approximates $\sigma_k(t)$. We have different approximations for different ranges of t, thus we need the function $t'(t)$ to map from the σ parameter to the parameter of the Bézier curve. The curve then becomes

$$\sum_{k=0}^{n-1} \sigma_k(t)\mathbf{x}_k \approx \sum_{k=0}^{n-1}\sum_{j=0}^{5} B_j^5(t'(t))p_{k,j}\mathbf{x}_k$$

$$= \sum_{j=0}^{5} B_j^5(t'(t)) \sum_{k=0}^{n-1} p_{k,j}\mathbf{x}_k \qquad (6.10)$$

for each range of t. The sum $\sum_{k=0}^{n-1} p_{k,j}\mathbf{x}_k$ can be precomputed before rendering so that we have a regular Bézier patch that is sent through the rendering process.

We take each segment of the curve and sample 3 points on the curve. At these 3 points, we calculate both σ_k and σ_k'. These 6 values are used to determine the Bézier coefficients. The coefficients and values form a system of 6 linear equations which is easily solved using standard techniques. If the interval is $[a, b]$ then the sample points are a, b and $(a + b)/2$.

When selecting segments (sample points) we search for the roots of σ_k' for every valid k. Once all these roots are found, segments can be identified for approximation. If we don't use all the roots for determining the segments, then the Bézier coefficients are defined over different ranges and equation 6.10 is not valid. If we have distinct ranges in t over which the curves are all defined, then these form Bézier patches. These patches are piecewise smooth. Since we sample at the ends of the intervals, and use the derivative at these points, two adjacent Bézier curves have the same gradient, and are thus piecewise smooth. Unfortunately, we do not have a guarantee that the data points will be interpolated.

Bézier patches of degree 6 are not common primitives in graphics software. However Cubic Bézier patches are. It would thus be desirable to approximate $\sigma_k(t)$ by cubic Bézier curves. That is

$$\sigma_k(t) \approx \sum_{j=0}^{3} B_j^3(t'(t))p_{k,j} \ .$$

In this case we make use of the properties of Bézier curve to choose the approximation intervals. We choose intervals of the form $[\frac{a}{n}, \frac{a+1}{n}]$ and approximate $\sigma_k(t)$ by a cubic Bézier curve over this interval (as above). Bézier curves interpolate their endpoints, so we know that the approximation of $\sigma_k(t)$ will also interpolate the control points. We may use the values of

$\sigma_k(t)$ at $\frac{a}{n}$ and $\frac{a+1}{n}$ for approximation. We need two more equations to solve for the Bézier coefficients. One option is to use the derivative at these parameter values. We use two more equally spaced values of the function $\sigma_k(t)$. The curve can then be calculated by

$$\sum_{k=0}^{n-1} \sigma_k(t)\mathbf{x}_k \approx \sum_{k=0}^{n-1} \sum_{j=0}^{3} B_j^3(t'(t))p_{k,j}^i \mathbf{x}_k, \qquad \frac{i}{n} \le t < \frac{i+1}{n}$$

$$= \sum_{j=0}^{3} B_j^3(t'(t)) \sum_{k=0}^{n-1} p_{k,j}^i \mathbf{x}_k,$$

so that we can pre-calculate the control points of the Bézier curve. We see that different control points are used for different portions of the curve, indicated by i. We also use the Bézier parameter t' such that

$$t = (1 - t')\frac{i}{n} + t'\frac{i+1}{n}.$$

We can construct Bézier surfaces in a similar manner. We assume that the interpolation points are arranged in a square, the discussion is easily modified for rectangles. The tensor product surface is given by

$$\sum_{k=0}^{n-1} \sigma_k(u) \sum_{\ell=0}^{n-1} \sigma_\ell(v)\mathbf{x}_{k,\ell} \approx \sum_{k=0}^{n-1} \sum_{j=0}^{3} B_j^3(u')p_{k,j} \sum_{\ell=0}^{n-1} \sum_{i=0}^{3} B_i^3(v')p_{\ell,i}\mathbf{x}_{k,\ell}$$

$$= \sum_{j=0}^{3} \sum_{i=0}^{3} B_j^3(u')B_i^3(v') \sum_{k=0}^{n-1} \sum_{\ell=0}^{n-1} p_{k,j}p_{\ell,i}\mathbf{x}_{k,\ell}$$

so that we can calculate the control points of the patch beforehand. Using this approach, we have the ability to approximately represent harmonic tensor product surfaces as Bézier patches. In addition, we can use harmonic interpolation for surface fitting to produce a set Bézier patches that smoothly interpolates the surface. To illustrate this approach we have placed the previous example of a harmonic tensor product surface (figure 6.53) next to an approximation using Bézier patches (using the algorithm to produce cubic Bézier patches). The results are displayed in figure 6.54. Since there are 4×4 interpolation points we produce 16 Bézier patches to approximate the surface. The Bézier patches are illustrated in figure 6.55. The patches have been color coded in figure 6.55(b) to allow easy identification.

6.16   Combined Results

To illustrate the techniques discussed throughout this section, we have applied the approximation algorithm to a tensor product surface created from

(a) Harmonic tensor product surface   (b) Approximation

Figure 6.54: Approximation of harmonic tensor product surface.

(a) Surface   (b) Color coded Bézier patches

Figure 6.55: Bézier patches used to approximate figure 6.53.

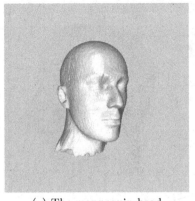
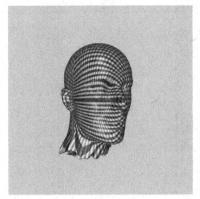

(a) The mannequin head   (b) Color coded Bézier patches

Figure 6.56: Final rendering of mannequin head formed from Bézier patches.

a geometry image of the mannequin and Spock data sets. For the geometry image we chose to use a flattened octahedron. We also chose to sample at a higher rate than required so that we can apply theorem 6.3 to reduce the size of the geometry image. We reduce the smoothed geometry image to approximately 25% of its original size. Finally, we approximate the obtained harmonic surface by a series of cubic Bézier patches. Figure 6.56 displays the results for the mannequin data set. Figure 6.56(b) displays the Bézier patches in a color coded form to highlight how Bézier patches have been used. For the mannequin data set we used a 150×150 geometry image (reduced from 400×400). The same procedure has been applied to the Spock data set in figure 6.57. Once again we have included color coded Bézier patches in figure 6.57(b).

6.17 Curvature

We have seen a few problems with harmonic interpolation. One of the greatest problems encountered was the undulation of the surfaces produced. In this section we measure the curvature of a few surfaces produced by harmonic interpolation. We use the measures introduced in section 6.6 to determine curvature. To measure the curvature of surfaces produced by harmonic interpolation, we sampled known parametric surfaces. We then compare the curvature of the parametric surface with the curvature of the harmonic surface. In each case, we only sampled 24×4 points on the parametric surface. The surfaces tested are as follows

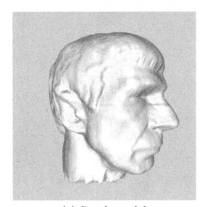

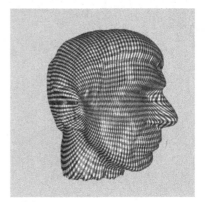

(a) Spock model   (b) Color coded Bézier patches

Figure 6.57: Final rendering of Spock formed from Bézier patches.

- A quadrilateral

$$\mathbf{f}(u,v) = \begin{pmatrix} 3u - 1.5 \\ 3v - 1.5 \\ 0 \end{pmatrix}.$$

- A partial sphere

$$\mathbf{f}(u,v) = \begin{pmatrix} r\cos\rho\cos\theta \\ r\cos\rho\sin\theta \\ r\sin\rho \end{pmatrix}$$

with $\rho := 0.9(\pi v - \frac{\pi}{2})$ and $\theta := 2\pi u$.

- A sphere

$$\mathbf{f}(u,v) = \begin{pmatrix} r\cos\rho\cos\theta \\ r\cos\rho\sin\theta \\ r\sin\rho \end{pmatrix}$$

with $\rho := 2\pi v - \frac{\pi}{2}$ and $\theta := 2\pi u$.

- A torus

$$\mathbf{f}(u,v) = \begin{pmatrix} (r\cos\rho + R)\cos\theta \\ r\sin\rho \\ (r\cos\rho + R)\sin\theta \end{pmatrix}$$

with $\rho := -2\pi v$ and $\theta := 2\pi u$.

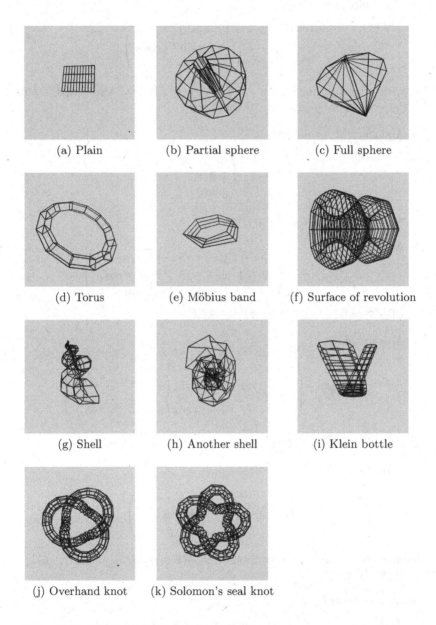

(a) Plain   (b) Partial sphere   (c) Full sphere

(d) Torus   (e) Möbius band   (f) Surface of revolution

(g) Shell   (h) Another shell   (i) Klein bottle

(j) Overhand knot   (k) Solomon's seal knot

Figure 6.58: Control points for interpolation of various parametric surfaces.

- The *Möbius band*

$$\mathbf{f}(u,v) = \begin{pmatrix} \left(2 - t\sin\frac{s}{2}\right)\sin s \\ \left(2 - t\sin\frac{s}{2}\right)\cos s \\ t\cos\frac{s}{2} \end{pmatrix}$$

with $s := 4\pi u$ and $t := v - 0.5$. We actually have two strips in this case to ensure periodicity of the data.

- A *surface of revolution*

$$\mathbf{f}(u,v) = \begin{pmatrix} \theta \\ (\sin\theta + 2)\cos\rho \\ (\sin\theta + 2)\sin\rho \end{pmatrix}$$

with $\theta := 2\pi u - \pi$ and $\rho := 2\pi v$.

- A *shell*

$$\mathbf{f}(u,v) = \begin{pmatrix} (r-1)\cos\theta + (r-1)\cos\theta\cos\rho \\ (r-1)\sin\theta + (r-1)\sin\theta\cos\rho \\ -(r^2-1) + (r-1)\sin\rho \end{pmatrix}$$

with $\theta := 6\pi u$, $\rho := 2\pi v$ and $r := e^u$.

- Another *shell*

$$\mathbf{f}(u,v) = \begin{pmatrix} (r-1)\sin\rho \\ (r-1)\left(1+\cos\rho\right)\sin\left(\theta - \frac{\sin(2\rho+\pi/2)}{2}\right) \\ (r-1)\left(1+\cos\rho\right)\cos\left(\theta - \frac{\sin(2\rho+\pi/2)}{2}\right) \end{pmatrix}$$

with $\theta := 6\pi u$, $\rho := 2\pi v$ and $r := e^u$.

- A portion of the *Klein bottle*

$$\mathbf{f}(u,v) = \begin{pmatrix} x + r\cos(\rho+\pi) \\ 16\sin\theta \\ r\sin\rho \end{pmatrix}$$

with $\theta := \pi u + \pi$, $\rho := 2\pi v$, $r := 4(1 - \cos\theta/2)$ and $x := 6(1 + \sin\theta)\cos\theta$.

- An *overhand knot*

$$\mathbf{f}(t) = \begin{pmatrix} \cos\theta\left(10 + 4\sin\left(\frac{3}{2}\theta\right)\right) \\ \sin\theta\left(10 + 4\sin\left(\frac{3}{2}\theta\right)\right) \\ 4\cos\left(\frac{3}{2}\theta\right) \end{pmatrix}$$

with $\theta := 4\pi t$. This formula produces a curve. To obtain a surface, we compute the *Frenet frame* for each point on the curve and construct a circle, using this coordinate system, around the curve and in a plane perpendicular to the curve. The construction produces a tube following the path of the curve.

- The *Solomon's Seal knot*

$$\mathbf{f}(t) = \begin{pmatrix} \cos(2\theta)\left(1 + \frac{2}{5}\cos(5\theta)\right) \\ \sin(2\theta)\left(1 + \frac{2}{5}\cos(5\theta)\right) \\ \frac{1}{2}\sin(5\theta) \end{pmatrix}$$

with $\theta := 2\pi t$. This formula produces a curve. As in the case above, we use the *Frenet frame* to produce a tube that follows the path of the curve.

A few of the surfaces cover certain areas twice. The sphere is one such surface. To render the surface we place restrictions on the u and v parameters so that each portion of the surface is only covered once. In general the values are such that $0 < u < 1$ and $0 < v < 1$. In the case of the sphere we add the restriction $0 < v < 0.5$. In each case, we have rendered the original parametric surface as well as curvature values. Both Gaussian and mean curvature are used to provide a complete picture. Lighting is omitted on the curvature diagrams to emphasize the measured values. Black indicates little or no curvature, and white indicates high curvature. The control points (drawn as a polygon mesh) for these surfaces are shown in figure 6.58. Curvature is determined numerically for parametric surfaces and analytically for the harmonic surfaces.

We find that harmonic interpolation extends the plane (figure 6.59) a little bit, but otherwise the surface properties appear to be the same.

The shape of the partial sphere differs from the surface produced by harmonic interpolation (figure 6.60) because the partial sphere is not a completely periodic parameterization of the sphere. High curvature is clearly visible at the ends of the harmonic surface.

As we have seen, harmonic interpolation can produce a torus precisely. Figure 6.61 shows the constant Gaussian curvature for the torus. We also see that the harmonic interpolation matches the curvature of the parametric torus. The mean curvature does not match precisely, this can only be due to numerical inaccuracy.

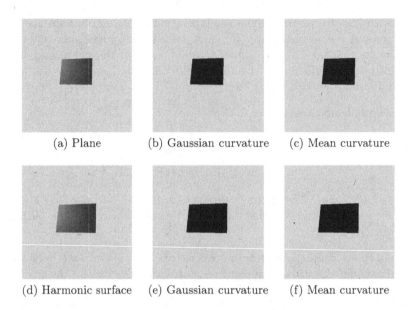

(a) Plane   (b) Gaussian curvature   (c) Mean curvature

(d) Harmonic surface   (e) Gaussian curvature   (f) Mean curvature

Figure 6.59: Comparison of plane and harmonic surface.

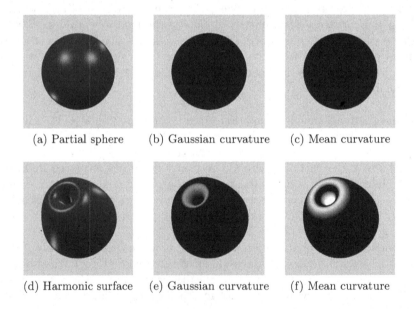

(a) Partial sphere   (b) Gaussian curvature   (c) Mean curvature

(d) Harmonic surface   (e) Gaussian curvature   (f) Mean curvature

Figure 6.60: Comparison of partial sphere and harmonic surface.

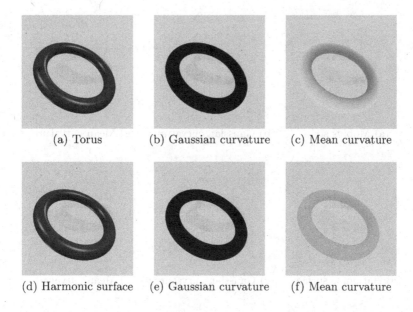

(a) Torus   (b) Gaussian curvature   (c) Mean curvature

(d) Harmonic surface   (e) Gaussian curvature   (f) Mean curvature

Figure 6.61: Comparison of torus and harmonic surface.

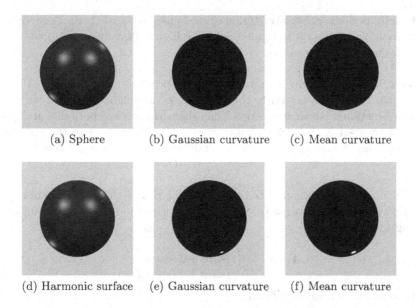

(a) Sphere   (b) Gaussian curvature   (c) Mean curvature

(d) Harmonic surface   (e) Gaussian curvature   (f) Mean curvature

Figure 6.62: Comparison of sphere and harmonic surface.

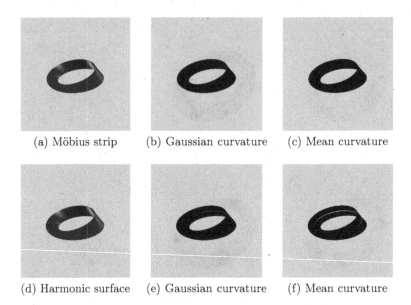

(a) Möbius strip   (b) Gaussian curvature   (c) Mean curvature

(d) Harmonic surface   (e) Gaussian curvature   (f) Mean curvature

Figure 6.63: Comparison of Möbius strip and harmonic surface.

The fully periodic parameterization of the sphere is correctly duplicated by harmonic interpolation in figure 6.62. The high curvature at the poles are due to numerical inaccuracy.

When the Möbius strip is parameterized to produce two strips, as in figure 6.63, the results are fairly consistent with the original strip. If we use the conventional parameterization, then the surface is not periodic, and we have a reversal of the order of the interpolation points where the strip is joined. This reversal of order causes undulations for a large portion of the surface.

Harmonic interpolation fails to interpolate the points on the surface of revolution (figure 6.64) correctly. If we parameterize the surface of revolution using

$$\mathbf{f}(u, v) = \begin{pmatrix} g(\theta) \\ (\sin\theta + 2)\cos\rho \\ (\sin\theta + 2)\sin\rho \end{pmatrix}$$

with $\theta = 4\pi u - \pi$, $\rho = 2\pi v$ and

$$g(\theta) = \begin{cases} \theta, & \theta < \pi \\ 2\pi - \theta, & \text{otherwise} \end{cases}$$

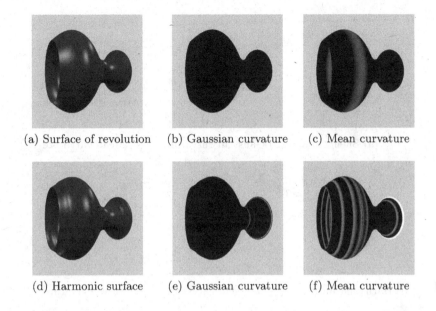

(a) Surface of revolution   (b) Gaussian curvature   (c) Mean curvature

(d) Harmonic surface   (e) Gaussian curvature   (f) Mean curvature

Figure 6.64: Comparison of surface of revolution and harmonic surface.

we obtain a periodic surface. We then add the restriction $0 < u < 0.5$ to obtain the results in figure 6.64. To achieve periodicity, the control points are mirrored. The resulting surface has a sharp change at the edge, but duplicated the parametric surface fairly well. The results are illustrated in figure 6.65.

Although the shape of the harmonic surface in figure 6.66 does not match the parametric surface, it seems to have the same character. The control points are duplicated to obtain a peroidic surface which causes the extension and flattening of the edge.

The Klein bottle is also not periodic. Duplicating control points yields the results in figure 6.67. The harmonic interpolation has high curvature even though artifacts are not really visible.

The overhand knot (figure 6.68) changes direction frequently as indicated by the curvature. The original control points indicate the points where the Frenet frame rotates quickly There is undulation in the segment where the rotation takes place which causes earlier portions of the surface to be enlarged. This region is also characterized by high curvature. The un-

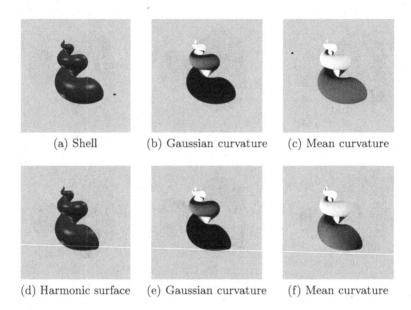

(a) Shell   (b) Gaussian curvature   (c) Mean curvature

(d) Harmonic surface   (e) Gaussian curvature   (f) Mean curvature

Figure 6.65: Comparison of shell and harmonic surface.

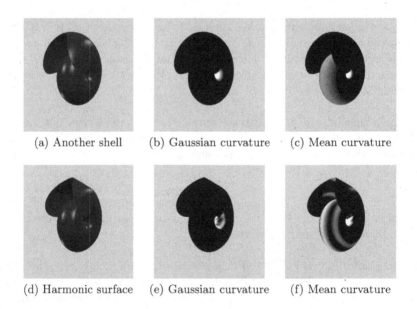

(a) Another shell   (b) Gaussian curvature   (c) Mean curvature

(d) Harmonic surface   (e) Gaussian curvature   (f) Mean curvature

Figure 6.66: Comparison of another shell and harmonic surface.

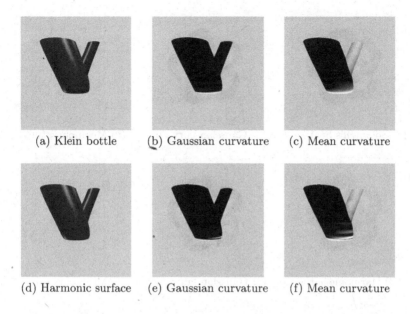

(a) Klein bottle   (b) Gaussian curvature   (c) Mean curvature

(d) Harmonic surface   (e) Gaussian curvature   (f) Mean curvature

Figure 6.67: Comparison of partial Klein bottle and harmonic surface.

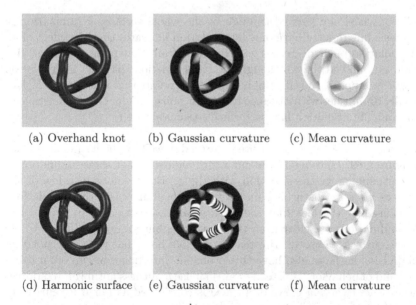

(a) Overhand knot   (b) Gaussian curvature   (c) Mean curvature

(d) Harmonic surface   (e) Gaussian curvature   (f) Mean curvature

Figure 6.68: Comparison of overhand knot and harmonic surface.

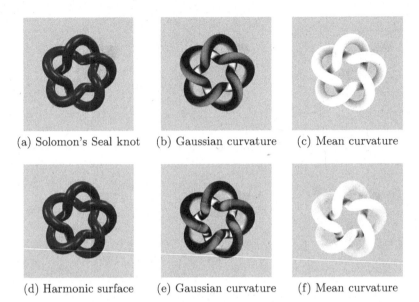

(a) Solomon's Seal knot   (b) Gaussian curvature   (c) Mean curvature

(d) Harmonic surface   (e) Gaussian curvature   (f) Mean curvature

Figure 6.69: Comparison of Solomon's Seal knot and harmonic surface.

dulations have not carried through to the whole surface. Examination of the basis functions of harmonic interpolation indicates that the effect of an interpolation point decreases with distance from that point (although this is not guaranteed). Even though the basis functions have all interpolation points as support, the effect of interpolation points that disturb the surface usually diminishes with distance from that point. Under the circumstances, harmonic interpolation has performed reasonably well.

Solomon's Seal knot is represented reasonably well by the harmonic surface in figure 6.69. Once again the curvature indicates that some undulation is present, similar to the situation with the overhand knot. In a few of the surfaces we note disturbing undulations. In many cases the undulations are caused by the fact that the surfaces are not periodic. In many cases the undulations are clear from the curvature, but are more difficult to see on the surface. However, Halstead et al. [53] note that their interpolating subdivision surfaces also have this problem. Interpolation can often cause this kind of behavior. Halstead et al. [53] use a fairness norm [14] to address these issues, where a curve or surface is considered as *fair* if its curvature plot is continuous and consists of only a few monotone pieces [32].

6.18   C# Implementation

Subdivision surfaces as well as geometry images are implemented in the Mesh class. The SparseMatrix class solves the equations for parameterization. Since the number of vertices involved are large, but connectivity is limited, the SparseMatrix class increases performance significantly. The meshes are visualized using TAO (*www.taoframework.com*).

```
//SparseMatrix.cs
using System;

public class SparseElement {
   public SparseRow row;
   public int col;
   public double x; //the value of the entry
   public SparseElement(SparseRow parent,int col,double x) {
      row=parent; this.col=col; this.x=x;
   }

   public SparseElement(SparseRow parent,SparseElement e) {
      row=parent; col=e.col; x=e.x;
   }
}

public class SparseRow {
   public int row;
   public SparseElement[] data;
   public int n;
   public SparseRow(int row) { this.row=row; data=null; n=0; }

   public SparseRow(SparseRow r) {
      this.row=r.row; this.data=null; n=0;
      for(int i=0;i<r.n;i++) SetValue(r.data[i].col,r.data[i].x);
   }

   public void SetValue(int col,double x) {
      SparseElement[] newdata=null;
      for(int i=0;i<n;i++)
         if(data[i].col==col) { data[i].x=x; return; }
      //not found, add the element
      newdata=new SparseElement[n+1];
      for(i=0;i<n;i++) newdata[i]=data[i];
      data=newdata;
      data[n]=new SparseElement(this,col,x);
      n++;
   }

   public double GetValue(int col) {
      for(int i=0;i<n;i++) if(data[i].col==col) return data[i].x;
      //not found
```

```
      return 0;
   }

   public bool Exists(int col) {
      for(int i=0;i<n;i++)
         if(data[i].col==col) return true;
      //not found
      return false;
   }
}

public class SparseMatrix {
   public SparseRow[] rows;
   public int maxrows, maxcols;
   public SparseMatrix() { maxrows=maxcols=0; rows=null; }
   public SparseMatrix(int rows,int cols) {
      maxrows=rows; maxcols=cols;
      this.rows=new SparseRow[maxrows];
   }

   public SparseMatrix(SparseMatrix M) {
      Resize(M.maxrows,M.maxcols);
      for(int i=0;i<maxrows;i++)
         if(M.rows[i]!=null) rows[i]=new SparseRow(M.rows[i]);
   }

   public double this[int row,int col] {
      get {return rows[row].GetValue(col);}
      set {if(rows[row]==null) rows[row]=new SparseRow(row);
         rows[row].SetValue(col,value);}
   }
   public void Resize(int rows,int cols) {
      if((this.maxrows==rows)&&(this.maxcols==cols)) return;
      if((rows<0)||(cols<0)) {
         maxrows=0; maxcols=0;
         this.rows=null;
      } else {
         maxrows=rows; maxcols=cols;
         this.rows=new SparseRow[maxrows];
      }
   }

   public bool isZero(int row,int col) {
      if(rows[row]==null) return true;
      if(rows[row].Exists(col)) return false;
      return true;
   }

   //Note: number of rows should be the same as columns
   //return value <=0 implies failed.
   // 0 = failed to converge
```

```
// <0 = underdetermined system of equations
public int Jacobi(double[] b,int maxiter,double eps) {
   return Jacobi(b,maxiter,eps,null);
}
public int Jacobi(double[] b,int maxiter,double eps,double[] guess) {
   double[] e, bnew, cb, ob, temp;
   double diff, Mii=0.0;
   int i, j, col;
   bool converged=false;
   if(guess==null)
      if(!Prepare(0)) return -1;

   e=new double[maxrows];
   bnew=new double[maxrows];
   for(i=0;i<maxrows;i++) e[i]=b[i];
   if(guess!=null)
      for(i=0;i<maxrows;i++) b[i]=guess[i];

   cb=b; ob=bnew;

   while((!converged)&&(maxiter>0)) {
      temp=cb; cb=ob; ob=temp;
      diff=0.0;
      for(i=0;i<maxrows;i++) {
         cb[i]=e[i];
         if(rows[i]!=null)
         for(j=0;j<rows[i].n;j++) {
            col=rows[i].data[j].col;
            if(i!=col) {
               cb[i]-=rows[i].data[j].x*ob[col];
            } else Mii=rows[i].data[j].x;
         }
         cb[i]/=Mii;
         diff+=(cb[i]-ob[i])*(cb[i]-ob[i]);
      }
      maxiter--;
      if(diff<eps) converged=true;
   }
   if(cb!=b)
      for(i=0;i<maxrows;i++) b[i]=cb[i];
   return maxiter;
}

//Note: number of rows should be the same as columns
//return value <=0 implies failed.
// 0 = failed to converge
// <0 = underdetermined system of equations
public int GaussSeidel(double[] b,int maxiter,double eps) {
   return GaussSeidel(b,maxiter,eps,null);
}
public int GaussSeidel(double[] b,int maxiter,double eps,double[] guess) {
```

```
    double[] e;
    double diff, bnew, Mii=0.0;
    int i, j, col;
    bool converged=false;
    if(guess==null)
        if(!Prepare(0)) return -1;

    e=new double[maxrows];
    for(i=0;i<maxrows;i++) e[i]=b[i];
    if(guess!=null)
        for(i=0;i<maxrows;i++) b[i]=guess[i];

    while((!converged)&&(maxiter>0)) {
        diff=0.0;
        for(i=0;i<maxrows;i++) {
            bnew=e[i];
            if(rows[i]!=null)
            for(j=0;j<rows[i].n;j++) {
                col=rows[i].data[j].col;
                if(i!=col) bnew-=rows[i].data[j].x*b[col];
                else Mii=rows[i].data[j].x;
            }
            bnew/=Mii;
            diff+=(bnew-b[i])*(bnew-b[i]);
            b[i]=bnew;
        }
        maxiter--;
        if(diff<eps) converged=true;
    }
    return maxiter;
}

//Note: number of rows should be the same as columns
//return value <=0 implies failed.
//  0 = failed to converge
//  <0 = underdetermined system of equations
//  A is the areas provided by radiosity
//  Only suitable for radiosity!
public int Shooting(double[] e,double[] a,int maxiter,double eps) {
    double[] b, db;
    double diff, bnew;
    int i, j, k, col;
    bool converged=false;
    if(!Prepare(0)) return -1;
    b=new double[maxrows];
    db=new double[maxrows];
    for(i=0;i<maxrows;i++) b[i]=0;
    for(i=0;i<maxrows;i++) db[i]=e[i];

    while((!converged)&&(maxiter>0)) {
        diff=0.0; j=0;
```

```
        for(i=1;i<maxrows;i++)
            if(db[i]*a[i]>db[j]*a[j]) j=i;
        b[j]+=db[j];
        for(i=0;i<maxrows;i++) {
            bnew=db[i];
            if(rows[i]!=null)
            for(k=0;k<rows[i].n;k++) {
                col=rows[i].data[k].col;
                if(k==col) bnew+=rows[i].data[k].x*b[j]; }
            }
            diff+=(bnew-db[i])*(bnew-db[i]);
            db[i]=bnew;
        }
        db[j]=0; maxiter--;
        if(diff<eps) converged=true;
    }
    return maxiter;
}
//Make sure that the elements on the diagonal are nonzero. If this can't be done
//then Gauss-Seidel and Jacobi iteration will not work. Very quick check to try
//ordering, if it fails then it reverts to the backtracking version
private bool Prepare(int start) {
    int i,j,k;
    double max;
    bool found;
    SparseElement col;
    SparseRow trow;

    if(start==0) {
        for(i=0;i<maxrows;i++) if(rows[i]==null) return false;
    }
    for(i=0;i<maxrows;i++) {
        found=false; max=0.0;
        for(j=i;(!found) && (j<maxrows);j++) {
            if(rows[j]!=null)
            for(k=0;k<rows[j].n;k++) {
                col=rows[j].data[k];
                if(col.col==i) {
                    if(Math.Abs(col.x)>1e-8)
                    if(Math.Abs(col.x)>max) {
                        //found a later row, swap the rows
                        trow=rows[i]; rows[i]=rows[j]; rows[j]=trow;
                        found=true;
                        max=Math.Abs(col.x);
                        break;
                    }
                }
            }
        }
        if(!found) return PrepareBacktrack(start);
    }
```

```
    return true;
}


//Make sure that the elements on the diagonal are nonzero. If this can't be done
//then Gauss-Seidel and Jacobi iteration will not work.
//This version backtracks to test all options
private bool PrepareBacktrack(int start) {
    int i,j,k;
    bool found;
    SparseElement col;
    SparseRow trow;

    if(start==0)
        for(i=0;i<maxrows;i++)
            if(rows[i]==null) return false;
    //found a solution
    if(start>=maxrows) return true;
    //See if we can get a value in the diagonal for this row
    // if so, we are done, otherwise backtrack and try another option
    i=start;
    found=false;
    //include row i, so that we include the current row
    for(j=i;(!found) && (j<maxrows);j++) {
        if(rows[j]!=null)
        for(k=0;k<rows[j].n;k++) {
            col=rows[j].data[k];
            if(col.col==i) {
                if(Math.Abs(col.x)>1e-8) {
                    //found a later row, swap the rows
                    trow=rows[i]; rows[i]=rows[j]; rows[j]=trow;
                    found=(PrepareBacktrack(start+1));
                    if(!found) {
                        //this did not work, undo the row swap
                        trow=rows[i]; rows[i]=rows[j]; rows[j]=trow;
                    }
                }
            }
        }
    }
    return found;
}


public object Clone() {
    Object o=new SparseMatrix(this); return o;
}
}
```

The Mesh class implements many of the algorithms discussed in this chapter. This class also has several methods for rasterizing geometry images and a corresponding normal map, and saving the texture coordinates used to create the geometry images. The coordinates can be saved in a variety of formats including OFF, Wavefront object gile, METAPOST and the Renderman bytestream format. The Renderman format can be used to render the geometry image with a Renderman compliant renderer. A Set class is provided to manage lists of vertices, edges and faces. It is important that no duplicates are stored and the Set class ensures that this is the case. Each Vertex, Face and Edge contains a set of adjacent edges, faces or vertices (as appropriate). These adjacency sets are used extensively to implement cutting, parameterization and subdivision.

```
//Mesh.cs
using System;
using System.IO;

public class Set {
    public Set() { n=0; size=0; set=null; }

    private void push_back(object x) {
        int ns, i;
        object[] newset;
        if(n<size) set[n]=x;
        else {
            if(size==0) ns=1;
            //Grow by ten percent, but at least 1 position
            else ns=size*110/100+1;
            newset=new object[ns];
            for(i=0;i<size;i++) newset[i]=set[i];
            size=ns; set=newset;
            set[n]=x;
        }
    }

    public void clear() { n=0; size=0; set=null; }

    public int add(object x) {
        for(int i=0;i<n;i++)
            if(set[i].Equals(x)) return i;
        push_back(x); n++;
        return n-1;
    }

    public int addWithoutCheck(object x) {
        push_back(x); n++;
        return n-1;
    }

    public void remove(object x) {
        for(int i=0;i<n;i++) {
            if(set[i].Equals(x)) { set[i]=set[n-1]; n--; return; }
```

```
    }
}

public void remove(int i) {
   if(i<0) return;
   if(i>=n) return;
   set[i]=set[n-1];
   pop_back(); n--;
}

public int index(object x) {
   for(int i=0;i<n;i++) if(set[i].Equals(x)) return i;
   return -1;
}

public bool contains(object x) {
   int i=index(x);
   if(i!=-1) return true;
   else return false;
}

public object match(object x) {
   int i=index(x);
   if(i!=-1) return set[i];
   else return null;
}

public int getCount() { return n; }

public object this[int i] {
   get {return set[i];}
   set {if(i>=n) n=i+1; set[i]=value;}
}

public void setIndex(int i,object x) { set[i]=x; }

//Union operator
public static Set operator+(Set s1,Set s2) {
   int i;
   Set s=new Set();

   for(i=0;i<s1.n;i++) s.add(s1.set[i]);
   for(i=0;i<s2.n;i++) s.add(s2.set[i]);
   return s;
}
//Reserve a minimum of so many items
public void reserve(int s) {
   object[] newset;
   if(s<=size) return;
   else {
      if(s==0) s=1;
```

```
            newset=new object[s];
            for(int i=0;i<size;i++) newset[i]=set[i];
            size=s; set=newset;
        }
    }

    protected object[] set;
    protected int n, size;
}

public class VertexSet: Set {
    public new Vertex match(object x) {
        int i=index(x);
        if(i!=-1) return (Vertex)set[i];
        else return null;
    }

    public new Vertex this[int i] {
        get {return (Vertex)set[i];} set {set[i]=value;}
    }

    public VertexSet Clone() {
        VertexSet v=new VertexSet();
        v.set=(object[])set.Clone();
        v.n=n; v.size=size;
        return v;
    }
}

public class EdgeSet: Set {
    public new Edge match(object x) {
        int i=index(x);
        if(i!=-1) return (Edge)set[i];
        else return null;
    }

    public new Edge this[int i] {
        get {return (Edge)set[i];} set {set[i]=value;}
    }

    public EdgeSet Clone() {
        EdgeSet e=new EdgeSet();
        e.set=(object[])set.Clone();
        e.n=n; e.size=size;
        return e;
    }
}

public class FaceSet: Set {
    public new Face match(object x) {
        int i=index(x);
```

```
      if(i!=-1) return (Face)set[i];
      else return null;
   }

   public new Face this[int i] {
      get {return (Face)set[i];} set {set[i]=value;}
   }

   public FaceSet Clone() {
      FaceSet f=new FaceSet();
      f.set=(object[])set.Clone();
      f.n=n; f.size=size;
      return f;
   }
}

// Although the face class is fairly general in what it can represent,
// many of the methods assume triangles only
public class Face {
   public Face() {
      label=0;
      edges=new EdgeSet();
      vertices=new VertexSet();
      normal=new Vector();
      vertices.reserve(3);
      edges.reserve(3);
   }

   public Face Clone() {
      Face f=new Face();
      f.edges=edges.Clone();
      f.label=label;
      f.normal=(Vector)normal.Clone();
      f.vertices=vertices.Clone();
      return f;
   }

   public Edge adjacent(Face f) {
      for(int i=0;i<edges.getCount();i++)
         for(int j=0;j<f.edges.getCount();j++)
            if(edges[i].Equals(f.edges[j])) return edges[i];
      return null;
   }

   public Vertex OffEdge(Edge e) {
      for(int i=0;i<vertices.getCount();i++)
         if((vertices[i]!=e.ends[0])&&
         (vertices[i]!=e.ends[1])) return vertices[i];
      return null;
   }
```

```csharp
public void replace(Edge eold,Edge enew) {
   for(int i=0;i<edges.getCount();i++)
      if(edges[i].Equals(eold)) {
         eold.remove(this);
         edges[i]=enew;
         enew.add(this);
      }
}

public void replace(Vertex vold,Vertex vnew) {
   for(int i=0;i<vertices.getCount();i++)
      if(vertices[i].Equals(vold)) {
         vold.faces.remove(this);
         vertices[i]=vnew;
         vnew.faces.add(this);
      }
}

public void disconnect() {
   int i;
   for(i=0;i<vertices.getCount();i++) vertices[i].faces.remove(this);
   for(i=0;i<edges.getCount();i++) edges[i].remove(this);
   edges.clear();
   vertices.clear();
}

public void ComputeNormal() {
   normal=(vertices[1].v-vertices[0].v)^
      (vertices[2].v-vertices[0].v);
   normal.normalize();
}

public void ComputeNormalTex() {
   normal=(vertices[1].tex-vertices[0].tex)^
      (vertices[2].tex-vertices[0].tex);
   normal.normalize();
}

public double area() {
   Vector e1, e2;
   e1=vertices[1].v-vertices[0].v;
   e2=vertices[2].v-vertices[0].v;
   return Math.Abs((e1^e2).norm()/2);
}

public double texarea() {
   Vector e1, e2;
   e1=vertices[1].tex-vertices[0].tex;
   e2=vertices[2].tex-vertices[0].tex;
   return Math.Abs((e1^e2).norm()/2);
}
```

```
//See: Texture mapping progressive meshes, by Sander et al.
public double stretch() {
    Vector Ss, St;
    double a, b, c, A;
    Vertex q1, q2, q3;
    q1=vertices[0]; q2=vertices[1]; q3=vertices[2];
    // x= s coordinate
    // y= t coordinate
    //Area of parameterized triangle
    A=((q2.tex.x-q1.tex.x)*(q3.tex.y-q1.tex.y)-
    (q3.tex.x-q1.tex.x)*(q2.tex.y-q1.tex.y))/2.0;
    A=Math.Abs(A);
    if(A<1e-10) A=1e-10;
    Ss=q1.v*(q2.tex.y-q3.tex.y)+q2.v*(q3.tex.y-q1.tex.y)+
        q3.v*(q1.tex.y-q2.tex.y);
    St=q1.v*(q3.tex.x-q2.tex.x)+q2.v*(q1.tex.x-q3.tex.x)+
        q3.v*(q2.tex.x-q1.tex.x);
    Ss/=2*A; St/=2*A;
    a=Ss*Ss; b=Ss*St; c=St*St;
    //L^2 stretch metric from Sander et al.
    return Math.Sqrt((a+c)/2.0);
}
public bool boundary() {
    if(edges[0].boundary()) return true;
    if(edges[1].boundary()) return true;
    if(edges[2].boundary()) return true;
    return false;
}
//Neglects to check if vertices are in the same order. But we don't want a mesh
//where the same vertices occur in several faces but cross/overlap in some way.
public override bool Equals(object obj) {
    int i, j, sum;
    int[] tag;
    Face f2;
    f2=(Face)obj;
    tag=new int[vertices.getCount()];
    for(i=0;i<vertices.getCount();i++) tag[i]=0;
    if(vertices.getCount()!=f2.vertices.getCount()) return false;
    for(i=0;i<vertices.getCount();i++)
        for(j=0;j<f2.vertices.getCount();j++)
            if(vertices[i].Equals(f2.vertices[j])) tag[i]=1;
    sum=0;
    for(i=0;i<vertices.getCount();i++) sum+=tag[i];
    if(sum==vertices.getCount()) return true;
    else return false;
}
//For fast access
public VertexSet vertices;
public EdgeSet edges;
public Vector normal;
```

```
    public int label;
}

public class Vertex {
    public Vertex() {
        label=0; pos=0; dist=1e15; next=null;
        edges=new EdgeSet(); faces=new FaceSet();
        normal=new Vector(); tex=new Vector();
        n=new Vector(); v=new Vector();
    }

    public Vertex Clone() {
        Vertex v=new Vertex();
        v.dist=dist; v.label=label;
        v.faces=faces.Clone();
        v.n=(Vector)n.Clone();
        v.normal=(Vector)normal.Clone();
        v.next=next; v.pos=pos;
        v.tex=(Vector)tex.Clone();
        v.v=(Vector)this.v.Clone();
        v.wij=null;
        return v;
    }

    public int valence() { return edges.getCount(); }

    public void ComputeNormal() {
        normal=new Vector(0,0,0,1);
        for(int i=0;i<faces.getCount();i++) normal+=faces[i].normal;
        normal.normalize();
    }

    public bool adjacent(Vertex v) {
        for(int i=0;i<edges.getCount();i++) {
            if(edges[i].ends[0]==v) return true;
            if(edges[i].ends[1]==v) return true;
        }
        return false;
    }

    public void add(Face f) { faces.add(f); }

    public void remove(Face f) { faces.remove(f); }

    public void add(Edge e) { edges.add(e); }

    public void remove(Edge e) { edges.remove(e); }

    public bool boundary() {
        for(int i=0;i<edges.getCount();i++)
            if(edges[i].boundary()) return true;
```

```
      return false;
  }

  public override bool Equals(object o) {
     if(this==o) return true;
     else return false;
  }
  public Vector v, n, tex;
  //Vertex normal (may also be used for other purposes)
  public Vector normal;
  public EdgeSet edges;
  public FaceSet faces;
  public int label, pos;
  //Geodesic dist;
  public double dist;
  //Weights for parameterisation per vertex,
  //So that weights on opposite ends of an edge can differ
  public double[] wij;
  //For the creation of a path
  public Vertex next;
}


//For most algorithms an edge must be adjacent to only two faces
public class Edge {
  public Edge() {
     ends=new Vertex[2];
     ends[0]=ends[1]=null;
     label=0;
     faces=new FaceSet();
     faces.reserve(2);
  }

  public Edge Clone() {
     Edge e=new Edge();
     e.ends=(Vertex[])ends.Clone();
     e.faces=faces.Clone();
     e.label=label;
     return e;
  }
  public void add(Face f) { faces.add(f); }

  public void remove(Face f) { faces.remove(f); }

  public double length() {
     return (ends[0].v-ends[1].v).norm(); }

  public bool boundary() {
     if(faces.getCount()<2) return true;
     return false;
  }
```

```csharp
public bool orphan() {
   if(faces.getCount()==0) return true;
   return false;
}

public void disconnect() {
   //only called if orphaned
   if(ends[0]!=null) ends[0].edges.remove(this);
   if(ends[1]!=null) ends[1].edges.remove(this);
   ends[0]=ends[1]=null;
   faces.clear();
}

public void replace(Vertex vold,Vertex vnew) {
   for(int i=0;i<2;i++)
      if(ends[i]==vold) {
         vold.edges.remove(this);
         ends[i]=vnew;
         vnew.edges.add(this);
      }
}

public override bool Equals(object obj) {
   Edge e1=this;
   Edge e2=(Edge)obj;
   if(e1.ends[0].Equals(e2.ends[0])) {
      if(e1.ends[1].Equals(e2.ends[1])) return true;
      else return false;
   } else if(e1.ends[0].Equals(e2.ends[1])) {
      if(e1.ends[1].Equals(e2.ends[0])) return true;
      else return false;
   } else return false;
}

public Vertex []ends;
public FaceSet faces;
public int label;
}

public class Mesh {
   public const int FODEL=1<<16;
   public const int F1DEL=2<<16;
   public const int SINGLEFACE=3<<16;
   public const int DELETED=4<<16;
   public const int SPLIT=8<<16;
   public const int BOUNDARY=16<<16;
   public const int LABELMASK=65535;
   public const int BOUNDARY_RECTANGLE=1;
   public const int BOUNDARY_CIRCLE=2;
   public const int BOUNDARY_CHORD_RECTANGLE=3;
   public const int BOUNDARY_CHORD_CIRCLE=4;
```

```
public const int BOUNDARY_PRESET=5;
public const int GEOMETRY_IMAGE=1;
public const int NORMAL_MAP=2;

public bool test(int i)
{ if(i==0) return false; else return true; }

public void copy(Mesh M) {
    int i;
    destroy();
    for(i=0;i<M.vertices.getCount();i++) {
        int p=AddVertex(M.vertices[i].v);
        M.vertices[i].pos=p;
        vertices[p].tex=(Vector)M.vertices[i].tex.Clone();
        vertices[p].normal=(Vector)M.vertices[i].normal.Clone();
        vertices[p].n=(Vector)M.vertices[i].n.Clone();
    }
    for(i=0;i<M.faces.getCount();i++) {
        AddTriangle(M.faces[i].vertices[0].pos,
            M.faces[i].vertices[1].pos,
            M.faces[i].vertices[2].pos);
    }
}

public Mesh Clone()
{   Mesh m=new Mesh(); m.copy(this); return m; }

public Mesh(Mesh M) {
    vertices=new VertexSet(); edges=new EdgeSet();
    faces=new FaceSet();
    copy(M);
}

public Mesh() {
    vertices=new VertexSet(); edges=new EdgeSet();
    faces=new FaceSet();
}

public void destroy()
{ vertices.clear(); edges.clear(); faces.clear(); }

// Will always return vertices in sequence, unless vertices are deleted
public int AddVertex(Vector v) {
    Vertex vert=new Vertex();
    vert.v=(Vector)v.Clone();
    vert.n=new Vector(0.0,1.0,0.0);
    vert.normal=new Vector(0.0,1.0,0.0);
    vert.tex=new Vector(0.0,0.0,0.0);
    return vertices.addWithoutCheck(vert);
}
```

```
public void SetTex(int v,Vector tex) {
   if(v<0) return;
   if(v>=vertices.getCount()) return;
   vertices[v].tex=(Vector)tex.Clone();
}

public void SetVertex(int v,Vector vert) {
   if(v<0) return;
   if(v>=vertices.getCount()) return;
   vertices[v].v=(Vector)vert.Clone();
}

public void SetNormal(int v,Vector n) {
   if(v<0) return;
   if(v>=vertices.getCount()) return;
   vertices[v].n=(Vector)n.Clone();
   vertices[v].normal=(Vector)n.Clone();
}

public Vertex getVertex(int i) {
   if(i<0) return null;
   if(i>=vertices.getCount()) return null;
   return vertices[i];
}

public void Recenter() {
   int i;
   Vector min, max, c;
   if(vertices.getCount()==0) return;
   min=(Vector)vertices[0].v.Clone();
   max=(Vector)vertices[0].v.Clone();
   for(i=1;i<vertices.getCount();i++) {
      if(vertices[i].v.x<min.x) min.x=vertices[i].v.x;
      if(vertices[i].v.y<min.y) min.y=vertices[i].v.y;
      if(vertices[i].v.z<min.z) min.z=vertices[i].v.z;
      if(vertices[i].v.x>max.x) max.x=vertices[i].v.x;
      if(vertices[i].v.y>max.y) max.y=vertices[i].v.y;
      if(vertices[i].v.z>max.z) max.z=vertices[i].v.z;
   }
   c=(max+min)/2.0;
   for(i=0;i<vertices.getCount();i++) vertices[i].v-=c;
}

public void Rescale() {
   int i;
   Vector min, max;
   double maxw;
   if(vertices.getCount()==0) return;
   min=(Vector)vertices[0].v.Clone();
   max=(Vector)vertices[0].v.Clone();
   for(i=1;i<vertices.getCount();i++) {
```

```
      if(vertices[i].v.x<min.x) min.x=vertices[i].v.x;
      if(vertices[i].v.y<min.y) min.y=vertices[i].v.y;
      if(vertices[i].v.z<min.z) min.z=vertices[i].v.z;
      if(vertices[i].v.x>max.x) max.x=vertices[i].v.x;
      if(vertices[i].v.y>max.y) max.y=vertices[i].v.y;
      if(vertices[i].v.z>max.z) max.z=vertices[i].v.z;
    }
    maxw=max.x-min.x;
    if(max.y-min.y>maxw) maxw=max.y-min.y;
    if(max.z-min.z>maxw) maxw=max.z-min.z;
    for(i=0;i<vertices.getCount();i++) vertices[i].v/=maxw;
}

public int AddTriangle(int v1,int v2,int v3) {
    Vertex v;
    if((v1==v2)||(v1==v3)||(v2==v3)) return -1;
    Edge e1=AddEdge(v1,v2);
    Edge e2=AddEdge(v2,v3);
    Edge e3=AddEdge(v3,v1);
    Face f=new Face();
    f.vertices.add(vertices[v1]);
    f.vertices.add(vertices[v2]);
    f.vertices.add(vertices[v3]);
    f.edges.add(e1); f.edges.add(e2); f.edges.add(e3);
    //Check for duplicate triangles. If the face exists, all vertices
    //will have the face in their adjacency lists
    v=vertices[v1];
    for(int i=0;i<v.faces.getCount();i++)
       if(f.Equals(v.faces[i])) return faces.index(v.faces[i]);
    vertices[v1].add(f); vertices[v2].add(f);
    vertices[v3].add(f);
    e1.add(f); e2.add(f); e3.add(f);
    return faces.addWithoutCheck(f);
}

//Take a triangle already in the mesh and re-add it
public void AddTriangle(int v1,int v2,int v3,Face f) {
    Vertex v;
    Edge e1=AddEdge(v1,v2);
    Edge e2=AddEdge(v2,v3);
    Edge e3=AddEdge(v3,v1);
    f.vertices.add(vertices[v1]);
    f.vertices.add(vertices[v2]);
    f.vertices.add(vertices[v3]);
    f.edges.add(e1); f.edges.add(e2); f.edges.add(e3);
    //Check for duplicate triangles. If the face exists, all vertices
    //will have the face in their adjacency lists
    v=vertices[v1];
    for(int i=0;i<v.faces.getCount();i++)
       if(f.Equals(v.faces[i])) return;
    vertices[v1].add(f); vertices[v2].add(f);
```

```
      vertices[v3].add(f);
      e1.add(f); e2.add(f); e3.add(f);
}

public void ReverseNormals() {
   int i;
   for(i=0;i<vertices.getCount();i++)
      vertices[i].normal=-vertices[i].normal;
   for(i=0;i<faces.getCount();i++)
      faces[i].normal=-faces[i].normal;
}

public int Genus() {
   int i, j;
   int N, F, E, G, B;
   bool loop=true;
   //Euler-Poincare formula: N+F-E=2-2G-B
   //N=no. vertices, F=no. faces, E=no. edges, G=genus
   //B=no. of boundary loops
   //thus G=(2-B-N-F+E)/2;

   N=vertices.getCount();
   F=faces.getCount(); E=edges.getCount();
   for(i=0;i<E;i++) edges[i].label=0;
   B=0;
   //visit boundaries
   while(loop) {
      loop=false;
      for(i=0;i<E;i++) {
         if((edges[i].label==0)&&(edges[i].boundary())) {
            loop=true;
            B++;
            Edge e=edges[i];
            while(e!=null) {
               e.label=1;
               Edge e2=null;
               EdgeSet es=e.ends[0].edges;
               for(j=0;j<es.getCount();j++)
                  if((es[j].label==0)&&(es[j].boundary())) e2=es[j];
               es=e.ends[1].edges;
               if(e2==null)
               for(j=0;j<es.getCount();j++)
                  if((es[j].label==0)&&(es[j].boundary())) e2=es[j];
               e=e2;
            }
         } else edges[i].label=1;
      }
   }
   G=(2-B-N-F+E);
   return G/2;
}
```

```
public void ComputeFaceNormals()
{ for(int i=0;i<faces.getCount();i++) faces[i].ComputeNormal(); }

public void ComputeVertexNormals() {
  ComputeFaceNormals();
  for(int i=0;i<vertices.getCount();i++)
    vertices[i].ComputeNormal();
}

public bool Connected() {
  if(!ConnectedFaces()) return false;
  if(!ConnectedEdges()) return false;
  return true;
}

public bool ConnectedFaces() {
  int i;
  if(faces.getCount()==0) return true;
  for(i=0;i<faces.getCount();i++) faces[i].label=0;
  CheckConnected(faces[0]);
  for(i=0;i<faces.getCount();i++)
    if(faces[i].label==0) return false;
  return true;
}

public bool ConnectedEdges() {
  int i;
  if(edges.getCount()==0) return true;
  for(i=0;i<edges.getCount();i++) edges[i].label=0;
  for(i=0;i<vertices.getCount();i++) vertices[i].label=0;
  CheckConnected(edges[0]);
  for(i=0;i<edges.getCount();i++)
    if(edges[i].label==0) return false;
  for(i=0;i<vertices.getCount();i++)
    if(vertices[i].label==0) return false;
  return true;
}

// Only 2-manifold meshes can be cut and parameterized.
public bool Manifold() {
  for(int i=0;i<edges.getCount();i++)
    if(edges[i].faces.getCount()>2) return false;
  return true;
}

// Check that no vertex is connected to two or more triangle fans
// If so, split the fans. This happens if the mesh touches itself at exactly
// one point, a vertex (i.e. not an edge or face).
public void CheckFans() {
  int i,j,k;
```

```csharp
bool recheck=false;
for(i=0;i<vertices.getCount();i++) {
   Vertex v=vertices[i];
   for(j=0;j<v.faces.getCount();j++) v.faces[j].label=0;
   if(v.faces.getCount()==0) continue;
   v.faces[0].label=1;
   bool changed=true;
   while(changed) {
      changed=false;
      for(j=0;j<v.faces.getCount();j++) {
         for(k=j+1;k<v.faces.getCount();k++) {
            if((v.faces[j].label==0)||(v.faces[k].label==0)) {
               Edge e=v.faces[j].adjacent(v.faces[k]);
               if(e!=null) {
                  if(v.faces[j].label>0) {
                     v.faces[k].label=v.faces[j].label;
                     changed=true;
                  } else if(v.faces[k].label>0) {
                     v.faces[j].label=v.faces[k].label;
                     changed=true;
                  }
               }
            }
         }
      }
   }

   bool touch=false;
   for(j=0;j<v.faces.getCount();j++)
      if(v.faces[j].label==0) touch=true;
   if(touch==true) {
      Console.Write("Found touching vertex\n");
      Vertex vnew=new Vertex();
      vnew.dist=v.dist;
      vnew.label=v.label;
      vnew.n=(Vector)v.n.Clone();
      vnew.normal=(Vector)v.normal.Clone();
      vnew.tex=(Vector)v.tex.Clone();
      vnew.v=(Vector)v.v.Clone();
      FaceSet vfaces=v.faces.Clone();
      vertices.addWithoutCheck(vnew);
      recheck=true;
      for(j=0;j<vfaces.getCount();j++) {
         if(vfaces[j].label==1) {
            vfaces[j].replace(v,vnew);
            for(k=0;k<vfaces[j].edges.getCount();k++)
               vfaces[j].edges[k].replace(v,vnew);
         }
      }
   }
}
```

```
    if(recheck) CheckFans();
}

//Cut mesh to be equivalent to a disc, only works if the mesh does not
// "cross" itself. That is, inside and outside is always clear.
public void DiscCut() {
    int i, j;
    EdgeSet cutpath=new EdgeSet();
    EdgeSet candidates=new EdgeSet();
    Edge selected;
    double min;
    int valence, x;
    Vertex v;
    bool changed;
    bool boundary=false;

    //Mark boundary edges
    for(i=0;i<edges.getCount();i++) {
        //Mark boundaries, marked as split as well, so
        //that we don't try to split them
        if(edges[i].faces.getCount()<2) {
            edges[i].label|=F1DEL|BOUNDARY|SPLIT;
            boundary=true;
        } else edges[i].label=0;
    }

    //No faces are deleted
    for(i=0;i<faces.getCount();i++) faces[i].label=0;

    //For computation of geodesic distance
    for(i=0;i<vertices.getCount();i++) vertices[i].dist=1e15;
    //Remove a seed triangle
    int fs=0;
    DiscDeleteFace(faces[fs],candidates);
    //Update geodesic distance for each of the seed triangle vertices
    VertexSet border=new VertexSet();
    border.add(faces[fs].vertices[0]);
    border.add(faces[fs].vertices[1]);
    border.add(faces[fs].vertices[2]);
    Console.Write("Distance...\n");
    CalculateGeodesicDistance(border);

    //Successively remove edges that are only adjacent
    // to one triangle, and remove the edge and triangle
    Console.Write("Removing triangles...\n");
    selected=candidates[0];
    while(selected!=null) {
        selected=null;
        min=-1.0;
        for(i=0;i<candidates.getCount();i++) {
            if((!(test(candidates[i].label&BOUNDARY)))&&
```

```
            ((candidates[i].label&SINGLEFACE)>0)) {
            if(!((test(candidates[i].label&F0DEL))
                &&(test(candidates[i].label&F1DEL)))) {
                if(candidates[i].ends[0].dist>min) {
                    selected=candidates[i];
                    min=selected.ends[0].dist;
                }
                if(candidates[i].ends[1].dist>min) {
                    selected=candidates[i];
                    min=selected.ends[1].dist;
                }
            }
        }
    }
    if(selected!=null) {
        //One of the two must be deleted, one is deleted already
        //DiscDeleteFace checks if the face is already deleted
        //the corresponding edge is also deleted.
        candidates.remove(selected);
        DiscDeleteEdge(selected);
        DiscDeleteFace(selected.faces[0],candidates);
        DiscDeleteFace(selected.faces[1],candidates);
    }
}

//the cut path can now be built
for(i=0;i<edges.getCount();i++) {
    if((!(test(edges[i].label&DELETED)))&&
    (!(test(edges[i].label&BOUNDARY)))) cutpath.add(edges[i]);
}

Console.Write("Pruning...{0}\n",cutpath.getCount());
//Prune vertices that are connected to only one edge,
//delete the edge also. Repeat until only loops remain
changed=true;
while(changed) {
    changed=false;
    for(i=cutpath.getCount()-1;i>=0;i--) {
        valence=0;
        v=cutpath[i].ends[0];
        for(j=0;j<v.edges.getCount();j++)
            if(!(test(v.edges[j].label&DELETED))) valence++;
        //store the valence in the label
        v.label=valence;
        //if the valence is one, prune the edge
        if(valence==1) {
            cutpath[i].label|=DELETED;
            cutpath.remove(i);
            changed=true; continue;
        }
        //Recompute valence by disregarding boundary edges, since they are not
```

```
//part of the cut. However, if a boundary is found, then the valence
//should be increased by one, since a boundary can be regarded as a cut
//that has already been made. A vertex can be joined to a maximum of two
//boundary edges, any more and the graph is not connected nicely.
valence=0; x=0;
for(j=0;j<v.edges.getCount();j++) {
    if(test(v.edges[j].label&BOUNDARY)) x=1;
    if((!(test(v.edges[j].label&DELETED)))&&
        (!(test(v.edges[j].label&BOUNDARY)))) valence++;
}
//store the valence in the label
v.label=valence+x;
valence=0;
v=cutpath[i].ends[1];
for(j=0;j<v.edges.getCount();j++)
    if(!(test(v.edges[j].label&DELETED))) valence++;
//store the valence in the label
v.label=valence;
//if the valence is one, prune the edge
if(valence==1) {
    cutpath[i].label|=DELETED;
    cutpath.remove(i);
    changed=true; continue;
}
//Recompute valence by disregarding boundary edges,
//since they are not part of the cut
valence=0;
x=0;
for(j=0;j<v.edges.getCount();j++) {
    if(test(v.edges[j].label&BOUNDARY)) x=1;
    if((!(test(v.edges[j].label&DELETED)))&&
        (!(test(v.edges[j].label&BOUNDARY)))) valence++;
}
//store the valence in the label
v.label=valence+x;
    }
}


//Now try to remove serrations in the path we do this by checking the triangles
//adjacent to each edge in the path, if another edge on the path is part of the
//triangle, then we check the third edge. If the length of the third edge is shorter
//than the first two, then we replace the two edges by the third edge.
Console.Write("Smoothing cut...\n");
while(SmoothCut(cutpath));
Random rnd=new Random();

//Test for genus 0 surface
if((cutpath.getCount()==0)&&(!boundary)) {
    //If we get a genus 0 surface, we should rather use
    // an alternative parameterization and avoid the disc cut
```

```csharp
//Create a random connected path to cut along
VertexSet cutvert=new VertexSet();
i=rnd.Next()%edges.getCount();
cutpath.add(edges[i]);
min=8;
v=edges[i].ends[1];
cutvert.add(edges[i].ends[0]); cutvert.add(edges[i].ends[1]);
//remark edges
for(i=0;i<edges.getCount();i++) edges[i].label=DELETED;
for(i=0;i<min;i++) {
    selected=v.edges[rnd.Next()%(v.edges.getCount())];
    while(cutpath.contains(selected)) {
        selected=v.edges[rnd.Next()%(v.edges.getCount())];
    }
    Vertex nv;
    if(selected.ends[0]==v) nv=selected.ends[1];
    else nv=selected.ends[0];
    if(!cutvert.contains(nv)) {
        cutvert.add(nv); v=nv;
        cutpath.add(selected);
    }
}
//remark edges
for(i=0;i<cutpath.getCount();i++) cutpath[i].label=0;
//compute valences for path
for(i=0;i<cutvert.getCount();i++) {
    valence=0;
    v=cutvert[i];
    for(j=0;j<v.edges.getCount();j++)
        if(!(test(v.edges[j].label&DELETED))) valence++;
    //store the valence in the label
    v.label=valence;
}
}
if((cutpath.getCount()==0)&&(!boundary)) {
    //Failed to cut the surface! we should hopefully never get here
}
Console.Write("Performing cut...{0}\n",cutpath.getCount());
CutMesh(cutpath);
Console.Write("Cut done.\n");
}


//Cut for geometry image using the technique described in Gu's thesis
//on geometry images. C# doesn't support default parameters, so two
//methods are required
public void GuCut() { GuCut(false); }
public void GuCut(bool flipedge) {
    EdgeSet eboundary=new EdgeSet();
    VertexSet vboundary=new VertexSet();
    Edge e, ce;
    Vertex v, vp;
```

```
Face f;
int i, j, c;
double maxstretch, stretch, Eold, Enew;
EdgeSet cutpath=new EdgeSet();
Mesh opt=null;
int iter=1000;
//first cut into a disc
Console.Write("Cutting\n");
DiscCut();
//then compute Floater parameterisation
Console.Write("Floater param to circle\n");
ParamFloater(BOUNDARY_CIRCLE);
Enew=AllStretch();
Eold=Enew+1.0;
Console.Write("Stretch before: {0}\n",Enew);
//refine until stretch increases
while((Eold>Enew)&&(--iter>0)) { //save curent mesh
   opt=this.Clone();
   if(!flipedge) {
      //If any border triangle is degenerate in parameter space,
      // split all edges not on the border.
      // Degeneracy occurs if three vertices are on the border.
      // This creates 4 new triangles (usually), and 2 are discarded
      cutpath.clear();
      for(i=0;i<faces.getCount();i++) {
         c=0;
         for(j=0;j<3;j++)
            if(faces[i].vertices[j].boundary()) c++;
         if(c==3) {
            for(j=0;j<3;j++)
               if(!(faces[i].edges[j].boundary()))
                  cutpath.add(faces[i].edges[j]);
         }
      }
      if(cutpath.getCount()>0) {
         for(i=0;i<cutpath.getCount();i++)
            SplitEdge(cutpath[i]);
         //reparameterize
         Console.Write("Parameterize...\n");
         ParamFloater(BOUNDARY_CIRCLE);
         //check if stretch is minimised
         Eold=Enew; Enew=AllStretch(); Eold=Enew+1.0;
         Console.Write("Stretch new: {0}\n",Enew);
         continue;
      }
   } else {
      //flip the offending edge instead of introducing new vertices
      for(i=0;i<vertices.getCount();i++) vertices[i].pos=i;
      for(i=0;i<faces.getCount();i++) {
         c=0;
         for(j=0;j<3;j++)
```

```
                if(faces[i].vertices[j].boundary()) c++;
           if(c==3) {
               Edge et=null;
               for(j=0;j<3;j++) {
                   if(!faces[i].edges[j].boundary())
                       et=faces[i].edges[j];
               }
               if(et!=null) {
                   Vertex v1, v2, v3=null, v4=null;
                   v1=et.ends[0]; v2=et.ends[1];
                   for(j=0;j<3;j++) {
                       if((et.faces[0].vertices[j]!=v1)&&
                          (et.faces[0].vertices[j]!=v2))
                           v3=et.faces[0].vertices[j];
                       if((et.faces[1].vertices[j]!=v1)&&
                          (et.faces[1].vertices[j]!=v2))
                           v4=et.faces[1].vertices[j];
                   }
                   RemoveFace(et.faces[0]); RemoveFace(et.faces[1]);
                   edges.remove(et);
                   AddTriangle(v1.pos,v3.pos,v4.pos);
                   AddTriangle(v2.pos,v3.pos,v4.pos);
               }
           }
       }

       //reparameterize
       Console.Write("Parameterize...\n");
       ParamFloater(BOUNDARY_CIRCLE);
       //check if stretch is minimised
       Eold=Enew; Enew=AllStretch(); Eold=Enew+1.0;
       Console.Write("Stretch new: {0}\n",Enew);
       continue;
   }
   maxstretch=-1;
   f=null;
   for(i=0;i<faces.getCount();i++) {
       //don't consider triangles on the boundary
       if(faces[i].edges[0].boundary()) continue;
       if(faces[i].edges[1].boundary()) continue;
       if(faces[i].edges[2].boundary()) continue;
       stretch=faces[i].stretch();
       if(maxstretch<stretch) {
           maxstretch=stretch; f=faces[i];
       }
   }
   if(f==null) Console.Write("No maximal stretch!\n");
   //Check for high stretch. If found, join vertex of high stretch to
   //current border using shortest path
   eboundary.clear();
   vboundary.clear();
```

```
     ComputeBoundary(eboundary,vboundary);

     Console.Write("Calculating distances...\n");
     CalculateGeodesicDistance(vboundary);

     v=f.vertices[0];
     cutpath.clear();
     //follow path from vertex to boundary
     Console.Write("Building cutpath...\n");
     while(v.next!=null) {
       vp=v.next;
       ce=new Edge();
       ce.ends[0]=v; ce.ends[1]=vp;
       //find matching edge
       e=v.edges.match(ce);
       //add to cutpath
       cutpath.add(e);
       //advance to next node
       v=vp;
     }

     Console.Write("Cutting...\n");
     //cut the mesh
     CutMesh(cutpath);

     //reparameterize
     Console.Write("Parameterize...\n");
     ParamFloater(BOUNDARY_CIRCLE);
     //check if stretch is minimised
     Eold=Enew; Enew=AllStretch();
     Console.Write("Stretch new: {0}\n",Enew);
   }
   //revert to previous mesh (stretch was better)
   copy(opt);
   Enew=AllStretch();
   Console.Write("Stretch after: {0}\n",Enew);
 }

 public void SplitEdge(Edge e) {
   Face f;
   Vector pos;
   int v1, v2, v3, vpos, i, j;
   pos=(e.ends[0].v + e.ends[1].v)/2.0;
   vpos=AddVertex(pos);
   //remove edge
   e.ends[0].edges.remove(e);
   e.ends[1].edges.remove(e);
   edges.remove(e);

   for(i=0;i<2;i++) {
     f=e.faces[i];
```

```
        if(f!=null) {
          for(j=0;j<3;j++) {
            f.vertices[j].faces.remove(f);
            f.edges[j].remove(f);
          }
          for(j=0;j<3;j++) {
            if((f.vertices[j]!=e.ends[0])
              &&(f.vertices[j]!=e.ends[1])) {
              Vertex tmp=f.vertices[0];
              f.vertices[0]=f.vertices[j];
              f.vertices[j]=tmp;
            }
          }
          v1=vertices.index(f.vertices[0]);
          v2=vertices.index(f.vertices[1]);
          v3=vertices.index(f.vertices[2]);
          faces.remove(f);
          AddTriangle(v1,v2,vpos);
          AddTriangle(v1,vpos,v3);
        }
      }
  }

  public void CutMesh(EdgeSet cutpath) {
    int i, j, k, valence, x, count;
    VertexSet cutvert=new VertexSet();
    Vertex[] newvert;
    Vertex v;
    Edge adj, e;
    bool changed;

    //label edges as if they are not in the cutpath
    for(i=0;i<edges.getCount();i++) {
      if(edges[i].boundary()) edges[i].label=BOUNDARY|SPLIT;
      else edges[i].label=DELETED;
    }

    //label edges in cutpath as not deleted
    for(i=0;i<cutpath.getCount();i++) {
      //label edge as not deleted
      if(!cutpath[i].boundary()) cutpath[i].label=0;
      else {
        Console.Write("Boundary in cutpath!\n");
        cutpath.remove(i); i--;
      }
    }

    //label vertices according to valence (undeleted edges)
    for(i=0;i<cutpath.getCount();i++) {
      valence=0;
```

```
v=cutpath[i].ends[0];
x=0;
for(j=0;j<v.edges.getCount();j++) {
    if(test(v.edges[j].label&BOUNDARY)) x=1;
    if((!(test(v.edges[j].label&DELETED)))
        &&(!(test(v.edges[j].label&BOUNDARY))))  valence++;
}
//store the valence in the label
v.label=valence+x;
valence=0;
v=cutpath[i].ends[1];
x=0;
for(j=0;j<v.edges.getCount();j++) {
    if(test(v.edges[j].label&BOUNDARY)) x=1;
    if((!(test(v.edges[j].label&DELETED)))
        &&(!(test(v.edges[j].label&BOUNDARY))))  valence++;
}
//store the valence in the label
v.label=valence+x;
}


//find the vertices in the cut
for(i=0;i<cutpath.getCount();i++) {
    //Check valence
    //For genus 0 surfaces, the cut will not necessarily be a loop
    if(cutpath[i].ends[0].label>=2)
        cutvert.add(cutpath[i].ends[0]);
    if(cutpath[i].ends[1].label>=2)
        cutvert.add(cutpath[i].ends[1]);
}

for(i=0;i<cutvert.getCount();i++) {
    count=0;
    v=cutvert[i];
    //Create a new vertex for each edge
    // entering this vertex (each edge on a cutpath)
    newvert=new Vertex[v.label];
    newvert[0]=v;
    for(j=1;j<v.label;j++) {
        newvert[j]=new Vertex();
        newvert[j].v=(Vector)v.v.Clone();
        newvert[j].tex=(Vector)v.tex.Clone();
        newvert[j].normal=(Vector)v.normal.Clone();
        newvert[j].n=(Vector)v.n.Clone();
        newvert[j].dist=v.dist;
        vertices.add(newvert[j]);
    }
    //reset labels for cut
    for(j=0;j<v.faces.getCount();j++) v.faces[j].label=-1;
    changed=true;
    //label the faces
```

```
while(changed) {
  changed=false;
  //first label a triangle next to a cut edge
  for(j=0;(!changed) && (j<v.faces.getCount());j++) {
    if(v.faces[j].label<0)
    for(k=0;(!changed) && (k<3);k++) {
      if((!(test(v.faces[j].edges[k].label&DELETED)))
      &&(!(test(v.faces[j].edges[k].label&BOUNDARY)))) {
        v.faces[j].label=count;
        changed=true; count++;
      }
    }
  }

  if(changed==false) break;
  //now propogate the information to the surrounding faces
  while(changed) {
    changed=false;
    for(j=0;j<v.faces.getCount();j++) {
      for(k=j+1;k<v.faces.getCount();k++) {
        if((v.faces[j].label<0)||(v.faces[k].label<0)) {
          adj=v.faces[j].adjacent(v.faces[k]);
          if(adj!=null) {
            if(test(adj.label&DELETED)) {
              //faces should have same label
              if(v.faces[j].label>=0) {
                v.faces[k].label=v.faces[j].label;
                changed=true;
              } else if(v.faces[k].label>=0) {
                v.faces[j].label=v.faces[k].label;
                changed=true;
              }
            } else {
              //Faces should have different labels
              //Later iterations will determine the label
            }
          }
        }
      }
    }
  }
  //go to next iteration, to choose a new cut face to label
  changed=true;
}

//Now, update the edges to use the correct vertex.
//If the edge was a cut edge, split the edge and use the
//face labels to determine which edge belongs
//to which face. These new edges are no longer cut edges.
//go backwards, because we will be removing edges while working
for(j=v.edges.getCount()-1;j>=0;j--) {
```

```
if((test(v.edges[j].label&DELETED))
   ||(test(v.edges[j].label&SPLIT))) {
//edge not part of cutpath: just change the vertex
   e=v.edges[j];
   if(e.faces[0]!=null) {
      if(e.ends[0]==v) {
         v.edges.remove(e);
         e.ends[0]=newvert[e.faces[0].label];
         e.ends[0].edges.add(e);
      } else if(e.ends[1]==v) {
         v.edges.remove(e);
         e.ends[1]=newvert[e.faces[0].label];
         e.ends[1].edges.add(e);
      }
   } else {
      if(e.ends[0]==v) {
         v.edges.remove(e);
         e.ends[0]=newvert[e.faces[1].label];
         e.ends[0].edges.add(e);
      } else if(e.ends[1]==v) {
         v.edges.remove(e);
         e.ends[1]=newvert[e.faces[1].label];
         e.ends[1].edges.add(e);
      }
   }
} else { //change the existing edge to use the correct vertex
   Edge newedge;
   newedge=v.edges[j].Clone();
   e=v.edges[j];
   if(e.ends[0]==v) {
      v.edges.remove(e);
      e.ends[0]=newvert[e.faces[0].label];
      e.ends[0].edges.add(e);
   } else if(e.ends[1]==v) {
      v.edges.remove(e);
      e.ends[1]=newvert[e.faces[0].label];
      e.ends[1].edges.add(e);
   }
   //edge part of cutpath: split edge
   if(newedge.ends[0]==v) {
      newedge.ends[0]=newvert[newedge.faces[1].label];
   } else if(newedge.ends[1]==v) {
      newedge.ends[1]=newvert[newedge.faces[1].label];
   }
   newedge.ends[0].add(newedge);
   newedge.ends[1].add(newedge);
   newedge.faces.remove(0);
   //don't have to set the face to null, since replace will do it
   newedge.faces[0].replace(e,newedge);
   newedge.label|=SPLIT;
   e.label|=SPLIT;
```

```
                    edges.add(newedge);
                }
            }
        //now update the triangles
        for(j=v.faces.getCount()-1;j>=0;j--)
            v.faces[j].replace(v,newvert[v.faces[j].label]);
        }
    }

    public bool SmoothCut(EdgeSet cutpath) {
        int i, j, k, valence, x;
        Edge other;
        Face tri;
        Face f=new Face();
        int[] tag=new int[3] {0,0,0};
        Edge e1, e2;
        Vertex v;

        for(i=0;i<cutpath.getCount();i++) {
            //check for later connecting edges
            for(j=i+1;j<cutpath.getCount();j++) {
                //Test if they share an endpoint, but there must be only two
                //edges sharing this vertex, thus the valence (stored in the
                //label) must be 2
                tri=null;
                if(cutpath[i].ends[0].label==2) {
                    if(cutpath[j].ends[0]==cutpath[i].ends[0]) {
                        f.vertices[0]=cutpath[i].ends[0];
                        f.vertices[1]=cutpath[i].ends[1];
                        f.vertices[2]=cutpath[j].ends[1];
                        tri=faces.match(f);
                    }
                    if(cutpath[j].ends[1]==cutpath[i].ends[0]) {
                        f.vertices[0]=cutpath[i].ends[0];
                        f.vertices[1]=cutpath[i].ends[1];
                        f.vertices[2]=cutpath[j].ends[0];
                        tri=faces.match(f);
                    }
                }
                if(cutpath[i].ends[1].label==2) {
                    if(cutpath[j].ends[0]==cutpath[i].ends[1]) {
                        f.vertices[0]=cutpath[i].ends[0];
                        f.vertices[1]=cutpath[i].ends[1];
                        f.vertices[2]=cutpath[j].ends[1];
                        tri=faces.match(f);
                    }
                    if(cutpath[j].ends[1]==cutpath[i].ends[1]) {
                        f.vertices[0]=cutpath[i].ends[0];
                        f.vertices[1]=cutpath[i].ends[1];
                        f.vertices[2]=cutpath[j].ends[0];
                        tri=faces.match(f);
                    }
```

```
        }
    }
    //If we find such a triangle, find the other edge
    //and see if it is shorter
    if(tri!=null) {
        for(k=0;k<3;k++) tag[k]=0;
        for(k=0;k<3;k++) {
            if(tri.edges[k]==cutpath[j]) tag[k]=1;
            if(tri.edges[k]==cutpath[i]) tag[k]=1;
        }
        other=null;
        for(k=0;k<3;k++) if(tag[k]==0) other=tri.edges[k];
        if(other.length()<cutpath[i].length()+cutpath[j].length()) {
            //the edge is shorter, replace the other two by this edge
            e1=cutpath[i]; e2=cutpath[j];
            cutpath.add(other);
            cutpath.remove(i); cutpath.remove(j);
            e1.label|=DELETED; e2.label|=DELETED;
            other.label&=~DELETED;

            //Recompute valence by disregarding boundary edges, since they are not
            //part of the cut. However, if a boundary is found, then the valence
            //should be increased by one, since a boundary can be regarded as a cut
            //that has already been made. A vertex can be joined to a maximum of
            //two boundary edges, any more and the graph is not connected nicely.
            v=other.ends[0];
            valence=0; x=0;
            for(j=0;j<v.edges.getCount();j++) {
                if(test(v.edges[j].label&BOUNDARY)) x=1;
                if((!(test(v.edges[j].label&DELETED)))
                    &&(!(test(v.edges[j].label&BOUNDARY)))) valence++;
            }
            //store the valence in the label
            v.label=valence+x;
            v=other.ends[1];
            valence=0; x=0;
            for(j=0;j<v.edges.getCount();j++) {
                if(test(v.edges[j].label&BOUNDARY)) x=1;
                if((!(test(v.edges[j].label&DELETED)))
                    &&(!(test(v.edges[j].label&BOUNDARY)))) valence++;
            }
            //store the valence in the label
            v.label=valence+x;
            return true;
        }
    }
  }
}
return false;
}
```

```
//Calculate the geodesic distance, the shortest path on the surface,
//between this vertex and all other vertices. Uses Dijkstra's algorithm (approximate).
//The next value of vertices are set to point to the next in the path to v
public void CalculateGeodesicDistance(Vertex v) {
    VertexSet set=new VertexSet();
    set.add(v); Dijkstra(set);
}

public void CalculateGeodesicDistance(VertexSet set)
{ Dijkstra(set); }

public void Dijkstra(VertexSet known) {
    int i, j;
    VertexSet S=new VertexSet();
    VertexSet W=new VertexSet();
    Vertex x, v;
    double min, d;

    for(j=0;j<vertices.getCount();j++) {
        vertices[j].label=-1; vertices[j].dist=1e15; vertices[j].next=null;
    }
    //apply Dijkstra's algorithm
    for(j=0;j<known.getCount();j++) {
        v=known[j]; v.dist=0; v.label=0;
    }
    for(j=0;j<known.getCount();j++) {
        v=known[j];
        //set distance for neighboring edges
        for(i=0;i<v.edges.getCount();i++) {
            d=v.edges[i].length();
            if(v.edges[i].ends[0]==v) {
                if(v.edges[i].ends[1].dist>d) {
                    v.edges[i].ends[1].dist=d; v.edges[i].ends[1].next=v;
                }
            } else {
                if(v.edges[i].ends[0].dist>d) {
                    v.edges[i].ends[0].dist=d; v.edges[i].ends[0].next=v;
                }
            }
        }
    }
    S.add(v);

    //compute W, the set of all vertices connected to S, but not in S
    for(i=0;i<v.edges.getCount();i++) {
        if(v.edges[i].ends[0]==v) {
            if(!S.contains(v.edges[i].ends[1]))
                W.add(v.edges[i].ends[1]);
        } else {
            if(!S.contains(v.edges[i].ends[0]))
                W.add(v.edges[i].ends[0]);
        }
    }
```

```
      }
   }

   while((S.getCount()!=vertices.getCount())
      &&(W.getCount()>0)) {
      //Find the vertex X in W for which the distance is minimum
      //there will be at least one element in W, because we stop when
      //W is empty (and S contains all vertices);
      x=W[0];
      min=x.dist;
      for(i=1;i<W.getCount();i++) {
         if(W[i].dist<min) { x=W[i]; min=x.dist; }
      }
      //Add X to S
      S.add(x);
      //Update W, the set of all vertices connected to S, but not in S
      W.remove(x);
      //Update closest distance for all vertices outside S
      //(but only if they are connected to X), and update W
      for(i=0;i<x.edges.getCount();i++) {
         if(!(S.contains(x.edges[i].ends[0]))) {
            d=x.edges[i].length();
            if(d+x.dist<x.edges[i].ends[0].dist) {
               x.edges[i].ends[0].dist=d+x.dist;
               //label prior vertex in sequence
               x.edges[i].ends[0].next=x;
            }
            W.add(x.edges[i].ends[0]);
         }
         if(!(S.contains(x.edges[i].ends[1]))) {
            d=x.edges[i].length();
            if(d+x.dist<x.edges[i].ends[1].dist) {
               x.edges[i].ends[1].dist=d+x.dist;
               //label prior vertex in sequence
               x.edges[i].ends[1].next=x;
            }
            W.add(x.edges[i].ends[1]);
         }
      }
      //next iteration
   }
}

public void DiscDeleteEdge(Edge e) {
   if(test(e.label&BOUNDARY)) return;
   e.label|=DELETED;
}

public void DiscDeleteFace(Face f,EdgeSet candidates) {
   if(test(f.label&DELETED)) return;
   f.label|=DELETED;
```

```
      for(int i=0;i<3;i++) {
        if(f.edges[i].faces[0]==f) f.edges[i].label|=F0DEL;
        else f.edges[i].label|=F1DEL;
        if((test(f.edges[i].label&F0DEL))
           &&(test(f.edges[i].label&F1DEL))) {
        } else candidates.add(f.edges[i]);
      }
    }

    public Edge AddEdge(int v1,int v2) {
      int i;
      Vertex v;
      Edge e=new Edge();
      e.ends[0]=vertices[v1];
      e.ends[1]=vertices[v2];
      //If the edge exists, both vertices will have the edge
      //in their adjacency lists
      v=vertices[v1];
      for(i=0;i<v.edges.getCount();i++) {
        if(e.Equals(v.edges[i])) return v.edges[i];
      edges.addWithoutCheck(e);
      vertices[v1].add(e); vertices[v2].add(e);
      return e;
    }

    public VertexSet ComputeRing(Vertex v,int level) {
      VertexSet ring=new VertexSet();
      ring.add(v);
      if(level<=0) return ring;
      return ComputeRing(ring,level);
    }

    public VertexSet ComputeRing(VertexSet set,int level) {
      VertexSet ring=new VertexSet();
      Vertex v;
      int i, j;
      for(i=0;i<set.getCount();i++) ring.add(set[i]);
      if(level<=0) return ring;
      for(i=0;i<set.getCount();i++) {
        v=set[i];
        for(j=0;j<v.edges.getCount();j++) {
          ring.add(v.edges[j].ends[1]); ring.add(v.edges[j].ends[0]);
        }
      }
      if(level==1) return ring;
      return ComputeRing(ring,level-1);
    }

    public VertexSet ComputeExclusiveRing(Vertex v,int level) {
      VertexSet ring=new VertexSet();
      if(level<=0) return ring;
```

```
      ring.add(v);
      return ComputeExclusiveRing(ring,level);
}

public VertexSet ComputeExclusiveRing(Face t,int level) {
      VertexSet ring=new VertexSet();
      if(level<=0) return ring;
      ring.add(t.vertices[0]); ring.add(t.vertices[1]); ring.add(t.vertices[2]);
      return ComputeExclusiveRing(ring,level);
}

public VertexSet ComputeExclusiveRing(VertexSet set,int level) {
      VertexSet ring, inner;
      Vertex v;
      inner=ComputeRing(set,level-1);
      ring=ComputeRing(set,level);
      for(int i=0;i<inner.getCount();i++)
      { v=inner[i]; ring.remove(v); }
      return ring;
}

public void CircleBoundary(VertexSet vboundary) {
      int n;
      Vector p=new Vector();
      //Circle boundary
      n=vboundary.getCount();
      for(int i=0;i<n;i++) {
          p.z=0;
          p.x=Math.Cos(i*2.0*Math.PI/n)*0.5+0.5;
          p.y=Math.Sin(i*2.0*Math.PI/n)*0.5+0.5;
          vboundary[i].tex=(Vector)p.Clone();
      }
}

public void CircleChordBoundary(VertexSet vboundary) {
      int i, n;
      double dist, cd;
      Vector p=new Vector();
      //Circle boundary
      n=vboundary.getCount();
      dist=0;
      for(i=1;i<n;i++) dist+=(vboundary[i].v-vboundary[i-1].v).norm();
      dist+=(vboundary[n-1].v-vboundary[0].v).norm();
      cd=0;
      for(i=0;i<n;i++) {
          p.x=Math.Cos(cd/dist*2.0*Math.PI)*0.5+0.5;
          p.y=Math.Sin(cd/dist*2.0*Math.PI)*0.5+0.5;
          p.z=0; vboundary[i].tex=(Vector)p.Clone();
          if(i<n-1) cd+=(vboundary[i+1].v-vboundary[i].v).norm();
      }
}
```

```csharp
public void RectangleBoundary(VertexSet vboundary) {
    int i, n, basei, corner;
    double min;
    Vector p=new Vector();
    //parameterize in a straight line
    n=vboundary.getCount();
    if(n==0) return;
    p.x=p.y=p.z=0.0;
    for(i=0;i<n;i++) {
        p.x=i/((double)n);
        vboundary[i].tex=(Vector)p.Clone();
    }
    //find point closest to 1/4 distance, make it the corner
    basei=0; corner=0;
    min=Math.Abs(vboundary[basei].tex.x-1.0/4.0);
    for(i=basei;i<n;i++) {
        if(Math.Abs(vboundary[i].tex.x-1.0/4.0)<min) {
            min=Math.Abs(vboundary[i].tex.x-1.0/4.0);
            corner=i;
        }
    }
    for(i=basei;i<corner;i++) {
        p.x=p.z=0.0;
        p.y=i/((double)corner);
        vboundary[i].tex=(Vector)p.Clone();
    }

    //find point closest to 2/4 distance, make it the corner
    basei=corner; corner=basei;
    min=Math.Abs(vboundary[basei].tex.x-2.0/4.0);
    for(i=basei;i<n;i++) {
        if(Math.Abs(vboundary[i].tex.x-2.0/4.0)<min) {
            min=Math.Abs(vboundary[i].tex.x-2.0/4.0);
            corner=i;
        }
    }
    for(i=basei;i<corner;i++) {
        p.z=0.0; p.y=1.0;
        p.x=(i-basei)/((double)(corner-basei));
        vboundary[i].tex=(Vector)p.Clone();
    }

    //find point closest to 3/4 distance, make it the corner
    basei=corner; corner=basei;
    min=Math.Abs(vboundary[basei].tex.x-3.0/4.0);
    for(i=basei;i<n;i++) {
        if(Math.Abs(vboundary[i].tex.x-3.0/4.0)<min) {
            min=Math.Abs(vboundary[i].tex.x-3.0/4.0);
            corner=i;
        }
```

```
    }
    for(i=basei;i<corner;i++) {
        p.z=0.0;  p.x=1.0;
        p.y=1.0-(i-basei)/((double)(corner-basei));
        vboundary[i].tex=(Vector)p.Clone();
    }

    //parameterize last stretch of boundary
    basei=corner;
    for(i=basei;i<n;i++) {
        p.z=0.0;  p.y=0.0;
        p.x=1.0-(i-basei)/((double)(n-basei));
        vboundary[i].tex=(Vector)p.Clone();
    }
}

public void RectangleChordBoundary(VertexSet vboundary) {
    int i, j, n, corner;
    double min, dist, cd;
    Vector p=new Vector();
    //parameterize in a straight line
    n=vboundary.getCount();
    if(n==0) return;
    p.x=p.y=p.z=0.0;
    dist=0;
    for(i=1;i<n;i++) dist+=(vboundary[i].v-vboundary[i-1].v).norm();
    dist+=(vboundary[n-1].v-vboundary[0].v).norm();
    cd=0;
    for(i=0;i<n;i++) {
        p.x=cd/dist;
        vboundary[i].tex=(Vector)p.Clone();
        if(i<n-1) cd+=(vboundary[i+1].v-vboundary[i].v).norm();
    }

    //find corners, first corner is already at 0,0. Last corner is the first corner
    for(j=1;j<4;j++) {
        //find closest parameter
        min=Math.Abs(vboundary[0].tex.x-j/4.0);
        corner=0;
        for(i=1;i<n;i++) {
            if(Math.Abs(vboundary[i].tex.x-j/4.0)<min) {
                min=Math.Abs(vboundary[i].tex.x-j/4.0);
                corner=i;
            }
        }
        //set the parameter value
        vboundary[corner].tex.x=j/4.0;
    }
    //move each parameter to the correct segment
    for(i=0;i<n;i++) {
        p=(Vector)vboundary[i].tex.Clone();
```

```
    //first segment
    if(p.x<1.0/4.0) { p.y=p.x/0.25; p.x=p.z=0.0; }
    else if(p.x<2.0/4.0) {
        p.x=(p.x-1.0/4.0)/0.25; p.y=1.0; p.z=0.0;
    } else if(p.x<3.0/4.0) {
        p.y=1.0-(p.x-2.0/4.0)/0.25; p.x=1.0; p.z=0.0;
    } else {
        p.x=1.0-(p.x-3.0/4.0)/0.25; p.y=0.0; p.z=0.0;
    }
    vboundary[i].tex=(Vector)p.Clone();
  }
}

public void ComputeBoundary(EdgeSet eboundary) {
  //mark boundary edges
  for(int i=0;i<edges.getCount();i++)
    if(edges[i].faces.getCount()<2) eboundary.add(edges[i]);
}

//Only works if there is precisely one boundary loop!!
public void ComputeBoundary(EdgeSet eboundary,VertexSet vboundary) {
  int i;
  Edge e;
  Vertex v;

  //mark boundary edges
  Console.Write("Total edges: {0}\n",edges.getCount());
  for(i=0;i<edges.getCount();i++) {
    edges[i].label=0;
    //mark boundaries
    if(edges[i].faces.getCount()<2) {
      edges[i].label|=BOUNDARY;
      eboundary.add(edges[i]);
    }
  }
  Console.Write("Boundary edges: {0}\n",eboundary.getCount());

  //remove edges one for one to get boundary vertices
  if(eboundary.getCount()==0)
    Console.Write("Fatal: boundary count=0\n");
  e=eboundary[0];
  v=e.ends[1];
  vboundary.add(e.ends[0]); vboundary.add(e.ends[1]);
  eboundary.remove(0);

  while(eboundary.getCount()>0) {
    for(i=0;i<eboundary.getCount();i++) {
      e=eboundary[i];
      if(e.ends[0]==v) {
        vboundary.add(e.ends[1]);
        eboundary.remove(i);
```

```
          v=e.ends[1]; e=null; break;
        } else if(e.ends[1]==v) {
          vboundary.add(e.ends[0]);
          eboundary.remove(i);
          v=e.ends[0]; e=null; break;
        }
      }
      if(e!=null) Console.Write("Broken loop! \n");
      if(e!=null) break;
    }

}

// Tutte
public void ParamBarycentric(int boundary_type) {
    int i, j, n, c;
    double lambda;
    EdgeSet eboundary=new EdgeSet();
    VertexSet vboundary=new VertexSet();
    Vertex v, v2;
    SparseMatrix M=new SparseMatrix();
    double[] bu, bv, scu, scv;

    ComputeBoundary(eboundary,vboundary);
    if(vboundary.getCount()==0) {
        Console.Write("No boundary, perhaps the mesh is too small?\n");
        return;
    }
    switch (boundary_type) {
        case BOUNDARY_CIRCLE: CircleBoundary(vboundary); break;
        case BOUNDARY_RECTANGLE: RectangleBoundary(vboundary); break;
        case BOUNDARY_CHORD_CIRCLE: CircleChordBoundary(vboundary); break;
        case BOUNDARY_CHORD_RECTANGLE: RectangleChordBoundary(vboundary);
            break;
        case BOUNDARY_PRESET: break;
        default: RectangleBoundary(vboundary); break;
    }

    //label non-border vertices according to equation variable number
    n=0;
    for(i=0;i<vertices.getCount();i++) {
        if(!vboundary.contains(vertices[i])) {
            vertices[i].label=n; n++;
        } else vertices[i].label=-1;
    }

    M.Resize(n,n);
    bu=new double[n]; bv=new double[n];
    for(i=0;i<n;i++) bu[i]=0.0;
    for(i=0;i<n;i++) bv[i]=0.0;
    scu=new double[n]; scv=new double[n];
```

```
//Border is paramerised. Set up system of equations setting each
//vertex to the barycentre of its neighbors (Tutte)
for(i=0;i<vertices.getCount();i++) {
    //check for a boundary
    v=vertices[i];
    if(v.label!=-1) {
        c=v.label;
        M[c,c]=1.0;
        //Compute the 1 ring
        VertexSet ring;
        ring=ComputeExclusiveRing(v,1);
        //From Floater: lambda=w_ij/sum(w_ij), for barycentric w_ij=1
        lambda=1.0/(ring.getCount());
        for(j=0;j<ring.getCount();j++) {
            v2=ring[j];
            if(v2==v) continue;
            //boundary goes into b
            if(v2.label==-1) {
                bu[c]+=lambda*v2.tex.x; bv[c]+=lambda*v2.tex.y;
            } else M[c,v2.label]=-lambda;
        }
    }
}

for(i=0;i<n;i++) scu[i]=bu[i];
for(i=0;i<n;i++) scv[i]=bv[i];
c=M.GaussSeidel(bu,100000,1e-7);
if(c<0) { Console.Write("Failed to solve\n"); return; }
if(c==0) {
    //failed to obtain accuracy, try again
    c=M.GaussSeidel(scu,100000,1e-7,bu);
    if(c==0) Console.Write("Failed to solve to desired accuracy\n");
    for(i=0;i<n;i++) bu[i]=scu[i];
}
c=M.GaussSeidel(bv,100000,1e-7);
if(c<0) { Console.Write("Failed to solve\n"); return; }
if(c==0) {
    //failed to obtain accuracy, try again
    c=M.GaussSeidel(scv,100000,1e-7,bv);
    if(c==0) Console.Write("Failed to solve to desired accuracy\n");
    for(i=0;i<n;i++) bv[i]=scv[i];
}

for(i=0;i<vertices.getCount();i++) {
    //check for a boundary
    v=vertices[i];
    if(v.label!=-1) {
        c=v.label;
        v.tex.x=bu[c]; v.tex.y=bv[c]; v.tex.z=0.0;
    }
}
```

```
}

public double angle(Vector v1,Vector v2) {
    double proj, ang;
    v1=(Vector)v1.Clone(); v2=(Vector)v2.Clone();
    v2.normalize(); v1.normalize();
    proj=v1*v2;
    ang=Math.Acos(proj);
    return ang;
}

//Stretch for a vertex
public double Sigma(Vertex v) {
    double sumarea=0.0, sumstretch=0.0;
    double area, stretch;

    for(int i=0;i<v.faces.getCount();i++) {
        area=v.faces[i].area();
        sumarea+=area;
        stretch=v.faces[i].stretch();
        sumstretch+=area*stretch*stretch;
    }
    return Math.Sqrt(sumstretch/sumarea);
}

//Stretch for entire mesh
public double AllStretch() {
    double sumarea=0.0, sumstretch=0.0;
    double area, stretch;

    for(int i=0;i<faces.getCount();i++) {
        area=faces[i].area();
        sumarea+=area;
        stretch=faces[i].stretch();
        sumstretch+=area*stretch*stretch;
    }

    return Math.Sqrt(sumstretch/sumarea);
}

//Determine if the vector from v1 to v2 and onwards crosses
//the vector from v3 to v4
public bool cross(Vector v1,Vector v2,Vector v3,Vector v4) {
    Vector dir, e1, e2, p1, p2;
    dir=v2-v1;
    dir.normalize();
    e1=v3-v2; e2=v4-v2;
    //check if either of the points are behind
    if(e1*dir<0) return false;
    if(e2*dir<0) return false;
    p1=e1-(e1*dir)*dir; p2=e2-(e2*dir)*dir;
```

```
    //don't care about positive crossings of v1-v2 and v3-v4
    //check if the perpendicular vectors are on opposite sides of dir
    if(p1*p2<=0.0) return true;
    return false;
}

//area of triangle
public double area(Vector v1,Vector v2,Vector v3)
{ return ((v2-v1)^(v3-v1)).norm()/2.0; }

public void ParamFloater(int boundary_type) {
    int i, j, k, n, c;
    double lambda, sumtheta, theta, totalw;
    EdgeSet eboundary=new EdgeSet();
    VertexSet vboundary=new VertexSet();
    Vertex v, v2=null, v3=null;
    SparseMatrix M=new SparseMatrix();
    double[] bu, bv, scu, scv;
    bool trianglesleft=true;
    Console.Write("Boundary\n");
    ComputeBoundary(eboundary,vboundary);
    if(vboundary.getCount()==0) {
        Console.Write("No boundary, perhaps the mesh is too small?\n");
        return;
    }
    Console.Write("Boundary param\n");
    switch (boundary_type) {
        case BOUNDARY_CIRCLE: CircleBoundary(vboundary); break;
        case BOUNDARY_RECTANGLE: RectangleBoundary(vboundary); break;
        case BOUNDARY_CHORD_CIRCLE: CircleChordBoundary(vboundary); break;
        case BOUNDARY_CHORD_RECTANGLE: RectangleChordBoundary(vboundary);
            break;
        case BOUNDARY_PRESET: break;
        default: RectangleBoundary(vboundary); break;
    }

    //label non-border vertices according to equation variable number
    n=0;
    for(i=0;i<vertices.getCount();i++) {
        if(!vboundary.contains(vertices[i])) {
            vertices[i].label=n; n++;
        } else vertices[i].label=-1;
    }

    Console.Write("Main param...\n");
    M.Resize(n,n);
    bu=new double[n]; bv=new double[n];
    for(i=0;i<n;i++) bu[i]=0.0;
    for(i=0;i<n;i++) bv[i]=0.0;
    scu=new double[n]; scv=new double[n];
    //Border is paramerised. Set up system of equations setting
```

```
//each vertex to a weighted average of its neighbors (Floater)
for(i=0;i<vertices.getCount();i++) {
  //check for a boundary
  v=vertices[i];
  //corresponds to edges
  v.wij=new double[v.valence()];
  for(j=0;j<v.valence();j++) v.wij[j]=0.0;
  if(v.label!=-1) {
    VertexSet ring;
    ring=ComputeExclusiveRing(v,1);
    //save texture coordinates of boundary in normals
    for(j=0;j<ring.getCount();j++) {
      ring[j].n=(Vector)ring[j].tex.Clone();
    }
    c=v.label;
    M[c,c]=1.0;
    //Now do local parameterisation according to Floater, set p in the middle
    v.tex=new Vector(0,0,0);
    //determine sum of angles
    sumtheta=0.0;
    for(j=0;j<v.faces.getCount();j++) {
      if(v==v.faces[j].vertices[0]) {
        v2=v.faces[j].vertices[1]; v3=v.faces[j].vertices[2];
      } else if(v==v.faces[j].vertices[1]) {
        v2=v.faces[j].vertices[0]; v3=v.faces[j].vertices[2];
      } else if(v==v.faces[j].vertices[2]) {
        v2=v.faces[j].vertices[0]; v3=v.faces[j].vertices[1];
      }
      sumtheta+=Math.Abs(angle(v2.v-v.v,v3.v-v.v));
      //this face has not been parameterized yet
      v.faces[j].label=0;
    }

    //place first adjacent vertex horizontally, preserving distance
    j=0;
    if(v==v.faces[j].vertices[0]) {
      v2=v.faces[j].vertices[1]; v3=v.faces[j].vertices[2];
    } else if(v==v.faces[j].vertices[1]) {
      v2=v.faces[j].vertices[0]; v3=v.faces[j].vertices[2];
    } else if(v==v.faces[j].vertices[2]) {
      v2=v.faces[j].vertices[0]; v3=v.faces[j].vertices[1];
    }
    theta=0.0;
    theta+=2*Math.PI*Math.Abs(angle(v2.v-v.v,v3.v-v.v))/sumtheta;
    v2.tex.x=(v2.v-v.v).norm();
    v2.tex.y=v2.tex.z=0.0;
    v3.tex.x=Math.Cos(theta); v3.tex.y=Math.Sin(theta);
    v3.tex.z=0.0;
    v3.tex*=(v3.v-v.v).norm();
    v2=v3;
```

```
//Place vertices at shape preserving angles around the vertex
//This creates a local shape preserving parameterization
trianglesleft=true;
while(trianglesleft) {
    //Find a triangle adjacent to the current one, that
    //has not been computed
    Edge e=new Edge();
    e.ends[0]=v; e.ends[1]=v2;

    trianglesleft=false;
    for(j=0;j<v.faces.getCount();j++) {
        if(v.faces[j].label==0) {
            //check to see if common edge is shared
            if(v.faces[j].edges[0].Equals(e)) break;
            if(v.faces[j].edges[1].Equals(e)) break;
            if(v.faces[j].edges[2].Equals(e)) break;
        }
    }
    //found an adjacent triangle
    if(j<v.faces.getCount()) {
        int[] tag=new int [3]{0,0,0};
        for(k=0;k<3;k++) {
            if(v==v.faces[j].vertices[k]) tag[k]=1;
            if(v2==v.faces[j].vertices[k]) tag[k]=1;
        }
        for(k=0;k<3;k++) {
            if(tag[k]==0) v3=v.faces[j].vertices[k];
        }
        //The undetermined vertex is placed according to
        //its angle to the vertex, and the parametric distance
        //is set to be the same as the real distance
        theta+=2*Math.PI*Math.Abs(angle(v2.v-v.v,v3.v-v.v))/sumtheta;
        v3.tex.x=Math.Cos(theta); v3.tex.y=Math.Sin(theta);
        v3.tex.z=0.0;
        v3.tex*=(v3.v-v.v).norm();
        v2=v3;
        trianglesleft=true;
        v.faces[j].label=1;
    }
}

//For each vertex determine a triangle that v lies in, and then
//adjust the weights according to the barycentric coordinates
//Note: ring.getCount()==v.valence()
for(k=0;k<ring.getCount();k++) {
    for(j=0;j<v.faces.getCount();j++) {
        if(v==v.faces[j].vertices[0]) {
            v2=v.faces[j].vertices[1]; v3=v.faces[j].vertices[2];
        } else if(v==v.faces[j].vertices[1]) {
            v2=v.faces[j].vertices[0]; v3=v.faces[j].vertices[2];
        } else if(v==v.faces[j].vertices[2]) {
```

```
            v2=v.faces[j].vertices[0]; v3=v.faces[j].vertices[1];
          }
          //determine if this is the triangle
          if(cross(ring[k].tex,v.tex,v2.tex,v3.tex)) {
            double l1, l2, l3, a;
            int i2, i3;
            i2=ring.index(v2); i3=ring.index(v3);
            a=area(ring[k].tex,v2.tex,v3.tex);
            l1=area(v.tex,v2.tex,v3.tex)/a;
            l2=area(ring[k].tex,v.tex,v3.tex)/a;
            l3=area(ring[k].tex,v2.tex,v.tex)/a;
            v.wij[k]+=l1; v.wij[i2]+=l2; v.wij[i3]+=l3;
          }
        }
      }

      totalw=0.0;
      for(j=0;j<ring.getCount();j++) {
        totalw+=v.wij[j];
        //if it is a border vertex, put the normal back in the texture
        if(ring[j].label==-1) ring[j].tex=(Vector)ring[j].n.Clone();
      }

      for(j=0;j<ring.getCount();j++) {
        v2=ring[j];
        lambda=v.wij[j]/totalw;
        if(v2==v) continue;
        //boundary goes into b
        if(v2.label==-1) {
          bu[c]+=lambda*v2.tex.x; bv[c]+=lambda*v2.tex.y;
        } else M[c,v2.label]=-lambda;
      }
    }
  }

for(i=0;i<n;i++) scu[i]=bu[i];
for(i=0;i<n;i++) scv[i]=bv[i];
Console.Write("Solving\n");
c=M.GaussSeidel(bu,100000,1e-7);
if(c<0) { Console.Write("Failed to solve\n"); return; }
if(c==0) {
  //failed to obtain accuracy, try again
  c=M.GaussSeidel(scu,100000,1e-7, bu);
  if(c==0) Console.Write("Failed to solve to desired accuracy\n");
  for(i=0;i<n;i++) bu[i]=scu[i];
}
c=M.GaussSeidel(bv,100000,1e-7);
if(c<0) { Console.Write("Failed to solve\n"); return; }
if(c==0) {
  //failed to obtain accuracy, try again
  c=M.GaussSeidel(scv,100000,1e-7, bv);
```

```
      if(c==0) Console.Write("Failed to solve to desired accuracy\n");
      for(i=0;i<n;i++) bv[i]=scv[i];
   }

   for(i=0;i<vertices.getCount();i++) {
     //check for a boundary
     v=vertices[i];
     if(v.label!=-1) {
        c=v.label; v.tex.x=bu[c]; v.tex.y=bv[c]; v.tex.z=0.0;
     }
   }
}

//Mean value parameterisation, also due to Floater
public void ParamMeanValue(int boundary_type) {
   int i, j, k, n, c;
   double lambda, sumtheta, theta, totalw;
   EdgeSet eboundary=new EdgeSet();
   VertexSet vboundary=new VertexSet();
   Vertex v, v2=null, v3=null;
   SparseMatrix M=new SparseMatrix();
   double[] bu, bv, scu, scv;
   bool trianglesleft=true;

   ComputeBoundary(eboundary,vboundary);
   if(vboundary.getCount()==0) {
      Console.Write("No boundary, perhaps the mesh is too small?\n");
      return;
   }
   switch (boundary_type) {
      case BOUNDARY_CIRCLE: CircleBoundary(vboundary); break;
      case BOUNDARY_RECTANGLE: RectangleBoundary(vboundary); break;
      case BOUNDARY_CHORD_CIRCLE: CircleChordBoundary(vboundary); break;
      case BOUNDARY_CHORD_RECTANGLE: RectangleChordBoundary(vboundary);
         break;
      case BOUNDARY_PRESET: break;
      default:  RectangleBoundary(vboundary); break;
   }

   //label non-border vertices according to equation variable number
   n=0;
   for(i=0;i<vertices.getCount();i++) {
      if(!vboundary.contains(vertices[i])) {
         vertices[i].label=n; n++;
      } else vertices[i].label=-1;
   }

   M.Resize(n,n);
   bu=new double[n]; bv=new double[n];
   for(i=0;i<n;i++) bu[i]=0.0;
   for(i=0;i<n;i++) bv[i]=0.0;
```

```
scu=new double[n]; scv=new double[n];
//Border is paramerised. Set up system of equations setting
//each vertex to a weighted average of its neighbors (Mean value)
for(i=0;i<vertices.getCount();i++) {
   //check for a boundary
   v=vertices[i];
   //corresponds to edges
   v.wij=new double[v.valence()];
   for(j=0;j<v.valence();j++) v.wij[j]=0.0;

   if(v.label!=-1) {
      VertexSet ring;
      ring=ComputeExclusiveRing(v,1);
      //save texture coordinates of boundary in normals
      for(j=0;j<ring.getCount();j++)
         ring[j].normal=(Vector)ring[j].tex.Clone();
      c=v.label;
      M[c,c]=1.0;
      //Now do local parameterisation according to Floater
      //set p in the middle
      v.tex=new Vector(0,0,0);
      //determine sum of angles
      sumtheta=0.0;
      for(j=Q;j<v.faces.getCount();j++) {
         if(v==v.faces[j].vertices[0]) {
            v2=v.faces[j].vertices[1]; v3=v.faces[j].vertices[2];
         } else if(v==v.faces[j].vertices[1]) {
            v2=v.faces[j].vertices[0]; v3=v.faces[j].vertices[2];
         } else if(v==v.faces[j].vertices[2]) {
            v2=v.faces[j].vertices[0]; v3=v.faces[j].vertices[1];
         }
         sumtheta+=Math.Abs(angle(v2.v-v.v,v3.v-v.v));
         //this face has not been parameterized yet
         v.faces[j].label=0;
      }

      //place first adjacent vertex horizontally, preserving distance
      j=0;
      if(v==v.faces[j].vertices[0]) {
         v2=v.faces[j].vertices[1]; v3=v.faces[j].vertices[2];
      } else if(v==v.faces[j].vertices[1]) {
         v2=v.faces[j].vertices[0]; v3=v.faces[j].vertices[2];
      } else if(v==v.faces[j].vertices[2]) {
         v2=v.faces[j].vertices[0]; v3=v.faces[j].vertices[1];
      }
      theta=0.0;
      theta+=2*Math.PI*Math.Abs(angle(v2.v-v.v,v3.v-v.v))/sumtheta;
      v2.tex.x=(v2.v-v.v).norm();
      v2.tex.y=v2.tex.z=0.0;
      v3.tex.x=Math.Cos(theta); v3.tex.y=Math.Sin(theta);
      v3.tex.z=0.0;
```

```
v3.tex*=(v3.v-v.v).norm();
v2=v3;

//Place vertices at shape preserving angles around the vertex
//This creates a local shape preserving parameterization
trianglesleft=true;
while(trianglesleft) {
    //Find a triangle adjacent to the current one, that
    //has not been computed
    Edge e=new Edge();
    e.ends[0]=v; e.ends[1]=v2;

    trianglesleft=false;
    for(j=0;j<v.faces.getCount();j++) {
        if(v.faces[j].label==0) {
            //check to see if common edge is shared
            if(v.faces[j].edges[0].Equals(e)) break;
            if(v.faces[j].edges[1].Equals(e)) break;
            if(v.faces[j].edges[2].Equals(e)) break;
        }
    }
    //found an adjacent triangle
    if(j<v.faces.getCount()) {
        int[] tag=new int[3]{0,0,0};
        for(k=0;k<3;k++) {
            if(v==v.faces[j].vertices[k]) tag[k]=1;
            if(v2==v.faces[j].vertices[k]) tag[k]=1;
        }
        for(k=0;k<3;k++)
            if(tag[k]==0) v3=v.faces[j].vertices[k];
        //The undetermined vertex is placed according to
        //its angle to the vertex, and the parametric distance
        //is set to be the same as the real distance
        theta+=2*Math.PI*Math.Abs(angle(v2.v-v.v,v3.v-v.v))/sumtheta;
        v3.tex.x=Math.Cos(theta);
        v3.tex.y=Math.Sin(theta); v3.tex.z=0.0;
        v3.tex*=(v3.v-v.v).norm(); v2=v3;
        trianglesleft=true;
        v.faces[j].label=1;
    }
}

for(k=0;k<ring.getCount();k++) {
    double alpha,beta;
    Edge e;
    Edge e2=new Edge();

    e2.ends[0]=v; e2.ends[1]=v2;
    v2=ring[k];
    e=v.edges.match(e2);
    //find angles adjacent to edge
```

```
            Face f=e.faces[0];
            if(v==f.vertices[0]) { v2=f.vertices[1]; v3=f.vertices[2]; }
            else if(v==f.vertices[1]) { v2=f.vertices[0]; v3=f.vertices[2]; }
            else if(v==f.vertices[2]) { v2=f.vertices[0]; v3=f.vertices[1]; }
            alpha=angle(v3.v-v.v,v2.v-v.v);

            f=e.faces[1];
            if(v==f.vertices[0]) { v2=f.vertices[1]; v3=f.vertices[2]; }
            else if(v==f.vertices[1]) { v2=f.vertices[0]; v3=f.vertices[2]; }
            else if(v==f.vertices[2]) { v2=f.vertices[0]; v3=f.vertices[1]; }
            beta=angle(v3.v-v.v,v2.v-v.v);

            //Formula from mean-value paper by Floater
            v.wij[k]=(Math.Tan(alpha/2.0)+Math.Tan(beta/2.0))
                /(v2.v-v.v).norm();
        }

        totalw=0.0;
        for(j=0;j<ring.getCount();j++) {
            totalw+=v.wij[j];
            //if it is a border vertex, put the normal back in the texture
            if(ring[j].label==-1)
                ring[j].tex=(Vector)ring[j].normal.Clone();
        }

        for(j=0;j<ring.getCount();j++) {
            v2=ring[j];
            lambda=v.wij[j]/totalw;
            if(v2==v) continue;
            //boundary goes into b
            if(v2.label==-1) {
                bu[c]+=lambda*v2.tex.x; bv[c]+=lambda*v2.tex.y;
            } else M[c,v2.label]=-lambda;
        }
    }
}

for(i=0;i<n;i++) scu[i]=bu[i];
for(i=0;i<n;i++) scv[i]=bv[i];
c=M.GaussSeidel(bu,100000,1e-7);
if(c<0) { Console.Write("Failed to solve\n"); return; }
if(c==0) {
    //failed to obtain accuracy, try again
    c=M.GaussSeidel(scu,100000,1e-7,bu);
    if(c==0) Console.Write("Failed to solve to desired accuracy\n");
    for(i=0;i<n;i++) bu[i]=scu[i];
}
c=M.GaussSeidel(bv,100000,1e-7);
if(c<0) { Console.Write("Failed to solve\n"); return; }
if(c==0) {
    //failed to obtain accuracy, try again
```

```
        c=M.GaussSeidel(scv,100000,1e-7,bv);
        if(c==0) Console.Write("Failed to solve to desired accuracy\n");
        for(i=0;i<n;i++) bv[i]=scv[i];
    }

    for(i=0;i<vertices.getCount();i++) {
        //check for a boundary
        v=vertices[i];
        if(v.label!=-1) {
            c=v.label; v.tex.x=bu[c]; v.tex.y=bv[c]; v.tex.z=0.0;
        }
    }
}

//Use Floater parameterisation, followed by stretch minimisation of
//Yoshizawa, Belyaev and Seidel (2004)
public void ParamStretchmin(int boundary_type,double eta) {
    int i, j, n, c;
    double lambda, sigma, totalw, Enew, Eold;
    EdgeSet eboundary=new EdgeSet();
    VertexSet vboundary=new VertexSet();
    Vertex v, v2;
    SparseMatrix M=new SparseMatrix();
    double[] bu, bv, su, sv, scu, scv;
    int iter=500;
    Mesh opt=null;

    ParamFloater(boundary_type);
    ComputeBoundary(eboundary,vboundary);
    if(vboundary.getCount()==0) {
        Console.Write("No boundary, perhaps the mesh is too small?\n");
        return;
    }
    switch (boundary_type) {
        case BOUNDARY_CIRCLE: CircleBoundary(vboundary); break;
        case BOUNDARY_RECTANGLE: RectangleBoundary(vboundary); break;
        case BOUNDARY_CHORD_CIRCLE: CircleChordBoundary(vboundary); break;
        case BOUNDARY_CHORD_RECTANGLE: RectangleChordBoundary(vboundary);
            break;
        case BOUNDARY_PRESET: break;
        default: RectangleBoundary(vboundary); break;
    }

    //label non-border vertices according to equation variable number
    n=0;
    for(i=0;i<vertices.getCount();i++) {
        if(!vboundary.contains(vertices[i])) {
            vertices[i].label=n; n++;
        } else vertices[i].label=-1;
    }
    Console.Write("variables={0}\n",n);
```

```
M.Resize(n,n);
bu=new double[n]; bv=new double[n];
for(i=0;i<n;i++) bu[i]=0.0;
for(i=0;i<n;i++) bv[i]=0.0;
su=new double[n]; sv=new double[n];
scu=new double[n]; scv=new double[n];

Eold=AllStretch()+1.0;
while(--iter>0) {
  Enew=AllStretch();
  Console.Write("Eold={0} Enew={1}\n",Eold,Enew);
  if((Enew>=Eold)||(Double.IsNaN(Enew))) break;
  Eold=Enew; opt=this.Clone();
  Console.Write("Stretchmin iter {0}\n",iter);

  for(i=0;i<n;i++) bu[i]=0.0;
  for(i=0;i<n;i++) bv[i]=0.0;
  for(i=0;i<vertices.getCount();i++) { //check for a boundary
    v=vertices[i];

    if(v.label!=-1) {
      c=v.label;
      M[c,c]=1.0;
      VertexSet ring;
      ring=ComputeExclusiveRing(v,1);
      for(j=0;j<ring.getCount();j++) {
        sigma=Sigma(ring[j]);
        sigma=Math.Pow(sigma,eta);
        if(sigma!=0.0) v.wij[j]/=sigma;
      }

      totalw=0.0;
      for(j=0;j<ring.getCount();j++) totalw+=v.wij[j];

      for(j=0;j<ring.getCount();j++) {
        v2=ring[j];
        lambda=v.wij[j]/totalw;
        if(lambda<0) Console.Write("-lambda\n");
        if(v2==v) continue;
        //boundary goes into b
        if(v2.label==-1) {
          bu[c]+=lambda*v2.tex.x;
          bv[c]+=lambda*v2.tex.y;
        } else M[c,v2.label]=-lambda;
      }
    }
  }

  for(i=0;i<vertices.getCount();i++) {
    //check for a boundary
```

```
            v=vertices[i];
            if(v.label!=-1) {
                c=v.label; su[c]=v.tex.x; sv[c]=v.tex.y;
            }
        }

        for(i=0;i<n;i++)  scu[i]=bu[i];
        for(i=0;i<n;i++)  scv[i]=bv[i];
        c=M.GaussSeidel(bu,100000,1e-7);
        if(c<0) {
            Console.Write("Failed to solve\n");
            copy(opt); return;
        }
        if(c==0) {
            //failed to obtain accuracy, try again
            c=M.GaussSeidel(scu,100000,1e-7,bu);
            if(c==0) {
                Console.Write("Failed to solve to desired accuracy\n");
                eta/=2.0; continue;
            }
            for(i=0;i<n;i++)  bu[i]=scu[i];
        }
        c=M.GaussSeidel(bv,100000,1e-7);
        if(c<0) {
            Console.Write("Failed to solve\n");
            copy(opt); return;
        }
        if(c==0) {
            //failed to obtain accuracy, try again
            c=M.GaussSeidel(scv,100000,1e-7,bv);
            if(c==0) {
                Console.Write("Failed to solve to desired accuracy\n");
                eta/=2.0; continue;
            }
            for(i=0;i<n;i++)  bv[i]=scv[i];
        }
        for(i=0;i<vertices.getCount();i++) {
            //check for a boundary
            v=vertices[i];
            if(v.label!=-1) {
                c=v.label;
                v.tex.x=bu[c]; v.tex.y=bv[c]; v.tex.z=0.0;
            }
        }
    }
    Console.Write("Stretchmin done\n");
    copy(opt);
    Console.Write("opt assigned\n");
}

//Loop subdivision only works on triangle meshes
```

```
//Loop subdivision only works on 2-manifold meshes
public Mesh SubdivideLoop() {
    int i,j,k;
    Vector nv;
    Mesh nm=new Mesh();

    for(i=0;i<vertices.getCount();i++) {
        nv=new Vector(0.0,0.0,0.0);
        if(vertices[i].boundary()) {
            //Find two boundary edges, each opposite end contributes 1
            //while this vertex contributes 6/8
            for(j=0;j<vertices[i].edges.getCount();j++) {
                Edge e=vertices[i].edges[j];
                if(e.boundary()) {
                    nv+=1.0/8.0*e.ends[0].v;
                    nv+=1.0/8.0*e.ends[1].v;
                }
            }
            //this vertex has been added with weight 2*1.0/8.0
            //still need 4.0/8.0
            nv+=0.5*vertices[i].v;
        } else {
            VertexSet ring=ComputeExclusiveRing(vertices[i],1);
            //the valence
            int n=vertices[i].valence(); //==ring.getCount()
            //To use Loop's method uncomment the next two lines
            //double num=(3.0+2.0*Math.Cos(2.0*Math.PI/n));
            //double beta=1.0/n*(5.0/8.0-num*num/64.0);
            //Warren and Weimer's method
            double beta=3.0/(n*(n+2.0));
            nv=vertices[i].v*(1-n*beta);
            for(j=0;j<n;j++) {
                nv+=beta*ring[j].v;
            }
        }
        vertices[i].label=nm.AddVertex(nv);
    }
    for(i=0;i<edges.getCount();i++) {
        nv=new Vector();
        Edge e=edges[i];
        if(e.boundary()) {
            nv=0.5*e.ends[0].v;  nv+=0.5*e.ends[1].v;
        } else {
            nv=3.0/8.0*e.ends[0].v;  nv+=3.0/8.0*e.ends[1].v;
            //for each face find the vertex not on the edge
            for(k=0;k<2;k++) {
                nv+=1.0/8.0*e.faces[k].OffEdge(e).v;
            }
        }
        e.label=nm.AddVertex(nv);
    }
```

```
//vertices are created, now add the triangles
for(i=0;i<faces.getCount();i++) {
    Face f=faces[i];
    //center triangle
    nm.AddTriangle(f.edges[0].label,f.edges[1].label,f.edges[2].label);
    //triangles connected to existing vertices
    for(j=0;j<3;j++) {
        for(k=j+1;k<3;k++) {
            Vertex v=null;
            //find common vertex
            if(f.edges[j].ends[0]==f.edges[k].ends[0]) v=f.edges[j].ends[0];
            if(f.edges[j].ends[0]==f.edges[k].ends[1]) v=f.edges[j].ends[0];
            if(f.edges[j].ends[1]==f.edges[k].ends[1]) v=f.edges[j].ends[1];
            if(f.edges[j].ends[1]==f.edges[k].ends[0]) v=f.edges[j].ends[1];
            nm.AddTriangle(f.edges[j].label,v.label,f.edges[k].label);
        }
    }
}
return nm;
}

//This is an interpolating subdivision scheme
//so existing vertices are left unaltered
public Mesh SubdivideButterfly() {
    int i,j,k;
    Vector nv;
    Mesh nm=new Mesh();

    //add existing vertices with no changes
    for(i=0;i<vertices.getCount();i++)
        vertices[i].label=nm.AddVertex(vertices[i].v);
    //create new vertices for each edge
    for(i=0;i<edges.getCount();i++) {
        nv=new Vector();
        Edge e=edges[i];
        if(e.boundary()) {
            nv=9.0/16.0*e.ends[0].v; nv+=9.0/16.0*e.ends[1].v;
            //find adjacent boundary edges
            for(k=0;k<2;k++) {
                for(j=0;j<e.ends[k].edges.getCount();j++) {
                    Edge eb=e.ends[k].edges[j];
                    if((eb!=e)&&(eb.boundary())) {
                        if(eb.ends[0]==e.ends[k]) nv-=1.0/16.0*eb.ends[1].v;
                        else nv-=1.0/16.0*eb.ends[0].v;
                    }
                }
            }
        } else {
            //number of irregular settings encountered, to compute average
            int irreg=0;
```

```
//check for regular setting
if((e.ends[0].valence()==6)&&(e.ends[1].valence()==6)) {
    nv+=0.5*e.ends[0].v; nv+=0.5*e.ends[1].v;
    //for each face find the vertex not on the edge
    for(k=0;k<2;k++)
        nv+=1.0/8.0*e.faces[k].OffEdge(e).v;
    //Now find the other faces adjacent to the
    //edge faces, and find the point not on the
    //edge faces (4 of them).
    for(k=0;k<2;k++) {
        for(j=0;j<3;j++) {
            if(e.faces[k].edges[j]!=e) {
                Face adj=null;
                if(e.faces[k]==e.faces[k].edges[j].faces[0])
                    adj=e.faces[k].edges[j].faces[1];
                else adj=e.faces[k].edges[j].faces[0];
                if(adj!=null)
                    nv-=1.0/16.0*adj.OffEdge(e.faces[k].edges[j]).v;
                else {} //use a reflection, left to the reader
            }
        }
    }

    //since we will divide set irreg to something not zero
    irreg=1;
}
//and now the irregular setting
for(k=0;k<2;k++) {
    if(e.ends[k].valence()!=6) {
        double sumwi=0.0;
        VertexSet ring=ComputeExclusiveRing(e.ends[k],1);
        ring=OrderRing(e.ends[k],e.ends[1-k],ring);
        if(e.ends[k].valence()==3) {
            nv+=5.0/12.0*ring[0].v; sumwi+=5.0/12.0;
            nv-=1.0/12.0*ring[1].v; sumwi+=-1.0/12.0;
            nv-=1.0/12.0*ring[2].v; sumwi+=-1.0/12.0;
        } else
        if(e.ends[k].valence()==4) {
            nv+=3.0/8.0*ring[0].v; sumwi+=3.0/8.0;
            //ring[1] weight is zero
            nv-=1.0/8.0*ring[2].v; sumwi+=-1.0/8.0;
            //ring[3] weight is zero
        } else {
            int n=ring.getCount();
            for(j=0;j<ring.getCount();j++) {
                double wi=0.25+Math.Cos(2.0*Math.PI*j/n)+
                    0.5*Math.Cos(4.0*Math.PI*j/n);
                wi/=n; sumwi+=wi; nv+=wi*ring[j].v;
            }
        }
        nv+=(1.0-sumwi)*e.ends[k].v;
```

```
                 irreg++;
            }
        }
        nv/=irreg;
    }
    e.label=nm.AddVertex(nv);
}


//vertices are created, now add the triangles
for(i=0;i<faces.getCount();i++) {
    Face f=faces[i];
    //center triangle
    nm.AddTriangle(f.edges[0].label,f.edges[1].label,f.edges[2].label);
    //triangles connected to existing vertices
    for(j=0;j<3;j++) {
        for(k=j+1;k<3;k++) {
            Vertex v=null;
            //find common vertex
            if(f.edges[j].ends[0]==f.edges[k].ends[0]) v=f.edges[j].ends[0];
            if(f.edges[j].ends[0]==f.edges[k].ends[1]) v=f.edges[j].ends[0];
            if(f.edges[j].ends[1]==f.edges[k].ends[1]) v=f.edges[j].ends[1];
            if(f.edges[j].ends[1]==f.edges[k].ends[0]) v=f.edges[j].ends[1];
            nm.AddTriangle(f.edges[j].label,v.label,f.edges[k].label);
        }
    }
}
return nm;
}

//m is the vertex for which ring is the 1-ring
//start is the first vertex in the ordered ring
public VertexSet OrderRing(Vertex m,Vertex start,VertexSet ring) {
    int i, j, miss=0;
    bool found;
    Vertex v=start;
    VertexSet r=new VertexSet();
    ring.remove(start);
    r.add(start);

    while(ring.getCount()>0) {
        found=false;
        for(i=0;i<m.faces.getCount();i++) {
            for(j=0;j<m.faces[i].edges.getCount();j++) {
                Edge e=m.faces[i].edges[j];
                if((e.ends[0]==v)&&(ring.contains(e.ends[1]))) {
                    v=e.ends[1]; r.add(v); ring.remove(v);
                    found=true;
                    break;
                } else if((e.ends[1]==v)&&(ring.contains(e.ends[0]))) {
                    v=e.ends[0]; r.add(v); ring.remove(v);
                    found=true;
```

```
            break;
        }
    }
    if(found) break;
}
//no edge found, this could be a problem
if(!found) miss++;
//The ring of vertices is probably broken by a boundary, we should
//use reflection to create virtual interpolation points. Instead
//we just look for the other edge of the boundary. It is not sufficient
//that this is a boundary point, it must also only have one face in common
//with the vertex for which the ring has been computed
if(miss>5) {
    miss=0;
    for(i=0;i<m.edges.getCount();i++) {
        if(m.edges[i].boundary()) {
            if(m.edges[i].ends[0]==m) v=m.edges[i].ends[1];
            else v=m.edges[i].ends[0];
            if(ring.contains(v)) {
                r.add(v); ring.remove(v); found=true;
                break;
            }
        }
    }
}
    return r;
}

//Boundary specifies whether the boundary edge must be subdivided
//this must only happen every second iteration
public Mesh SubdivideSqrt3(bool boundary) {
    int i, j, k;
    int v1, v2, v3, v4, v5;
    Mesh nm=new Mesh();
    //edge flipping happens as a second pass so we have two meshes
    Mesh nm2=new Mesh();
    Vector nv;
    //smooth exisitng vertices
    for(i=0;i<vertices.getCount();i++) {
        VertexSet ring;
        nv=new Vector();
        if(vertices[i].boundary()) {
            if(boundary) {
                //Find two boundary edges each opposite end contributes 4/27
                //while this vertex contributes 19/27
                for(j=0;j<vertices[i].edges.getCount();j++) {
                    Edge e=vertices[i].edges[j];
                    if(e.boundary()) {
                        nv+=4.0/27.0*e.ends[0].v; nv+=4.0/27.0*e.ends[1].v;
                    }
```

```
                    }
                    // This vertex has been added with weight 2*4.0/27.0
                    // still need 11.0/27.0
                    nv+=11.0/27.0*vertices[i].v;
                } else nv=(Vector)vertices[i].v.Clone();
            } else {
                int n=vertices[i].valence();
                double alpha=4.0-2.0*Math.Cos(2.0*Math.PI/n);
                alpha/=9.0;
                nv=(1.0-alpha)*vertices[i].v;
                ring=ComputeExclusiveRing(vertices[i],1);
                for(j=0;j<ring.getCount();j++)
                    nv+=alpha/n*ring[j].v;
            }
            vertices[i].label=nm.AddVertex(nv);
            // label this as : not a new vertex
            nm.vertices[vertices[i].label].label=0;
        }
        // add a new vertex for each face
        for(i=0;i<faces.getCount();i++) {
            nv=new Vector();
            if((faces[i].boundary())&&(boundary)) {
                Edge e=null;
                // There should be precisely one boundary edge. In the first pass any
                // triangle with two boundary edges is subdivided so that each new triangle
                // has only one boundary edge. Since this code should only be invoked every
                // second iteration only one boundary edge should be present.
                for(j=0;j<faces[i].edges.getCount();j++) {
                    if(faces[i].edges[j].boundary()) e=faces[i].edges[j];
                }
                // split the boundary edge, first find two boundary edges
                nv=new Vector();
                for(k=0;k<e.ends[0].edges.getCount();k++) {
                    Edge e2=e.ends[0].edges[k];
                    if(e2.boundary()&&(e2!=e)) {
                        if(e2.ends[0]!=e.ends[0])
                            nv=1.0/27.0*(e2.ends[0].v+16.0*e.ends[0].v+10.0*e.ends[1].v);
                        else
                            nv=1.0/27.0*(e2.ends[1].v+16.0*e.ends[0].v+10.0*e.ends[1].v);
                    }
                }
                v4=nm.AddVertex(nv);

                nv=new Vector();
                for(k=0;k<e.ends[1].edges.getCount();k++) {
                    Edge e2=e.ends[1].edges[k];
                    if(e2.boundary()&&(e2!=e)) {
                        if(e2.ends[0]!=e.ends[1])
                            nv=1.0/27.0*(e2.ends[0].v+16.0*e.ends[1].v+10.0*e.ends[0].v);
                        else
                            nv=1.0/27.0*(e2.ends[1].v+16.0*e.ends[1].v+10.0*e.ends[0].v);
```

```
        }
    }
    v5=nm.AddVertex(nv);
    //since vertices are added sequntially we have v5=v4+1
    faces[i].label=v4;
    nm.vertices[v4].label=1;
    nm.vertices[v5].label=1;
} else {
    nv=faces[i].vertices[0].v/3.0;
    nv+=faces[i].vertices[1].v/3.0;
    nv+=faces[i].vertices[2].v/3.0;
    faces[i].label=nm.AddVertex(nv);
    //label this as : a new vertex
    nm.vertices[faces[i].label].label=1;
    }
}
//Now create the new triangles
//Edge flips are done later
for(i=0;i<faces.getCount();i++) {
    if((faces[i].boundary())&&(boundary)) {
        //Boundary edges are only subdivided every second iteration
        //and are not subject to edge flips.
        Edge e=null;
        //Tthere should be precisely one boundary edge. In the first pass any
        //triangle with two boundary edges is subdivided so that each new triangle
        //has only one boundary edge. Since this code should only be invoked every
        //second iteration only one boundary edge should be present.
        for(j=0;j<faces[i].edges.getCount();j++) {
            if(faces[i].edges[j].boundary()) e=faces[i].edges[j];
        }
        v1=faces[i].OffEdge(e).label;
        v2=e.ends[0].label; v3=e.ends[1].label; v4=faces[i].label;
        v5=v4+1;
        nm.AddTriangle(v1,v2,v4); nm.AddTriangle(v1,v4,v5);
        nm.AddTriangle(v1,v5,v3);
    } else {
        v4=faces[i].label;
        v1=faces[i].vertices[0].label;
        v2=faces[i].vertices[1].label;
        v3=faces[i].vertices[2].label;
        nm.AddTriangle(v1,v2,v4); nm.AddTriangle(v2,v3,v4);
        nm.AddTriangle(v3,v1,v4);
    }
}

//now do edge flipping, create a new mesh with the same vertices
for(i=0;i<nm.vertices.getCount();i++) //add the vertex and store the index
    nm.vertices[i].pos=nm2.AddVertex(nm.vertices[i].v);
//now add the triangles in such a way that the edgesi are flipped
for(i=0;i<nm.faces.getCount();i++) //not added yet
    nm.faces[i].label=0;
```

```
for(i=0;i<nm.edges.getCount();i++) {
  //only non boundary edges need to be flipped
  Edge e=nm.edges[i];
  if(!e.boundary()) {
    //only flip if both ends of the edge are "old vertices"
    if((e.ends[0].label==0)&&(e.ends[1].label==0)) {
      //and if oppposite ends are "new vertices"
      if((e.faces[0].OffEdge(e).label==1)
      &&(e.faces[1].OffEdge(e).label==1)) {
        v1=e.ends[0].pos; v2=e.ends[1].pos;
        v3=e.faces[0].OffEdge(e).pos;
        v4=e.faces[1].OffEdge(e).pos;
        nm2.AddTriangle(v1,v3,v4); nm2.AddTriangle(v3,v2,v4);
        //these triangles are added
        e.faces[0].label=1; e.faces[1].label=1;
      }
    }
  }
}
for(i=0;i<nm.faces.getCount();i++) {
  if(nm.faces[i].label==0) {
    v1=nm.faces[i].vertices[0].pos;
    v2=nm.faces[i].vertices[1].pos;
    v3=nm.faces[i].vertices[2].pos;
    nm2.AddTriangle(v1,v2,v3);
  }
}
return nm2;
}

public void AlignAdjacentFaces(FaceSet queue) {
  int i;
  Face f;
  while(queue.getCount()>0) {
    f=queue[0];
    queue.remove(0);
    if(f.label==0) return;
    for(i=0;i<f.edges.getCount();i++) {
      Edge e=f.edges[i];
      Face adj;
      if(!e.boundary()) {
        if(e.faces[0]==f) adj=e.faces[1];
        else adj=e.faces[0];
        //might cause acute angles to face inward!
        if((adj.normal*f.normal<0.0)&&(adj.label==0)) {
          //flip adj to have same orientation as this face
          Vertex tmp;
          tmp=adj.vertices[0];
          adj.vertices[0]=adj.vertices[2];
          adj.vertices[2]=tmp;
          adj.normal=-adj.normal;
```

```
            }
            if(adj.label==0) { adj.label=1; queue.add(adj); }
        }
    }
}
}
// Try to fix problems in alignment of normals caused by incorrect
// triangle vertex orders. Only works on triangles.
public void AlignNormals() {
    ComputeFaceNormals();
    for(int i=0;i<faces.getCount();i++) faces[i].label=0;
    faces[0].label=1;
    FaceSet queue=new FaceSet();
    queue.add(faces[0]);
    AlignAdjacentFaces(queue);
    ComputeVertexNormals();
}

public void SaveTexInNormal() {
    for(int i=0;i<vertices.getCount();i++)
        vertices[i].normal=vertices[i].tex;
}

public void WriteOFF(string filename) {
    int nv, nf, i, v1, v2, v3;
    StreamWriter f= new StreamWriter(filename);
    if(f==null) return;

    f.Write("OFF\n");
    nv=vertices.getCount();
    nf=faces.getCount();
    f.Write("{0} {1} 0\n",nv,nf);
    for(i=0;i<nv;i++) {
        f.Write("{0} {1} {2}\n",vertices[i].v.x,vertices[i].v.y,
            vertices[i].v.z);
        vertices[i].label=i;
    }
    for(i=0;i<nf;i++) {
        v1=faces[i].vertices[0].label; v2=faces[i].vertices[1].label;
        v3=faces[i].vertices[2].label;
        f.Write("3 {0} {1} {2}\n",v1,v2,v3);
    }
    f.Close();
}

//wavefront obj
public void WriteOBJ(string filename) {
    int nv, nf, i, v1, v2, v3;
    StreamWriter f=new StreamWriter(filename);
    if(f==null) return;
```

```
        nv=vertices.getCount();
        nf=faces.getCount();
        for(i=0;i<nv;i++) {
            f.Write("v {0} {1} {2}\n",vertices[i].v.x,vertices[i].v.y,
                vertices[i].v.z);
            vertices[i].label=i+1;
        }
        for(i=0;i<nf;i++) {
            v1=faces[i].vertices[0].label; v2=faces[i].vertices[1].label;
            v3=faces[i].vertices[2].label;
            f.Write("f {0} {1} {2}\n",v1,v2,v3);
        }
        f.Close();
    }

    public void WriteParamOBJ(string filename) {
        int nv, nf, i, v1, v2, v3;
        StreamWriter f=new StreamWriter(filename);
        if(f==null) return;

        nv=vertices.getCount();
        nf=faces.getCount();
        for(i=0;i<nv;i++) {
            f.Write("v {0} {1} {2}\n",vertices[i].tex.x,
                vertices[i].tex.y,vertices[i].tex.z);
            vertices[i].label=i+1;
        }
        for(i=0;i<nf;i++) {
            v1=faces[i].vertices[0].label; v2=faces[i].vertices[1].label;
            v3=faces[i].vertices[2].label;
            f.Write("f {0} {1} {2}\n",v1,v2,v3);
        }
        f.Close();
    }

    public void WriteParamOFF(string filename) {
        int nv, nf;
        int i, v1, v2, v3;
        StreamWriter f=new StreamWriter(filename);
        if(f==null) return;

        f.Write("OFF\n");
        nv=vertices.getCount();
        nf=faces.getCount();
        f.Write("{0} {1} 0\n",nv,nf);
        for(i=0;i<nv;i++) {
            f.Write("{0} {1} {2}\n",vertices[i].tex.x,
                vertices[i].tex.y,vertices[i].tex.z);
            vertices[i].label=i;
        }
        for(i=0;i<nf;i++) {
```

```
        v1=faces[i].vertices[0].label;  v2=faces[i].vertices[1].label;
        v3=faces[i].vertices[2].label;
        f.Write("3 {0} {1} {2}\n",v1,v2,v3);
    }
    f.Close();
}

//Size is the recommended size, but it may have to be larger to avoid
//vertices being placed in the same cell
public Vector [,]CreateGeometryImage(int size,bool resize) {
    return CreateGeometryImage(size,resize,GEOMETRY_IMAGE); }
public Vector [,]CreateGeometryImage(int size,bool resize,int type) {
    int[,] occupied;
    Vector[,] gim=null;
    int i, j, x, y, newsize, closest;
    bool restart=true;
    double minx, maxx, miny, maxy, tx, ty, alpha, beta, gamma;
    double basearea, min;
    Face f;

    newsize=size;
    while(restart) {
        restart=false; size=newsize;
        //no vertices have been placed
        occupied=new int[size,size];
        for(y=0;y<size;y++)
            for(x=0;x<size;x++) occupied[y,x]=-1;

        //place the vertices in cells
        for(i=0;i<vertices.getCount();i++) {
            x=(int)(vertices[i].tex.x*(size-1)+0.4);
            y=(int)(vertices[i].tex.y*(size-1)+0.4);
            //if not occupied, then use the vertex
            if(occupied[y,x]==-1) occupied[y,x]=i;
            else {
                //Occupied cell, either don't use the
                //current vertex, or resize and start again
                if((resize)&&(size<1024)) {
                    newsize=size*2; restart=true; break;
                }
            }
        }

        //if there is no need to restart, then search through cells for unoccupied cells
        if(!restart) {
            gim=new Vector[size,size];
            for(y=0;y<size;y++) {
                FaceSet linecandidates=new FaceSet();
                ty=((y)/(double)(size-1));
                if(y==0) ty=0.0;
                if(y==size-1) ty=1.0;
```

```
for(i=0;i<faces.getCount();i++) {
    //compute the bounding box of the triangle
    miny=maxy=faces[i].vertices[0].tex.y;
    for(j=1;j<3;j++) {
        if(faces[i].vertices[j].tex.y>maxy)
            maxy=faces[i].vertices[j].tex.y;
        if(faces[i].vertices[j].tex.y<miny)
            miny=faces[i].vertices[j].tex.y;
    }
    //check to see if it is in the bounding box
    if((miny<=ty)&&(ty<=maxy)) linecandidates.add(faces[i]);
}

for(x=0;x<size;x++) {
    if(occupied[y,x]!=-1) {
        if(type==NORMAL_MAP) {
            gim[y,x]=vertices[occupied[y,x]].normal;
        } else gim[y,x]=vertices[occupied[y,x]].v;
    } else
    if(occupied[y,x]==-1) {
        //Take the unnocupied cell and compute in which triangle the
        //centre of the cell lies
        FaceSet candidates=new FaceSet();
        tx=((x)/(double)(size-1));
        // handle borders specially
        if(x==0) tx=0.0;
        if(x==size-1) tx=1.0;
        Vector v=new Vector();
        v.x=tx; v.y=ty; v.z=0.0;
        for(i=0;i<linecandidates.getCount();i++) {
            //compute the bounding box of the triangle
            minx=maxx=linecandidates[i].vertices[0].tex.x;
            for(j=1;j<3;j++) {
                if(linecandidates[i].vertices[j].tex.x>maxx)
                    maxx=linecandidates[i].vertices[j].tex.x;
                if(linecandidates[i].vertices[j].tex.x<minx)
                    minx=linecandidates[i].vertices[j].tex.x;
            }
            //check to see if it is in the bounding box
            if((minx<=tx)&&(tx<=maxx))
                candidates.add(linecandidates[i]);
        }
        closest=-1;
        min=1e10;
        Vector v1, v2, v3;
        for(i=0;i<candidates.getCount();i++) {
            //Compute barycentric coordinates and use them to determine
            //the euclidean 3d-space position. The point is inside
            //the triangle if the sum of the barycentric coordinates is 1
            //and all coordinates are greater than 0.
```

```
                    f=candidates[i]; v1=f.vertices[0].tex;
                    v2=f.vertices[1].tex; v3=f.vertices[2].tex;
                    basearea=area(v1,v2,v3);
                    alpha=area(v,v2,v3)/basearea;
                    beta=area(v1,v,v3)/basearea;
                    gamma=area(v1,v2,v)/basearea;
                    //alpha, beta and gamma are all positive by definition
                    if(Math.Abs(alpha+beta+gamma-1.0)<min) {
                        closest=i;
                        min=Math.Abs(alpha+beta+gamma-1.0);
                    }
                }
                f=candidates[closest];
                v1=f.vertices[0].tex;
                v2=f.vertices[1].tex;
                v3=f.vertices[2].tex;
                basearea=area(v1,v2,v3);
                alpha=area(v,v2,v3)/basearea;
                beta=area(v1,v,v3)/basearea;
                gamma=area(v1,v2,v)/basearea;
                if(type==NORMAL_MAP) {
                    v=alpha*f.vertices[0].normal+beta*f.vertices[1].normal+
                        gamma*f.vertices[2].normal;
                } else {
                    v=alpha*f.vertices[0].v+beta*f.vertices[1].v+
                        gamma*f.vertices[2].v;
                }
                gim[y,x]=v;
            }
        }
    }
}

    return gim;
}


public void WriteGeometryImageRIB(string filename,
    string tiffname,int size) {
    int i;
    StreamWriter f=new StreamWriter(filename);
    Vector v1, v2, v3, v4;

    if(f==null) return;
    f.Write("Format {0} {1} 1\n",size,size);
    f.Write("Clipping 0.1 100.0\n");
    f.Write("PixelSamples 2 2\n");
    f.Write("Sides 2\n");
    f.Write("ShadingRate 0.5\n");
    f.Write("Quantize \"rgba\" 0 0 0 0\n");
    f.Write("Display \"{0}\" \"file\" \"rgba\"\n",tiffname);
```

```csharp
f.Write("Scale {0} {1} 1\n",2.0-1.0/size,2.0-1.0/size);
f.Write("Translate 0 0 1\n");
f.Write("WorldBegin\n");
f.Write("\tSurface \"constant\"\n");

for(i=0;i<vertices.getCount();i++) {
    vertices[i].tex.x-=0.5; vertices[i].tex.y-=0.5;
    vertices[i].label=i;
}
f.Write("\t PointsPolygons [\n");
for(i=0;i<faces.getCount();i++) f.Write("\t\t 3\n");
f.Write("\t ] [\n");
for(i=0;i<faces.getCount();i++)
    f.Write("\t\t {0} {1} {2}\n",faces[i].vertices[0].label,
            faces[i].vertices[1].label,faces[i].vertices[2].label);
f.Write("\t [\n"); f.Write("\t \"P\" [\n");
for(i=0;i<vertices.getCount();i++)
    f.Write("\t\t {0} {1} {2} \n",
            vertices[i].tex.x,vertices[i].tex.y,vertices[i].tex.z);
f.Write("\t [\n"); f.Write("\t \"Cs\" [\n");
for(i=0;i<vertices.getCount();i++)
    f.Write("\t\t {0} {1} {2} \n",
            vertices[i].v.x,vertices[i].v.y,vertices[i].v.z);
f.Write("\t [\n");
f.Write("\tTranslate 0.0 0.0 0.5\n");
for(i=0;i<edges.getCount();i++) {
    if(edges[i].boundary()) {
        v1=edges[i].ends[0].tex*0.5; v2=edges[i].ends[0].tex*1.5;
        v3=edges[i].ends[1].tex*1.5; v4=edges[i].ends[1].tex*0.5;
        f.Write("\t Polygon \"Cs\" [ ");
        f.Write("{0} {1} {2} ",
            edges[i].ends[0].v.x,edges[i].ends[0].v.y,edges[i].ends[0].v.z);
        f.Write("{0} {1} {2} ",
            edges[i].ends[0].v.x,edges[i].ends[0].v.y,edges[i].ends[0].v.z);
        f.Write("{0} {1} {2} ",
            edges[i].ends[1].v.x,edges[i].ends[1].v.y,edges[i].ends[1].v.z);
        f.Write("{0} {1} {2} ",
            edges[i].ends[1].v.x,edges[i].ends[1].v.y,edges[i].ends[1].v.z);
        f.Write("]\n\t\t \"P\" [ ");
        f.Write("{0} {1} {2} ",v1.x,v1.y,v1.z);
        f.Write("{0} {1} {2} ",v2.x,v2.y,v2.z);
        f.Write("{0} {1} {2} ",v3.x,v3.y,v3.z);
        f.Write("{0} {1} {2} ",v4.x,v4.y,v4.z);
        f.Write("]\n");
    }
}
f.Write("WorldEnd\n");
f.Close();

for(i=0;i<vertices.getCount();i++) {
    vertices[i].tex.x+=0.5; vertices[i].tex.y+=0.5;
```

```
      }
}

public void WriteParamMetaPost(string filename) {
    int i;
    StreamWriter f=new StreamWriter(filename);
    if(f==null) return;
    Vector v1, v2;
    f.Write("u:=5cm;\n");
    f.Write("beginfig(1);\n");
    for(i=0;i<edges.getCount();i++) {
        v1=edges[i].ends[0].tex; v2=edges[i].ends[1].tex;
        f.Write("\tdraw ({0},{1})-({0},{1});\n",v1.x,v1.y,v2.x,v2.y);
    }
    f.Write("endfig;\n");
    f.Write("end;\n");
    f.Close();
}

public void WriteNormalMapRIB(string filename,
        string tiffname,int size) {
    int i;

    StreamWriter f=new StreamWriter(filename);
    Vector v1, v2, v3, v4;
    if(f==null) return;
    f.Write("Format {0} {1} 1\n",size,size);
    f.Write("Clipping 0.1 100.0\n");
    f.Write("PixelSamples 2 2\n");
    f.Write("Sides 2\n");
    f.Write("ShadingRate 0.5\n");
    f.Write("Quantize \"rgba\" 0 0 0 0\n");
    f.Write("Display \"{0}\" \"file\" \"rgba\"\n",tiffname);
    f.Write("Scale {0} {1} 1\n",2.0-1.0/size,2.0-1.0/size);
    f.Write("Translate 0 0 1\n");
    f.Write("WorldBegin\n");
    f.Write("\tSurface \"constant\"\n");
    for(i=0;i<vertices.getCount();i++) {
        vertices[i].tex.x-=0.5; vertices[i].tex.y-=0.5;
        vertices[i].label=i;
    }

    f.Write("\t PointsPolygons /\n");
    for(i=0;i<faces.getCount();i++) f.Write("\t\t 3\n");
    f.Write("\t ] /\n");
    for(i=0;i<faces.getCount();i++) {
        f.Write("\t\t {0} {1} {2}\n",faces[i].vertices[0].label,
            faces[i].vertices[1].label,faces[i].vertices[2].label);
    }
    f.Write("\t /\n"); f.Write("\t \"P\" /\n");
    for(i=0;i<vertices.getCount();i++) {
```

```
        f.Write("\t\t {0} {1} {2} \n",
           vertices[i].tex.x,vertices[i].tex.y,vertices[i].tex.z);
    }
    f.Write("\t /\n"); f.Write("\t \"Cs\" /\n");
    for(i=0;i<vertices.getCount();i++) {
        f.Write("\t\t {0} {1} {2} \n",
           vertices[i].normal.x,vertices[i].normal.y,vertices[i].normal.z);
    }
    f.Write("\t /\n");
    f.Write("\tTranslate 0.0 0.0 0.5\n");
    for(i=0;i<edges.getCount();i++) {
        if(edges[i].boundary()) {
            v1=edges[i].ends[0].tex*0.5;  v2=edges[i].ends[0].tex*1.5;
            v3=edges[i].ends[1].tex*1.5;  v4=edges[i].ends[1].tex*0.5;
            f.Write("\t Polygon \"Cs\" [ ");
            f.Write("{0} {1} {2} ",
                edges[i].ends[0].normal.x,edges[i].ends[0].normal.y,
                edges[i].ends[0].normal.z);
            f.Write("{0} {1} {2} ",
                edges[i].ends[0].normal.x,edges[i].ends[0].normal.y,
                edges[i].ends[0].normal.z);
            f.Write("{0} {1} {2} ",
                edges[i].ends[1].normal.x,edges[i].ends[1].normal.y,
                edges[i].ends[1].normal.z);
            f.Write("{0} {1} {2} ",
                edges[i].ends[1].normal.x,edges[i].ends[1].normal.y,
                edges[i].ends[1].normal.z);
            f.Write("/n\t\t \"P\" [ ");
            f.Write("{0} {1} {2} ",v1.x,v1.y,v1.z);
            f.Write("{0} {1} {2} ",v2.x,v2.y,v2.z);
            f.Write("{0} {1} {2} ",v3.x,v3.y,v3.z);
            f.Write("{0} {1} {2} ",v4.x,v4.y,v4.z);
            f.Write("/n");
        }
    }
    f.Write("WorldEnd\n");
    f.Close();

    for(i=0;i<vertices.getCount();i++) {
        vertices[i].tex.x+=0.5; vertices[i].tex.y+=0.5;
    }
}

public VertexSet vertices;
public EdgeSet edges;
public FaceSet faces;

//Compute the genus of the mesh (assuming all vertices
//and edges are used) and assuming there are no boundaries
//see Computer Aided Geometric Design (Farin) pg. 395
public int SimpleGenus() { //Euler-Poincare formula
```

```
      return (vertexCount()-edgeCount()+faceCount()-2)/2;
}

public int faceCount() { return faces.getCount(); }

public int edgeCount() { return edges.getCount(); }

public int vertexCount() { return vertices.getCount(); }

public void RemoveFace(Face f) {
   for(int i=0;i<3;i++) { f.vertices[i].remove(f); f.edges[i].remove(f); }
   faces.remove(f);
}

public void RemoveFace(int j) {
   Face f=faces[j];
   for(int i=0;i<3;i++) {
      f.vertices[i].remove(f); f.edges[i].remove(f);
   }
   faces.remove(j);
}

public int RemoveOrphanedEdges() {
   int i=0, n=0;
   Edge e;
   while(i<edges.getCount()) {
      if(edges[i].faces.getCount()==0) {
         edges[i].ends[0].remove(edges[i]);
         edges[i].ends[1].remove(edges[i]);
         e=edges[i]; edges.remove(i); n++;
      } else i++;
   }
   return n;
}

public int RemoveOrphanedVertices() {
   int i=0, n=0;
   while(i<vertices.getCount()) {
      if((vertices[i].edges.getCount()==0)
         &&(vertices[i].faces.getCount()==0)) {
         v=vertices[i]; vertices.remove(i); n++;
      } else i++;
   }
   return n;
}

private void CheckConnected(Edge e) {
   int i;
   Vertex v;
   if(e.label==1) return;
   e.label=1;
```

```
      v=e.ends[0];i v.label=1;
      for(i=0;i<v.edges.getCount();i++) CheckConnected(v.edges[i]);
      v=e.ends[1]; v.label=1;
      for(i=0;i<v.edges.getCount();i++) CheckConnected(v.edges[i]);
    }

  private void CheckConnected(Face f) {
    if(f==null) return;
    if(f.label==1) return;
    f.label=1;
    for(int i=0;i<3;i++) {
      CheckConnected(f.edges[i].faces[0]);
      CheckConnected(f.edges[i].faces[1]);
    }
  }
}
```

The `GeometryFile` class separates the loading of triangle meshes from the `Mesh` class. Methods are provided for loading OFF and Wavefront object files. Meshes are triangulated during loading.

```
//GeometryFile.cs
using System;
using System.IO;
using System.Collections;
using System.Runtime.InteropServices;

//For console output in a GUI application
public class Win32
{
    [DllImport("kernel32.dll") ]
    public static extern Boolean AllocConsole();
    [DllImport("kernel32.dll") ]
    public static extern Boolean FreeConsole();
}

public class GeometryFile {
    private static void SkipWhite(TextReader f) {
      int c;
      c=f.Peek();
      while((c!=-1)&&(Char.IsWhiteSpace((char)c))) {
        c=f.Read(); c=f.Peek();
      }
    }

    private static int ReadInt(TextReader f) {
      SkipWhite(f);
      return ReadIntNoSkip(f);
    }
```

```
private static int ReadIntNoSkip(TextReader f) {
    int c,d;
    string text="";
    c=f.Peek();
    while((c!=-1)&&(Char.IsDigit((char)c))) {
        c=f.Read(); text+=(char)c; c=f.Peek();
    }
    if(Int32.TryParse(text,out d)) return d;
    else return 0;
}

private static double ReadDouble(TextReader f) {
    int c;
    double d;
    string text="";
    SkipWhite(f);
    c=f.Peek();
    //seek till next white space
    while((c!=-1)&&(!Char.IsWhiteSpace((char)c))) {
        c=f.Read(); text+=(char)c; c=f.Peek();
    }
    if(Double.TryParse(text,out d)) return d;
    else return 0.0;
}

private static Vector ReadVector(TextReader f) {
    Vector v=new Vector();
    v.x=ReadDouble(f); v.y=ReadDouble(f); v.z=ReadDouble(f);
    v.w=1.0;
    return v;
}

public static Mesh LoadOFF(string filename) {
    char[] magic=new char[3];
    int nv, nf, tmp;
    Vector v;
    int i, j, c, v1, v2, v3;
    Mesh m;

    Console.Write("Loading OFF {0}\n",filename);
    StreamReader f=new StreamReader(filename);
    if(f==null) return null;
    f.ReadBlock(magic,0,3);
    if(new string(magic)!="OFF") { f.Close(); return null; }
    nv=ReadInt(f); nf=ReadInt(f); tmp=ReadInt(f);
    Console.Write("{0} vertices, {1} faces\n",nv,nf);
    m=new Mesh();
    for(i=0;i<nv;i++) {
        v=ReadVector(f); m.AddVertex(v);
        if(i%100==0) Console.Write("Vertices: {0}%\r",i*100/nv);
```

```
   }
   Console.Write("Vertices loaded.\n");
   for(i=0;i<nf;i++) {
      c=ReadInt(f); v1=ReadInt(f); v2=ReadInt(f);
      for(j=2;j<c;j++) {
         v3=ReadInt(f); m.AddTriangle(v1,v2,v3); v2=v3;
      }
      if(i%100==0) Console.Write("Faces: {0}%\r",i*100/nf);
   }
   Console.Write("Faces loaded.\n");
   f.Close();
   return m;
}

public static Mesh LoadOBJ(string filename) {
   Vector v;
   int nv, nf, nn, nt, c, v1, v2, v3, n1, n2, n3, t1, t2, t3;
   Mesh m;
   ArrayList normals=new ArrayList();
   ArrayList tex=new ArrayList();
   string line;

   StreamReader f=new StreamReader(filename);
   if(f==null) return null;
   m=new Mesh();

   nf=nv=nn=nt=0;
   while(!f.EndOfStream) {
      line=f.ReadLine();
      StringReader str=new StringReader(line);
      c=str.Read();
      if(c==-1) continue;
      if((char)c=='v') {
         c=str.Read();
         if((char)c=='n') {
            v=ReadVector(str); normals.Add(v); nn++;
         }
         if(Char.IsWhiteSpace((char)c)) {
            v=ReadVector(str); m.AddVertex(v); nv++;
         }
      }
      if((char)c=='t') {
         v=ReadVector(str);
         //add to texture coordinates
         tex.Add(v); nt++;
      }
      if((char)c=='f') {
         v1=ReadInt(str); c=str.Read();
         if((char)c=='/') {
            t1=ReadIntNoSkip(str); c=str.Read();
            n1=ReadIntNoSkip(str);
```

```
            } else t1=n1=-1;
            v2=ReadInt(str); c=str.Read();
            if((char)c=='/') {
                t2=ReadIntNoSkip(str); c=str.Read();
                n2=ReadIntNoSkip(str);
            } else t2=n2=-1;
            v3=ReadInt(str); c=str.Read();
            if((char)c=='/') {
                t3=ReadIntNoSkip(str); c=str.Read();
                n3=ReadIntNoSkip(str);
            } else t3=n3=-1;
            if(t1>0) m.SetTex(v1-1,(Vector)tex[t1-1]);
            if(t2>0) m.SetTex(v2-1,(Vector)tex[t2-1]);
            if(t3>0) m.SetTex(v3-1,(Vector)tex[t3-1]);
            if(n1>0) m.SetNormal(v1-1,(Vector)normals[n1-1]);
            if(n2>0) m.SetNormal(v2-1,(Vector)normals[n2-1]);
            if(n3>0) m.SetNormal(v3-1,(Vector)normals[n3-1]);
            if((v1>0)&&(v2>0)&&(v3>0)) {
                m.AddTriangle(v1-1,v2-1,v3-1); nf++;
            }
            while(str.Peek()>0) {
                v2=v3;
                v3=ReadInt(str); c=str.Read();
                if((c!=-1)&&((char)c=='/')) {
                    t3=ReadIntNoSkip(str); c=str.Read();
                    n3=ReadIntNoSkip(str);
                } else t3=n3=-1;
                if(t3>0) m.SetTex(v3-1,(Vector)tex[t3-1]);
                if(n3>0) m.SetNormal(v3-1,(Vector)normals[n3-1]);
                if((v1>0)&&(v2>0)&&(v3>0)) {
                    m.AddTriangle(v1-1,v2-1,v3-1); nf++;
                }
            }
        }
    }
    Console.Write("{0} vertices, {1} faces\n",nv,nf);
    f.Close();
    return m;
}

public static Mesh Load(string filename) {
    Win32.AllocConsole();
    Console.Write("Loading {0}\n",filename);
    if(filename.EndsWith("obj")) return LoadOBJ(filename);
    if(filename.EndsWith("off")) return LoadOFF(filename);
    Console.Write("Not recognized:\n",filename);
    return null;
}
}
```

Chapter 7

Raytracing

7.1 Raytracing Process

We know that light has a wave and particle nature; we are most interested in the wave nature. Light is emitted from a source, for example a laser or LED. This source can emit light in various ways. The light source has various attributes including

- Color (RGB triple)

- Position

- Amount of light emitted in each direction.

The most common lights considered here are

- Point light (Equal energy in all directions)

- Spot light (Maximum energy emitted in one direction, with linear or quadratic falloff from that point)

- Infinite light (The light is placed infinitely far away, so only the direction of the light is needed).

The emitted light travels through the scene and reflects (or transmits) from various objects. At each reflection, some of the light may be absorbed by the surface of the object. Certain frequencies may be reduced in intensity. Eventually some of the light rays reach the eye. These light rays stimulate the rods and cones on the retina to produce the image we see. In most cases, it is sufficient to determine the intensity (and color) of all light rays hitting a particular point in space. The intensity at this point is the sum

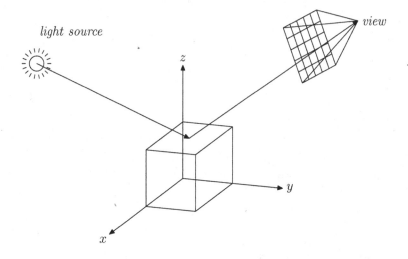

light source

Figure 7.1: A scene and viewpoint.

of the intensities of the rays hitting that point. So we model the eye as a
rectangle in 3D, divided into squares. Each square will represent a pixel in
the final image. The color of the square is approximated by the intensity
at the point in the center of the square (more accurate answers can be
obtained by using more than one sample point). Figure 7.1 shows a simple
scene and a viewpoint (pyramid). It is clear that the number of rays coming
from the lightsource that actually hit the viewing area (front panel of the
pyramid) is far fewer than those that do not. It will take a very long time
(and many rays) before a reasonable image is obtained using this method.
Instead we try to do the reverse. Consider a ray coming directly into the
view area toward the viewer. This ray of light constributes directly to the
image seen by the viewer. However, rays of light that do not go directly
to the viewer are not taken into account. It is worthwhile to try to extract
some information from these rays to increase the speed at which an image
can be produced. We presume that light that does not enter directly in the
right direction, can be modeled as light that enters directly with a lower
intensity. This assumption will be incorporated in the lighting models that
are presented later. We can now simply trace a ray from the viewer back
to where it came from, back to the light source, to determine how it was
affected and what color should be seen. So instead of casting rays from the
light source, cast rays from the viewer. If the ray does not arrive back at
the light source, then the lighting model will determine the contribution
from the light source taking into account the effect of the position of the

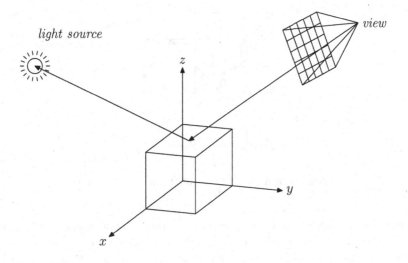

Figure 7.2: Raytracing by casting rays from the viewer into the scene.

light source. Figure 7.2 illustrates this process. There are two options when tracing the rays back to the source,

- If the camera transform is $C = M_1 M_2 M_3 \ldots M_n$ then transform each object by $C^{-1} = M_n^{-1} \ldots M_3^{-1} M_2^{-1} M_1^{-1}$ where M_j^{-1} is the inverse of M_j. For the transforms we have covered it is easy to calculate the inverse, so C and C^{-1} can be built up simultaneously and used as necessary. Now rays can be cast in the discrete directions $(x \ y \ z)^T$ for $x, y \in [-1, 1]$ and $z = -d$. The choice of d determines the field of view. Choosing limits for x, y and z determine the field of view.

- Store an axis system for the camera, and transform it by C. Now $(x \ y \ z)^T$ can be used exactly as before, but the actual vector used in the ray cast is $C(0 \ 0 \ 0)^T \rightarrow C(x \ y \ z)^T$. $C(x \ y \ z)^T$ can be quickly calculated as

$$C(x \ y \ z)^T = x\mathbf{u} + y\mathbf{v} + z\mathbf{w}$$

where $\mathbf{u}$, $\mathbf{v}$ and $\mathbf{w}$ are the transformed axis vectors of the camera.

Note that each object has a transform matrix (and possibly) inverse associated with it, even the camera. No projection is needed. Projection is implicitly done by the raycast process. The scene from the perspective of the camera would now look like figure 7.3 To determine where the light came from, and what color and intensity it has, a ray is cast from the viewpoint through the pixel for which a color must be determined. The first

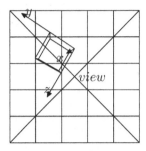

Figure 7.3: View of the scene from the camera.

object the ray intersects with determines where the ray would have come from. The intersection with the *nearest* object is thus used. Hidden surface removal is an automatic consequence of selecting the nearest object. This makes sense, since the light did not come through the object (unless it is transparent). Now that we know where the ray intersects the object we should determine where that ray came from. We calculate the reflection vector, and determine what light came from that direction. The light from that direction is affected by the surface in some way and so a lighting model is appled to determine what effect the surface has. It is clear that the same algorithm can be used to determine what the color of this reflected ray is! Raytracing is thus implemented with a recursive algorithm. If the ray does not intersect anything, then we should use a lighting model to try to approximate the indirect lighting in the scene. To apply the lighting model to a reflected ray, it is necessary to determine if light from the light sources actually reaches the object (in which case we apply our model), or does not (in which case the object is in shadow, and we don't apply the model).

The above discussion leads to the following algorithm

```
Color raycast(Ray r)
begin
    Color result=(0,0,0)
    Find nearest intersection between r and the set of objects O.
    if there is an intersection
    begin
        Let the intersected object be o.
        Calculate the reflected ray x using r and the normal to object o.
        Set c:=raycast(x).
        Apply the lighting model of o to the result c using the properties of o
```

Set $result:=c$.
for each light source l
begin
    Cast a ray x in the direction of the light source l
    if x intersects an object set $c:=(0,0,0)$
    else use the lighting model to calculate c
        using the properties of o and the light source l.
    Set $result:=result + c$.
 end
else
    Apply lighting model to approximate global illumination.
    The simplest option is to set $result:=backgroundcolor$.
    end
    return $result$
end

Note that contributions are additive. This model ignores refracted rays. The effect that the object has on the intensity of the light is given by the *Beer-Lambert law* as discussed in chapter 2. The raytracing algorithm with refractions is given by

Color raycast(Ray r)
begin
    Color $result=(0,0,0)$
    Find nearest intersection between r and the set of objects O.
    if there is an intersection
    begin
        Let the intersected object be o.
        Calculate the reflected ray x using r and the normal to object o.
        Set $c:=$raycast(x).
        Apply the lighting model of o to the result c
            using the properties of o
        Set $result:=c$.
        Calculate the refracted ray y using r and the properties of object o.
        Set $c:=$raycast(y).
        Apply the lighting model of o to the result c
            using the properties of o
        Set $result:=result + c$.
        for each light source l
        begin
            Cast a ray x in the direction of the light source l
            if x intersects an object set $c:=(0,0,0)$

```
        else use the lighting model to calculate c
            using the properties of o and the light source l.
            Set result:=result + c.
        end
    else
        Apply lighting model to approximate global illumination.
        The simplest option is to set result:=backgroundcolor.
    end
    return result
end
```

On occasion, numerical inaccuracy can cause a ray reflected off an object to intersect that object again in close proximity to the original intersection. It may be necessary to put in a minimum required intersection distance to avoid this problem. Or, if only convex objects are used, the object at which the ray originated can be stored and this object is then ignored in the next intersection calculation for this ray.

7.2 Representation of a Ray

A ray can be represented parametrically as

$$\mathbf{o} + t\mathbf{d}$$

where $\mathbf{o}$ is the origin of the ray, and $\mathbf{d}$ is the unit vector identifying the direction in which the ray is travelling. This is useful, since if $\mathbf{d}$ is normalized then the parameter t represents the distance from the point $\mathbf{o}$. If we calculate intercepts, we need only consider answers with $t > 0$. Anything else must be behind the ray.

7.3 Reflection

Reflections are relatively easy to calculate if the normal to the surface is available. Since the normal will be required for lighting calculations, the normal should be available at the point of intersection between the ray and the surface. The normal at a point $\mathbf{p}$ for a

- **Sphere** of the form $(x - a)^2 + (y - b)^2 + (z - c)^2 = r^2$ is $\mathbf{p} - \mathbf{o}$ where $\mathbf{o}$ is $(a \ b \ c)^T$.

- **infinite plane** of the form $ax + by + cz + d = 0$ is $(a \ b \ c)^T$.

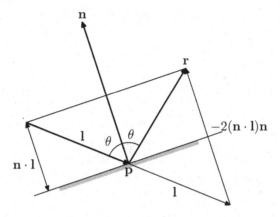

Figure 7.4: Computation of the reflected vector **r**.

- **Triangle** specified by $\mathbf{v}_1$, $\mathbf{v}_2$, $\mathbf{v}_3$ is of the form $(\mathbf{v}_2 - \mathbf{v}_1) \times (\mathbf{v}_3 - \mathbf{v}_1)$, where $\times$ denotes the vector product.

Figure 7.4 illustrates the process used to compute the reflected vector given the unit normal **n**. The reflected vector **r** is given by

$$\mathbf{r} = -2(\mathbf{n} \cdot \mathbf{l})\mathbf{n} + \mathbf{l}$$

where $\mathbf{n} \cdot \mathbf{l}$ denotes the scalar product of **n** and **l**. If we were to construct a ray to represent the reflection, the origin would clearly be **p** and the direction would be given by **r**.

7.4 Refraction

The refracted ray can be computed using *Snell's law* after analysis of figure 7.5. Snell's law gives us

$$n_1 \sin(\theta_1) = n_2 \sin(\theta_2) \tag{7.1}$$

where θ_1 is the angle at which the ray enters the material, θ_2 is the angle the ray travels in due to refraction, n_1 is the index of refraction of the exterior material and n_2 is the index of refraction of the interior material.

We define $r := n_1/n_2$ so that

$$r \sin(\theta_1) = \sin(\theta_2) \tag{7.2}$$

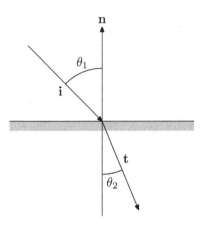

Figure 7.5: Computation of the refracted vector **t**.

If both **i** and **n** are unit vectors and $\mathbf{n}^\perp$ is the unit vector perpendicular to **n** in the plane defined by **i** and **n**, then

$$\mathbf{i} = \sin\left(-\left(\frac{\pi}{2} - \theta_1\right)\right)\mathbf{n} + \cos\left(-\left(\frac{\pi}{2} - \theta_1\right)\right)\mathbf{n}^\perp$$
$$= -\cos(\theta_1)\mathbf{n} + \sin(\theta_1)\mathbf{n}^\perp$$

and

$$\mathbf{t} = -\cos(\theta_2)\mathbf{n} + \sin(\theta_2)\mathbf{n}^\perp = -\cos(\theta_2)\mathbf{n} + r\sin(\theta_1)\mathbf{n}^\perp.$$

We have

$$r^2 \sin^2(\theta_1) = \sin^2(\theta_2) = 1 - \cos^2(\theta_2)$$
$$\cos^2(\theta_2) = 1 - r^2 \sin^2(\theta_1)$$
$$\cos(\theta_2) = \sqrt{1 - r^2 \sin^2(\theta_1)}.$$

It follows that

$$\mathbf{t} = -\sqrt{1 - r^2 \sin^2(\theta_1)}\mathbf{n} + r\sin(\theta_1)\mathbf{n}^\perp .$$

We now set $w := -(\mathbf{i} \cdot \mathbf{n})r = r\cos(\theta_1)$ and $k := \sqrt{1 + (w - r)(w + r)}$ so that

$$\mathbf{t} = -\sqrt{1 - r^2 \sin^2(\theta_1)}\mathbf{n} + r\sin(\theta_1)\mathbf{n}^\perp$$
$$= -\sqrt{1 - r^2(1 - \cos^2(\theta_1))}\mathbf{n} + r\sin(\theta_1)\mathbf{n}^\perp$$

$$= -\sqrt{1 - r^2 + r^2 \cos^2(\theta_1)}\,\mathbf{n} + r\sin(\theta_1)\mathbf{n}^\perp$$
$$= -\sqrt{1 - r^2 + w^2}\,\mathbf{n} + r\sin(\theta_1)\mathbf{n}^\perp$$
$$= -\sqrt{1 + w^2 - r^2}\,\mathbf{n} + r\sin(\theta_1)\mathbf{n}^\perp$$
$$= -\sqrt{1 + (w - r)(w + r)}\,\mathbf{n} + r\sin(\theta_1)\mathbf{n}^\perp$$
$$= -k\mathbf{n} + r\mathbf{i} + r\cos(\theta_1)\mathbf{n}$$
$$= -k\mathbf{n} + r\mathbf{i} - r(\mathbf{i} \cdot \mathbf{n})\mathbf{n}$$
$$= -k\mathbf{n} + r\mathbf{i} + w\mathbf{n}$$
$$= r\mathbf{i} + (w - k)\mathbf{n}\,.$$

Note that if $1 + (w - r)(w + r) < 0$ then k is a complex number. In this case we have total internal reflection and the reflection vector should be used for lighting calculations. Total internal reflection results in a mirror like surface so the result should not simply be discarded.

When dealing with several materials a ray can enter and exit materials several times, it is necessary to remember which material the ray is currently passing through. For the purpose of refraction, the index of refraction between the two materials is sufficient to compute the refracted ray. One way to approach the problem is to create a stack of refraction indices. Initially the stack contains one value, namely the index of refraction of the material that the camera is in. Usually this value can be taken to be 1.0. Each time a material is entered, the index of refraction of the material is pushed onto the stack. The value that was on the stack is n_1, whereas the material provides n_2 for the calculation. When we exit the object, the value at the top of the stack should be popped off. The value popped off the stack is now n_1 and the value at the top of the stack is n_2.

To determine if the ray is exiting or entering the object it is sufficient to test $\mathbf{d} \cdot \mathbf{n}$. If the $\mathbf{d} \cdot \mathbf{n} < 0$ then the ray enters the surface. If $\mathbf{d} \cdot \mathbf{n} > 0$ then the ray exits the surface, and $-\mathbf{n}$ must be used where a normal is expected.

7.5 Intersections

To compute reflected and refracted rays, the normal at the surface and the point of intersection must be known. This section derives the formulas required to compute the point of intersection with a few simple objects. The normal to the surface can be computed from the point of intersection as described in section 7.3.

7.5.1   Sphere

The implicit formula for a sphere is given by

$$f(\mathbf{p}) = \|\mathbf{p} - \mathbf{c}\| - r = 0.$$

The point of intersection $\mathbf{p}$ between the ray $\mathbf{o} + t\mathbf{d}$ and sphere should be on the sphere and the ray. The point of intersection is described by t and the point is given by $\mathbf{o} + t\mathbf{d}$. It is thus necessary to solve for t given that $\mathbf{o} + t\mathbf{d}$ is a point on the sphere. In this case we have

$$f(\mathbf{o} + t\mathbf{d}) = \|\mathbf{o} + t\mathbf{d} - \mathbf{c}\| - r = 0.$$

We simplify and solve for t

$$f(\mathbf{o} + t\mathbf{d}) = \|\mathbf{o} + t\mathbf{d} - \mathbf{c}\| - r = 0$$
$$\|\mathbf{o} + t\mathbf{d} - \mathbf{c}\| = r$$
$$(\mathbf{o} + t\mathbf{d} - \mathbf{c}) \cdot (\mathbf{o} + t\mathbf{d} - \mathbf{c}) = r^2$$
$$t^2(\mathbf{d} \cdot \mathbf{d}) + 2t(\mathbf{d} \cdot (\mathbf{o} - \mathbf{c})) + (\mathbf{o} - \mathbf{c}) \cdot (\mathbf{o} - \mathbf{c}) - r^2 = 0.$$

If $\mathbf{d}$ is normalized it is possible to simplify even further. The standard formula for solving a quadratic equation $at^2 + bt + c = 0$ is used

$$t = \frac{-b \pm \sqrt{b^2 - 4ac}}{2a}$$

to calculate t. Thus the point of intersection is $\mathbf{o} + t\mathbf{d}$, where $a = \mathbf{d} \cdot \mathbf{d}$, $b = 2\mathbf{d} \cdot (\mathbf{o} - \mathbf{c})$ and $c = (\mathbf{o} - \mathbf{c}) \cdot (\mathbf{o} - \mathbf{c}) - r^2$. If $b^2 - 4ac < 0$ then there is no intersection. Since there are usually two values of t that satisfy the equation, the smallest, positive value of t is taken as the point of intersection.

Real-Time Rendering [1] can be consulted for faster algorithms.

7.5.2   Infinite Plane

Once again we substitute $\mathbf{o} + t\mathbf{d}$ into the plane equation

$$ax + by + cz + d = 0$$

or $\mathbf{n} \cdot \mathbf{p} + d = 0$. After the substitution $\mathbf{p} = \mathbf{o} + t\mathbf{d}$ we obtain

$$\mathbf{n} \cdot (\mathbf{o} + t\mathbf{d}) + d = 0$$
$$\mathbf{n} \cdot \mathbf{o} + t(\mathbf{n} \cdot \mathbf{d}) + d = 0$$
$$t(\mathbf{n} \cdot \mathbf{d}) = -d - \mathbf{n} \cdot \mathbf{o}.$$

Thus

$$t = \frac{-d - \mathbf{n} \cdot \mathbf{o}}{\mathbf{n} \cdot \mathbf{d}}.$$

Substitute t into the ray equation to get the point of intersection.

7.5.3   Triangles

We use *barycentric coordinates* to describe a triangle with two parameters, u and v, i.e.

$$\mathbf{v}_0 + u(\mathbf{v}_1 - \mathbf{v}_0) + v(\mathbf{v}_2 - \mathbf{v}_0) = (1 - u - v)\mathbf{v}_0 + u\mathbf{v}_1 + v\mathbf{v}_2$$

where $0 \le u \le 1$, $0 \le v \le 1$ and $0 \le u + v \le 1$. To determine the point of intersection we calculate

$$\mathbf{o} + t\mathbf{d} = (1 - u - v)\mathbf{v}_0 + u\mathbf{v}_1 + v\mathbf{v}_2$$
$$\mathbf{o} - \mathbf{v}_0 = (-u - v)\mathbf{v}_0 + u\mathbf{v}_1 + v\mathbf{v}_2 - t\mathbf{d}$$
$$\mathbf{o} - \mathbf{v}_0 = u(\mathbf{v}_1 - \mathbf{v}_0) + v(\mathbf{v}_2 - \mathbf{v}_0) - t\mathbf{d}$$
$$\mathbf{o} - \mathbf{v}_0 = (\,-\mathbf{d} \quad \mathbf{v}_1 - \mathbf{v}_0 \quad \mathbf{v}_2 - \mathbf{v}_0\,) \begin{pmatrix} t \\ u \\ v \end{pmatrix}.$$

To simplify we define

$$\mathbf{e}_1 := \mathbf{v}_1 - \mathbf{v}_0, \qquad \mathbf{e}_2 := \mathbf{v}_2 - \mathbf{v}_0, \qquad \mathbf{s} := \mathbf{o} - \mathbf{v}_0$$
$$\mathbf{M} := (\,-\mathbf{d} \quad \mathbf{v}_1 - \mathbf{v}_0 \quad \mathbf{v}_2 - \mathbf{v}_0\,).$$

Now multiplying by $\mathbf{M}^{-1}$ gives t, u and v. We use *Cramer's rule* to find the solution

$$\begin{pmatrix} t \\ u \\ v \end{pmatrix} = \frac{1}{\det(-\mathbf{d}, \mathbf{e}_1, \mathbf{e}_2)} \begin{pmatrix} \det(\mathbf{s}, \mathbf{e}_1, \mathbf{e}_2) \\ \det(-\mathbf{d}, \mathbf{s}, \mathbf{e}_2) \\ \det(-\mathbf{d}, \mathbf{e}_1, \mathbf{s}) \end{pmatrix}.$$

Using the identity $\det(\mathbf{a}, \mathbf{b}, \mathbf{c}) \equiv |\mathbf{abc}| \equiv -(\mathbf{a} \times \mathbf{c}) \cdot \mathbf{b} \equiv -(\mathbf{c} \times \mathbf{b}) \cdot \mathbf{a}$ and setting

$$\mathbf{p} := \mathbf{d} \times \mathbf{e}_2, \qquad \mathbf{q} := \mathbf{s} \times \mathbf{e}_1$$

the solution is then

$$\begin{pmatrix} t \\ u \\ v \end{pmatrix} = \frac{1}{(\mathbf{d} \times \mathbf{e}_2) \cdot \mathbf{e}_1} \begin{pmatrix} (\mathbf{s} \times \mathbf{e}_1) \cdot \mathbf{e}_2 \\ (\mathbf{d} \times \mathbf{e}_2) \cdot \mathbf{s} \\ (\mathbf{s} \times \mathbf{e}_1) \cdot \mathbf{d} \end{pmatrix}$$
$$= \frac{1}{\mathbf{p} \cdot \mathbf{e}_1} \begin{pmatrix} \mathbf{q} \cdot \mathbf{e}_2 \\ \mathbf{p} \cdot \mathbf{s} \\ \mathbf{q} \cdot \mathbf{d} \end{pmatrix}.$$

Solving for t, u, and v is required to make sure that the constraints on each are satisfied. If the constraints are not satisfied, there is no intersection. Real-Time Rendering by Möller and Haines [1] describes how the algorithm can be implemented in such a way as to reject failed intersections quickly. They give a complete algorithm listing.

7.5.4 Effect of Transforms

If a scale transform is applied to an object (for example to create an ellipsoid from a sphere) then the direction of the ray must be modified by the inverse transform. The direction is no longer necessarily a unit vector. If this direction vector can be used directly in the intersection test, then the calculated value for t will correspond to geometric distance. However, if the direction vector $\mathbf{d}$ must be normalized to apply the intersection test, then t is no longer a measure of geometric distance. To convert t to a geometric distance, which allows for comparison to the distance of other objects, we use

$$t' = \frac{t}{\|\mathbf{d}\|} \, .$$

7.6 C# Implementation of a Raytracer

Base classes for lights and primitives are provided. Some spatial partitioning is also included in the `SceneTree` class. The modular approach allows each light type an each object type to be implemented in their own class files.

```
//Light.cs
abstract public class Light {
    public Vector l;
    public Colour Ia, Id, Is;
    public double cub_att, lin_att, const_att;
    //for photon mapping
    public int photons;
    public Light() {
        const_att=1.0;
        lin_att=0.0;
        cub_att=0.0;
        l=new Vector(0.0,0.0,0.0,1.0);
        Ia=new Colour(1.0,1.0,1.0);
        Id=new Colour(1.0,1.0,1.0);
        Is=new Colour(1.0,1.0,1.0);
        photons=0;
    }
    public abstract double intensity(Vector p);
    public abstract double dist(Vector p);
```

```csharp
    public abstract Vector lightdir(Vector p);
    public abstract object Clone();
}


//PointLight.cs
public class PointLight:Light {
  public override double dist(Vector p) { return (p-l).norm(); }

  public override double intensity(Vector p) {
     double d=(p-l).norm();
     return 1.0/(const_att+d*lin_att+d*d*cub_att);
  }

  public override Vector lightdir(Vector p) {
     Vector x=l-p;
     x.normalize();
     return x;
  }

  public override object Clone() {
     PointLight lt=new PointLight();
     lt.l=(Vector)l.Clone();
     lt.Ia=(Colour)Ia.Clone();
     lt.Id=(Colour)Id.Clone();
     lt.Is=(Colour)Is.Clone();
     lt.cub_att=cub_att; lt.lin_att=lin_att; lt.const_att=const_att;
     return (object)lt;
  }
}


//InfiniteLight.cs
using System;

public class InfiniteLight:Light {
  public override double dist(Vector p) { return 1e10; }
  public override double intensity(Vector p) { return 1.0; }
  public override Vector lightdir(Vector p) {
     l.normalize(); l.w=0.0;
     return l;
  }

  public override object Clone() {
     InfiniteLight lt=new InfiniteLight();
     lt.l=(Vector)l.Clone();
     lt.Ia=(Colour)Ia.Clone();
     lt.Id=(Colour)Id.Clone();
     lt.Is=(Colour)Is.Clone();
     lt.cub_att=cub_att; lt.lin_att=lin_att; lt.const_att=const_att;
     return (object)lt;
  }
}
```

```csharp
//SpotLight.cs
using System;

public class SpotLight:Light {
    public Vector dir;
    public double falloff;
    public override double dist(Vector p)
    { return (p-l).norm(); }
    public override double intensity(Vector p) {
        double c;
        double d=(p-l).norm();
        Vector x=p-l;
        x.normalize();
        c=x*dir;
        if(c<0.0) return 0.0;
        c=Math.Pow(c,falloff);
        return c/(const_att+d*lin_att+d*d*cub_att);
    }

    public override Vector lightdir(Vector p) {
        Vector x=l-p;
        x.normalize();
        return x;
    }

    public override object Clone() {
        SpotLight lt=new SpotLight();
        lt.l=(Vector)l.Clone();
        lt.Ia=(Colour)Ia.Clone();
        lt.Id=(Colour)Id.Clone();
        lt.Is=(Colour)Is.Clone();
        lt.cub_att=cub_att; lt.lin_att=lin_att; lt.const_att=const_att;
        lt.dir=(Vector)dir.Clone();
        lt.falloff=falloff;
        return (object)lt;
    }
}


//Primitive.cs
abstract public class Primitive
{
    public Primitive()
    { T=new Matrix(); W=new Matrix(); TI=new Matrix(); }

    public abstract IntersectInfo intersect(Vector o,Vector d);

    public virtual void Translate(double x,double y,double z) {
        T=T*Matrix.Translate(new Vector(x,y,z));
        W=Matrix.Translate(new Vector(-x,-y,-z))*W;
```

```
        TI=W.Transpose();
}

public virtual void Rotate(double theta,double x,double y,double z) {
    T=T*Matrix.Rotate(new Vector(x,y,z),theta);
    W=Matrix.Rotate(new Vector(x,y,z),-theta)*W;
    TI=W.Transpose();
}

public virtual void Scale(double x,double y,double z) {
    T=T*Matrix.Scale(x,y,z);
    W=Matrix.Scale(1.0/x,1.0/y,1.0/z)*W;
    TI=W.Transpose();
}

public virtual void Scale(double s) {
    T=T*Matrix.Scale(s);
    W=Matrix.Scale(1.0/s)*W;
    TI=W.Transpose();
}

//get an axis aligned bound in world space, null if not possible
public virtual BBox getExtent() {
        BBox b, bw;
        Vector c=new Vector();
        b=getLocalExtent();
        if(b==null) return null;
        bw=new BBox();
        for(int i=0;i<8;i++) {
            if((i&1)==1) c.x=b.min.x; else c.x=b.max.x;
            if((i&2)==2) c.y=b.min.y; else c.y=b.max.y;
            if((i&4)==4) c.z=b.min.z; else c.z=b.max.z;
            c.w=1.0; c=T*c;
            if(i==0) { bw.min=new Vector(c); bw.max=new Vector(c); }
            if(c.x<bw.min.x) bw.min.x=c.x;
            if(c.y<bw.min.y) bw.min.y=c.y;
            if(c.z<bw.min.z) bw.min.z=c.z;
            if(c.x>bw.max.x) bw.max.x=c.x;
            if(c.y>bw.max.y) bw.max.y=c.y;
            if(c.z>bw.max.z) bw.max.z=c.z;
        }
        return bw;
}

//get an axis aligned bound in object space, null if not possible
public abstract BBox getLocalExtent();
//transform on object
public Matrix T;
//transform of the world relative to the object
public Matrix W;
//inverse transform for normals
```

```csharp
    public Matrix TI;
    public Material M;

    public virtual object Clone() { return null; }
}


//Plane.cs
using System;

//defined by n*p+d=0;
public class Plane:Primitive {
    //normal to plane and constant d
    public Plane() {
        this.n=new Vector(0.0,1.0,0.0,0.0);
        this.d=0.0;
    }

    public Plane(Vector n,double d) {
        this.n=(Vector)n.Clone();
        this.n.w=0.0;
        this.d=d;
    }
    //normal to plane+point on plane
    public Plane(Vector n,Vector p) {
        this.n=(Vector)n.Clone();
        this.n.w=0.0;
        this.d=-n*p;
    }

    public override IntersectInfo intersect(Vector o,
        Vector dir) {
        double denom=n*dir;
        IntersectInfo i;
        if(Math.Abs(denom)<1e-7) return null;
        i=new IntersectInfo();
        i.obj=this;
        i.n=n; i.t=(-n*o-d)/denom;
        return i;
    }

    public override BBox getLocalExtent() { return null; }

    public Vector n;
    public double d;

    public override object Clone() { object o=new Plane(n,d); return o; }

    public override string ToString() { return "Primitive::Plane()"; }

}
```

```
//Sphere.cs
using System;

//A unit sphere, scale and translate to change position and size
public class Sphere:Primitive {
  public Sphere() { }

  public override IntersectInfo intersect(Vector o,Vector dir) {
    double a, b, c, d, t, t1, t2;
    Vector p;
    IntersectInfo i;
    a=dir*dir; b=2.0*o*dir; c=o*o-1.0; d=b*b-4*a*c;
    if(d<0.0) return null;
    t1=(-b-Math.Sqrt(d))/(2.0*a); t2=(-b+Math.Sqrt(d))/(2.0*a);
    if(t1<0.0) t=t2; else t=t1;
    if(t<=0.0) return null;
    i=new IntersectInfo();
    p=o+t*dir; p.w=0.0;
    i.obj=this; i.n=p; i.t=t;
    return i;
  }

  public override BBox getLocalExtent() {
    BBox b=new BBox();
    b.min=new Vector(-1.0,-1.0,-1.0);
    b.max=new Vector(1.0,1.0,1.0);
    return b;
  }

  public override object Clone() { object o=new Sphere(); return o; }

  public override string ToString() { return "Primitive::Sphere()"; }
}


//Triangle.cs
using System;

public class Triangle:Primitive {
  public Triangle() {
    this.v0=new Vector(0.0,0.0,0.0);
    this.v1=new Vector(0.0,0.0,0.0);
    this.v2=new Vector(0.0,0.0,0.0);
    this.n0=new Vector(0.0,1.0,0.0);
    this.n1=new Vector(0.0,1.0,0.0);
    this.n2=new Vector(0.0,1.0,0.0);
  }

  public Triangle(Vector v0,Vector v1,Vector v2) {
    Vector n;
```

```
    n=(v1-v0)^(v2-v0);
    n.normalize();
    this.v0=(Vector)v0.Clone();
    this.v1=(Vector)v1.Clone();
    this.v2=(Vector)v2.Clone();
    this.n0=n; this.n1=n; this.n2=n;
}

public Triangle(Vector v0,Vector v1,Vector v2,
    Vector n0,Vector n1,Vector n2) {
    this.v0=(Vector)v0.Clone();
    this.v1=(Vector)v1.Clone();
    this.v2=(Vector)v2.Clone();
    this.n0=(Vector)n0.Clone();
    this.n1=(Vector)n1.Clone();
    this.n2=(Vector)n2.Clone();
}

//From Real-Time Rendering, by Moller and Haines
public override IntersectInfo intersect(Vector o,Vector d) {
    Vector e1, e2, p, s, q;
    IntersectInfo info;
    double a, f, u, v, t;
    e1=v1-v0; e2=v2-v0;
    p=d^e2; a=e1*p;
    if((a>-1e-7)&&(a<1e-7)) return null;
    f=1.0/a; s=o-v0; u=f*(s*p);
    if((u<0.0)||(u>1.0)) return null;
    q=s^e1; v=f*(d*q);
    if((v<0.0)||(u+v>1.0)) return null;
    t=f*(e2*q);
    info=new IntersectInfo();
    info.n=(1.0-u-v)*n0+u*n1+v*n2;
    info.n.normalize();
    info.obj=this;
    info.t=t;
    return info;
}

public override BBox getLocalExtent() {
    BBox b=new BBox();
    b.min=new Vector(v0); b.max=new Vector(v0);
    if(v1.x<b.min.x) b.min.x=v1.x;
    if(v1.y<b.min.y) b.min.y=v1.y;
    if(v1.z<b.min.z) b.min.z=v1.z;
    if(v1.x>b.max.x) b.max.x=v1.x;
    if(v1.y>b.max.y) b.max.y=v1.y;
    if(v1.z>b.max.z) b.max.z=v1.z;
    if(v2.x<b.min.x) b.min.x=v2.x;
    if(v2.y<b.min.y) b.min.y=v2.y;
    if(v2.z<b.min.z) b.min.z=v2.z;
```

```
    if(v2.x>b.max.x) b.max.x=v2.x;
    if(v2.y>b.max.y) b.max.y=v2.y;
    if(v2.z>b.max.z) b.max.z=v2.z;
    return b;
}

public Vector v0, v1, v2, n0, n1, n2;

public override object Clone() {
    object o=new Triangle(v0,v1,v2,n0,n1,n2);
    return o; }

public override string ToString() { return "Primitive::Triangle()"; }
}
```

The MeshTriangle class is almost identical to the Triangle class, except that it is designed to share vertices and normals with other triangles which makes the class better suited to triangles meshes.

```
//MeshTriangle.cs
//A mesh triangle differs from a triangle in that vertices and normals
//are shared with other triangles, therefore no cloning is done.
using System;

//never transform a MeshTriangle, should only be used as a part of mesh
public class MeshTriangle:Primitive {
    public MeshTriangle() {
        this.v0=new Vector(0.0,0.0,0.0);
        this.v1=new Vector(0.0,0.0,0.0);
        this.v2=new Vector(0.0,0.0,0.0);
        this.n0=new Vector(0.0,1.0,0.0);
        this.n1=new Vector(0.0,1.0,0.0);
        this.n2=new Vector(0.0,1.0,0.0);
    }

    public MeshTriangle(Vector v0,Vector v1,Vector v2) {
        Vector n;
        n=(v1-v0)^(v2-v0);
        n.normalize();
        this.v0=v0; this.v1=v1; this.v2=v2;
        this.n0=n; this.n1=n; this.n2=n;
    }

    public MeshTriangle(Vector v0,Vector v1,Vector v2,
        Vector n0,Vector n1,Vector n2) {
        this.v0=v0; this.v1=v1; this.v2=v2;
        this.n0=n0; this.n1=n1; this.n2=n2;
    }

    //from Real-Time Rendering, by Moller and Haines
```

```
public override IntersectInfo intersect(Vector o,Vector d) {
  Vector e1, e2, p, s, q;
  IntersectInfo info;
  double a, f, u, v, t;
  e1=v1-v0; e2=v2-v0;
  p=d^e2; a=e1*p;
  if((a>-1e-7)&&(a<1e-7)) return null;
  f=1.0/a; s=o-v0; u=f*(s*p);
  if((u<0.0)||(u>1.0)) return null;
  q=s^e1; v=f*(d*q);
  if((v<0.0)||(u+v>1.0)) return null;
  t=f*(e2*q);
  info=new IntersectInfo();
  info.n=(1.0-u-v)*n0+u*n1+v*n2;
  info.n.normalize();
  info.obj=this;
  info.t=t;
  return info;
}

public override BBox getLocalExtent() {
  BBox b=new BBox();
  b.min=new Vector(v0);
  b.max=new Vector(v0);
  if(v1.x<b.min.x) b.min.x=v1.x;
  if(v1.y<b.min.y) b.min.y=v1.y;
  if(v1.z<b.min.z) b.min.z=v1.z;
  if(v1.x>b.max.x) b.max.x=v1.x;
  if(v1.y>b.max.y) b.max.y=v1.y;
  if(v1.z>b.max.z) b.max.z=v1.z;
  if(v2.x<b.min.x) b.min.x=v2.x;
  if(v2.y<b.min.y) b.min.y=v2.y;
  if(v2.z<b.min.z) b.min.z=v2.z;
  if(v2.x>b.max.x) b.max.x=v2.x;
  if(v2.y>b.max.y) b.max.y=v2.y;
  if(v2.z>b.max.z) b.max.z=v2.z;
  return b;
}

public Vector v0, v1, v2i, n0, n1, n2;

public override object Clone() {
  object o=new MeshTriangle(v0,v1,v2,n0,n1,n2);
  return o; }

public override string ToString()
{ return "Primitive::MeshTriangle()"; }

}
```

```
//Mesh.cs
using System;
using System.IO;

public class Mesh:Primitive {
    Scene trilist;
    public Mesh() { trilist=new SceneTree(); }

    //Read a wavefront obj file
    public Mesh(String file) {
        int nv, nn, nt;
        nv=nn=nt=0;
        trilist=new SceneTree();
        try {
            //count number of vertices, triangles and normals
            using (StreamReader sr=new StreamReader(file)) {
                String line;
                while((line=sr.ReadLine())!=null) {
                    if(line.Length>=2) {
                        if(line[0]=='v') {
                            if(line[1]=='n') nn++; //vertex normal
                            else nv++; //vertex
                        }
                        if(line[0]=='f') nt++;
                    }
                }
            }
            //Create an extra normal for each triangle for per triangle information
            n=new Vector[nn+nt];
            int basen=nn;
            v=new Vector[nv];
            nn=nv=nt=0;
            char[] sep=new char[1];
            char[] subsep=new char[1];
            String[] parts, subparts;
            sep[0]=' '; subsep[0]='/';
            double[] d=new double[5];
            int[] vnum=new int[5];
            int[] nnum=new int[5];
            int c, i;

            using (StreamReader sr=new StreamReader(file)) {
                String line;
                while((line=sr.ReadLine())!=null) {
                    if(line.Length>=2) {
                        if(line[0]=='v') {
                            if(line[1]=='n') { //vertex normal
                                parts=line.Split(sep);
                                c=0;
                                for(i=1;i<parts.GetLength(0);i++) {
```

```
                  if(parts[i].Length>0)
                      d[c++]=Double.Parse(parts[i]);
                }
                n[nn]=new Vector(d[0],d[1],d[2],0.0);
                nn++;
              } else { //vertex
                parts=line.Split(sep);
                c=0;
                for(i=1;i<parts.GetLength(0);i++) {
                  if(parts[i].Length>0)
                      d[c++]=Double.Parse(parts[i]);
                }
                v[nv]=new Vector(d[0],d[1],d[2],1.0);
                nv++;
              }
            }
            if(line[0]=='f') {
              parts=line.Split(sep);
              c=0;
              for(i=1;i<parts.GetLength(0);i++){
                if(parts[i].Length>0) {
                  subparts=parts[i].Split(subsep);
                  vnum[c]=Int32.Parse(subparts[0])-1;
                  nnum[c]=Int32.Parse(subparts[2])-1;
                  c++;
                }
              }
              for(i=0;i<3;i++) if(nnum[i]<0) nnum[i]=basen+nt;
              n[basen+nt]=(v[vnum[1]]-v[vnum[0]])^
                (v[vnum[2]]-v[vnum[0]]);
              trilist.add(new MeshTriangle(
                v[vnum[0]],v[vnum[1]],v[vnum[2]],
                n[nnum[0]],n[nnum[1]],n[nnum[2]]));
              nt++;
            }
          }
        }
      }
    }
  }
  catch(Exception e)
  {
    Console.WriteLine("The file could not be read:");
    Console.WriteLine(e.Message);
  }
  trilist.prepare_for_render();
}

public Mesh(Mesh m) {
  v=(Vector[])m.v.Clone();
  n=(Vector[])m.n.Clone();
  trilist=(Scene)m.trilist.Clone();
```

```
}

public void recenter() {
   int i, n;
   Vector c=new Vector(0.0,0.0,0.0);
   if(v==null) return;
   n=v.GetLength(0);
   for(i=0;i<n;i++) c+=v[i];
   c/=n;
   for(i=0;i<n;i++) { v[i].x-=c.x; v[i].y-=c.y; v[i].z-=c.z; }
}

public void rescale() {
   int i, n;
   double max=-1.0;
   if(v==null) return;
   n=v.GetLength(0);
   for(i=0;i<n;i++) {
      if(Math.Abs(v[i].x)>max) max=Math.Abs(v[i].x);
      if(Math.Abs(v[i].y)>max) max=Math.Abs(v[i].y);
      if(Math.Abs(v[i].z)>max) max=Math.Abs(v[i].z);
   }
   for(i=0;i<n;i++) { v[i].x/=max; v[i].y/=max; v[i].z/=max;}
}

public override IntersectInfo intersect(Vector o,Vector d) {
   IntersectInfo info=null;

   if(trilist==null) return null;
   info=trilist.intersect(o,d);
   if(info!=null) { info.obj=this; }
   return info;
}

public override BBox getLocalExtent() {
   BBox b=new BBox();
   if(v==null) return null;
   if(v.GetLength(0)<=0) return null;
   b.min=new Vector(v[0]); b.max=new Vector(v[0]);
   for(int i=1;i<v.GetLength(0);i++) {
      if(v[i].x<b.min.x) b.min.x=v[i].x;
      if(v[i].y<b.min.y) b.min.y=v[i].y;
      if(v[i].z<b.min.z) b.min.z=v[i].z;
      if(v[i].x>b.max.x) b.max.x=v[i].x;
      if(v[i].y>b.max.y) b.max.y=v[i].y;
      if(v[i].z>b.max.z) b.max.z=v[i].z;
   }
   return b;
}

public Vector[] v, n;
```

```
    public override object Clone() { object o=new Mesh(this); return o; }

    public override string ToString() { return "Primitive::Mesh()"; }
}


//BBox.cs
using System;

public class BBox {
    public Vector min;
    public Vector max;
    public bool intersect(BBox b2) {
        int overlap=0;
        if((min.x<=b2.min.x)&&(b2.min.x<=max.x)) overlap++;
        else if((min.x<=b2.max.x)&&(b2.max.x<=max.x)) overlap++;
        else if((b2.min.x<=min.x)&&(min.x<=b2.max.x)) overlap++;
        else if((b2.min.x<=max.x)&&(max.x<=b2.max.x)) overlap++;
        if((min.y<=b2.min.y)&&(b2.min.y<=max.y)) overlap++;
        else if((min.y<=b2.max.y)&&(b2.max.y<=max.y)) overlap++;
        else if((b2.min.y<=min.y)&&(min.y<=b2.max.y)) overlap++;
        else if((b2.min.y<=max.y)&&(max.y<=b2.max.y)) overlap++;
        if((min.z<=b2.min.z)&&(b2.min.z<=max.z)) overlap++;
        else if((min.z<=b2.max.z)&&(b2.max.z<=max.z)) overlap++;
        else if((b2.min.z<=min.z)&&(min.z<=b2.max.z)) overlap++;
        else if((b2.min.z<=max.z)&&(max.z<=b2.max.z)) overlap++;
        return (overlap==3);
    }

    public IntersectInfo intersect(Vector o,Vector d) {
        double t1, t2, temp;
        double tmin, tmax;
        IntersectInfo info=new IntersectInfo();
        //check if the ray starts from inside the box
        if((o.x>=min.x)&&(o.x<=max.x)&&(o.y>=min.y)&&(o.y<=max.y)
            &&(o.z>=min.z)&&(o.z<=max.z))
            { info.t=1e-7; return info; }
        //check if the ray is parallel to one of the planes
        // and then if it is outside the box
        if(Math.Abs(d.x)<1e-15) {
            if(o.x<min.x) return null; if(o.x>max.x) return null;
        }
        if(Math.Abs(d.y)<1e-15) {
            if(o.y<min.y) return null; if(o.y>max.y) return null;
        }
        if(Math.Abs(d.z)<1e-15) {
            if(o.z<min.z) return null; if(o.z>max.z) return null;
        }

        //check intersection point with AABB planes
```

```
            t1=(min.x-o.x)/d.x;  t2=(max.x-o.x)/d.x;
            if(t1>t2) { temp=t1;  t1=t2;  t2=temp; }
            tmin=t1; tmax=t2;
            t1=(min.y-o.y)/d.y;  t2=(max.y-o.y)/d.y;
            if(t1>t2) { temp=t1;  t1=t2;  t2=temp; }
            if(t1>tmin) tmin=t1; if(t2<tmax) tmax=t2;
            t1=(min.z-o.z)/d.z;  t2=(max.z-o.z)/d.z;
            if(t1>t2) { temp=t1;  t1=t2;  t2=temp; }
            if(t1>tmin) tmin=t1; if(t2<tmax) tmax=t2;
            if(tmin>tmax) return null;
            if(tmax<0.0) return null;
            if(tmin>0.0) info.t=tmin;
            else info.t=tmax;
            return info;
        }

        public BBox union(BBox b2) {
            BBox r=new BBox();
            r.min=(Vector)min.Clone();
            r.max=(Vector)max.Clone();
            if(r.min.x>b2.min.x) r.min.x=b2.min.x;
            if(r.min.y>b2.min.y) r.min.y=b2.min.y;
            if(r.min.z>b2.min.z) r.min.z=b2.min.z;
            if(r.max.x<b2.max.x) r.max.x=b2.max.x;
            if(r.max.y<b2.max.y) r.max.y=b2.max.y;
            if(r.max.z<b2.max.z) r.max.z=b2.max.z;
            return r;
        }

        public object Clone() {
            BBox b=new BBox();
            b.min=(Vector)min.Clone();
            b.max=(Vector)max.Clone();
            return (object)b;
        }
    }
}


//BoundingVolume.cs
using System;

//Bounding volume, do not set transforms in any way! The values are
//returned directly, so the inverse must be stored directly with the object.
public class BoundingVolume:Primitive {
    public Primitive bv;
    public Primitive obj;

    public BoundingVolume() { }

    public BoundingVolume(Primitive bv,Primitive obj)
    { this.bv=bv; this.obj=obj; }
```

```
//prevent (partially) setting of transforms
public override void Translate(double x,double y,double z)
{ throw new Exception("Transforms not supported on BV!"); }
public override void Rotate(double theta,double x,double y,double z)
{ throw new Exception("Transforms not supported on BV!"); }
public override void Scale(double x,double y,double z)
{ throw new Exception("Transforms not supported on BV!"); }
public override void Scale(double s)
{ throw new Exception("Transforms not supported on BV!"); }

public override IntersectInfo intersect(Vector o,Vector dir) {
    Vector to, td;
    IntersectInfo info;

    to=bv.W*o; td=bv.W*dir;
    info=bv.intersect(to,td);
    if(info!=null) {
        to=obj.W*o; td=obj.W*dir;
        info=obj.intersect(to,td);
    }
    return info;
}

public override object Clone()
{ object o=new BoundingVolume(bv,obj); return o; }

public override BBox getExtent() { return bv.getExtent(); }

public override BBox getLocalExtent()
{ return bv.getLocalExtent(); }

public override string ToString()
{ return "Primitive::BoundingVolume()"; }
}


//IntersectInfo.cs
public class IntersectInfo {
    public Vector n;
    //p is set by the raytracer core
    public Vector p;
    public Primitive obj;
    public double t;
    public object Clone() {
        IntersectInfo i=new IntersectInfo();
        i.n=(Vector)n.Clone();
        if(p!=null) i.p=(Vector)p.Clone();
        i.obj=obj; i.t=t;
        return (object)i;
    }
```

```
}
```

The **Feedback** handles information regarding the progress of rendering a scene. This allows the interface to be changed at any time. Both console and GUI applications can then use the raytracer.

```
// Feedback.cs
using System;

abstract public class Feedback
{
   public Feedback() { }
   abstract public void complete(double guess,int x,int y,Colour[,] img);
}
```

Scene and **SceneTree** manage the objects in a scene. **SceneTree** creates a binary space partition to accelerate intersection testing.

```
//Scene.cs
using System;

public class Scene {
   protected Primitive[] scene;
   public Light[] lights;
   public Scene()
   { lights=new Light[0]; scene=new Primitive[0]; }
   public virtual void add(Light l) {
      Array.Resize(ref lights,lights.GetLength(0)+1);
      lights[lights.GetLength(0)-1]=l;
   }

   public virtual void add(Primitive p) {
      Array.Resize(ref scene,scene.GetLength(0)+1);
      scene[scene.GetLength(0)-1]=p;
   }

   public virtual IntersectInfo intersect(Vector o,Vector d) {
      Vector to,td;
      IntersectInfo closest=null;
      IntersectInfo next;
      int i, n;

      d.w=0.0;
      n=scene.GetLength(0);
      for(i=0;i<n;i++) {
         to=scene[i].W*o;  td=scene[i].W*d;
         next=scene[i].intersect(to,td);
         if((next!=null)&&(next.t>1e-7)) {
            if((closest==null)||(next.t<closest.t)) closest=next;
```

```
      }
    }
    return closest;
}

public virtual void prepare_for_render() { }

public object Clone() {
    int i;
    Scene s=new Scene();
    for(i=0;i<lights.GetLength(0);i++) s.add((Light)lights[i].Clone());
    for(i=0;i<scene.GetLength(0);i++) s.add((Primitive)scene[i].Clone());
    object o=s;
    return o;
}
}


//SceneTree.cs
using System;

public class SceneNode {
    public BBox bbox;
    public int splitaxis; //0-x 1-y 2-z
    public SceneNode left, right;
    public Primitive[] objects;
    public SceneNode()
    { objects=new Primitive[0]; left=null; right=null; }

    public void add(Primitive p) {
        Array.Resize(ref objects,objects.GetLength(0)+1);
        objects[objects.GetLength(0)-1]=p;
    }

    public void split(int depth,int maxprimitives) {
        int i, n;
        Vector diff;
        BBox b;
        n=objects.GetLength(0);
        if(n<=0) { bbox=null; return; }
        if(bbox==null) {
            bbox=objects[0].getExtent();
            if(n==1) return;
            for(i=1;i<n;i++) {
                b=objects[i].getExtent(); bbox=bbox.union(b);
            }
        }

        if(depth==0) return;
        if(n<=maxprimitives) return;
```

```csharp
    diff=bbox.max-bbox.min;
    if((diff.x>=diff.y)&&(diff.x>=diff.z)) splitaxis=0;
    else if(diff.y>=diff.z) splitaxis=1;
    else splitaxis=2;

    left=new SceneNode(); right=new SceneNode();
    left.bbox=(BBox)bbox.Clone();
    right.bbox=(BBox)bbox.Clone();
    if(splitaxis==0) {
        left.bbox.max.x=bbox.min.x+diff.x/2.0;
        right.bbox.min.x=left.bbox.max.x;
    }
    else if(splitaxis==1) {
        left.bbox.max.y=bbox.min.y+diff.y/2.0;
        right.bbox.min.y=left.bbox.max.y;
    }
    else if(splitaxis==2) {
        left.bbox.max.z=bbox.min.z+diff.z/2.0;
        right.bbox.min.z=left.bbox.max.z;
    }
    for(i=0;i<n;i++) {
        b=objects[i].getExtent();
        if(left.bbox.intersect(b)) left.add(objects[i]);
        if(right.bbox.intersect(b)) right.add(objects[i]);
    }
    left.split(depth-1,maxprimitives);
    right.split(depth-1,maxprimitives);
}

public IntersectInfo intersect(Vector o,Vector d,
        IntersectInfo best) {
    Vector to, td;
    IntersectInfo closest=null;
    IntersectInfo next, infol, infor;
    int i, n;

    if(bbox==null) return null;
    next=bbox.intersect(o,d);
    if(next==null) return null;
    if(best!=null) if(next.t>best.t) return null;
    if(left!=null) {
        infol=left.intersect(o,d,best);
        if(best==null) best=infol;
        else if((infol!=null)&&(infol.t<best.t)) best=infol;
        infor=right.intersect(o,d,best);
        if(infol==null) return infor;
        if(infor==null) return infol;
        if(infol.t<infor.t) return infol;
        else return infor;
    } else {
        d.w=0.0; n=objects.GetLength(0);
```

```
      for(i=0;i<n;i++) {
         to=objects[i].W*o; td=objects[i].W*d;
         next=objects[i].intersect(to,td);
         if((next!=null)&&(next.t>1e-7))
            if((closest==null)||(next.t<closest.t)) closest=next;
      }
      return closest;
   }
  }
}

public class SceneTree:Scene {
   public Primitive[] infinite;
   public SceneNode root;
   public int maxdepth, maxprimitives;
   public SceneTree() {
      lights=new Light[0];
      scene=new Primitive[0];
      infinite=new Primitive[0];
      maxdepth=25;
      maxprimitives=4;
   }

   public override void add(Light l) {
      Array.Resize(ref lights,lights.GetLength(0)+1);
      lights[lights.GetLength(0)-1]=l; }

   public override void add(Primitive p) {
      Array.Resize(ref scene,scene.GetLength(0)+1);
      scene[scene.GetLength(0)-1]=p; }

   public override IntersectInfo intersect(Vector o,Vector d) {
      Vector to, td;
      IntersectInfo closest=null;
      IntersectInfo next;
      int i, n;
      d.w=0.0;
      n=infinite.GetLength(0);
      for(i=0;i<n;i++) {
         to=scene[i].W*o; td=scene[i].W*d;
         next=infinite[i].intersect(to,td);
         if((next!=null)&&(next.t>1e-7))
            if((closest==null)||(next.t<closest.t)) closest=next;
      }

      next=root.intersect(o,d,closest);
      if((next!=null)&&(next.t>1e-7))
         if((closest==null)||(next.t<closest.t)) closest=next;
      return closest;
   }
```

```
public override void prepare_for_render() {
    int i, n;
    root=new SceneNode();
    infinite=new Primitive[0];
    n=scene.GetLength(0);
    for(i=0;i<n;i++) {
        if(scene[i].getExtent()!=null) root.add(scene[i]);
        else {
            Array.Resize(ref infinite,infinite.GetLength(0)+1);
            infinite[infinite.GetLength(0)-1]=scene[i];
        }
    }
    root.split(maxdepth,maxprimitives);
}
}
```

The majority of the work is done in the **Raytracer** class. Primitives handle intersections, but the **Raytracer** class manages the scene, the recursive raycast process and some additional features.

```
//Raytracer.cs
using System;

public class Raytracer {
    public Colour bg, ambient;
    //refraction stack
    private double[] rstack;
    private int rst;
    //current medium refraction index
    private double ri=1.0;
    private double baseri=1.0;
    //ambient occlusion settings
    public bool ao;
    public int aorays, supersample;
    public double ao_lin, ao_const, ao_cub, jitter;
    private Random rnd;
    public Matrix camera;
    public Vector cpos;
    public int maxdepth=5;
    public Scene scene;
    //photon mapping
    public bool photonmapping, show_photonmap;
    private PhotonTrace photontracer;
    private PhotonMap photonmap;
    public int photons, photonsamples;
    public double photonradius;

    public Raytracer() {
        bg=new Colour(0.0,0.0,0.0);
        ambient=new Colour(0.0,0.0,0.0);
```

```
    rst=0;
    rstack=new double[1024];
    ao=false;
    aorays=512;
    ao_lin=0.0; ao_cub=0.0; ao_const=0.0;
    rnd=new Random();
    supersample=1;
    jitter=0.0;
    camera=new Matrix();
    scene=null;
    photonmapping=false; show_photonmap=false;
    photontracer=null;
    photons=500000; photonmap=null;
    photonsamples=100; photonradius=1e10;
}

public void pushri() { if(rst>=1024) return; rstack[rst]=ri; rst++; }

public void popri() { if(rst<=0) return; rst--; ri=rstack[rst]; }

public void resetri() { rst=0; ri=baseri; }

public void add(Light l) {
    if(scene==null) scene=new Scene(); scene.add(l);
}

public void add(Primitive p) {
    if(scene==null) scene=new Scene(); scene.add(p);
}

IntersectInfo intersect(Vector o,Vector d) {
    if(scene==null) return null; return scene.intersect(o,d);
}

Vector rand_vector(Vector n) {
    Vector p=new Vector();
    p.x=rnd.NextDouble()*2.0-1.0;
    p.y=rnd.NextDouble()*2.0-1.0;
    p.z=rnd.NextDouble()*2.0-1.0;
    while((p*p>1.0)||(p*n<0)) {
        p.x=rnd.NextDouble()*2.0-1.0;
        p.y=rnd.NextDouble()*2.0-1.0;
        p.z=rnd.NextDouble()*2.0-1.0;
    }
    p.normalize();
    return p;
}.

double ambient_occlusion(Vector n,Vector p) {
    double ao=0.0;
    double aototal=0.0;
```

```
        double d, rn;
        Vector r;
        IntersectInfo occlusion;

        for(int i=0;i<aorays;i++) {
            r=rand_vector(n);
            occlusion=intersect(p,r);
            rn=r*n; aototal+=rn;
            if(occlusion!=null) {
                d=occlusion.t;
                d=1.0/(ao_const+d*ao_lin+d*d*ao_cub);
                if(d>1.0) d=1.0;
                ao+=d*rn;
            }
        }
        ao=ao/aototal;
        return 1.0-ao;
    }

    Colour raycast(Vector o,Vector d,int depth) {
        IntersectInfo info, shadow;
        Vector p,l,r,v;
        Colour accum=new Colour(0.0,0.0,0.0);
        int i, n;
        double pa=1.0;
        double I;
        Material m;
        if(depth==0) return accum;
        info=intersect(o,d);
        if(info==null) return bg;
        p=o+info.t*d;
        info.p=p;
        info.n=info.obj.TI.Transpose()*info.n;
        info.n.normalize();
        v=cpos-p;
        if(scene!=null) n=scene.lights.GetLength(0);
        else n=0;
        pa=info.obj.M.pa; m=info.obj.M;
        if(ao) pa*=ambient_occlusion(info.n,p);
        accum=ambient*m.ambient*pa;
        accum+=m.emissive*m.pe;
        for(i=0;i<n;i++) {
            accum+=scene.lights[i].Ia*m.ambient*pa;
            l=scene.lights[i].lightdir(p);
            l.normalize();
            l.w=0.0;
            shadow=intersect(p,l);
            if((shadow==null)||(shadow.t>scene.lights[i].dist(p))) {
                I=scene.lights[i].intensity(p);
                accum+=m.Light(info.n,l,v,new Colour(0.0,0.0,0.0),
                    scene.lights[i].Id*I, scene.lights[i].Is*I);
```

```
      }
   }

   if(m.pr>0.0) {
      r=Vector.reflect(-d,info.n); r.w=0.0;
      //use the specular colour to filter reflections
      accum+=m.pr*m.specular*raycast(p+r*1e-7,r,depth-1);
   }

   //add photon map contribution if required
   if(photonmapping) {
      if(show_photonmap) accum=photonmap.ViewMap(p,0.01);
      else accum+=photonmap.Irradiance(p,info.n,v,info.obj.M);
   }

   if(m.pt>0.0) {
      bool enter=(info.n*d<0.0);
      if(!enter) popri(); //leaving material, restore old material
      r=Vector.transmit(d,info.n,ri,m.ir);
      r.w=0.0; p.w=1.0;
      if(enter) //going into material, save old material
      { pushri(); ri=m.ir; }
      //use the diffuse component as a filter
      accum+=m.pt*m.diffuse*raycast(p+r*1e-7,r,depth-1);
   }
   return accum;
}

//field of view refers to the x direction, always assume square pixels
public Colour raytrace(int x,int y,int w,int h,double fov) {
   Colour accum=new Colour(0.0,0.0,0.0);
   double dx, dy, d, jx, jy;
   Vector dir=new Vector();
   d=-1.0/Math.Tan(fov/2.0);
   //find pixel coordinate as value between -1 and 1
   dx=(2.0*x-w)/w; dy=(2.0*y-w)/w;
   cpos=camera*new Vector(0.0,0.0,0.0);
   for(x=0;x<supersample;x++) {
      for(y=0;y<supersample;y++) {
         resetri();
         //get random offset in subpixel
         jx=rnd.NextDouble()*2.0-1.0;
         //add offset to center of subpixel
         jx=(x+0.5+jx*0.5*jitter)/(w*supersample);
         jy=rnd.NextDouble()*2.0-1.0;
         jy=(y+0.5+jy*0.5*jitter)/(w*supersample);
         //add jittered subpixel offset to pixel. Note the jittered subpixel
         //is multiplied by 2 because coordinates lie between -1 and 1.
         dir.x=dx+2.0*jx; dir.y=dy+2.0*jy;
         dir.z=d; dir.w=0.0; dir=camera*dir; dir.normalize();
         accum+=raycast(cpos,dir,maxdepth);
```

```csharp
        }
    }
    accum/=supersample*supersample;
    return accum;
}

public Colour[,] raytrace(int w,int h,double fov,int adaptive,double eps,
        Feedback progress) {
    int x, y;
    Colour c;
    Colour[,] bmp=new Colour[h,w];
    bool[,] redo=new bool[h,w];

    scene.prepare_for_render();
    //if adaptive supersampling is enabled, first disable supersampling
    if(adaptive>0) { supersample=1; jitter=0.0; }

    //if photonmapping is enabled, create photon map
    if(photonmapping) {
        photontracer=new PhotonTrace();
        photonmap=photontracer.createPhotonMap(scene,photons);
        photonmap.maxdist=photonradius;
        photonmap.maxsamples=photonsamples;
    }
    //raytrace each pixel
    for(y=0;y<h;y++) {
        for(x=0;x<w;x++) {
            redo[y,x]=false;
            c=raytrace(x,y,w,h,fov);
            bmp[y,x]=c;
            progress.complete((double)(y*w+x)/(h*w),x,y,bmp);
        }
    }
    if(adaptive>0) {
        //adaptive supersampling, enable supersampling
        supersample=adaptive;
        jitter=1.0;
        //rerender all pixels where difference is large
        for(y=0;y<h-1;y++) {
            for(x=0;x<w-1;x++) {
                if((bmp[y,x]-bmp[y+1,x]).norm()>eps)
                    { redo[y,x]=true; redo[y+1,x]=true; }
                if((bmp[y,x]-bmp[y,x+1]).norm()>eps)
                    { redo[y,x]=true; redo[y+1,x]=true; }
                if((bmp[y,x]-bmp[y+1,x+1]).norm()>eps)
                    { redo[y,x]=true; redo[y+1,x+1]=true; }
                if(redo[y,x]) { c=raytrace(x,y,w,h,fov); bmp[y,x]=c; }
                progress.complete((double)(y*w+x)/(h*w),x,y,bmp);
            }
        }
    }
```

```
    //clamp final results
    for(y=0;y<h;y++)
        for(x=0;x<w;x++) bmp[y,x]=bmp[y,x].clamp();
    return bmp;
}

public void Translate(double x,double y,double z)
{ camera=camera*Matrix.Translate(new Vector(x,y,z)); }

public void Rotate(double theta,double x,double y,double z)
{ camera=camera*Matrix.Rotate(new Vector(x,y,z),theta); }
}
```

7.7 Implicit Surfaces

Most of the surfaces described in this section are implicit surfaces. However, we have described the triangle as an explicit surface. By explicit we mean that given parameter values u and v we can obtain points on the triangle. The sphere as we have described it is an implicit surface since points on the sphere satisfy the equation

$$x^2 + y^2 + z^2 - r^2 = 0 \,.$$

There is no explicit mechanism for deriving points. For the implicit surfaces presented so far, it is possible to obtain the point of intersection by substituting the ray equation $\mathbf{o} + t\mathbf{d}$ into the implicit formula and solving for t. On occasion it is quite difficult to solve such an equation analytically and it is necessary to resort to numerical methods. One such method is *Newton-Rhapson*. Even numerical methods sometimes fail. Consider the torus, in some situtations a ray will intersect a torus as many as 4 times. In raytracing it is important that we obtain the nearest intersection point depending on the initial values for the method. But no such guarantee is provided by Newton-Rhapson type techniques. It is quite possible that the numerical method will provide the intersection point furthest from the viewer depending on the initial value for the Newton-Rhapson method. It is possible to obtain the correct intersection point if some bound on the intersection is kown, but that is seldom the case.

Next we present an algorithm due to Hart [58] that can be used to effectively render implicit surfaces.

7.7.1 Sphere Tracing

Sphere tracing makes use of *distance surfaces*. For the purposes of sphere tracing, it is necessary to use *geometric distance* as opposed to *algebraic distance*. Geometric distance corresponds precisely to the *Euclidean distance*. For example the sphere described by the distance function

$$x^2 + y^2 + z^2 - r^2$$

describes algebraic distance since the value of the function increases quadratically at points further from the surface. Geometric distance for the sphere is given by

$$\|\mathbf{p}\| - r.$$

This implicit formulation gives the geometric distance to the nearest point on the surface of the sphere. The geometric distance gives exact measures that can be used to determine how far a ray can travel before intersecting the surface. Note that both equations have the same value for points on the surface (that is 0). However, the values differ for points off the surface. Points inside the surface are assigned a negative distance, and points outside are assigned a positive value.

Let $f : \mathbb{R}^n \to \mathbb{R}$ be the function that explicitly describes the set of points $P \subset \mathbb{R}^n$ such that

$$P = \{x : f(\mathbf{p}) \le 0\}.$$

The function f has value 0 on the boundary of P, and this boundary forms the implicit surface of f. Points for which $f < 0$ are regarded as inside the surface and points for which $f > 0$ are regarded as outside. If f is strictly negative over the interior of P, then f^{-1} represents the implicit surface of f exactly. Note that f^{-1} is a multivalued function.

The distance from a point $\mathbf{x} \in \mathbb{R}^3$ to a set $P \subset \mathbb{R}^3$ is given by the distance from $\mathbf{x}$ to the closest point in P [58],

$$d(\mathbf{x}, P) := \min_{\mathbf{y} \in P} \|\mathbf{x} - \mathbf{y}\|$$

where $\|\mathbf{x} - \mathbf{y}\|$ denotes the Euclidean distance between $\mathbf{x}$ and $\mathbf{y}$. The distance function d implicitly defines P. A function $g : \mathbb{R}^3 \to \mathbb{R}$ is a *signed distance bound* of the implicit surface it describes ($g^{-1}(0)$) if

$$|g(\mathbf{x})| \le d(\mathbf{x}, g^{-1}(0)).$$

The function g is known as a *signed distance function*.

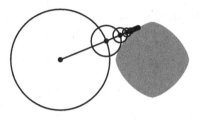

Figure 7.6: Sphere tracing: Hit.

The signed distance function describes the maximum distance that can be advanced along the ray without moving into the interior of P. The function g is not necessarily exact, all that is required is that g be conservative. The closer g is to geometric distance the faster convergence will be. The algorithm to trace the ray to intersection point is given by

```
SphereTrace(Ray o + td)
begin
    t=0
    while(t < D)
    begin
        d = |g(o + td)|
            if(d < ε) then return INTERSECTION(t).
            t = t + d.
    end
    return NO INTERSECTION
end
```

At each iteration of the algorithm, where d is calculated, a sphere centered at $\mathbf{o} + t\mathbf{d}$ with radius d will definitely *not* intersect the implicit surface. Hence the name sphere tracing. Since d is always positive, and the algorithm guarantees that the step size is less than the distance to the surface, the algorithm will converge to the surface or miss entirely. There is also no possibility that the algorithm returns a point on the surface other than the closest point. Figure 7.6 shows how the sphere is used as a measure of how far along the ray it is safe to advance, and the resulting intersection. Figure 7.7 shows the situation where the ray misses the object. Note how sphere tracing ensures that we rapidly reach the limit of the ray as soon as the ray passes the surface. It may be sufficient in certain cases to use an increase in distance to the surface as termination criteria. However, this will not work in general.

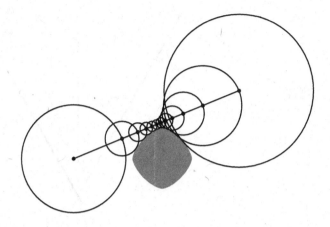

Figure 7.7: Sphere tracing: Miss.

The next section lists some signed distance functions for various surfaces as described by Hart [58].

7.7.2   Distance Functions

Sphere

As seen in the previous section the sphere can be described by the distance function

$$g(\mathbf{p}) = \|\mathbf{p}\| - r\,.$$

Here $\|\mathbf{p}\|$ is the distance from the origin to point $\mathbf{p}$. Thus points on the sphere of radius r have distance 0. Points outside have a distance value greater than 0. Points inside have a distance value smaller than 0.

Cylinder

The *infinite cylinder* with radius 1 can be described by the distance function

$$g(\mathbf{p}) = \|(p_0 \ \ p_1)^T\| - 1\,.$$

Thus only the first two components of any points are needed for the calculation. There are no conditions placed on p_2 and so the cylinder is an infinite cylinder.

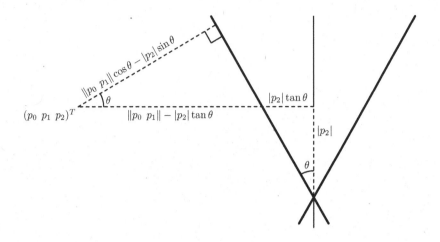

Figure 7.8: Distance to a cone (after [58]).

Cone

A *cone* is described by the signed distance function

$$g(\mathbf{p}) = \|(p_0 \ p_1)^T\| \cos\theta - |p_2| \sin\theta \,.$$

This distance function is very similar to the cylinder. The angle θ is the divergence from the z-axis and is required to compute the correct geometric distance (see figure 7.8).

Torus

A *torus* with radius with major radius a and minor radius b is described by the implicit surface

$$\left(\sqrt{p_0^2 + p_1^2} - a\right)^2 + p_2^2 - b^2 = 0 \,.$$

The distance function for the torus is

$$g(\mathbf{p}) = \left\|\left(\left\|(p_0 \ p_1)^T\right\| - a, p_2\right)\right\| - b \,.$$

Superquadrics

A *superquadric* is a surface defined by

$$\left(\left(\frac{p_0}{r_0}\right)^{2/s_2} + \left(\frac{p_1}{r_1}\right)^{2/s_2}\right)^{s_2/s_1} + \left(\frac{p_2}{r_2}\right)^{2/s_1} - 1 = 0 \,.$$

Figure 7.9: A superquadric.

The parametric version of the surface is then

$$p_0(\phi, \theta) = r_0 \cos^{s_1}(\phi) \cos^{s_2}(\theta), \quad -\pi/2 \le \phi \le \pi/2$$
$$p_1(\phi, \theta) = r_1 \cos^{s_1}(\phi) \sin^{s_2}(\theta), \quad -\pi \le \theta \le \pi$$
$$p_2(\phi, \theta) = r_2 \sin^{s_1}(\phi) .$$

The parameters s_1 and s_2 control the shape of the surface, and r_0, r_1 and r_2 determines the size of the surface in the x, y and z directions. To define the signed distance function for a superellipsoid, we need the p-norm. The p-norm is defined on $\mathbb{R}^2$ as

$$\|(x \; y)^T\|^p := (|x|^p + |y|^p)^{1/p} .$$

The pq-norm is defined in a similar fashion on $\mathbb{R}^3$ as

$$\|(x \; y \; z)^T\|^{pq} := \|(\|(x \; y)^T\|^p, z)\|^q .$$

The superellipsoid is defined in the same way as the sphere except that the pq-norm is used instead of the conventional norm. The distance function for the superellipsoid is given by

$$g(\mathbf{p}) = \|\mathbf{p}\|^{pq} - r .$$

Likewise supertori can be created using the p-norm. The distance function for a supertorus is given by

$$g(\mathbf{p}) = \left\| \left(\left\| (p_0 \; p_1)^T \right\|^p - a, p_2 \right) \right\|^q - b .$$

The pq-norm does not necessarily measure Euclidean distance. The distance computed with the pq-norm should thus be converted to an Euclidean distance to be comparable with other distance functions defined in Euclidean space. If r_s is the distance specified by the pq-norm, then the Euclidean distance can be taken as [58]

$$r_e = \begin{cases} r_s/ \left\| \left(\frac{1}{\sqrt{3}} \ \frac{1}{\sqrt{3}} \ \frac{1}{\sqrt{3}}\right)^T \right\|^{pq}, & \text{if } p \text{ or } q < 2 \\ r_s, & \text{otherwise.} \end{cases}$$

An example of a superquadric rendered with our C# implementation is displayed in figure 7.9.

7.7.3   C# Implementation

The `Implicit` class provides a starting point for implicit surfaces. Most implicit surfaces only define a distance function and inherit the intersection test from `Implicit`.

```
//Implicit.cs
using System;

//A unit Implicit, scale and translate to change position and size
public class Implicit:Primitive {
    double eps=1e-7;
    public Implicit() { }

    public virtual double func(Vector p)
    { double dist=p*p-1.0; return dist; }

    public virtual double dist(Vector p)
    { double dist=Math.Sqrt(p*p)-1.0; return dist; }

    public virtual Vector grad(Vector p) {
        double dx, dy, dz, f;
        f=func(p);
        dx=(func(p+new Vector(eps,0.0,0.0))-f)/eps;
        dy=(func(p+new Vector(0.0,eps,0.0))-f)/eps;
        dz=(func(p+new Vector(0.0,0.0,eps))-f)/eps;
        return new Vector(dx,dy,dz,0.0);
    }

    public override IntersectInfo intersect(Vector o,Vector dir) {
        Vector p=(Vector)o.Clone();
        double t=0.0, d=1e5;
        Vector dn;
        dn=(Vector)dir.Clone();
        dn.normalize();
        while((d>eps)&&(t<1e7)) {
            d=dist(o+t*dn);
            if(d>eps) { t=t+Math.Abs(d); }
        }
```

```
        if(t>=1e7) return null;
        IntersectInfo i=new IntersectInfo();
        p=o+t*dn; p.w=0.0;
        i.obj=this;
        i.n=grad(p); i.n.normalize(); i.t=t/dir.norm();
        return i;
    }

    public override BBox getLocalExtent() { return null; }

    public override object Clone() { object o=new Implicit(); return o; }

    public override string ToString() { return "Primitive::Implicit()"; }
}
```

Two examples of implicit surfaces are included, namely the torus and superellipsoid.

```
// Torus.cs
using System;

public class Torus:Implicit {
    public double rminor, rmajor;
    public Torus() { rminor=0.1; rmajor=1.0; }
    public Torus(double rminor,double rmajor)
    { this.rminor=rminor; this.rmajor=rmajor; }

    public override double dist(Vector p) {
        double dist;
        dist=Math.Sqrt(p.x*p.x+p.y*p.y)-rmajor;
        dist=Math.Sqrt(dist*dist+p.z*p.z)-rminor;
        return dist;
    }

    public override double func(Vector p) {
        double dist;
        dist=Math.Pow(Math.Sqrt(p.x*p.x+p.y*p.y)-rmajor,2.0)+
                p.z*p.z-rminor*rminor;
        return dist;
    }

    public override object Clone()
    { object o=new Torus(rminor,rmajor); return o; }

    public override string ToString() { return "Primitive::Torus()"; }

}


// SuperEllipsoid.cs
using System;
```

```
public class SuperEllipsoid:Implicit {
  public double s1, s2, rx, ry, rz;
  public SuperEllipsoid() { rx=ry=rz=1.0; s1=s2=1.0; }
  public SuperEllipsoid(double s1,double s2) {
    rx=ry=rz=1.0; this.s1=s1; this.s2=s2;
  }

  public SuperEllipsoid(double s1,double s2,double rx,
      double ry,double rz) {
    this.rx=rx; this.ry=ry; this.rz=rz; this.s1=s1; this.s2=s2;
  }

  public double pqnorm(double x,double y,double z) {
    double norm;
    x=Math.Abs(x); y=Math.Abs(y); z=Math.Abs(z);
    norm=Math.Pow(Math.Pow(x,s1)+Math.Pow(y,s1),1.0/s1);
    norm=Math.Pow(Math.Pow(norm,s2)+Math.Pow(z,s2),1.0/s2);
    return norm;
  }

  public override double dist(Vector p) {
    double root3=Math.Sqrt(3.0)/3.0;
    double dist=pqnorm(p.x/rx,p.y/ry,p.z/rz);
    //convert from pqnorm to euclidean metric
    if((s1<2.0)||(s2<2.0)) dist=dist/pqnorm(root3,root3,root3);
    return dist-1.0;
  }

  public override double func(Vector p) {
    double dist=Math.Pow((Math.Pow(p.x/rx,s1)+Math.Pow(p.y/ry,s1)),
      s2/s1)+Math.Pow(p.z/rz,s2);
    return dist-1.0;
  }

  public override object Clone()
  { object o=new SuperEllipsoid(s1,s2,rx,ry,rz); return o; }

  public override string ToString()
  { return "Primitive::SuperEllipsoid()"; }
}
```

7.8 CSG Objects

Computational Solid Geometry (CSG) defines objects according to set operations. Typical operations include the union, intersection and difference. The union of two objects is trivially calculated using the existing ray tracing algorithm. Simply take the closest intersection between the two objects whose union is to be computed. This is already the standard operation of the raytracer. Union and difference operations are slightly more complicated. In this case it is necessary to compute all intersections with the surfaces, both in front and behind the point of origin. These points define intervals where the ray is inside the object, and intervals where the ray is outside. If the appropriate operation is then applied to these sets, the closest intersection point can be found.

An alternative solution is offered by sphere tracing. In this case the signed distance function for the union of two surfaces A and B is a combination of the distance functions of the surfaces

$$g_{A \cup B}(\mathbf{x}) = \min\{g_A(\mathbf{x}), g_B(\mathbf{x})\}.$$

The difference operator $A - B$ can be defined in terms of the complement of a set, that is

$$A - B := A \cap (\mathbb{R}^3 \backslash B).$$

If a surface A is defined by the signed distance function $g_A(\mathbf{x})$ then the signed distance function for the complement $\mathbb{R}^3 \backslash A$ is [58]

$$g_{\mathbb{R}^3 \backslash A}(\mathbf{x}) = -g_A(\mathbf{x}).$$

Sphere tracing only requires a conservative estimate of the distance to the surface, that is the distance provided must be less than or equal to the real distance to the surface. Additional conditions may be required for convergence, but in many cases conservative estimates provide reasonable results. To compute the intersection between two surfaces, the following property can be used [58]

$$d(\mathbf{x}, A \cap B) \geq \max\{g_A(\mathbf{x}), g_B(\mathbf{x})\}.$$

7.8.1   C# Implementation

Since CSG objects are easily implemented as implicit surfaces using sphere tracing, both the difference and intersection surfaces inherit from the class Implicit. Union is not included since a raytracer already computes the union of surfaces fairly effectively (except perhaps in the interior of the surface).

//Difference.cs
using System;

```
//Intersection of obj1 with the complement of obj2. The complement of
//obj2 is given by the negative of the signed distance function
public class Difference:Implicit {
   public Implicit obj1, obj2;
   public Difference() { obj1=obj2=null; }

   public Difference(Implicit i1,Implicit i2) { obj1=i1; obj2=i2; }

   public override double dist(Vector p) {
      double dist1, dist2;
      Vector tp;
      .tp=obj1.W*p; dist1=obj1.dist(tp);
      tp=obj2.W*p; dist2=-obj2.dist(tp);
      if(dist1>dist2) return dist1;
      else return dist2;
   }

   public override double func(Vector p) {
      double dist1, dist2;
      Vector tp;
      tp=obj1.W*p; dist1=obj1.func(tp);
      tp=obj2.W*p; dist2=-obj2.func(tp);
      if(dist1>dist2) return dist1;
      else return dist2;
   }

   public override object Clone()
   { object o=new Difference(obj1,obj2); return o; }

   public override string ToString()
   { return "Primitive::Difference()"; }
}


//Intersection.cs
using System;

public class Intersection:Implicit {
   public Implicit obj1, obj2;
   public Intersection() { obj1=obj2=null; }

   public Intersection(Implicit i1,Implicit i2) { obj1=i1; obj2=i2; }

   public override double dist(Vector p) {
      double dist1, dist2;
      Vector tp;
      tp=obj1.W*p; dist1=obj1.dist(tp);
      tp=obj2.W*p; dist2=obj2.dist(tp);
      if(dist1>dist2) return dist1;
      else return dist2;
```

```
    }

    public override double func(Vector p) {
        double dist1, dist2;
        Vector tp;
        tp=obj1.W*p; dist1=obj1.func(tp);
        tp=obj2.W*p; dist2=obj2.func(tp);
        if(dist1>dist2) return dist1;
        else return dist2;
    }

    public override object Clone()
    { object o=new Intersection(obj1,obj2); return o; }

    public override string ToString()
    { return "Primitive::Intersection()"; }
}
```

7.9 Parametric Surfaces

A variety of techniques have been applied for rendering parametric polynomial patches. We mention a few of these techniques and see if any are applicable for rendering harmonic tensor product surfaces. A number of the techniques accelerate intersection testing, using properties of the surface or bounding volumes. Several other acceleration techniques are also available. We are not concerned with acceleration, but rather with techniques that correctly yield a point of intersection. We concentrate on results that may be applicable to harmonic surfaces. To ray trace a tensor product surface we need to find the intersection point between the parametric surface given by

$$\mathbf{f}(u,v) = \begin{pmatrix} x_0(u,v) \\ x_1(u,v) \\ x_2(u,v) \end{pmatrix}$$

and a ray given by

$$\mathbf{p}(t) = \mathbf{o} + t\mathbf{d}$$

where $\mathbf{o}$ is the origin of the ray and $\mathbf{d}$ is the direction of the ray. We must solve the system of nonlinear equations

$$\mathbf{f}(u,v) = \mathbf{p}(t)$$

for u, v and t. One possibility is to use the multi-dimensional Newton-Raphson technique, however the results are seldom stable. Kajiya [71] provides one of the first techniques for ray tracing parametric patches. Kajiya represents a ray as the intersection between two planes. The system of equations then reduces to two variables, u and v. The equations are nonlinear, so Kajiya proceeds to explain how these equations may be solved. Sederberg and Anderson [113] apply a similar technique to Steiner patches. Applying this technique to harmonic interpolation yields trigonometric polynomials. Numerical techniques such as interval Newton-Raphson are thus preferable. Joy [70] used quasi-Newton methods to determine the point of intersection. We found that the Newton-methods were not stable enough using the trigonometric functions. Further work on the intersection test on cubic parametric surfaces, in various forms have been published by Wang [136], Lischinksi [83]. Nishita [97], Roth [106], and Stürzlinger [131] discuss ray tracing of trimmed and triangular Bézier surfaces. A variety of intersection algorithms are discussed by Manocha [91]. The majority of the algorithms presented rely on Newton's method, subdivision and the convex hull property of the surfaces discussed. A bounding volume for the surface can be produced using the convex hull so that portions of the surface can be identified that definitely do not intersect the ray. Chebyshev polynomials may be used for boxing [41], and a bounding volume hierarchy or Bézier clipping [10, 97] can also be used. Harmonic tensor product surfaces do not have the convex hull property, and Newton's method fails to converge in a stable manner. Subdivision surfaces can also be ray traced [75], but the lack of local support in harmonic interpolation makes this approach difficult. We turn our attention to the use of interval arithmetic as demonstrated by Toth [133].

7.9.1   Interval Arithmetic

Interval arithmetic [93] is an arithmetic defined on sets of intervals. An *interval* X is defined as

$$X := \{\, x \mid x_\ell \leq x \leq x_u \,\} = [x_\ell,\, x_u]\,.$$

Elementary operations for *idealized interval arithmetic* are defined by

$$X \circ Y := \{\, x \circ y \mid x \in X \quad \text{and} \quad y \in Y \,\}$$

where $\circ$ is $+$, $-$, $\times$ or $\div$. It is not always feasible to perform these operations, we therefore prefer the *operational definitions*

$$X + Y := [x_\ell + y_\ell,\, x_u + y_u]$$
$$X - Y := [x_\ell - y_u,\, x_u - y_\ell]$$
$$X \times Y := [\min\{x_\ell y_\ell, x_\ell y_u, x_u y_\ell, x_u y_u\},\, \max\{x_\ell y_\ell, x_\ell y_u, x_u y_\ell, x_u y_u\}]$$
$$\frac{1}{X} := [1/x_u, 1/x_\ell], \qquad 0 \notin X$$

$$X \div Y := X \times 1/Y \,.$$

Using these operations we can compute bounds on the ranges of functions. If we use the correct rounding on a computer then we can obtain accurate bounds in which a solution must lie. If f is a continuous function of a real variable, then an *inclusion monotonic interval extension* F is a function that maps from intervals to intervals such that

$$\{\, f(x) \mid x \in X \,\} \subset F(X) \,.$$

Evaluating polynomials using the operational definitions provides us with an inclusion monotonic interval extension.

Transcendental Functions

We can also obtain interval extensions of the transcendental functions. For example [120]

$$\cos([x_\ell, x_u]) = \begin{cases} [-1, 1], & \text{if } 1 + \left\lceil \frac{x_\ell}{\pi} \right\rceil \leq \frac{x_u}{\pi} \\ [-1, b], & \text{if } \left\lceil \frac{x_\ell}{\pi} \right\rceil \leq \frac{x_u}{\pi} \text{ and } \left\lceil \frac{x_\ell}{\pi} \right\rceil \bmod 2 = 1 \\ [a, 1], & \text{if } \left\lceil \frac{x_\ell}{\pi} \right\rceil \leq \frac{x_u}{\pi} \text{ and } \left\lceil \frac{x_\ell}{\pi} \right\rceil \bmod 2 = 0 \\ [a, b], & \text{otherwise} \end{cases}$$

with

$$a = \min\{\cos(x_\ell), \cos(x_u)\}, \qquad b = \max\{\cos(x_\ell), \cos(x_u)\} \,.$$

and $\lceil a \rceil$ is the ceiling of a. That is, the smallest integer that is larger than or equal to a. We can use similar results for the sine function, or we can use identities to reuse the cosine function. We can thus create interval extensions for polynomial functions, and functions such as σ. Next we consider root finding using intervals.

7.9.2 Interval Root Finding — Bisection

Using the interval extension F of a function f, the bisection method can simply determine where the roots of the function lie. The algorithm is [20]

```
set interval_bisection([a, b]) {
    real c;
    set S;
    if(0 ∈ F([a, b])) {
        c ← (a + b)/2;
```

```
if(b − a < ε) {
        return set(c);
} else {
        S ←interval_bisection([a, c]);
        S ← S ∪ interval_bisection([c, b]);
        return S;
    }
} else {return ∅;}
}
```

The above algorithm returns all the roots with a maximum error of ϵ. The algorithm is easily modified to return intervals in which the roots are found. We can also apply the bisection method to multidimensional root finding, we would typically choose one dimension two divide at each step. We can obtain faster convergence if we modify the Newton-Raphson algorithm for use with intervals.

7.9.3   Interval Root Finding — Newton-Raphson

The Newton-Raphson, or Newton method can be used to solve the system of equations [125]

$$f_1(x_1, x_2, \ldots, x_n) = 0$$
$$f_2(x_1, x_2, \ldots, x_n) = 0$$
$$\vdots$$
$$f_n(x_1, x_2, \ldots, x_n) = 0.$$

Let $\mathbf{f} = (f_1 \ f_2 \ \ldots \ f_n)^T$ and $\mathbf{x} = (x_1 \ x_2 \ \ldots \ x_n)^T$. Then the system of equations can be written as $\mathbf{f}(\mathbf{x}) = \mathbf{0}$. The gradients of the components are given by the entries of the Jacobian matrix [125]

$$J := \begin{pmatrix} \frac{\partial f_1}{\partial x_1} & \frac{\partial f_1}{\partial x_2} & \cdots & \frac{\partial f_1}{\partial x_n} \\ \frac{\partial f_2}{\partial x_1} & \frac{\partial f_2}{\partial x_2} & \cdots & \frac{\partial f_2}{\partial x_n} \\ \vdots & & & \\ \frac{\partial f_n}{\partial x_1} & \frac{\partial f_n}{\partial x_2} & \cdots & \frac{\partial f_n}{\partial x_n} \end{pmatrix}.$$

Suppose we want to solve the problem $\mathbf{f}(\mathbf{x}) = \mathbf{0}$, and our present approximation is $\mathbf{x}$ which can be written as $\mathbf{x} = \mathbf{y} + \mathbf{h}$, where $\mathbf{y}$ is the exact solution. We compute

$$f_i(x_1, x_2, \ldots, x_n) = g_i.$$

Using the Taylor expansion, and neglecting higher order terms, we find that $J\mathbf{h} = \mathbf{g}$ and consequently

$$\mathbf{h} = J^{-1}\mathbf{g}\,.$$

We assume that the matrix J is nonsingular. We can now compute $\mathbf{h}$ to obtain a better approximation of the correct answer $\mathbf{y}$. The Newton iteration is then given by

$$\mathbf{x}_{n+1} = \mathbf{x}_n - J^{-1}\mathbf{f}(\mathbf{x}_n)\,.$$

To apply a Newton-Raphson algorithm to intervals, we need to introduce the *midpoint* (which we have used in interval bisection) and the *width* of an interval. We use the syntax of Toth [133]. The *midpoint* of an interval $X = [x_\ell,\ x_u]$ is given by

$$m(X) := (x_\ell + x_u)/2$$

and the *width* is defined as

$$w(X) := x_u - x_\ell\,.$$

Since Newton-Raphson involves vectors and matrices it is useful to define interval vectors and matrices. These are quite naturally just vectors and matrices with intervals as entries. Now we can define the *max norm* of a vector $\mathbf{x} = (x_0\ \ldots\ x_{n-1})^T$ to be

$$\|\mathbf{x}\| = \max_{0 \le j \le n-1} |x_j|\,.$$

If we have two interval vectors,

$$\mathbf{X} = (X_0\ \ldots\ X_{n-1})^T, \qquad \mathbf{Y} = (Y_0\ \ldots\ Y_{n-1})^T$$

with $X_i = [a_i, b_i]$ and $Y_i = [c_i, d_i]$, we define $\mathbf{a} = (a_0\ \ldots\ a_{n-1})^T$, $\mathbf{b} = (b_0\ \ldots\ b_{n-1})^T$ and likewise for $\mathbf{c}$ and $\mathbf{d}$. We define a distance metric on the interval vectors as

$$d(\mathbf{X}, \mathbf{Y}) = \max(\|\mathbf{a} - \mathbf{c}\|, \|\mathbf{b} - \mathbf{d}\|)\,.$$

Using this metric continuity can be defined in the normal manner. We can now define the interval vector norm as

$$\|\mathbf{X}\| := \max_{0 \le i \le n-1} (|X_i|)$$

where $X_i = [a_i, b_i]$ and $|X_i| := \max(|a_i|, |b_i|)$. For an interval matrix A (a matrix with interval entries) we define the maximum row sum norm as

$$\|A\| := \max_i \Big(\sum_j |A_{ij}|\Big)\,.$$

The interval vector norm and interval matrix norm are compatible, that is

$$\|A\mathbf{X}\| \leq \|A\|\|\mathbf{X}\|$$

for an interval matrix A and interval vector $\mathbf{X}$. We need a mean value theorem for intervals [133].

Theorem 7.1 (The Mean Value Theorem for Intervals). *If $\mathbf{x}$ and $\mathbf{y}$ are any real vectors in $\mathbf{X}$, then $\mathbf{f}(\mathbf{x}) - \mathbf{f}(\mathbf{y}) \in F'(\mathbf{X})(\mathbf{x} - \mathbf{y})$, where $F(\mathbf{X})$ is the interval extension of f.*

The following lemma [133] will assist in developing the Newton method for interval arithmetic. We consider the Newton step

$$\mathbf{p}(\mathbf{x}) := \mathbf{x} - Y\mathbf{f}(\mathbf{x})$$

with $Y = J^{-1}$.

Lemma 7.1. *Suppose that $\mathbf{p}(\mathbf{x}) = \mathbf{x} - Y\mathbf{f}(\mathbf{x})$ maps $\mathbf{X}$ onto itself and there is a constant $r < 1$ for which*

$$\|\mathbf{p}(\mathbf{x}) - \mathbf{p}(\mathbf{y})\| \leq r\|\mathbf{x} - \mathbf{y}\|$$

for any $\mathbf{x}$ and $\mathbf{y}$ in $\mathbf{X}$. Then the simple Newton sequence $\mathbf{x}_{n+1} = p(\mathbf{x}_n)$ converges to $\mathbf{x}^*$ in $\mathbf{X}$, where $\mathbf{x}^*$ is a unique solution to the equation $\mathbf{f}(\mathbf{x}) = \mathbf{0}$.

To determine if $\mathbf{p}(\mathbf{x})$ maps X to itself we define the Krawczyk operator [77]

$$K(\mathbf{X}, \mathbf{y}, Y) := \mathbf{y} - Y\mathbf{f}(\mathbf{y}) + (I - YF'(\mathbf{X}))(\mathbf{X} - \mathbf{y})$$

for an interval vector X, real vector $\mathbf{y}$ and nonsingular matrix Y. We then note that

$$\mathbf{p}(\mathbf{x}) = \mathbf{y} - Y\mathbf{f}(\mathbf{y}) + (\mathbf{x} - \mathbf{y}) - Y(\mathbf{f}(\mathbf{x}) - \mathbf{f}(\mathbf{y})).$$

The mean value theorem for intervals yields

$$Y(\mathbf{f}(\mathbf{x}) - \mathbf{f}(\mathbf{y})) \in YF'(\mathbf{X})(\mathbf{x} - \mathbf{y})$$

and consequently

$$\mathbf{p}(\mathbf{x}) \in \mathbf{y} - Y\mathbf{f}(\mathbf{y}) + (I - YF'(\mathbf{X}))(\mathbf{x} - \mathbf{y}) \subset K(\mathbf{X}, \mathbf{y}, Y).$$

Thus $K(\mathbf{X}, \mathbf{y}, Y)$ is an interval extension of $\mathbf{p}(\mathbf{x})$, and $\mathbf{p}(\mathbf{x})$ maps $\mathbf{X}$ onto itself. The operator K is in a *centered form*, i.e. it has the form

$$C(\mathbf{f}, \mathbf{X}, \mathbf{y}) = \mathbf{f}(c) + G(\mathbf{X} - \mathbf{y})(\mathbf{X} - \mathbf{y})$$

with $\mathbf{f}(\mathbf{x}) = \mathbf{p}(\mathbf{y})$. We are interested in a particular centered form, the *mean value form*

$$C(\mathbf{f}, \mathbf{X}, \mathbf{y}) = \mathbf{f}(c) + F'(X)(\mathbf{X} - \mathbf{y})$$

and we note that K is indeed in mean value form. We now examine the operator K with $\mathbf{y} = m(\mathbf{X})$. Using the norms defined earlier we calculate

$$r = \|I - YF'(\mathbf{X})\|$$

and with the mean value theorem we obtain

$$\mathbf{p}(\mathbf{x}) - \mathbf{p}(\mathbf{y}) \in (I - YF'(\mathbf{X}))(\mathbf{x} - \mathbf{y})$$

so that

$$\|\mathbf{p}(\mathbf{x}) - \mathbf{p}(\mathbf{y})\| \leq r\|\mathbf{x} - \mathbf{y}\|.$$

From lemma 7.1 we obtain the theorem

Theorem 7.2. *If $K(\mathbf{X}, \mathbf{y}, Y) \subset \mathbf{X}$ and $r < 1$ then the simple Newton sequence $\mathbf{x}_{n+1} = \mathbf{p}(\mathbf{x}_n)$ will converge to a unique solution $\mathbf{x}^* \in \mathbf{X}$ to $\mathbf{f}(\mathbf{x}) = \mathbf{0}$ from any starting point $\mathbf{x}_0$ in $\mathbf{X}$.*

Interval Newton iteration [77] is defined as

$$\mathbf{X}_{n+1} = K(\mathbf{X}_n, m(\mathbf{X}_n), Y_n) \cap \mathbf{X}_n$$

where

$$Y_n = \begin{cases} m(F'(\mathbf{X}_n))^{-1}, & r_n \leq r_{n-1} \\ Y_{n-1}, & \text{otherwise} \end{cases}$$

and $r_n = \|I - Y_n F'(\mathbf{X}_n)\|$. By applying interval Newton iteration, we either obtain the empty set (in which case there is no solution), or the solution to $\mathbf{f}(\mathbf{x}) = \mathbf{0}$. Toth [133] describes an algorithm using the interval Newton iteration to ray trace Bézier patches. In addition to the interval Newton method, the convex hull property of Bézier patches is used.

7.9.4 Ray Tracing Harmonic Surfaces

Applying interval Newton iteration or the interval bisection method to the problem of intersection between a ray and a tensor product harmonic surface does yield a solution. The torus in figure 6.36(b) was ray traced along with a few other objects. The result is shown in figure 7.10. The process of ray tracing the image is time consuming, and yet further accuracy is still desired. The methods mentioned take a considerable amount of time because the trigonometric functions cause difficulties in determining a tight

Figure 7.10: Ray traced harmonic surface (torus).

bound on the interval at each step, and we have no convex hull property to quickly discard portions of the surface for which there can be no intercept. Due to the time taken to render these simple images, we decided not to compare the interval Newton and interval bisection methods. Instead, we try to find alternative techniques to improve the rendering speed. We now try to answer the question: Can we obtain a convex hull for a harmonic tensor product surface? Our answer is obtained by approximating the harmonic surface by a series of Bézier patches. To obtain the Bézier patches we need to approximate the basis functions of harmonic interpolation.

7.10 Lighting Models

A lighting model can be selected from those in chapter 2 and should be applied to using the normal and point of intersection. The lighting model applies the properties of the object to the reflected ray and may change the color and intensity of the reflected light.

7.11 Supersampling

Initially we assumed that only one ray, cast through the center of each pixel is sufficient to capture the information. Although this provides reasonable images, the results suffer from *aliasing*. That is, a clear demarcation between objects and background that often results in a "stepped" appearance. This is due to the sampling rate required to capture the image in the scene.

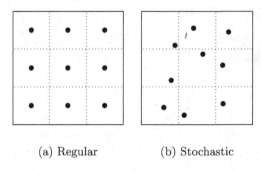

(a) Regular   (b) Stochastic

Figure 7.11: Supersampling.

The *Nyquist limit* [124] describes exactly how many samples are required to be able to correctly reconstruct a signal. The Nyquist limit is twice the maximum frequency present in the signal. An edge in an image requires an infinite number of samples (infinite frequency) to reproduce. For the purposes of raytracing it becomes clear that more samples (rays cast) per pixel will result in a better approximation of reality. Thus supersampling casts many rays per pixel to derive a better approximation of the image.

7.11.1   Regular Supersampling

If several samples are taken per pixel, how should these samples be distributed? One answer to this question is simply to divide the pixel into "subpixels" and cast a ray through each of these subpixels. Figure 7.11(a) illustrates a pixel divided into 9 subpixels. The dots in the middle of each subpixel indicate that all samples are taken at the center of each subpixel. One all subpixels have been sampled, the color of the pixel is taken to be the average of all samples. The choice of grid size influences both time and quality of rendering.

7.11.2   Stochastic Supersampling

Sampling in a regular grid structure still fails to capture all frequencies that may occur in a given scene. Irregular sampling can sample more frequencies and thus provide a better approximation of the scene. Naive irregular sampling simply uses random offsets within the pixel. Several rays at these random offsets are cast, and the results are averaged. However, there is no guarantee that the random offsets will result in a useful sampling of the scene. It may be possible that several offsets cluster together and so many parts of the scene are missed. To limit the frequencies selected for

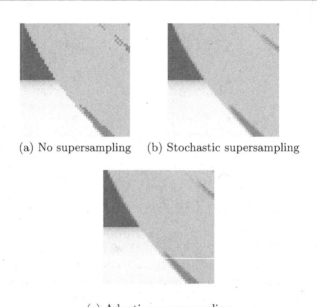

(a) No supersampling   (b) Stochastic supersampling

(c) Adaptive supersampling

Figure 7.12: Adaptive supersampling.

sampling, *jittering* can be used.

If jittering is used, then sampling occurs on a regular grid, but samples are offset by a random amount within each subpixel. There is thus a guarantee that samples are taken over many portions of the pixel. Figure 7.11(b) gives an example of samples that have been jittered. Note that new random offsets are used for every pixel, and so adjacent pixels may not be entirely consistent. This artifact of stochastic supersampling is visible as noise in the image. Noise is not always visible when using stochastic supersampling, but it may be visible on occasion. The human visual system is less sensitive to noise, however, and so the results are usually regarded as superior.

7.11.3 Adaptive Supersampling

Supersampling is very expensive and can slow rendering time several fold. Very high frequencies are usually only present at the edges of objects. Supersampling is thus often unneccesary for the center of objects, where two adjacent pixels yield similar results.

To increase performance supersampling should only be applied when samples taken on adjacent pixels differ by more than some predetermined amount. In this way supersampling is primarily used on edges where the technique is most effective and provides the most evident results. Note that all adjacent pixels should be taken into account, both horizontally and vertically.

One possible implementation would be to render the scene with one sample per pixel. As a second pass, flag all pixels that differ sufficiently from one or more neighbors. Rerender these pixels again using supersampling.

7.12 Ambient Occlusion

The ambient term in lighting models attempts to approximate indirect lighting (typical of global illumination models) by a constant term. The assumption is that light reflected several times (in a diffuse fashion) eventually reaches all surfaces, and that all surfaces receive an equal amount of this indirect light. This is seldom the case however.

Ambient occlusion [141, 80] assumes that there is a constant, equal amount of light coming in from all directions. No light source is taken into account. At a point on a surface, the light enters through a hemisphere of radius 1, specified by the surface normal, above the point under consideration. If no other objects are visible through this hemisphere, then the normal ambient term is applied. If objects are visible through this hemisphere, then the point on the surface is occluded. The *accessibility* [92] of the point on the surface is decreased by the occluding objects.

The proportion of hemisphere that is unoccluded is then used to determine how much light actually reaches the surface. The *obscurance* is given by

$$ao(\mathbf{p}, \mathbf{n}) = \frac{1}{\pi} \int_\Omega \rho(d(\mathbf{p}, \boldsymbol{\omega}))(\mathbf{n} \cdot \boldsymbol{\omega}) \, d\boldsymbol{\omega} \qquad (7.3)$$

where $\mathbf{p}$ is the point under consideration, $\mathbf{n}$ is the surface normal, Ω is the hemisphere above the point $\mathbf{p}$, $d(\mathbf{p}, \boldsymbol{\omega})$ is the distance function that determines the distance to the nearest surface from $\mathbf{p}$ in direction $\boldsymbol{\omega}$ and ρ is a function that maps the distance to some suitable value. ρ is used to determine the distance at which an occluder no longer has a significant effect on the ambient lighting. One option suggested in the literature is $\rho(d) = 1 - e^{-\tau d}$ [66]. In our implementation we have chosen

$$\rho(d) = \frac{1}{a + bd + cd^2}$$

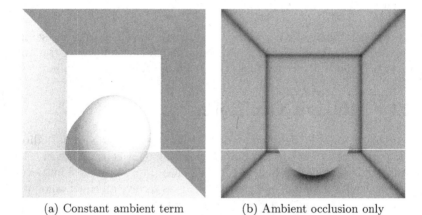

(a) Constant ambient term   (b) Ambient occlusion only

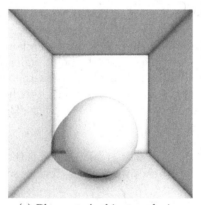

(c) Phong + Ambient occlusion

Figure 7.13: Ambient occlusion.

to provide more control. The factor $\frac{1}{\pi}$ in equation 7.3 ensures that the result of the integral is in the range $[0, 1]$ since

$$\int_\Omega (\mathbf{n} \cdot \boldsymbol{\omega})\, d\boldsymbol{\omega} = \pi \,.$$

The distance function $d(\mathbf{p}, \boldsymbol{\omega})$ acts as both a distance function, as well as a visibility function. If no surface is visible then $d(\mathbf{p}, \boldsymbol{\omega}) = \infty$ otherwise $d \in \mathbb{R}$.

To compute ambient occlusion, the integral is approximated by casting out a number of rays in random directions on the hemisphere. Random rays are created from random vectors of unit length. Vectors that do not point in the direction of the hemisphere are discarded, as well as those that have a length greater than 1. Vectors with length less than 1 do not lie on the hemisphere. These vectors are normalized (scaled so that they have length 1). The C# code to create such a random vector is thus

```
Vector rand_vector(Vector n) {
        Vector p=new Vector();
        p.x=rnd.NextDouble()*2.0-1.0;
        p.y=rnd.NextDouble()*2.0-1.0;
        p.z=rnd.NextDouble()*2.0-1.0;
        while((p*p>1.0)||(p*n<0.0)) {
                p.x=rnd.NextDouble()*2.0-1.0;
                p.y=rnd.NextDouble()*2.0-1.0;
                p.z=rnd.NextDouble()*2.0-1.0;
        }
        p.normalize();
        return p;
}
```

The simplest form of ambient occlusion simply casts out a number of these random rays and determines if any objects are intersected. The accessability to ambient lighting is given by

$$1 - ao(\mathbf{p}, \mathbf{n}) \approx \frac{\text{rays missing all objects}}{\text{total number of rays}} \,.$$

To improve the result the cosine term $\mathbf{n} \cdot \boldsymbol{\omega}$ can be included as well as the distance function. The cosine term decreases the importance of occluders that are near the horison of the surface.

Ambient occlusion is expensive since many rays are required to get a reasonable result (as many as 500 rays may be necessary). This expense is ameliorated by the fact that ambient occlusion is independant of light location and can thus be precomputed for several frames in an animation.

The results are usually stored in a texture. Since the effect of an occluder attenuates with distance, it may be possible to only consider self-shadowing with ambient occlusion. In this case, the algorithm can be executed once per object in the scene. Shadowing by other objects will then be handled by other algorithms.

If supersampling is enabled, then the number of rays can be decreased. For example, if the pixel is divided into 16 subpixels and 25 samples are taken for ambient occlusion, then a total of 400 samples are taken for one pixel. Adaptive supersampling can indirectly control the number of samples used for ambient occlusion. If an area is largely occluded then few samples tends to create a lot of noise. This noise will cause supersampling to be enabled, which results in a better approximation of ambient occlusion. The number of samples required for unshadowed areas is typically small. In these areas color should vary smoothly and supersampling is not used, and so very few ambient occlusion samples are used.

The lighting equation can be modified further by computing the *bent normal* [80]. The bent normal is obtained by computing the average direction of all rays that do not hit any objects. This bent normal can be used in the lighting model to look up the predominent color of the ambient environment in the direction from which most ambient light is arriving.

7.13   Ray Marching

Volumetric data such as smoke, clouds or dust require special techniques for raytracing. In this section we briefly discuss one method that can be used to render such volumetric data. The actual lighting equations for modelling of effects such as smoke and clouds are beyond the scope of this book. For the moment we assume that there is some function $d(\mathbf{q}, c)$ that describes the lighting at a point in the volume to be rendered, where $\mathbf{q}$ is the point in the volume and c is the accumulated contribution of light travelling in the direction of the camera. This function will typically take into account effects such as in-scattering and out-scattering. To determine the effect that the volume has in a specific view direction, the volume must be sampled at each point along the path. This information is then combined to determine what is seen along this path. It is not feasible to sample every point, so instead a predetermined number of steps (or distance) along the ray must be taken and the lighting at each point must be accumulated.

It is important to accumulate data from the last visible surface to the eye, so that light coming in the direction of the camera is filtered by the volume between that point and the camera. The following ray marching [27] algorithm implements this approach.

```
Color raymarch(Ray r = o + td)
begin
    Color result=(0,0,0)
    Find nearest intersection between r and the set of opaque objects O.
    Find s so that o + sd = p, where p is the point of intersection.
    while (s > 0.0)
    begin
        Compute the point q := o + sd.
        Set result:=d(q, result).
    end
    return result
end
```

If the ray does not intersect the volume data (a bounding volume test can be used to determine if this is the case) then the normal raytracing algorithm can be applied. This algorithm is expensive to execute and should not be used if no volumetric data needs to be rendered.

If the density throughout the volume is constant and the lighting model is simple, then ray marching is not required. In this case the result can be simplified to some expression related to the distance to the nearest intersection point. This might be the case if dust or fog is rendered. The Beer-Lambert law is often suitable in this situation.

7.14 Photon Mapping

One way to obtain better results for various scenes, is to combine radiosity (chapter 8) and raytracing. Radiosity then provides the diffuse term. Another option is provided by photon mapping [67]. The key feature of photon mapping is that the existing raytracing algorithm can be used for global illumination. Also, since the differences provided by global illumination tends to be rather subtle, we can choose how much time (and thus quality) we wish to expend on this stage. To introduce photon mapping, we first examine path tracing, an expensive (high quality) solution to the global illumination equation.

7.14.1 Transport Notation

We use light transport notation to describe what kind of lighting a model captures correctly [59]. Light transport notation describes which paths of light are captured correctly by the model. These paths are described by regular expressions consisting of the light source (L), diffuse reflection off a surface (D), specular reflection off a surface (S) and the camera or eye (E). Regular expressions consist of these symbols plus a number of operators

- Concatenation – If two symbols (or expressions) are placed consecutively, then the regular expression matches any light path consisting of the first path, followed by the second. For example LSDE, refers to light from the light source that reflects once in a specular fashion, followed by a second reflection in a diffuse fashion, which then reaches the eye without any further reflections.

- Grouping – Parenthesis are used to group symbols (or expressions) together to form a new expression. Operators can then be applied to the entire expression.

- Alternation – The selection operator A|B refers to either path A or path B. If a light path is of the form A then the regular expression matches it. If the light path is instead of form B, then the regular expression also matches this light path.

- Repetition – A* is the Kleene closure of A. The Kleene closure A is zero or more occurances of A.

These regular expressions also include the ϵ symbol, that matches an empty path. We write A+ as shorthand for AA*, and A? as shorthand for (A|ϵ).

7.14.2 Path Tracing

The standard raytracing algorithm uses a local lighting model in combination with pure reflection. The light paths sampled are of the form LD(S*)E. To support full global illumination we must sample the light coming in from all directions. In this way we sample light paths of the form L(D|S)*E. We can do this by numerically integrating over the visible space of the object we are considering, i.e., we cast rays in several random directions and see what answers we get. The answers should, of course, be adjusted by the properties of the surface (BRDF function). So we should calculate the diffuse and specular contribution according to our lighting equations. The more rays we cast out, the better our approximation for global illumination. This turns out to be costly. The recursive nature of ray tracing implies an exponential growth in the number of rays that needs to be cast.

Instead of using this computationally expensive approach, we sample light in only **one** direction. Now, we only have to follow a single path to its destination. However, this is clearly not sufficient to model the lighting in the scene. If we use many such paths and average the result, we get an estimate for the radiosity at that point. Usually 1000+ rays are needed to get acceptable quality. One problem with this random sampling technique is the amount of noise created in the image. Although path tracing is far faster than the naive approach it is still very expensive (1000 times slower for 1000 rays). This approach illustrates that raytracing techniques can produce global illumination results.

7.14.3   Creating the Photon Map

To get global illumination and effects such as caustics, we could trace rays of light from the light sources thorough the scene until they hit the eye. This technique was rejected for raytracing because a very small fraction of the light rays would ever reach the eye. So instead we trace rays backward from the eye. Photon mapping reintroduces the forward raytrace (but in a limited fashion). We implement the renderer in two passes.

- Trace photons into the scene (and store their positions).

- Render the scene using standard raytracing, but use the traced photons to improve the accuracy of the lighting calculations.

The advantages of this technique are

- All global illumination effects can be simulated.

- Arbitrary geometry is supported. (We are not forced to use patches)

- Low memory consumption.

- Little noise (variance).

- Consistency (will converge to the correct solution with enough photons).

These phases are discussed in more detail in the following sections.

7.14.4   Photon Tracing

Photon Emission

Photons are created at light sources. Any type of light source can be used, point lights, spotlights or even area lights. The power of the light source is divided among the emitted photons so that each carries a fraction of the light source power. For a point light we can simply emit photons evenly in all directions. For area lights we have to distribute the origin of the photons across the area of the light. For spotlights we concentrate photons in a particular direction. Both source points and directions of the photons can be generated randomly using the properties of the light. Rejection testing can be used to simplify the creation of the photons. Projection maps can be used to send photons in the direction of geometry (where they yield the greatest results).

Photon Scattering

An emitted photon is traced through the scene using standard raytracing techniques. When a photon hits an object it can be

- Reflected

- Transmitted

- Absorbed

The power of the photon should be scaled by the reflectivity (or other property). The photon **is not** stored for specular (mirror) reflection. The photon **is** stored for diffuse reflections. In that case the photon can be transmitted in a random direction, and it is scaled by the diffuse reflectivity coefficient.

Monte Carlo methods [127] can be used to reduce the number of photon traces required. Instead of scaling the power of the photon by the surface property (e.g. diffuse reflection coefficient), we determine if the photon should be reflected at all. If the surface has property $0 \leq \rho \leq 1$, then we generate a random number $0 \leq \xi \leq 1$. If $\xi < \rho$, then the photon is reflected, otherwise the photon is absorbed. The same approach can be used to decide if specular or diffuse reflection should be followed for the photon. If the diffuse coefficient is ρ_d and the specular coefficient is ρ_s, then if

$$\xi \in [0, \rho_d] \quad \text{then we use diffuse reflection}$$
$$\xi \in [\rho_d, \rho_d + \rho_s] \quad \text{then we use specular reflection}$$
$$\xi \in [\rho_d + \rho_s, 1] \quad \text{the photon is absorbed}$$

For colored surfaces we can use the average of the coefficient values for the different frequencies as the threshold value. The power should also be scaled according to the average value and the coefficient (unless Monte Carlo methods are used).

Photon Storing

Photons are stored in the *photon map* when they hit a diffuse (non-specular) surface. Specular reflections are handled (better) by standard raytracing. The photons are stored at **every** point that they hit a diffuse surface. Photons represent the incoming flux at the surface. So photons are not really isolated packets of light. If a conventional lighting model such as the Phong model or Cook-Torrance model is used in addition to photon mapping (which is certainly a good choice), then the first intersection between a photon and a diffuse surface should not be stored. The interaction between the photon and the surface is already captured by the selected lighting model.

7.14.5   Photon Map Data Structure

One of the strengths of the photon map is that it is decoupled from the geometry involved. The information regarding the photons is stored in a separate datastructure, and not in the datastructure of the geometry. The photon map and ray tracing algorithm allows any geometry to be used during rendering (even – for example – point clouds!).

Photons are stored during the photon tracing phase, they then have to be queried for nearest neighbors. The structure should thus be efficient (for speed) both in query time and in size (we plan to store millions of photons). The *kd-tree* is a suitable structure for this purpose. The *kd*-tree is a binary tree used for spacial partioning. Each node in the tree describes a volume of space. This volume is split in two to create the child nodes. One of the coordinate axes are used for this split. At the top level, the x-axis is used to split the volume into two equal halves. At the next level, the y-axis is used, and at the next level the z-axis is used and so forth. The query for k nearest neighbors is $O(k + \log n)$ on average, where n is the number of photons.

The *kd-tree* stores one photon at each node in the tree. Each node then divides the space into two half spaces. The left child is all photons on the left (positive) side of the half space, and the right child is all the photons in the right (negative) half space. Each split occurs along one of the coor-

dinate axes. First x, then y, then z and then x again for each level of the
kd-tree. We thus use a 3d-tree. It may be more convenient to decide on the
split based on the distribution of the points in the set. In other words, we
compute the axis aligned bounding box of the photons, and split according
to the longest edge of the bounding box.

Since the kd-tree will be used many times when rendering, it is important
that the kd-tree be balanced. We store the photons in a simple structure
during the photon trace phase, and then construct a balanced tree from this
information. If we store a balanced tree, then pointers to the child notes
are not necessary since we can store the photon map in an arrangement
similar to a heap. The root will be at index 1. A node in position i has $2i$
as left child and $2i + 1$ as right child. To build the balanced tree, we simply
repetitively split the set using the median value of the data.

We need to be able to locate photons to get an approximation of the lighting
near a point. The following algorithm finds the nearest photons within
maximum distance d of the point x:

locate_photons(p) {
    δ = signed distance to splitting plane of node $n(p)$
    if $(\delta < 0)$ **then**
        x is on the left hand side, examine the left subtree
        locate_photons $(2p)$
        if $(\delta^2 < d^2)$ **then**
            the right subtree is within range, check it
            locate_photons$(2p + 1)$
        end if
    else
        x is on the right hand side, examine the right subtree
        locate_photons $(2p + 1)$
        if $(\delta^2 < d^2)$ **then**
            the left subtree is within range, check it
            locate_photons$(2p)$
        end if
    end if
    check if this photon is within range and should be stored
    δ^2 = squared distance from photon p to x
    if $(\delta^2 < d^2)$ **then**
        insert photon p into list of nearest photons
        reduce maximum range to check, prune search
        d^2 = squared distance to median photon in list of nearest photons

```
    end if
}
```

7.14.6   Radiance Estimate

We calculate the radiance estimate using the photon map, by finding a number of photons in a certain range of the intersection point (during raytracing). This is a spherical volume. We want to calculate a density estimate using the area that the photons, are in. The sphere projects onto the flat surface as a circle with area πd^2. We can sum the values of the photons and divide by the area to get an approximation of the flux. However, we have to integrate this into the lighting equation as follows

$$L(\mathbf{x}, \mathbf{r}) \approx \frac{1}{\pi d^2} \sum_{p=1}^{n} f(\mathbf{x}, \mathbf{i}_p, \mathbf{r}) \Delta \Psi_p(\mathbf{x}, \mathbf{i}_p)$$

where

- d is the maximum radius of the nearest neighbor search

- n is the number of photons found

- $\mathbf{x}$ is the point of intersection

- L is the luminance

- f is the Bidirectional Reflectance Distribution Function (BRDF)

- $\mathbf{i}_p$ is the incoming direction of the photon (stored)

- $\mathbf{r}$ is the view direction (direction for evaluation)

- $\Delta \Psi_p(\mathbf{x}, \mathbf{i}_p)$ is the power of photon p, which hit from direction $\mathbf{i}_p$. We include Δ to indicate that this photon has a portion of the power of the light source from which it originated.

Photon mapping allows many other global illumination phenomena to be rendered (as illustrated in figures 7.14 and 7.15). Caustics are an excellent example of the phenomena that photon mapping can render. A global photon map can be used to capture caustics (eg. focussed light), but the detail of the caustic is not always sufficient. In this case a dedicated caustic photon map can be created to capture the caustic accurately.

Photon mapping can also be used to create soft shadows from area lights. Instead of storing and reflecting photons that hit a surface, the photon is

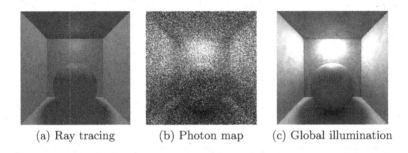

(a) Ray tracing   (b) Photon map   (c) Global illumination

Figure 7.14: Global illumination with photon mapping.

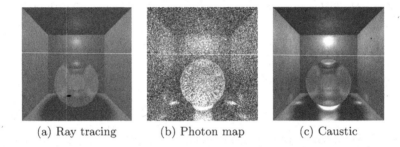

(a) Ray tracing   (b) Photon map   (c) Caustic

Figure 7.15: Caustics.

allowed to pass through the surface. The photon is only stored if the photon has passed through at least one surface. These photons are stored in a shadow map. The query for nearest shadow photons determine the degree of shadowing for a particular light source.

Photons can deal with participating media in a similar fashion to ray marching. Caustics projected onto a dust cloud can be captured quite effectively with this technique. The expense of marching a photon through a volume is reduced due to the Monte-Carlo techniques employed to sample the paths light can follow. Subsurface scattering can also be handled with these techniques. This situation occurs where there is a thin layer of translucent material at the surface of the object. Milk, skin and marble can effectively be modelled in this way. Photons penetrate the translucent outer surface and reflect of the inner surface.

7.14.7 C# Implementation

We have chosen to implement photon mapping with two classes. The PhotonTrace class traces photons through the scene and decides which photons must be stored and applies Monte Carlo methods to determine how photons are reflected or absorbed.

```
//PhotonTrace.cs
using System;

public class PhotonTrace {
    public Random rnd;
    private double[] rstack;
    private int rst;
    //current medium refraction index
    private double ri=1.0;
    private double baseri=1.0;

    public void pushri() { if(rst>=1024) return; rstack[rst]=ri; rst++; }

    public void popri() { if(rst<=0) return; rst--; ri=rstack[rst]; }

    public void resetri() { rst=0; ri=baseri; }

    public PhotonTrace()
    { rnd=new Random(); rst=0; rstack=new double[1024]; }

    Vector rand_vector(Vector n) {
        Vector p=new Vector();
        p.x=rnd.NextDouble()*2.0-1.0;
        p.y=rnd.NextDouble()*2.0-1.0;
        p.z=rnd.NextDouble()*2.0-1.0;
        while((p*p>1.0)||(p*n<0)) {
            p.x=rnd.NextDouble()*2.0-1.0;
            p.y=rnd.NextDouble()*2.0-1.0;
            p.z=rnd.NextDouble()*2.0-1.0;
        }
        p.normalize();
        return p;
    }

    public Vector rand_vector(Light l) {
        Vector v=new Vector();
        if(l.GetType().FullName=="InfiniteLight") return l.lightdir(v);
        Light ld=(Light)l.Clone();
        ld.const_att=1.0; ld.cub_att=0.0; ld.lin_att=0.0;
        do {
            v.x=rnd.NextDouble()*2.0-1.0;
            v.y=rnd.NextDouble()*2.0-1.0;
            v.z=rnd.NextDouble()*2.0-1.0;
```

```
    } while((rnd.NextDouble()>ld.intensity(1.1+v)));
    v.normalize();
    return v;
}

public PhotonMap createPhotonMap(Scene s,int nphotons) {
    PhotonMap map=new PhotonMap(nphotons);
    IntersectInfo info;
    Vector o=null, d=null;
    Light l=null;
    Colour Id=null, Is=null;
    int first=0;

    while(map.photons()<nphotons) {
        if(o==null) {
            l=s.lights[rnd.Next(s.lights.GetUpperBound(0))];
            //use intensity as probability distribution
            o=l.l; d=rand_vector(l);
            first=0; resetri();
            l.photons++;
            Id=(Colour)l.Id.Clone(); Is=(Colour)l.Is.Clone();
        }
        info=s.intersect(o,d);
        if(info!=null) {
            if(info.t>1e-7) {
                Primitive obj=info.obj;
                Vector n=info.obj.TI.Transpose()*info.n;
                Vector p=o+info.t*d;
                n.normalize();
                double pr=rnd.NextDouble();
                //check transparency
                if(pr<obj.M.pt) { //do refraction
                    bool enter=(n*d<0.0);
                    if(!enter) popri();//leaving material, restore old material
                    d=Vector.transmit(d,n,ri,obj.M.ir);
                    d.w=0.0; o=p+d*1e-7;
                    if(enter) //going into material, save old material
                    { pushri(); ri=obj.M.ir; }
                    Id=Id*obj.M.diffuse; Is=Is*obj.M.diffuse;
                    first++;
                } else {
                    if(n*d>0.0) n=-n;
                    //Only store if this is a reflection and not directly from the
                    //light source. The lighting model takes care of direct lighting.
                    if(first>0) map.store(p,d,l,Id,Is);
                    first++;
                    //do diffuse or specular reflection or absorb
                    pr=rnd.NextDouble();
                    if(pr<obj.M.pd) { //diffuse reflection
                        d=rand_vector(n);
                        while(rnd.NextDouble()>d*n) d=rand_vector(n);
```

```
                    o=p+1e-7*d;
                    Id=Id*obj.M.diffuse; Is=Is*obj.M.diffuse;
                } else if(pr<obj.M.ps+obj.M.pd) { //specular reflection
                    d=Vector.reflect(-d,n); o=p+1e-7*d;
                    Id=Id*obj.M.specular; Is=Is*obj.M.specular;
                } else { o=null; d=null; } //absorbed by surface
            }
        } else { o=null; d=null; }
      } else { o=null; d=null; }
    }
    map.buildHeap();
    return map;
  }
}
```

The `PhotonMap` class is responsible for storing the photons in a *kd*-tree and supports queries for the nearest photons to a particular point. We have adapted the code in [67] to C# and integrated the photon map with the raytracer.

```
//PhotonMap.cs
using System;
//Adapted from Realistic Image Synthesis Using Photon Mapping
//by Henrik Wann Jensen
//Photons are stored in a heap (after all photons have been accumulated)
//Note: a heap is a balanced binary tree stored in an array such that if
//a node is at index i, then its left child is at index 2*i and its right
//child is at 2*i+1. This implies that indices start at 1, and NOT 0.
public class PhotonMap {
  public PhotonMap(int n) {
    nphotons=0; max=n;
    orig=new Photon[max+1];
    //so that heap can be addressed from index 1
    heap=new Photon[max+1];
    maxdist=1.0; maxsamples=100;
    nearest=null;
  }
  public void store(Vector p,Vector dir,Light source,Colour Id,Colour Is) {
    if(nphotons>=max) return;
    Photon ph=new Photon(p,dir,source,Id,Is);
    nphotons++;
    orig[nphotons]=ph;
  }

  public int photons() { return nphotons; }

  private void swap(int i,int j) {
    Photon tmp;
    tmp=orig[i]; orig[i]=orig[j]; orig[j]=tmp;
  }
```

```
private void median_split(int start,int end,int median,int axis) {
  int left=start, right=end;
  double v=0.0;

  while(right>left) {
    if(axis==0) v=orig[right].p.x;
    if(axis==1) v=orig[right].p.y;
    if(axis==2) v=orig[right].p.z;
    int i=left-1, j=right;
    while(true) {
      if(axis==0) while(orig[i+1].p.x<v) i++;
      if(axis==1) while(orig[i+1].p.y<v) i++;
      if(axis==2) while(orig[i+1].p.z<v) i++;
      i++;
      if(axis==0) while((orig[j-1].p.x>v)&&(j-1>left)) j--;
      if(axis==1) while((orig[j-1].p.y>v)&&(j-1>left)) j--;
      if(axis==2) while((orig[j-1].p.z>v)&&(j-1>left)) j--;
      j--;
      if(i>=j) break;
      swap(i,j);
    }
    swap(i,right);
    if(i>=median) right=i-1;
    if(i<=median) left=i+1;
  }
}

private void balance_segment(int index,int start,int end) {
  Vector extent;
  //compute median
  int median=1;
  while(4*median<=(end-start+1)) median+=median;
  if(3*median<=(end-start+1)) { median+=median; median+=start-1; }
  } else median=end-median+1;

  //find splitting axis
  extent=bbox_max-bbox_min;
  int axis=0;
  if((extent.x>extent.y)&&(extent.x>extent.z)) axis=0;
  else if(extent.y>extent.z) axis=1;
  else axis=2;

  //partition photons around median
  median_split(start,end,median,axis);
  heap[index]=orig[median];
  heap[index].splitaxis=axis;

  //recursively balance left and right block
  if(median>start) { //balance left segment
    if(start<median-1) {
```

```
          Vector tmp=(Vector)bbox_max.Clone();
          if(axis==0) bbox_max.x=heap[index].p.x;
          if(axis==1) bbox_max.y=heap[index].p.y;
          if(axis==2) bbox_max.z=heap[index].p.z;
          balance_segment(2*index,start,median-1);
          bbox_max=tmp;
        } else heap[2*index]=orig[start];
    }

  if(median<end) { //balance right segment
    if(median+1<end) {
        Vector tmp=(Vector)bbox_min.Clone();
        if(axis==0) bbox_min.x=heap[index].p.x;
        if(axis==1) bbox_min.y=heap[index].p.y;
        if(axis==2) bbox_min.z=heap[index].p.z;
        balance_segment(2*index+1,median+1,end);
        bbox_min=tmp;
      } else heap[2*index+1]=orig[end];
    }
  }

public void buildHeap() {
  bbox_min=(Vector)orig[1].p.Clone();
  bbox_max=(Vector)orig[1].p.Clone();
  for(int i=2;i<=nphotons;i++) {
    heap[i]=orig[i];
    if(orig[i].p.x<bbox_min.x) bbox_min.x=orig[i].p.x;
    if(orig[i].p.y<bbox_min.y) bbox_min.x=orig[i].p.y;
    if(orig[i].p.z<bbox_min.z) bbox_min.x=orig[i].p.z;
    if(orig[i].p.x>bbox_max.x) bbox_max.x=orig[i].p.x;
    if(orig[i].p.y>bbox_max.y) bbox_max.x=orig[i].p.y;
    if(orig[i].p.z>bbox_max.z) bbox_max.x=orig[i].p.z;
  }

  balance_segment(1,1,nphotons);
  lastbranch=nphotons/2-1;
  Console.Write("Heap built.\n");
}

//visualize the photon map
public Colour ViewMap(Vector p,double tolerance) {
  nearest=new PhotonList(1);
  nearest.maxdist=maxdist;
  nearest.searchdist=maxdist*maxdist;
  nearest.p=p;
  locate_photons(1,p);
  if(nearest.searchdist<tolerance) return new Colour(1.0,1.0,1.0);
  else return new Colour(0.0,0.0,0.0);
}

//Irradiance at p, with surface normal n
```

```
public Colour Irradiance(Vector p,Vector n,Vector v,Material m) {
  double dist2;

  if(nearest==null) {
    nearest=new PhotonList(maxsamples);
    nearest.maxdist=maxdist;
    nearest.searchdist=maxdist*maxdist;
    nearest.p=p;
  } else {
    //reuse existing photons distance to increase search
    //speed (cached values) - only if all samples are found
    nearest.p=p;
    if(nearest.count()==maxsamples) {
      dist2=nearest.recomputeExistingDistance();
      dist2=dist2+1e-3;
    } else { dist2=maxdist*maxdist; }
    nearest.num=0;
    nearest.maxdist=maxdist;
    nearest.searchdist=dist2;
  }

  locate_photons(1,p);

  Colour irrad=new Colour(0.0,0.0,0.0);

  if(nearest.count()<2) return irrad;
  dist2=nearest.searchdist;
  double w=0.0,t=0.0;
  for(int i=0;i<nearest.count();i++) {
    if(nearest[i].dir*n<0.0) {
      irrad+=m.Light(n,-nearest[i].dir,v,new Colour(0.0,0.0,0.0),
      //The constant 10000.0 is fairly arbitrary, it is used to convert
      //between the intuitive values of Phong and the Irradiance of photons
      nearest[i].Id*10000.0/nearest[i].source.photons,
      nearest[i].Is*10000.0/nearest[i].source.photons);
    }
  }
  double tmp=(1.0/Math.PI)/(dist2+1e-7);
  irrad*=tmp;
  return irrad;
}

private void locate_photons(int index,Vector pos) {
  Photon p=heap[index];
  double dist1=0.0, dist2;
  if(index<lastbranch) {
    if(p.splitaxis==0) dist1=pos.x-p.p.x;
    if(p.splitaxis==1) dist1=pos.y-p.p.y;
    if(p.splitaxis==2) dist1=pos.z-p.p.z;
    if(dist1>0.0) { //search the right half
      locate_photons(2*index+1,pos);
```

```
            if(dist1*dist1<nearest.searchdist) { //interval overlaps left half
                locate_photons(2*index,pos);
            }
        } else { //search the left half
            locate_photons(2*index,pos);
            if(dist1*dist1<nearest.searchdist) { //interval overlaps right half
                locate_photons(2*index+1,pos);
            }
        }
    }

    //calculate distance from photon to point
    dist2=(p.p-pos)*(p.p-pos);
    if(dist2<nearest.searchdist) //the photon must be added
        nearest.addPhoton(p,dist2);
}
private int nphotons;
private Photon[] heap, orig;
private Vector bbox_max, bbox_min;
//last index before leaves
private int lastbranch;
//maximum distance to search for photons
public double maxdist;
//maximum number of photons
public int max;
//maximum number of photons per search
public int maxsamples;
private PhotonList nearest;

private class Photon {
    public Vector p, dir;
    public Light source;
    public int splitaxis;
    public Colour Id, Is;
    public Photon() { p=dir=source=Id=Is=null; }
    public Photon(Vector p,Vector dir,Light source,Colour Id,Colour Is) {
        this.p=(Vector)p.Clone(); this.dir=(Vector)dir.Clone();
        this.source=source;
        this.Id=(Colour)Id.Clone(); this.Is=(Colour)Is.Clone();
    }
}

private class PhotonList {
    public Photon[] photons;
    public int max, num;
    public double searchdist, maxdist;
    public double[] dists;
    public Vector p;
    public int count() { return num; }

    public PhotonList(int max) {
```

```
    this.max=max; num=0;
    photons=new Photon[max];
    dists=new double[max];
    searchdist=maxdist*maxdist;
}

public Photon this[int i] { get {return photons[i]; } set {} }

//recompute distances to photons, maxdist must
//be changed, but searchdist should not be changed!
public double recomputeExistingDistance() {
    int i;
    if(num<=0) return 1e-10;
    for(i=0;i<num;i++)
        dists[i]=(photons[i].p-p)*(photons[i].p-p);
    maxdist=dists[0];
    for(i=1;i<num;i++) if(dists[i]>maxdist) maxdist=dists[i];
    return maxdist;
}

public void addPhoton(Photon p,double dist) {
    int pos, i;
    //always keep the largest photon in position 0.
    if(num<max) {
        if(num==0) { photons[num]=p; dists[num]=dist; maxdist=dist; }
        else {
            if(dist>maxdist) {
                photons[num]=photons[0]; dists[num]=dists[0];
                photons[0]=p; dists[0]=dist; maxdist=dist;
            } else { photons[num]=p; dists[num]=dist; }
        }
        num++;
    } else if(dist<maxdist) { photons[0]=p; dists[0]=dist; }
        maxdist=dist; pos=0;
        for(i=1;i<max;i++)
            if(dists[i]>maxdist) { maxdist=dists[i]; pos=i; }
        if(pos!=0) {
            p=photons[0]; photons[0]=photons[pos]; photons[pos]=p;
            dists[pos]=dists[0]; dists[0]=maxdist;
        }
        searchdist=maxdist;
    }
  }
}
```

The Raytracer class already has a few lines that invoke the photon mapping module if requested. In this implementation, normal lighting models are applied and photon mapping is used to replace the ambient term of these lighting models.

Chapter 8

Radiosity

Raytracing yields impressive results, but fails to capture some of the lighting effects that we observe. In particular, raytracing handles mirror reflections well, but the environments we model have few highly reflective objects. Instead, most of the lighting is diffuse. We observe many subtle effects such as color bleeding in a closed diffuse environment. Raytracing does not model this effect since we only model certain kinds of light transport.

8.1 Light Transport Notation

We need to describe our models in terms of the possible light paths that can be modeled. We can use the notation of Heckbert [59] for this purpose. The vertices of a light path can be

- L - a light source.

- E - the eye.

- S - a specular reflection.

- D - a diffuse reflection.

We are only interested in light paths that begin at a light source and end at the eye. We can represent the light paths as regular expressions. Raytracing models light paths of the form LD?S*E, that is light (possibly reflected off a diffuse surface) reflected specularly zero or more times before reaching the eye. This is not a global illumination model, since indirect illumination from diffuse surfaces is not considered.

Radiosity attempts to model light paths of the form L(D+)E.

8.2   Radiosity Matrix

Radiosity algorithms approximate the lighting of a scene by dividing the scene into patches and calculating the energy transfer between patches. The radiosity of a patch, B is the total rate of energy leaving a surface and is equal to the sum of emitted and reflected energies. Consider two patches P_i and P_j,

$$B_i dA_i = E_i dA_i + \rho_i B_j dA_j F_{dA_j dA_i}$$

where dA_i is the area of patch i, B_i is the radiosity of path i and ρ_i is the portion of incoming energy reflected by this patch. The contribution for every patch P_j to patch P_i is then

$$B_i dA_i = E_i dA_i + \rho_i \int_j B_j dA_j F_{dA_j dA_i}$$

i.e. Radiosity $\times$ area = emitted energy + reflected energy.

- E_i is the light emitted from patch i.

- ρ_i is the reflectivity of patch i.

- $F_{dA_j dA_i}$ is the form factor between dA_i and dA_j, the fraction of energy leaving dA_j that arrives at dA_i.

In a closed environment this can be repeated for each patch to produce a system of equations. Normally the environment is discretized into n patches and constant radiosity for the patch is assumed so that

$$B_i A_i = E_i A_i + \rho_i \sum_{j=1}^{n} B_j F_{ji} A_j$$

with $F_{ij} A_i = F_{ji} A_j$. Thus $F_{ij} = F_{ji} A_j / A_i$ so that $B_i = E_i + \rho_i \sum_{j=1}^{n} B_j F_{ij}$. $F_{ii} = 0$ since we assume the surface is flat (or convex). This is the equation for one patch. For all the patches we have n simultaneous equations in n unknown B_i values given by

$$
\begin{pmatrix}
1 - \rho_1 F_{11} & -\rho_1 F_{12} & \cdots & -\rho_1 F_{1n} \\
-\rho_2 F_{21} & 1 - \rho_2 F_{22} & \cdots & -\rho_2 F_{2n} \\
\vdots & \vdots & \ddots & \vdots \\
-\rho_n F_{n1} & -\rho_n F_{n2} & \cdots & 1 - \rho_n F_{nn}
\end{pmatrix}
\begin{pmatrix}
B_1 \\ B_2 \\ \vdots \\ B_n
\end{pmatrix}
=
\begin{pmatrix}
E_1 \\ E_2 \\ \vdots \\ E_n
\end{pmatrix}.
$$

8.3 Solving for Radiosity Values

Solving for the radiosity values provides intensity values for the patches. Gauss-Jordan elimination, or Gaussian elimination with back substitution can be used to calculate the radiosity values. In practice many of the form factors are zero and other properties of the matrix ("diagonally dominant") allow techniques such as the Gauss-Seidel method to be used.

8.3.1 Solving: Jacobi Method

The Jacobi method calculates the total incoming energy from each of the other patches in order to calculate the new radiosity value for a particular patch. This process is repeated for each patch. The calculated values are stored in a separate array and then copied back to the first array, for the next iteration.

for $i = 1$ to n **do**
   $B[i] \leftarrow E[i]$
end for
while (not converged enough) **do**
   for $i = 1$ to n **do**
      $B_{new}[i] = E[i] + \sum_{j=1}^{n} M[i,j] \times B[j]$
   end for
   for $i = 1$ to n **do**
      $B[i] \leftarrow B_{new}[i]$
   end for
end while

8.3.2 Solving: Gauss-Seidel Iteration

Gauss-Seidel iteration converges more quickly to a solution than the Jacobi method. It can also be applied in place, no separate array is required.

for $i = 1$ to n **do**
   $B[i] \leftarrow E[i]$
end for
while (not converged enough) **do**
   for $i = 1$ to n **do**
      $B[i] = E[i] + \sum_{j=1}^{n} M[i,j] \times B[j]$
   end for
end while

This technique can be applied because the sum of each row of form factors should equal 1, since we cannot have more visibility than what we can see. Also ρ_i should be less than 1.

8.3.3 Solving: Shooting Method

Instead of determining how much energy a patch receives from other patches, we can determine how much energy a patch radiates to other patches. In this way, we can select bright patches to transmit energy first, and we should converge more quickly. The radiosity of a patch i at any time is $B[i]+\Delta B[i]$.

```
for i = 1 to n do
    B[i] ← 0
    ΔB[i] ← E[i]
end for
while (not converged enough) do
    Choose j so that ΔB[j] × A[j] is maximized
    B[j] = B[j] + ΔB[j]
    for i = 1 to n do
        ΔB[i] = ΔB[i] + M[i, j] × B[j]
    end for
    ΔB[j] = 0
end while
```

8.4 Form Factors

So far we have assumed that the form factors, or the visible portion of each patch from each other patch is known. We have to calculate these values in some way. Form factors are defined as

$$F_{A_i A_j} \equiv F_{ij} = \frac{\text{Radiative energy reaching } A_j \text{ from } A_i}{\text{Total radiative energy leaving } A_i \text{ in all directions}}$$

or

$$F_{ij} = \frac{1}{A_i} \int\limits_{A_i} \int\limits_{A_j} \frac{\cos \phi_i \cos \phi_j}{\pi r^2} dA_j dA_i$$

where r is the distance between the two patches, and ϕ_i, ϕ_j are the angles between the patches and the line connecting the two points under consideration. This approach does not take into account patches that may be in between the two patches for which we want to calculate the form factor.

The rest of this section presents some options for form factor calculation.

8.4.1 Numerical Solution

Convert the double area integral into a double contour integral using Stoke's theorem

$$F_{ij} = \frac{1}{2\pi A_i} \oint_{C_j} \oint_{C_i} (\ln(r)dx_i dy_i + \ln(r)dy_i dy_j + \ln(r)dz_i dz_j) \ .$$

This technique is expensive and requires the calculation of the contour of the visible area of the patch.

8.4.2 Raytracing Method

In this method we use an existing raytracing engine to approximate the form factor. We simply cast a number of rays from various points on patch j to patch i. Jittering should be used when selecting rays from a regular grid to obtain better results. Let the percentage of rays that make it from patch j to patch i be V_{ij}. We have $V_{ij} = V_{ji}$. Let r be the distance between the centers of the patches, then we approximate the form factor by

$$F_{ij} = V_{ij} \frac{A_j \cos \phi_i \cos \phi_j}{\pi r^2} \ .$$

The πr^2 term comes from the portion of the hemisphere above the center of the patch through which the other patch is visible (the area of the hemisphere is 2π) and the reduced visible size of the patch due to distance (inverse square law).

8.4.3 Hemicube Method

Ray casting can be an intensive process. The hemicube process uses rasterization techniques and can thus be accelerated by common graphics hardware. Instead of using a hemisphere on which projections are calculated, we use a hemicube (half a cube of side length 2). The hemicube is centered above the center of the patch. Now we render the scene from the viewpoint of the patch onto each side of the hemicube. A standard Z-buffer can be used for the for visibility calculations. Each patch is assigned a unique color (typically one of 16 million colors for a 24-bit color buffer). It is trivial to calculate the visibility V_{ij} by simply determining how many pixels on the surface of the hemicube are from the patch we investigate in proportion to the total number of pixels. The hemicube is illustrated in figure 8.1.

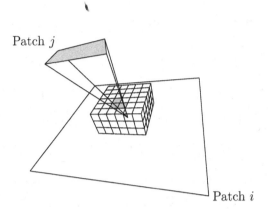

Figure 8.1: The Hemicube method.

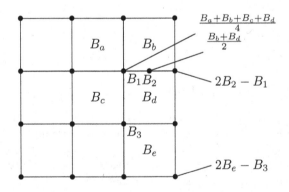

Figure 8.2: Determining radiosity values.

Figure 8.3: Examples of radiosity solutions.

8.5 Rendering

To render the scene, we simply render the patches using a rasterizer. We have the radiosity (brightness) for each patch, but this seldom provides smooth results. Instead we should try to calculate the radiosity value for each pixel using interpolation. Another option is to determine the radiosity at each vertex and then interpolate using Gouraud shading. Vertices that are not surrounded by patches can be calculated via extrapolation. The calculations are illustrated in figure 8.2. One drawback of the radiosity method is shadows. Shadows are seldom well defined. Subdivision of the patches in areas where radiosity varies greatly can reduce the problem. Examples of scenes rendered using the radiosity approach are displayed in figure 8.3.

8.6 C# Implementation

The C# implementation reuses the triangle Mesh class introduced for raytracing and the SparseMatrix class used for mesh parameterization. The raytracing intersection tests are used to determine the form factors for a mesh, and a sparse matrix is created for solving the radiosity equations. We use TAO (*www.taoframework.com*) to visualize the radiosity of triangles in the mesh. The radiosity of the polygons are not interpolated to obtain vertex radiosities, that is left to the reader as an exercise.

The MeshTriangle class is extended to include area and to support form factor computation using raytracing. Only the new methods are included here. Omitted code is indicated by vertical dots.

// MeshTriangle.cs

    ⋮

  //Omitted code

    ⋮

```
public Vector RandomPoint() {
  Vector p;
  double u=rnd.NextDouble(), v=rnd.NextDouble();
  while(u+v>1.0) { u=rnd.NextDouble(); v=rnd.NextDouble(); }
  p=u*v0+v*v1+(1-u-v)*v2;
  return p;
}

public double area() { return ((v1-v0)^(v2-v0)).norm()/2.0; }

public Vector center() { return (v0+v1+v2)/3.0; }

public Vector normal() {
  Vector n=(v1-v0)^(v2-v0);
  n.normalize(); return n;
}
```

  //pos is used to quickly identify which triangle has been intersected by a ray

```
public int pos;
```

    ⋮

  //Omitted code

    ⋮

The Mesh class has been modified so that the GeometryFile class can be used to load scenes. Since many scenes have a large variety of triangle sizes, subdivision is also included to attempt to produce a scene triangles of approximately equal size. The provided methods can subdivide, or only subdivide if a triangle's area exceeds some specified value. The longest edge is then split to create new triangles. The opposite face of an edge that is split should also be split. The implementation presented here does not do this, it is left to the reader to implement this enhancement.

// Mesh.cs
```
using System;
```

```csharp
using System.IO;

public class Mesh:Primitive {
   Scene trilist;
   public int ntriangles;
   public MeshTriangle[] triangles;

   public void add(MeshTriangle p) {
      Array.Resize(ref triangles,triangles.GetLength(0)+1);
      triangles[triangles.GetLength(0)-1]=p;
      p.pos=triangles.GetLength(0)-1;
      trilist.add(p); ntriangles++;
   }

   public int AddVertex(Vector vec) {
      Array.Resize(ref v,v.GetLength(0)+1);
      Array.Resize(ref n,n.GetLength(0)+1);
      v[v.GetLength(0)-1]=(Vector)vec.Clone();
      n[v.GetLength(0)-1]=new Vector(1.0,0.0,0.0);
      return v.GetLength(0)-1;
   }

   public void SetNormal(int i,Vector nl) { n[i]=(Vector)nl.Clone(); }

   public void AddTriangle(int v0,int v1,int v2) {
      MeshTriangle tri;
      tri=new MeshTriangle(v[v0],v[v1],v[v2],n[v0],n[v1],n[v2]);
      add(tri);
   }

   public void SetTex(int i,Vector n) { //not used for radiosity }

   public Mesh() {
      trilist=new SceneTree();
      triangles=new MeshTriangle[0];
      ntriangles=0;
      v=new Vector[0]; n=new Vector[0];
   }

   public void PrepareForIntersect() { trilist.prepare_for_render(); }

   public Mesh(Mesh m) {
      v=(Vector[])m.v.Clone(); n=(Vector[])m.n.Clone();
      trilist=(Scene)m.trilist.Clone();
      ntriangles=m.ntriangles;
      triangles=(MeshTriangle[])m.triangles.Clone();
   }

   public void recenter() {
      int i, n;
      Vector c=new Vector(0.0,0.0,0.0);
```

```
      if(v==null) return;
      n=v.GetLength(0);
      for(i=0;i<n;i++) c+=v[i];
      c/=n;
      for(i=0;i<n;i++) { v[i].x-=c.x; v[i].y-=c.y; v[i].z-=c.z; }
   }

   public void rescale() {
      int i, n;
      double max=-1.0;
      if(v==null) return;
      n=v.GetLength(0);
      for(i=0;i<n;i++) {
         if(Math.Abs(v[i].x)>max) max=Math.Abs(v[i].x);
         if(Math.Abs(v[i].y)>max) max=Math.Abs(v[i].y);
         if(Math.Abs(v[i].z)>max) max=Math.Abs(v[i].z);
      }
      for(i=0;i<n;i++) { v[i].x/=max; v[i].y/=max; v[i].z/=max; }
   }

   public override IntersectInfo intersect(Vector o,Vector d) {
      IntersectInfo info=null;
      if(trilist==null) return null;
      info=trilist.intersect(o,d);
      return info;
   }

   public override BBox getLocalExtent() {
      BBox b=new BBox();
      if(v==null) return null;
      if(v.GetLength(0)<=0) return null;
      b.min=new Vector(v[0]); b.max=new Vector(v[0]);
      for(int i=1;i<v.GetLength(0);i++) {
         if(v[i].x<b.min.x) b.min.x=v[i].x;
         if(v[i].y<b.min.y) b.min.y=v[i].y;
         if(v[i].z<b.min.z) b.min.z=v[i].z;
         if(v[i].x>b.max.x) b.max.x=v[i].x;
         if(v[i].y>b.max.y) b.max.y=v[i].y;
         if(v[i].z>b.max.z) b.max.z=v[i].z;
      }
      return b;
   }

   public Mesh Subdivide() {
      int i,p;
      Vector v0,v1,v2,e1,e2,e3;
      MeshTriangle tri;
      Vector v;
      Mesh m=new Mesh();
      m.v=(Vector[])this.v.Clone(); m.n=(Vector[])this.n.Clone();
      for(i=0;i<ntriangles;i++) {
```

```
        v0=triangles[i].v0; v1=triangles[i].v1; v2=triangles[i].v2;
        e1=v1-v0; e2=v2-v1; e3=v0-v2;
        if((e1.norm()>=e2.norm())&&(e1.norm()>=e3.norm())) {
            v=(triangles[i].v1+triangles[i].v0)/2.0;
            p=m.AddVertex(v);
            tri=new MeshTriangle(v1,v2,m.v[p]); m.add(tri);
            tri=new MeshTriangle(m.v[p],v2,v0); m.add(tri);
        } else if((e2.norm()>=e1.norm())&&(e2.norm()>=e3.norm())) {
            v=(triangles[i].v2+triangles[i].v1)/2.0;
            p=m.AddVertex(v);
            tri=new MeshTriangle(v2,v0,m.v[p]); m.add(tri);
            tri=new MeshTriangle(m.v[p],v0,v1); m.add(tri);
        } else {
            v=(triangles[i].v0+triangles[i].v2)/2.0;
            p=m.AddVertex(v);
            tri=new MeshTriangle(v0,v1,m.v[p]); m.add(tri);
            tri=new MeshTriangle(m.v[p],v1,v2); m.add(tri);
        }
    }
    return m;
}


//same as subdivide, but only subdivide triangles
// larger than the current minimum area triangle
public Mesh EqualizeArea() {
    int i;
    double minarea=1e10;
    double checkarea=1e12;
    double area;
    for(i=0;i<ntriangles;i++) {
        area=triangles[i].area();
        if(area<minarea) minarea=area;
    }
    Mesh m=SubdivideArea(minarea);
    while(checkarea>minarea) {
        checkarea=-1.0;
        for(i=0;i<m.ntriangles;i++) {
            area=m.triangles[i].area();
            if(area>checkarea) checkarea=area;
        }
        if(checkarea>minarea) m=m.SubdivideArea(minarea);
    }
    return m;
}

public Mesh EqualizeArea(double maxarea) {
    double minarea=maxarea;
    double checkarea=1e12;
    double area;
    Mesh m=SubdivideArea(minarea);
    while(checkarea>minarea) {
```

```
         checkarea=-1.0;
         for(int i=0;i<m.ntriangles;i++) {
            area=m.triangles[i].area();
            if(area>checkarea) checkarea=area;
         }
         if(checkarea>minarea)
            m=m.SubdivideArea(minarea);
      }
      return m;
   }

   public Mesh SubdivideArea(double minarea) {
      int i,p;
      MeshTriangle tri;
      Vector v0,v1,v2,e1,e2,e3,v;
      Mesh m=new Mesh();
      m.v=(Vector[])this.v.Clone(); m.n=(Vector[])this.n.Clone();
      for(i=0;i<ntriangles;i++) {
         v0=triangles[i].v0; v1=triangles[i].v1; v2=triangles[i].v2;
         if(triangles[i].area()<=minarea) {
            tri=new MeshTriangle(v0,v1,v2); m.add(tri);
            continue;
         }
         e1=v1-v0; e2=v2-v1; e3=v0-v2;
         if((e1.norm()>=e2.norm())&&(e1.norm()>=e3.norm())) {
            v=(triangles[i].v1+triangles[i].v0)/2.0;
            p=m.AddVertex(v);
            tri=new MeshTriangle(v1,v2,m.v[p]); m.add(tri);
            tri=new MeshTriangle(m.v[p],v2,v0); m.add(tri);
         } else if((e2.norm()>=e1.norm())&&(e2.norm()>=e3.norm())) {
            v=(triangles[i].v2+triangles[i].v1)/2.0;
            p=m.AddVertex(v);
            tri=new MeshTriangle(v2,v0,m.v[p]); m.add(tri);
            tri=new MeshTriangle(m.v[p],v0,v1); m.add(tri);
         } else {
            v=(triangles[i].v0+triangles[i].v2)/2.0;
            p=m.AddVertex(v);
            tri=new MeshTriangle(v0,v1,m.v[p]); m.add(tri);
            tri=new MeshTriangle(m.v[p],v1,v2); m.add(tri);
         }
      }
      return m;
   }

   public Vector[] v, n;

   public override object Clone() { object o=new Mesh(this); return o; }

   public override string ToString() { return "Primitive::Mesh()";}
}
```

Since form factor calculation requires the largest amount of time, the radiosity implementation allows the form factors to be saved and reloaded at a later time. The radiosity solution at each step of the iteration is displayed. The solution is fairly rapid, and some delays have been inserted into the implementation so that the steps during solution of the radiosity equations are visible.

```csharp
// Radiosity.cs
using System;
using System.Collections.Generic;
using System.Drawing;
using System.Windows.Forms;
using System.IO;
using Tao.OpenGl;
using Tao.FreeGlut;


namespace radiosity
{
    public partial class MainForm
    {
        double angle=0.0, area=0.3;
        bool wireframe=true, working=false, quitting=false;
        SparseMatrix formfactors=null, radmatrix=null;
        int glutwin, samples=20;
        double[] emittance=null, radiosity=null, radwork=null;
        // The reflectivity should be set per patch but a single value is
        // slightly simpler. The code is trivial to modify to support different values
        double rho=0.3, initial_power=10.0;
        Mesh m;
        System.Threading.Thread thread;
        public void ThreadStart() {
            Glut.glutInitDisplayMode(Glut.GLUT_RGB|Glut.GLUT_DOUBLE
                |Glut.GLUT_DEPTH);
            Glut.glutInit();
            glutwin=Glut.glutCreateWindow("Radiosity");
            Glut.glutDisplayFunc(
                    new Glut.DisplayCallback(this.DisplayCallback));
            Glut.glutIdleFunc(new Glut.IdleCallback(this.IdleCallback));
            Gl.glClearColor(0.0f,0.0f,0.0f,0.0f);
            Gl.glEnable(Gl.GL_DEPTH_TEST);
            Gl.glMatrixMode(Gl.GL_PROJECTION);
            Gl.glLoadIdentity();
            Glu.gluPerspective(60.0,1.0,0.001,1000.0);
            Glut.glutMainLoop();
        }

        [STAThread]
        public static void Main(string[] args)
        {
            Application.EnableVisualStyles();
```

```
    Application.SetCompatibleTextRenderingDefault(false);
    Application.Run(new MainForm());
}

public void IterateRadiosity() {
    int i;
    if((!working)&&(radiosity!=null)) {
        working=true;
        for(i=0;i<m.ntriangles;i++) {
            radiosity[i]=radwork[i]; radwork[i]=emittance[i];
        }
        radmatrix.GaussSeidel(radwork,10,1e-3,radiosity);
        for(i=0;i<m.ntriangles;i++) radiosity[i]=radwork[i];
        working=false;
    }
}

public void DisplayCallback() {
    int i;
    angle+=0.5;
    IterateRadiosity();
    Gl.glClear(Gl.GL_COLOR_BUFFER_BIT|Gl.GL_DEPTH_BUFFER_BIT);
    if(working) { Glut.glutSwapBuffers(); return; }
    Gl.glColor3d(1.0,1.0,1.0);
    Gl.glMatrixMode(Gl.GL_MODELVIEW);
    Gl.glLoadIdentity();
    Gl.glTranslated(0.0,0.0,-2.5);
    Gl.glRotated(angle,0.0,1.0,0.0);
    if(wireframe) Gl.glPolygonMode(Gl.GL_FRONT_AND_BACK,Gl.GL_LINE);
    else Gl.glPolygonMode(Gl.GL_FRONT_AND_BACK,Gl.GL_FILL);
    if(m!=null)
    for(i=0;i<m.ntriangles;i++) {
        Gl.glBegin(Gl.GL_POLYGON);
        if(wireframe) Gl.glColor3d(1.0,1.0,1.0);
        else Gl.glColor3d(radiosity[i],radiosity[i],radiosity[i]);
        Gl.glVertex3d(m.triangles[i].v0.x,
            m.triangles[i].v0.y,m.triangles[i].v0.z);
        Gl.glVertex3d(m.triangles[i].v1.x,
            m.triangles[i].v1.y,m.triangles[i].v1.z);
        Gl.glVertex3d(m.triangles[i].v2.x,
            m.triangles[i].v2.y,m.triangles[i].v2.z);
        Gl.glEnd();
    }
    Glut.glutSwapBuffers();
}

public void IdleCallback() {
    if(!working) Glut.glutPostRedisplay();
    else System.Threading.Thread.Sleep(250);
    if(quitting) Glut.glutLeaveMainLoop();
}
```

```csharp
public MainForm()
{
   InitializeComponent();
   thread=new System.Threading.Thread(this.ThreadStart);
   thread.Start();
}

void MainFormFormClosed(object sender,FormClosedEventArgs e)
{
   quitting=true; thread.Join();
   Glut.glutDestroyWindow(glutwin);
}

void InitRadiosity() {
   int i;
   Random rnd=new Random();
   emittance=new double[m.ntriangles];
   radiosity=new double[m.ntriangles];
   radwork=new double[m.ntriangles];
   for(i=0;i<m.ntriangles;i++) emittance[i]=0.0;
   emittance[rnd.Next()%m.ntriangles]=initial_power;
   for(i=0;i<m.ntriangles;i++) radwork[i]=emittance[i];
   radmatrix.GaussSeidel(radwork,10,1e-3);
   wireframe=false;
}

void CmdLoadClick(object sender,EventArgs e)
{
   working=true;
   openFileDialog1.Filter=
      "OFF (*.off)|*.off| Wavefront OBJ (*.obj)|*.obj| All files (*.*)|*.*";
   if(openFileDialog1.ShowDialog()==DialogResult.OK) {
      m=GeometryFile.Load(openFileDialog1.FileName);
      m.recenter(); m.rescale();
   }
   radiosity=null; wireframe=true; working=false;
}

void ComputeFormFactors() {
   double vij,fij,r,cosphi_i,cosphi_j;
   int i,j,k,hits;
   IntersectInfo info;
   MeshTriangle tri;
   Vector o,d;
   int ntri=m.ntriangles;
   formfactors=new SparseMatrix(ntri,ntri);
   radmatrix=new SparseMatrix(ntri,ntri);
   m.PrepareForIntersect();
   for(i=0;i<ntri;i++) {
      Console.Write("Form factor {0}/{1}\r",i+1,ntri);
```

```
//We assume that we have no convex surfaces
//So vii=0.0, that is the surface is not visible from itself
radmatrix[i,i]=1.0;
for(j=i+1;j<m.ntriangles;j++) {
    vij=0.0; hits=0;
    for(k=0;k<samples;k++) {
        o=m.triangles[i].RandomPoint();
        d=m.triangles[j].RandomPoint();
        d-=o; d.normalize();
        o=o+1e-5*d;
        info=m.intersect(o,d);
        if(info!=null) {
            tri=(MeshTriangle)info.obj;
            if(tri.pos==j) { vij+=1.0; hits++; }
        }
    }

    if(hits>0) {
        vij/=samples;
        d=m.triangles[j].center()-m.triangles[i].center();
        r=d.norm(); d.normalize();
        cosphi_i=Math.Abs(m.triangles[i].normal()*d);
        cosphi_j=Math.Abs(m.triangles[j].normal()*d);
        fij=vij*m.triangles[j].area()*cosphi_i*cosphi_j;
        fij/=Math.PI*r*r;
        formfactors[i,j]=fij; radmatrix[i,j]=-rho*fij;
        fij=vij*m.triangles[i].area()*cosphi_i*cosphi_j;
        fij/=Math.PI*r*r;
        formfactors[j,i]=fij; radmatrix[j,i]=-rho*fij;
    }
  }
 }
}

void CmdComputeFFClick(object sender,EventArgs e)
{
   working=true;
   ComputeFormFactors(); InitRadiosity();
   working=false;
   MessageBox.Show("Form factor computation complete.");
}


void CmdSaveFFClick(object sender,EventArgs e)
{
   int i,j,ne=0;
   working=true;
   saveFileDialog1.Filter="FF files (*.ff)|*.ff|All files (*.*)|*.*";
   if(saveFileDialog1.ShowDialog()==DialogResult.OK) {
       BinaryWriter bin=new BinaryWriter(File.Open(
           saveFileDialog1.FileName,FileMode.Create));
       int size=m.ntriangles;
```

```
        bin.Write(size);
        for(i=0;i<m.ntriangles;i++)
            for(j=0;j<m.ntriangles;j++)
                if(!formfactors.isZero(i,j)) ne++;
        bin.Write(ne);
        float fij;
        for(i=0;i<m.ntriangles;i++)
            for(j=0;j<m.ntriangles;j++)
                if(!formfactors.isZero(i,j)) {
                    bin.Write(i); bin.Write(j);
                    fij=(float)formfactors[i,j];
                    bin.Write(fij);
                }
        bin.Close();
    }
    working=false;
}

void CmdLoadFFClick(object sender,EventArgs e)
{
    int i,j,ne=0;
    float fij;
    double f;
    working=true;
    int ntri=m.ntriangles;
    openFileDialog1.Filter="FF files (*.ff)|*.ff|All files (*.*)|*.*";
    if(openFileDialog1.ShowDialog()==DialogResult.OK) {
        formfactors=new SparseMatrix(ntri,ntri);
        radmatrix=new SparseMatrix(ntri,ntri);
        BinaryReader bin=new BinaryReader(File.Open(
            openFileDialog1.FileName,FileMode.Open));
        int size=m.ntriangles;
        size=bin.ReadInt32(); ne=bin.ReadInt32();
        for(size=0;size<ne;size++) {
            i=bin.ReadInt32(); j=bin.ReadInt32();
            fij=bin.ReadSingle(); formfactors[i,j]=fij;
        }
        bin.Close();
        for(i=0;i<m.ntriangles;i++) {
            Console.Write("Form factor {0}/{1} \r",i+1,ntri);
            //We assume that we have no convex surfaces
            //So vii=0.0, that is the surface is not visible from itself
            radmatrix[i,i]=1.0;
            for(j=0;j<m.ntriangles;j++)
                if(!formfactors.isZero(i,j)) {
                    f=formfactors[i,j]; radmatrix[i,j]=-rho*f;
                }
        }
    }
    InitRadiosity(); working=false;
}
```

```
void CmdRestartClick(object sender,EventArgs e)
{ working=true; InitRadiosity(); working=false; }

void TxtRhoTextChanged(object sender,EventArgs e)
{ Double.TryParse(txtRho.Text,out rho); }

void TxtPowerTextChanged(object sender,EventArgs e)
{ Double.TryParse(txtPower.Text,out initial_power); }

void CmdSubdivClick(object sender,EventArgs e)
{
    working=true; radiosity=null;
    m=m.Subdivide(); working=false; wireframe=true;
}

void CmdAreaClick(object sender,EventArgs e)
{
    working=true; wireframe=true;
    Mesh newm=m.EqualizeArea(area);
    m=newm; working=false; radiosity=null;
}

void TxtAreaTextChanged(object sender,EventArgs e)
{ Double.TryParse(txtArea.Text,out area); }
}
}
```

Chapter 9

Animation

Animation is the process of controlling the movement of objects. The objective of animation is to produce a series of images which can be displayed in succession rapidly, thus giving the appearance of motion. In other words, we just need to render a suitable set of frames on the computer and then play back these frames rapidly. The difficult task is to define the motion that we wish to represent, and allow the motion to be defined easily.

9.1 Traditional Animation Techniques

In this section we discuss a few of the traditional animation techniques that are easily applied in a computer environment.

9.1.1 Keyframing

Each image in an animation sequence is known as a frame. Key frames are important frames in the animation that indicate key portions of the motion. After key frames have been produced, the in between frames can be interpolated from these frames. The in between frames must be generated carefully to provide the desired motion.

For computer animation we can specify the position and shape of objects at key frames. We then use some form of interpolation to obtain frames at in between values. In the worst case linear interpolation can be used. However, cubic splines (Bézier curves etc.) can also be used to provide smooth interpolation over time. We can move objects along various paths using piecewise smooth cubic curves. Interpolation on the computer is not restricted to position only. The velocity or acceleration of the object can also be modeled.

9.1.2 Motion Capture

Not all data need be fed into the animation system manually. Motion capture attempts to capture the motion of live actors. The actors will have devices placed on them that provide measurements of the position and/or orientation of various parts of the body. The information is then recorded and processed by the computer to provide animation. Sometimes spline curves will be used to approximate the data that has been acquired.

Various sensors can be used. Sensors may measure their position with respect to a magnetic field. Another approach is an optical system. Reflective spheres are placed on the actor, and the actor is recorded by several cameras. The information from the cameras allows the location of the spheres to be computed. However, this is not a trivial process since information from several cameras must be combined to provide reliable tracking information. As a result the data may contain a lot of noise.

9.2 Physics Models

For simple rigid objects, we can use classical physics models. Namely, compute the force and torque on the objects. The force determines acceleration, acceleration determines velocity and velocity determines position. We can then detect collisions between objects. Conservation of momentum, friction and other techniques can the be used to determine the new forces that apply to the object. Torque on the object determines rotation. The difficult part is the computation of collisions. Refer to Real-Time rendering [1] for details on collision detection algorithms.

If the force on an object is $\mathbf{F}$ then we have

$$\mathbf{F} = m\mathbf{a}_t$$

where m denotes the mass. Once the force and mass of the object are known the acceleration can be computed. $\mathbf{F}$ is the sum of all forces acting on the object. The velocity is then

$$\mathbf{v}_{t+1} = \mathbf{v}_t + (\Delta t)\mathbf{a}_t$$

and the position of the object

$$\mathbf{r}_{t+1} = \mathbf{r}_t + (\Delta t)\mathbf{v}_t.$$

Similar calculations can be performed to determine rotation using the torque.

9.3   Animation of Position

We can control camera movement or object movement by specifying curves that trace out the path of the object. These curves usually specify the center of mass of the object. The derivatives of cubic spline curves are available, so it is possible to also modify the velocity of the object. The curve will then alter accordingly.

Sometimes we want fairly dynamic situations. For example, we may want the camera to follow a certain object. It can be tedious and difficult to do so by hand. Another approach is to automatically build the spline curves required to follow the object.

As an example we can consider *ease-in*. In this case, we would like an object with some initial velocity to approach a point smoothly and stop at that point. This can be achieved using the formula

$$\mathbf{q}(u) = \mathbf{r}_0 H_0^3(u) + \mathbf{v}_0 H_1^3(u) + \mathbf{r}_1 H_3^3(u)$$

where $\mathbf{r}_0$ is the initials position of the object, $\mathbf{v}_0$ is the initial velocity of the object and $\mathbf{r}_1$ is the stopping point. The *cubic Hermite polynomials* H_j^3 are

$$H_0^3(u) = (1 + 2u)(1 - u)^2$$
$$H_1^3(u) = u(1 - u)^2$$
$$H_2^3(u) = -u^2(1 - u)$$
$$H_3^3(u) = u^2(3 - 2u).$$

We can change the time interval $0 \leq u \leq 1$ to $[u_0, u_1]$ with the simple substitution

$$J_i(u) = H_i^3 \left(\frac{u - u_0}{u_1 - u_0} \right).$$

In the case of a moving target, this approach is less effective. If the target does not change direction or velocity rapidly, linear interpolation may provide a suitable solution, that is

$$\mathbf{c}_{i+1} = (1 - \alpha)\mathbf{c}_i + \alpha\mathbf{t}_{i+1}$$

where subscripts indicate time, $0 \leq \alpha \leq 1$ is a fixed parameter and $\mathbf{t}_i$ is the target position at time i.

9.3.1 Arc length parameterization

The splines do not have equal speed across the path of the curve. Velocity curves are thus also not entirely easy to work with. If we compare the differences $\|\mathbf{q}(t_1 + \Delta t) - \mathbf{q}(t_1)\|$ and $\|\mathbf{q}(t_2 + \Delta t) - \mathbf{q}(t_2)\|$ for small Δt we may very well find that distance differs even though we may not want this to be the case. Greater distance implies greater velocity. To obtain constant velocity may require the path to change and this may not be desirable. The solution is to reparameterize the curve so that we have constant speed throughout the curve. The parameterization $\mathbf{q}(t) = \mathbf{q}(t(s))$ is known as the arclength parameterization of the curve. The arclength of a curve is given by

$$s(t') = \int_{t_0}^{t'} \sqrt{\left(\frac{dx}{dt}\right)^2 + \left(\frac{dy}{dt}\right)^2 + \left(\frac{dz}{dt}\right)^2} \, dt.$$

There is often no analytical solution to this integral, so the arclength would have to be found numerically. The Trapezoid rule, Simpson's rule or Rhomberg integration can be used to integrate the function numerically depending on the desired accuracy. Computing s is not our primary concern, however. Rather, we wish to compute $t(s)$, the value of t which produces the arclength s. The function $s(t)$ is often not analytic, neither is $t(s)$. We can use the bisection method to numerically find $t(s)$. Start with two guesses of the interval in which t lies. Let the interval be given by $[t_1, t_2]$. Compute the parameter halfway along the interval $t_m = 0.5(t_1 + t_2)$. Compute s_m for this parameter. If $s_m > s$ then apply the bisection method to $[t_1, t_m]$, otherwise, apply the bisection method to $[t_m, t_2]$.

This approach may be time consuming, so forward differencing can be used to quickly determine points on the curve that can be used as estimates for arclength parameterization. The estimate is given by

$$\sum_{k=1}^{n} \|\mathbf{q}(u_k) - \mathbf{q}(u_{k-1})\|.$$

where n is the number of curve segments used to approximate arclength, and u_k are the parameters at which the curve is evaluated. Watt & Watt [138] provide more details.

9.3.2 Orientation

We have already discussed orientation of objects to some extent. We briefly list some of the results.

Rotation matrices can be used to represent the orientation of an object. To do so we need a consistent way to represent the rotation of the object. One technique is to use *Euler angles*. Euler angles represent *yaw*, *pitch* and *roll* angles that correspond to rotation around the y, x and z-axes respectively. We can the specify our angles for an object and it will be rotated accordingly. However, we may encounter *Gimbal Lock* where we lose a degree of freedom. This is due to the limited way in which the orientation is presented.

Quaternions offer an alternative solution to representing rotations. One of the advantages of quaternions is relative simplicity of the calculation. Matrices may also be multiplied in the same way, however. Matrices can also represent translation (which quaternions cannot do). Details regarding quaternions can be found in section 1.5.

In terms of animation, it is relatively easy to construct a quaternion to indicate the direction in which a camera should be looking. One the destination direction has been determined, we can use spherical linear interpolation to smoothly transition from the one view to another. This technique can be used very effectively for a pilot that needs to look over his shoulder.

It is also possible to convert between representations, e.g. between a quaternion and a matrix. We do not have to exclusively use one technique or the other.

9.4 Articulated Structures (Kinematics)

An articulated structure or multibody is a series of rigid links which are joined in a tree structure. We consider joints with 1 degree of freedom. An example of an articulated structure is shown in figure 9.1. We consider the use of *kinematics* for the animation of articulated structures. Kinematics refers to the motion without respect to physical properties such as mass, acceleration etc. We can use one of several techniques to animate articulated structures, namely

- **Forward kinematics** - Given the angles of all joints, determine their positions.

- **Inverse kinematics** - Given the desired position of one or more joints, determine possible angles that satisfy these constraints.

- **Forward dynamics** - Given initial positions, velocities, forces, masses etc. determine the position of each joint at a particular time.

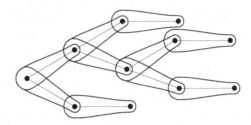

Figure 9.1: An articulated structure.

- **Inverse dynamics** - Given the motion of an object, determine what forces must be applied to the joints to achieve this motion.

Articulated structures are very useful for animation as they allow a structure or skeleton to be used to drive the animation. The skeleton can be used to deform a model.

9.4.1   Forward Kinematics

To describe the position of the model we specify the angle θ_i for each link. The angle is specified relative to the orientation of the parent link. The relative positions of the joints (initial state) are specified by the position vectors $\mathbf{r}_i$.

Using these values we can determine the positions of the joints and *end effectors* $\mathbf{s}_i$ for the articulated structure.

The calculation is trivially performed using the recursive evaluation

$$M_i = M_p R_{\theta_i} T_{\mathbf{r}_i}$$

of the matrix to be applied to each joint. In this case p represents the parent joint, and $T_{\mathbf{r}_i}$ is the translation required to move the joint from the origin into position. The point $\mathbf{s}_i$ is then given by

$$\mathbf{s}_i = M_i \mathbf{0}$$

where $\mathbf{0}$ is the zero vector. This calculation assumes that we are always rotating around the same axis, which is correct for a two-dimensional model. For a three-dimensional model, we need to store the axis of rotation $\mathbf{v}_i$. During recursive evaluation, we first determine the axis of rotation

$$\mathbf{w}_i = M_i \mathbf{v}_i.$$

9.4.2 Vertex Blending

Using the articulated structure we can manipulate a model. We determine which links (or bones) effect each vertex in the mesh representing the object. We might use a cylinder to determine the area of influence of a link. If several links affect a vertex, then we assign a weight w_i to each link for this vertex. The weight might be determined by the distance from the link to the vertex. We have

$$\sum_{i=0}^{n-1} w_i = 1, \quad w_i \geq 0$$

for a particular vertex. The position of the vertex when the articulated structure is moved is a weighted sum of the effect of the individual links, thus

$$\mathbf{v}_t = \sum_{i=0}^{n-1} w_i B_i(t) M_i^{-1} \mathbf{p}$$

where $\mathbf{p}$ is the original vertex, the matrix M_i transforms from link i's coordinate system into the world coordinate system, and the matrix $B_i(t)$ is the transform of the link at time t. B_i can be determined by the formulae in the previous section. Other techniques such as the free form deformation can also be used once the position of the articulated structure has been determined.

9.4.3 Inverse Kinematics

Inverse kinematics attempts to find the angle θ_i such that we obtain a desired set of joint positions $\mathbf{s}_i'$ or angles θ_i' (some may not be specified) given the current state $\mathbf{s}_i$ and θ_i.

We can determine the effect of changing the angles θ_i by a small amount using the *Jacobian* matrix J

$$d\mathbf{X} = J(\Theta)d\Theta$$

where $\mathbf{X}$ is the vector of positions of the joints $\mathbf{s}_i$ and end effectors, and Θ is the current set of angles θ_i. The entries of the Jacobian matrix are given by

$$J_{ij} := \frac{\partial \mathbf{f}_i}{\partial \theta_j}$$

where $\mathbf{f}_i$ is the function that determines $\mathbf{s}_i$ given the angles θ_i. We thus have

$$\mathbf{X} = \mathbf{f}(\Theta).$$

If we can compute the Jacobian matrix, then we can compute the change in angles to achieve the desired position by

$$\Delta\Theta = J^{-1}\Delta\mathbf{X}.$$

The updates angles are given by

$$\Theta' = \Theta + \epsilon\Delta\Theta.$$

We use the ϵ term to try to keep the process numerically stable. We can determine the function $\mathbf{f}$ from the matrix M_i calculated above. Computing the symbolic form of the matrix can be difficult. One option is to use a numerical approximation, but this is likely to be unstable. We can use the formulation above to obtain a simpler technique for calculating the partial derivative. A more suitable option is to use the chain rule.

9.5   Mass Spring Systems

Not all objects are rigid, some objects are deformable. A typical example of a deformable object is a piece of cloth. The same techniques that are applied to rigid objects can be applied to deformable objects. Often the representation of the deformable object differs to accommodate the deformation.

One representation for deformable objects, is the mass spring system. In the mass spring system we have a number of point masses which are connected to other point masses by springs. If we arrange the masses linearly we may approximate a rope. If we arrange the point masses in a grid, then we can approximate a cloth. The springs in the system give flexibility and allow the object to stretch. But, with suitable constants, the springs may also be very rigid.

The force that a spring exerts is given by *Hooke's law*

$$\mathbf{F} = -k\frac{\mathbf{x}}{\|\mathbf{x}\|}(\|\mathbf{x}\| - \ell)$$

where k is the spring constant that determines the force exerted by the spring, ℓ is the rest length of the spring and $\mathbf{x}$ is the position of the end point of the spring under consideration.

The point masses may also be under the influence of gravity or other forces. Using these equations we can determine the motion of a rope or piece of cloth. More sophisticated objects may be simulated in a similar fashion. A cushion may be modeled using a cloth surface, a rigid interior with string springs that connect to the point masses.

9.6 Particle Systems

A number of natural phenomena may be modeled quickly (but not necessarily accurately) by particles. Particles are small objects that are animated under certain rules. These rules may be from physics (for example gravitation) or other suitable rules. Usually a large number of particles are required to produce the desired effect.

A simple example of particles, is a water fountain. A number of water particles are shot into the air and fall back to earth under the effect of gravity and air resistance. A pure physics model can be used in this case. Because there is minimal interaction between the fluid particles in this scenario, it is sufficient to simply model the water as numerous particles. If we want a more realistic simulation of water we may consider using the Navier-Stokes equations.

Fire may also be modeled by particles. In this case, the particles are fired out in the direction of the fire, probably with some turbulent motion until they cool sufficiently to be no longer visible. Instead of removing the particles, the particles may be used to produce smoke.

9.7 Free Form Deformations

Many of the tools described in the previous section used physics to model some environment. The user of such a system has limited control. The free form deformation (FFD) is a tool that allows an animator to choose the shape of an object using conventional tools. The FFD may be used to deform a rigid or soft object. The deformation is totally under the control of the animator and not physics based at all.

The great advantage of the FFD, is that it may be applied to any object and is very simple to implement. Free form deformations have been used successfully as an animation tool, as well as an automated control for more physically realistic applications. FFD's were used successfully for modeling muscles when controlled by a skeleton based kinematic system [138].

The free form deformation is based on Bézier volumes. In the same way that we extend Bézier curves to Bézier surfaces, we can further extend the Bézier surface to a Bézier volume. A Bézier volume is simply given by

$$\mathbf{q}(u,v,w) = \sum_{i=0}^{3}\sum_{j=0}^{3}\sum_{k=0}^{3} B_i(u)B_j(v)B_k(w)\mathbf{p}_{i,j,k}$$

where $\mathbf{p}_{i,j,k}$ are control points for the Bézier volume. Naturally we are not restricted to cubic curves, but this is the form we use for the FFD. There are thus 3 parameters describing the volume. Initially we arrange the control points in a grid fashion so that the boundaries are given by straight lines and planes. The Bézier volume is created so that it surrounds the object to be deformed. The object is represented in the coordinate system of the Bézier volume. For each vertex $\mathbf{s}$ we find s_u, s_v and s_w so that

$$\mathbf{s} = \sum_{i=0}^{3}\sum_{j=0}^{3}\sum_{k=0}^{3} B_i(s_u)B_j(s_v)B_k(s_w)\mathbf{p}_{i,j,k}.$$

We then use these parameters to represent the vertex rather than *world coordinates*. World coordinates are the real location of the points in space. It is trivial to determine these parameters due to the (grid) linear arrangement of the control points.

To deform the object, we simply move the control points of the FFD, thereby moving and warping the space in which the object lies. When we render the object we use the equation

$$\mathbf{q}(u,v,w) = \sum_{i=0}^{3}\sum_{j=0}^{3}\sum_{k=0}^{3} B_i(u)B_j(v)B_k(w)\mathbf{p}_{i,j,k}$$

to convert from the object space (s_u, s_v, s_w) to the world coordinates. The free form deformation can thus be applied to various kinds of objects.

It is important to remember that the space in which the object lies is warped. Straight lines in object space are not necessarily straight in the warped space produced by the FFD. We cannot necessarily just transform the control points. Rather the rendering process should be carefully controlled.

9.8 Fluids

The realistic animation of fluids is a complex task requiring knowledge of fluid mechanics. Particle systems can provide interesting fluid animations

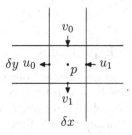

Figure 9.2: A fluid cell in the MAC-grid.

but seldom yield the same results as physically based fluid simulations. In this section we examine a two-dimensional fluid simulator as presented by Stam [121]. This simulator can be extended to handle free surfaces [29, 2], rigid bodies [11], or could even be modified to simulate smoke [33, 87]. There are several articles available that provide good summaries of the techniques involved [121, 57].

A number of properties must be known about fluid to be able to model the motion of fluid effectively. The most important property is the velocity of the fluid. The velocity at each point of the fluid must be known to be able to determine the velocities at each position during the next time step. It is thus necessary to store the velocities in a *vector field*. A simple approach is to divide the two-dimensional space into a grid, and store the properties of the fluid at the center of each grid cell [121, 57]. Another popular technique is the marker and cell method [56] (known as a MAC grid). In this case the velocites are stored at the edges of the cell (these velocities are stored at the faces of the cell for a three-dimensional simulation), and all other quantities are stored in the center of the cell. The marker and cell method is illustrated in figure 9.2. The left and right edges store the velocity in the horizontal direction at the middle of the edge. The upper and lower edges store the velocity in the vertical direction at the middle of the edge. The center of the cell stores the pressure of the fluid in the cell, and any other attributes that are required. The arrows illustrate the direction of the flow, horizontal or vertical. The velocity field is denoted $\mathbf{u}_{i,j} = (u_{i,j} \ v_{i,j})^T$. The width and height of the cell are δx and δy, respectively. If pressure is stored at the center of the cell then there are $n \times n$ pressure values, $(n + 1) \times n$ horizontal velocities and $n \times (n + 1)$ vertical velocities where n is the selected grid size.

Next we consider the Navier-Stokes equations to describe the physical motion of the fluid.

9.8.1   Navier-Stokes Equations

To simplify the fluid simulation we assume an incompressible, homogeneous fluid. A fluid is homogeneous if its density ρ is constant over space. The fluid is incompressible if the volume of fluid is constant over time. The *Navier-Stokes equations* for incompressible flow state that

$$\frac{\partial \mathbf{u}}{\partial t} = -(\mathbf{u} \cdot \nabla)\mathbf{u} - \frac{1}{\rho}\nabla p + \nu\nabla^2\mathbf{u} + \mathbf{F}$$

and

$$\nabla \cdot \mathbf{u} = 0$$

where ρ is the fluid density, ν is the kinematic viscosity and $\mathbf{F}$ is an external force acting on the fluid (such as gravity). The terms of the first equation represent forces acting on the fluid. These terms are

- **Advection** – The velocity of the fluid transports quantities in the direction of the fluid flow, which is determined the velocity field. The velocity itself is also *advected* by this field.

- **Pressure** – Force applied to a fluid is not propagated directly through the fluid. Rather the molecules are compressed and they intern exert forces on neighboring particles. These forces are captured in the pressure term. A pressure gradient will cause acceleration in the fluid.

- **Diffusion** – The *viscosity* of a fluid determines how easily the fluid flows past itself. A slow flowing fluid has high viscosity and the momentum is *diffused*.

- **External forces** – Fluid is usually under the influence of forces other than those that originate within the fluid. These forces include gravity, wind or simply forces put in place by an animator to achieve a desired effect.

The second equation enforces conservation of mass and prevents divergence in the system. This equation ensures that no fluid exits a cell if it does not enter another cell.

The operators in the Navier-Stokes equations in two dimensions are as follows

- *Gradient* –

$$\nabla p := \left(\frac{\partial p}{\partial x} \ \frac{\partial p}{\partial y}\right)^T .$$

- *Divergence –*

$$\nabla \cdot \mathbf{u} := \frac{\partial u}{\partial x} + \frac{\partial v}{\partial y}.$$

- *Laplacian –*

$$\nabla^2 p := \frac{\partial^2 p}{\partial x^2} + \frac{\partial^2 p}{\partial y^2}.$$

We also have the differential operator

$$\mathbf{u} \cdot \nabla := u\frac{\partial}{\partial x} + v\frac{\partial}{\partial y}$$

where $\mathbf{u} = (u \ v)^T$. The marker and cell method simplifies the finite difference form of these operators.

The *Helmholtz-Hodge Decomposition theorem* states that any vector field can be decomposed into the sum of two vector fields, namely a divergence-free vector field and the gradient of a scalar field. We can thus compute a new velocity field with divergence and then subtract the gradient of the pressure field to correct the divergence. The divergence free velocity field is given by

$$\mathbf{u} = \mathbf{w} - \nabla p$$

where $\mathbf{w}$ is the velocity field with divergence. We now have

$$\nabla \cdot \mathbf{w} = \nabla \cdot (\mathbf{u} + \nabla p) = \nabla \cdot \mathbf{u} + \nabla^2 p.$$

But conservation of mass requires that $\nabla \cdot \mathbf{u} = 0$. Thus we obtain the *Poisson equation*

$$\nabla^2 p = \nabla \cdot \mathbf{w}.$$

We can thus project a velocity field $\mathbf{w}$ onto its divergence free-component $\mathbf{u}$.

9.8.2 Advection

Advection describes the force exerted on a particle of fluid by the particles of fluid surrounding it. Advection represents the transport of fluid properties at a definite rate and direction, that of the fluid velocity, so that parcel trajectories are the characterisitics of the advection equation. To transport properties throught the fluid with advection the explicit scheme

$$\mathbf{q}(t + \delta t) = \mathbf{q}(t) + \mathbf{u}(t)\delta t$$

can be used where $\mathbf{q}$ is the new position of the quantity. The properties are transported forward in time to their new location. This scheme is unstable for large timesteps, so we rather use an implicit scheme [121]

$$\mathbf{q}(\mathbf{p}, t + \delta t) = \mathbf{q}(\mathbf{p} - \mathbf{u}(\mathbf{p}, t)\delta t), t).$$

The implicit scheme searches backwards in time to determine where the property for the next time step came from. This scheme is stable for arbitrarily large timesteps.

9.8.3   Diffusion

The viscous diffusion equation is given by

$$\frac{\partial \mathbf{u}}{\partial t} = \nu \nabla^2 \mathbf{u}$$

which can be discretised into an explicit form

$$\mathbf{u}(\mathbf{p}, t + \delta t) = \mathbf{u}(\mathbf{p}, t) + \nu \delta t \nabla^2 \mathbf{u}(\mathbf{p}, t).$$

To obtain an algorithm that is stable for large timesteps, the equation is rather discretised in implicit form [121]

$$(I - \nu \delta t \nabla^2) \mathbf{u}(\mathbf{p}, t + \delta t) = \mathbf{u}(\mathbf{p}, t)$$

where I is the identity matrix. This is a Poisson equation which can be expressed as the system of equations $A\mathbf{x} = \mathbf{b}$. In this case, $\mathbf{x}$ are the unknown variables $\mathbf{u}(\mathbf{p}, t + \delta t)$ and the known values $\mathbf{b}$ are the velocities $\mathbf{u}(\mathbf{p}, t)$. Poisson equations can be solved using Jacobi iteration or Gauss-Seidel iteration.

9.8.4   Projection

The projection step is repsonsible for ensuring that the vector field is divergence free, that is no fluid is being created or destroyed as a result of the simulation. The *Helmholtz-Hodge Decomposition Theorem* gives the equation

$$\nabla^2 p = \nabla \cdot \mathbf{w}$$

which can be used to determine the pressure field (a scalar field) from a divergent velocity field $\mathbf{w}$ which is obtained after advection and diffusion. This equation is also a Poisson equation and can be solved byt Jacobi iteration after discretization. After the pressure field has been determined, a divergence free velocity field is created using the equation

$$\mathbf{u} = \mathbf{w} - \nabla p.$$

Projection is only relevant to the velocity field, but advection and diffusion can be used to transport both velocity and other quantities (such as dye) through the fluid.

9.8.5 Boundary Conditions

Not all cells in the grid correspond to fluid. A more flexible fluid simulator allows the introduction of boundary conditions. That is, physical walls or obstructions are introduced in particular fluid cells. Naturally the fluid cannot cross a boundary. It is thus necessary to ensure that the velocity across a boundary is always zero. Boundaries are restricted to the walls of cells and so only one component of the velocity needs to be considered at a boundary. During the solution of the Poisson equations the velocity at boundaries are set to zero in the direction across the boundary. There are a few options for the velocity in the direction parallel to the boundary.

- Free slip - In this case the boundary has no friction and the velocity in the parallel direction remains unaltered.

- No slip - In this case friction slows the fluid down so that the parallel velocity at the interface between the fluid is set to zero. It may be necessary to set the fluid velocity at the opposite side of the cell to the negative of the parallel velocity of the fluid, so that the resulting velocity at the boundary is zero. This depends on the selected implementation, whether velocities are stored at the center of the fluid, or at the boundaries of each cell.

9.8.6 C# Implementation

The Poisson equations are solved using the Jacobi method. No matrix is used during the Jacobi iteration since the structure and coeffcients can be determined drectly from the fluid data structures. Dye density is advected and diffused through the fluid to visualize the velocity fields. The left mouse button is used to add velocity to the velocity field, and the right mouse button adds dye to the fluid. There is no free surface, the fluid fills the entire volume.

```
//Fluid.cs
using System;
using System.Threading;
using System.Collections.Generic;
using System.Drawing;
using System.Windows.Forms;

namespace fluid_mac
```

```
{
   public class FluidSolver {
      public double[,] vx, vy, dye;
      //pressure is stored to provide a good initial
      // guess for iteration methods
      public double[,] pressure;
      public bool[,] surface, fluid, boundary;
      private int i, j;
      public double dt=0.1;
      public double eps1=0.01f, eps2=0.02f;
      public int n=32;
      public double visc=0.0;
      public int maxiter=120;
      public double minerr=1e-5;
      public double dw, idw; //idw=1/dw

      public void Initialize() {
         vx=new double[n+1,n]; vy=new double[n,n+1];
         dye=new double[n,n];
         pressure=new double[n,n];
         surface=new bool[n,n];
         boundary=new bool[n,n];
         fluid=new bool[n,n];
         dw=1.0/n; idw=1.0/dw;
         for(i=0;i<n;i++) {
            for(j=0;j<n;j++) {
               if((i==0)||(i==n-1)||(j==0)||(j==n-1)) boundary[i,j]=true;
               else { boundary[i,j]=false; }
               surface[i,j]=false;
               fluid[i,j]=true; dye[i,j]=0.0; pressure[i,j]=0.0;
            }
         }
         for(i=0;i<n+1;i++)
            for(j=0;j<n;j++) vx[i,j]=0.0;
         for(i=0;i<n;i++)
            for(j=0;j<n+1;j++) vy[i,j]=0.0;
      }

      public void set_bounds_x(double[,] vxnew) {
         for(int i=0;i<n+1;i++) {
            for(int j=0;j<n;j++) {
               if(i-1>=0) if(boundary[i-1,j]) vxnew[i,j]=0.0;
               if(i+1<n) if(boundary[i+1,j]) vxnew[i,j]=0.0;
            }
         }
      }

      public void set_bounds_y(double[,] vynew) {
         int i, j;
         for(i=0;i<n;i++) {
            for(j=0;j<n+1;j++) {
```

```
                if(j-1>=0) if(boundary[i,j-1]) vynew[i,j]=0.0;
                if(j+1<n) if(boundary[i,j+1]) vynew[i,j]=0.0;
            }
        }
    }

    public void vel_diffuse() {
        double a=dt*visc*idw*idw;
        double c=1+4.0*a, diff=10.0, dv;
        int iter=maxiter;
        double[,] vxnew, vynew;
        vxnew=new double[n+1,n]; vynew=new double[n,n+1];

        //gauss seidel
        //initial guess is current velocities
        for(i=0;i<n+1;i++)
            for(j=0;j<n;j++) vxnew[i,j]=vx[i,j];
        for(i=0;i<n;i++)
            for(j=0;j<n+1;j++) vynew[i,j]=vy[i,j];

        //x and y velocities are done in two steps
        //first x
        while((diff>minerr)&&(0<iter--)) {
            diff=0.0f;
            for(i=1;i<n;i++) {
                for(j=1;j<n-1;j++) {
                    dv=vxnew[i,j];
                    vxnew[i,j]=(vx[i,j]+a*(vxnew[i-1,j]+
                        vxnew[i+1,j]+vxnew[i,j-1]+vxnew[i,j+1]))/c;
                    dv-=vxnew[i,j];
                    diff+=dv*dv;
                }
            }
            set_bounds_x(vxnew);
        }

        diff=10.0f;
        iter=maxiter;
        //then y
        while((diff>minerr)&&(0<iter--)) {
            diff=0.0f;
            for(i=1;i<n-1;i++) {
                for(j=1;j<n;j++) {
                    dv=vynew[i,j];
                    vynew[i,j]=(vy[i,j]+a*(vynew[i-1,j]+
                        vynew[i+1,j]+vynew[i,j-1]+vynew[i,j+1]))/c;
                    dv-=vxnew[i,j];
                    diff+=dv*dv;
                }
            }
            set_bounds_y(vynew);
```

```
      }
      vx=vxnew; vy=vynew;
}

public void dense_diffuse() {
    double a=dt*visc*idw*idw;
    double c=1+4.0f*a;
    double diff=10.0f;
    double dd;
    int iter=maxiter;
    double[,] dyenew=new double[n,n];

    //initial guess is current values
    for(i=0;i<n;i++)
       for(j=0;j<n;j++) dyenew[i,j]=dye[i,j];
    //gauss seidel
    while((diff>minerr)&&(0<iter--)) {
       diff=0.0;
       for(i=1;i<n-1;i++) {
          for(j=1;j<n-1;j++) {
             dd=dyenew[i,j];
             dyenew[i,j]=(dye[i,j]+a*(dyenew[i-1,j]+
             dyenew[i+1,j]+dyenew[i,j-1]+dyenew[i,j+1]))/c;
             dd-=dyenew[i,j];
             diff+=dd*dd;
          }
       }
    }
    dye=dyenew;
}

public void vel_advect() {
    Vector from;
    int x1, y1, x2, y2;
    double s1,s2,t1,t2,viy,vix;
    double dt0=dt*idw;
    Vector v;
    double[,] vxnew, vynew;
    vxnew=new double[n+1,n];
    vynew=new double[n,n+1];

    //x and y velocities are done in two steps
    //first x
    for(i=0;i<n+1;i++) {
       for(j=0;j<n;j++) {
          if((i>0)&&(i<n)) viy=(vy[i,j]+vy[i,j+1]+
             vy[i-1,j]+vy[i-1,j+1])/4.0;
          else if(i==n) viy=(vy[i-1,j]+vy[i-1,j+1])/2.0;
          else viy=(vy[i,j]+vy[i,j+1])/2.0;
          v=new Vector(vx[i,j],viy,0);
          from=new Vector(i,j,0)-v*dt0;
```

```
            x1=(int)from.x;  x2=x1+1;  y1=(int)from.y;  y2=y1+1;
            if(x1<0)  x1=0;  if(x1>=n+1)  x1=n;
            if(x2<0)  x2=0;  if(x2>=n+1)  x2=n;
            if(y1<0)  y1=0;  if(y1>=n)  y1=n-1;
            if(y2<0)  y2=0;  if(y2>=n)  y2=n-1;
            s1=(double)from.x-x1;  s2=1.0f-s1;
            t1=(double)from.y-y1;  t2=1.0f-t1;
            vxnew[i,j]=t1*(s1*vx[x2,y2]+s2*vx[x1,y2])+
               t2*(s1*vx[x2,y1]+s2*vx[x1,y1]);
        }
    }
    //then y
    for(i=0;i<n;i++) {
        for(j=0;j<n+1;j++) {
            if((j>0)&&(j<n))  vix=(vx[i,j]+vx[i+1,j]+
               vx[i,j-1]+vx[i+1,j-1])/4.0;
            else if(j==n)  vix=(vx[i,j-1]+vx[i+1,j-1])/2.0;
            else vix=(vx[i,j]+vx[i+1,j])/2.0;
            v=new Vector(vix,vy[i,j],0);
            from=new Vector(i,j,0)-v*dt0;
            x1=(int)from.x;  x2=x1+1;  y1=(int)from.y;  y2=y1+1;
            if(x1<0)  x1=0;  if(x1>=n)  x1=n-1;
            if(x2<0)  x2=0;  if(x2>=n)  x2=n-1;
            if(y1<0)  y1=0;  if(y1>=n+1)  y1=n;
            if(y2<0)  y2=0;  if(y2>=n+1)  y2=n;
            s1=(double)from.x-x1;  s2=1.0f-s1;
            t1=(double)from.y-y1;  t2=1.0f-t1;
            vynew[i,j]=t1*(s1*vy[x2,y2]+s2*vy[x1,y2])+
               t2*(s1*vy[x2,y1]+s2*vy[x1,y1]);
        }
    }
    vx=vxnew;  vy=vynew;
    set_bounds_x(vx);  set_bounds_y(vy);
}

public void dense_advect() {
    Vector from, v;
    int x1, y1, x2, y2;
    double s1,s2,t1,t2,vix,viy;
    double dt0=dt*idw;
    double[,] dyenew;
    dyenew=new double[n,n];
    for(i=0;i<n;i++) {
        for(j=0;j<n;j++) {
            vix=(vx[i,j]+vx[i+1,j])/2.0;  viy=(vy[i,j]+vy[i,j+1])/2.0;
            v=new Vector(vix,viy,0);
            from=new Vector(i,j,0)-v*dt0;
            x1=(int)from.x;  x2=x1+1;  y1=(int)from.y;  y2=y1+1;
            if(x1<0)  x1=0;  if(x1>=n)  x1=n-1;
            if(x2<0)  x2=0;  if(x2>=n)  x2=n-1;
            if(y1<0)  y1=0;  if(y1>=n)  y1=n-1;
```

```
            if(y2<0) y2=0; if(y2>=n) y2=n-1;
            s1=(double)from.x-x1; s2=1.0f-s1;
            t1=(double)from.y-y1; t2=1.0f-t1;
            dyenew[i,j]=t1*(s1*dye[x2,y2]+s2*dye[x1,y2])+
                t2*(s1*dye[x2,y1]+s2*dye[x1,y1]);
        }
    }
    dye=dyenew;
}

public void project() {
    double a=1.0f, c=4.0f, diff=10.0, dp;
    int iter=maxiter;
    double[,] pressurenew=new double[n,n];

    for(i=0;i<n;i++)
        for(j=0;j<n;j++) pressurenew[i,j]=pressure[i,j];
    //compute b=grad.w, b will be stored in pressure
    for(i=0;i<n;i++)
        for(j=0;j<n;j++)
            pressure[i,j]=-((vx[i+1,j]-vx[i,j])
            +(vy[i,j+1]-vy[i,j]));
    //gauss seidel
    while((diff>minerr)&&(0<iter--)) {
        diff=0.0;
        for(i=1;i<n-1;i++) {
            for(j=1;j<n-1;j++) {
                dp=pressurenew[i,j];
                pressurenew[i,j]=(pressure[i,j]+
                    a*(pressurenew[i-1,j]+pressurenew[i+1,j]+
                    pressurenew[i,j-1]+pressurenew[i,j+1]))/c;
                dp-=pressurenew[i,j];
                diff+=dp*dp;
            }
        }
    }

    pressure=pressurenew;
    for(i=1;i<n;i++)
        for(j=0;j<n;j++)
            vx[i,j]-=(pressure[i,j]-pressure[i-1,j]);

    for(i=0;i<n;i++)
        for(j=1;j<n;j++)
            vy[i,j]-=(pressure[i,j]-pressure[i,j-1]);

    set_bounds_x(vx); set_bounds_y(vy);
}

//Add some gravity. The additional force slows down the simulation
public void force() {
```

```
   for(i=0;i<n;i++)
      for(j=0;j<n;j++) if(fluid[i,j]) vy[i,j+1]+=0.03f*dt;
}

public void dense_step() { dense_diffuse(); dense_advect(); }

public void vel_step() {
   vel_diffuse();
   project();
   vel_advect();
   //uncomment the next line to add gravitational force
   //force();
   project();
}

public void RunFluid() { vel_step(); dense_step(); }
}

public partial class MainForm
{
   public FluidSolver fl;
   Thread thread;
   public bool quit=false;
   [STAThread]
   public static void Main(string[] args) {
      Application.EnableVisualStyles();
      Application.SetCompatibleTextRenderingDefault(false);
      Application.Run(new MainForm());
   }

   void ThreadStart() {
      while(!quit) { PicFluid.Invalidate(); Thread.Sleep(10); }
   }


   public MainForm() {
      InitializeComponent();
      fl=new FluidSolver();
      fl.Initialize();
      //rnd=new Random();
      thread=new Thread(this.ThreadStart);
      thread.Start();
   }

   void Draw(Graphics gfx,double x,double y,double r,
         double g,double b) {
      Pen pen=new Pen(Brushes.Black);
      pen.Color=Color.FromArgb(255,(int)(r*255),(int)(g*255),(int)(b*255));
      Brush brush=new SolidBrush(pen.Color);
      float rx=(float)x/fl.n*PicFluid.Width;
      float ry=(float)y/fl.n*PicFluid.Height;
```

```
    float w=PicFluid.Width/fl.n;
    float h=PicFluid.Height/fl.n;
    gfx.FillRectangle(brush,rx,ry,w,h);
}

void DrawVector(Graphics gfx,double x,double y,Vector v,
      double r,double g,double b) {
    Pen pen=new Pen(Brushes.Black);
    pen.Color=Color.FromArgb(255,(int)(r*255),(int)(g*255),(int)(b*255));
    float rx=(float)(x+0.5f)/fl.n*PicFluid.Width;
    float ry=(float)(y+0.5f)/fl.n*PicFluid.Height;
    float w=PicFluid.Width/fl.n;
    float h=PicFluid.Height/fl.n;
    gfx.DrawLine(pen,rx,ry,rx+(float)v.x*15.0f,
      ry+(float)v.y*15.0f);
}

public int ox, oy, mx, my;
public bool left=false, right=false;

void MainFormFormClosed(object sender,FormClosedEventArgs e)
{ quit=true; thread.Join(); }

void PicFluidMouseDown(object sender,MouseEventArgs e) {
    ox=(int)(fl.n*e.X/PicFluid.Width);
    oy=(int)(fl.n*e.Y/PicFluid.Height);
    mx=ox; my=oy;
    if(e.Button==MouseButtons.Left) left=true;
    else right=false;
    if(e.Button==MouseButtons.Right) right=true;
    else right=false;
    PicFluid.Invalidate();
}

void PicFluidMouseMove(object sender,MouseEventArgs e) {
    mx=(int)(fl.n*e.X/PicFluid.Width);
    my=(int)(fl.n*e.Y/PicFluid.Height);
    if(e.Button==MouseButtons.Left) left=true;
    else right=false;
    if(e.Button==MouseButtons.Right) right=true;
    else right=false;
    PicFluid.Invalidate();
}

void PicFluidMouseUp(object sender,MouseEventArgs e) {
    ox=(int)(fl.n*e.X/PicFluid.Width);
    oy=(int)(fl.n*e.Y/PicFluid.Height);
    mx=ox; my=oy;
    left=false; right=false;
    PicFluid.Invalidate();
}
```

```
void PicFluidPaint(object sender,PaintEventArgs e) {
    int i, j;
    double d;
    Vector v;
    if((mx!=ox)||(my!=oy)) {
        if(left) fl.vx[mx,my]+=(mx-ox)*100.0*fl.dw/PicFluid.Width;
        if(left) fl.vy[mx,my]+=(my-oy)*100.0*fl.dw/PicFluid.Height;
    }
    if(right) fl.dye[mx,my]+=5.0f;
    fl.RunFluid();
    for(i=0;i<fl.n;i++) {
        for(j=0;j<fl.n;j++) {
            d=fl.dye[i,j];
            if(d<0.0) d=0.0; if(d>1.0) d=1.0;
            if(fl.boundary[i,j]) Draw(e.Graphics,i,j,0.0,1.0,0.0);
            else Draw(e.Graphics,i,j,0.0,0.0,d);
            v=new Vector(0.5*(fl.vx[i,j]+fl.vx[i+1,j]),
            0.5*(fl.vy[i,j]+fl.vy[i,j+1]), 0);
            DrawVector(e.Graphics,i,j,v,1.0,0.0,0.0);
        }
    }
}
```

9.8.7   Free Surface

The fluid presented so far have no interface with the air. To create a free surface the location of the fluid within the grid must be determined. At the beginning of the simulation a number of particles are created within the fluid [40]. At each time step the particles are moved using the velocities stored in the vector field. The velocities are not stored at the precise locations of the particles, and so the velocities must be interpolated to obtain a velocity for the particle. The particle moves under the Newtonian laws. The grid is examined at the end of each timestep to determine which cells have fluid and which contain air. Cells that contain at least one particle are regarded as fluid cells. Otherwise the cell is an air cell.

If a particle moves into a cell, then the velocities in the cell must be initialized to be appropriate for the fluid motion.

The simulation must be adapted for the interface between the air and the fluid to try to prevent the dissipation of fluid volume, or the creation of

fluid. Boundary conditions must thus be applied at the free surface interface to ensure that there is no divergence.

Inflow and outflow boundaries can be created by ensuring that the velocity
in a cell is maintained thus creating a divergence. This divergence creates
fluid, or removes fluid from the simulation. It is very important that particles be introduced into the simulation at these points to ensure that surface
tracking is accurate.

Higher quality surfaces can be obtained using level-set methods [29] or
semi-Lagrangian contouring [2].

9.8.8 C# Implementation of Free Surfaces

A large part of the implementation of the free surface is omitted because it
is so similar to the conventional fluid simulation with no free surface. The
most significant changes involve surface tracking with particle physics, and
changes to the projection method to deal with the free surface. The right
mouse button is used to add boundaries, and the left mouse button is used
to toggle fluid in the grid. Omitted code is indicated by three vertical dots.

```
// FluidSurface.cs
using System;
using System.Threading;
using System.Collections.Generic;
using System.Drawing;
using System.Windows.Forms;

namespace fluid_mac
{
    public class FluidSolver {
        :
        :
        // Omitted code
        :
        :
        public double dw, idw; //idw=1/dw
        public double w=1.0;
        public Vector[] particles;
        public Vector[] pv; //particle velocity (to initialize cells only)
        public int np; //number of particles
        public int px=3, py=3;

        public void Initialize() {
            :
            :
            // Omitted code
```

```
                    ⋮
    particles=new Vector[n*n*px*py];
    pv=new Vector[n*n*px*py];

    rnd=new Random();

    np=0;
                    ⋮
    // Omitted code
                    ⋮
                    ⋮
}

public void set_surface(double[,] vxn,double[,] vyn) {
    int i, j, c;
    double v, b=0.0;
    for(i=1;i<n-1;i++) {
        for(j=1;j<n-1;j++) {
            if(surface[i,j]) {
                c=0; b=0.0;
                //calculate candidate cells for redistribution of divergence
                if(!fluid[i-1,j]&&!boundary[i-1,j]) c++;
                if(!fluid[i+1,j]&&!boundary[i+1,j]) c++;
                if(!fluid[i,j-1]&&!boundary[i,j-1]) c++;
                if(!fluid[i,j+1]&&!boundary[i,j+1]) c++;
                if(c!=0) { //compute divergence
                    b=0.0;
                    b-=vxn[i,j]; b+=vxn[i+1,j];
                    b-=vyn[i,j]; b+=vyn[i,j+1];
                    v=b/c;
                    //redistribute velocity
                    if(!fluid[i-1,j]&&!boundary[i-1,j]) vxn[i,j]+=v;
                    if(!fluid[i+1,j]&&!boundary[i+1,j]) vxn[i+1,j]+=-v;
                    if(!fluid[i,j-1]&&!boundary[i,j-1]) vyn[i,j]+=v;
                    if(!fluid[i,j+1]&&!boundary[i,j+1]) vyn[i,j+1]+=-v;
                }
            }
        }
    }
}

public void vel_diffuse() {
                    ⋮
    // Omitted code
                    ⋮
                    ⋮
    //The following is called whenever set_bounds is called
    set_surface(vxnew,vynew);
```

```
          ⋮
     // Omitted code
          ⋮
}

public void vel_advect() {
          ⋮
     // Omitted code
          ⋮

     // The following is called whenever set_bounds is called
     set_surface(vx,vy);
          ⋮
     // Omitted code
          ⋮
}

public void project() {
     double a=1.0f, c=4.0f, diff=10.0;
     double dp;
     int iter=maxiter;
     double[,] pressurenew;
     double[,] adj;
     pressurenew=new double[n,n];
     adj=new double[n,n];

     for(i=0;i<n;i++)
          for(j=0;j<n;j++) pressurenew[i,j]=pressure[i,j];
     //compute b=grad.w, b will be stored in pressure
     for(i=0;i<n;i++)
          for(j=0;j<n;j++)
               if(fluid[i,j]) pressure[i,j]=-((vx[i+1,j]-vx[i,j])
                    +(vy[i,j+1]-vy[i,j]));
               else pressure[i,j]=0.0;
     for(i=1;i<n-1;i++) {
          for(j=1;j<n-1;j++) {
               adj[i,j]=0.0;
               if(!boundary[i-1,j]) adj[i,j]+=1.0;
               if(!boundary[i+1,j]) adj[i,j]+=1.0;
               if(!boundary[i,j-1]) adj[i,j]+=1.0;
               if(!boundary[i,j+1]) adj[i,j]+=1.0;
          }
     }
     //gauss seidel
     while((diff>minerr)&&(0<iter--)) {
          diff=0.0;
          for(i=1;i<n-1;i++) {
```

```
        for(j=1;j<n-1;j++) {
            dp=pressurenew[i,j]; c=adj[i,j];
            if(c>0.0) {
                pressurenew[i,j]=pressure[i,j];
                if(!boundary[i-1,j])
                    pressurenew[i,j]+=a*pressurenew[i-1,j];
                if(!boundary[i+1,j])
                    pressurenew[i,j]+=a*pressurenew[i+1,j];
                if(!boundary[i,j-1])
                    pressurenew[i,j]+=a*pressurenew[i,j-1];
                if(!boundary[i,j+1])
                    pressurenew[i,j]+=a*pressurenew[i,j+1];
                pressurenew[i,j]/=c;
            }
            if(!fluid[i,j]) pressurenew[i,j]=0.0;
            dp-=pressurenew[i,j];
            diff+=dp*dp;
        }
    }
}

pressure=pressurenew;
for(i=1;i<n;i++)
    for(j=0;j<n;j++)
        vx[i,j]-=(pressure[i,j]-pressure[i-1,j]);

for(i=0;i<n;i++)
    for(j=1;j<n;j++)
        vy[i,j]-=(pressure[i,j]-pressure[i,j-1]);
set_bounds_x(vx); set_bounds_y(vy); set_surface(vx,vy);
}

public void compute_surface() {
    for(int i=1;i<n-1;i++) {
        for(int j=1;j<n-1;j++) {
            surface[i,j]=false;
            if((!boundary[i,j])&&(fluid[i,j])) {
                if((!fluid[i-1,j])&&(!boundary[i-1,j])) surface[i,j]=true;
                if((!fluid[i+1,j])&&(!boundary[i+1,j])) surface[i,j]=true;
                if((!fluid[i,j-1])&&(!boundary[i,j-1])) surface[i,j]=true;
                if((!fluid[i,j+1])&&(!boundary[i,j+1])) surface[i,j]=true;
            }
        }
    }
}

public void create_particles() {
    for(int i=0;i<n;i++) {
        for(int j=0;j<n;j++) {
            if(fluid[i,j]) {
                for(int x=0;x<px;x++) {
```

```
                  for(int y=0;y<py;y++) {
                     particles[np]=new Vector((double)x/px+i,
                        (double)y/py+j,0);
                     particles[np].x+=rnd.NextDouble()/px;
                     particles[np].y+=rnd.NextDouble()/py;
                     pv[np]=new Vector();
                     np++;
                  }
               }
            }
         }
      }
   }
}

public void particle_physics() {
   int x1, y1, x2, y2;
   double s1,s2,t1,t2,pvx,pvy;
   double dt0=dt*idw;
   for(int i=0;i<np;i++) {
      x1=(int)particles[i].x;  x2=x1+1;
      y1=(int)(particles[i].y-0.5);  y2=y1+1;
      if(x1<0) x1=0; if(x1>=n+1) x1=n;
      if(x2<0) x2=0; if(x2>=n+1) x2=n;
      if(y1<0) y1=0; if(y1>=n) y1=n-1;
      if(y2<0) y2=0; if(y2>=n) y2=n-1;
      s1=(double)particles[i].x-x1;  s2=1.0f-s1;
      t1=(double)(particles[i].y-0.5)-y1;  t2=1.0f-t1;
      pvx=t1*(s1*vx[x2,y2]+s2*vx[x1,y2])+
         t2*(s1*vx[x2,y1]+s2*vx[x1,y1]);
      x1=(int)(particles[i].x-0.5);  x2=x1+1;
      y1=(int)particles[i].y;  y2=y1+1;
      if(x1<0) x1=0; if(x1>=n) x1=n-1;
      if(x2<0) x2=0; if(x2>=n) x2=n-1;
      if(y1<0) y1=0; if(y1>=n+1) y1=n;
      if(y2<0) y2=0; if(y2>=n+1) y2=n;
      s1=(double)(particles[i].x-0.5)-x1;  s2=1.0f-s1;
      t1=(double)particles[i].y-y1;  t2=1.0f-t1;
      pvy=t1*(s1*vy[x2,y2]+s2*vy[x1,y2])+
         t2*(s1*vy[x2,y1]+s2*vy[x1,y1]);
      particles[i].x+=pvx*dt0;
      particles[i].y+=pvy*dt0;
      pv[i].x=pvx;
      pv[i].y=pvy;
   }
}

public void compute_fluid() {
   int i, j, x1, y1;
   bool[,] fluidnew=new bool[n,n];
   double s1, t1, s2, t2;
   for(i=0;i<n;i++)
```

```
      for(j=0;j<n;j++) fluidnew[i,j]=false;
   for(i=0;i<np;i++) {
      x1=(int)particles[i].x; y1=(int)particles[i].y;
      if(x1<0) x1=0; if(x1>=n) x1=n-1;
      if(y1<0) y1=0; if(y1>=n) y1=n-1;
      s1=particles[i].x-x1; s2=1.0-s1;
      t1=particles[i].y-y1; t2=1.0-t1;
      if(!boundary[x1,y1]) fluidnew[x1,y1]=true;
      else { particles[i].x=x1; particles[i].y=y1; }
   }
   fluid=fluidnew;
}

public void calc_safe_dt() {
   int i, j;
   double stp;
   dt=maxdt;
   for(i=0;i<n+1;i++)
      for(j=0;j<n;j++) { stp=Math.Abs(dw/vx[i,j]); if(stp<dt) dt=stp; }
   for(i=0;i<n;i++)
      for(j=0;j<n+1;j++) { stp=Math.Abs(dw/vy[i,j]); if(stp<dt) dt=stp; }
   dt/=2.0;
}

public void dense_step() { dense_diffuse(); dense_advect(); }

public void clear_air_velocity() {
   int i,j;
   for(i=1;i<n;i++)
      for(j=0;j<n;j++)
         if(!fluid[i-1,j]&&!boundary[i-1,j]
            &&!fluid[i,j]&&!boundary[i,j]) vx[i,j]=0.0;
   for(i=0;i<n;i++)
      for(j=1;j<n;j++)
         if(!fluid[i,j-1]&&!boundary[i,j-1]
            &&!fluid[i,j]&&!boundary[i,j]) vy[i,j]=0.0;
}

public void vel_step() {
   clear_air_velocity();
   vel_diffuse(); project();
   vel_advect(); force();
   set_bounds_x(vx); set_bounds_y(vy); set_surface(vx,vy);
   project();
   set_bounds_x(vx); set_bounds_y(vy); set_surface(vx,vy);
}

public void RunFluid() {
   calc_safe_dt();
   compute_fluid(); compute_surface();
   vel_step(); dense_step();
```

```
            particle_physics(); t+=dt;
     }
}

public partial class MainForm
{
   public FluidSolver fl;
   Thread thread;
   public bool quit=false;
   [STAThread]
   public static void Main(string[] args) {
      Application.EnableVisualStyles();
      Application.SetCompatibleTextRenderingDefault(false);
      Application.Run(new MainForm());
   }

   void ThreadStart() {
      while(!quit) { PicFluid.Invalidate(); Thread.Sleep(10); }
   }


   public MainForm() {
      InitializeComponent();
      fl=new FluidSolver();
      fl.Initialize();
      thread=new Thread(this.ThreadStart);
      thread.Start();
   }
      .
      .
      .
   // Omitted code

      .
      .
      .
   void DrawParticle(Graphics gfx,double x,double y,
         double r,double g,double b) {
      Pen pen=new Pen(Brushes.Black);
      pen.Color=Color.FromArgb(255,(int)(r*255),(int)(g*255),
         (int)(b*255));
      float rx=(float)(x)/fl.n*PicFluid.Width;
      float ry=(float)(y)/fl.n*PicFluid.Height;
      float w=PicFluid.Width/fl.n;
      float h=PicFluid.Height/fl.n;
      gfx.DrawLine(pen,rx,ry,rx+0.5f,ry);
   }

   public int ox, oy, mx, my;
   public bool left=false, right=false, active=false;

   void MainFormFormClosed(object sender,FormClosedEventArgs e)
   { quit=true; thread.Join(); }
```

```
void PicFluidMouseDown(object sender,MouseEventArgs e) {
   ox=(int)(fl.n*e.X/PicFluid.Width);
   oy=(int)(fl.n*e.Y/PicFluid.Height);
   mx=ox; my=oy;
   if(e.Button==MouseButtons.Left) left=true;
   else right=false;
   if(e.Button==MouseButtons.Right) right=true;
   else right=false;
   PicFluid.Invalidate();
}

void PicFluidMouseMove(object sender,MouseEventArgs e) {
   mx=(int)(fl.n*e.X/PicFluid.Width);
   my=(int)(fl.n*e.Y/PicFluid.Height);
   if(e.Button==MouseButtons.Left) left=true;
   else right=false;
   if(e.Button==MouseButtons.Right) right=true;
   else right=false;
   PicFluid.Invalidate();
}

void PicFluidMouseUp(object sender,MouseEventArgs e) {
   ox=(int)(fl.n*e.X/PicFluid.Width);
   oy=(int)(fl.n*e.Y/PicFluid.Height);
   mx=ox; my=oy;
   left=false; right=false;
   PicFluid.Invalidate();
}

void PicFluidPaint(object sender,PaintEventArgs e) {
   int i, j;
   double d;
   Vector v;

   if(active) {
      if((mx!=ox)||(my!=oy)) {
         if(left) fl.vx[mx,my]+=(mx-ox)*100.0*fl.dw/PicFluid.Width;
         if(left) fl.vy[mx,my]+=(my-oy)*100.0*fl.dw/PicFluid.Height;
      }
      if(right) fl.dye[mx,my]+=5.0f;
      fl.RunFluid();
      for(i=0;i<fl.n;i++) {
         for(j=0;j<fl.n;j++) {
            d=fl.dye[i,j];
            if(d<0.0) d=0.0; if(d>1.0) d=1.0;
            if(fl.boundary[i,j]) Draw(e.Graphics,i,j,0.0,1.0,0.0);
            else Draw(e.Graphics,i,j,0.0,0.0,d);
            if(fl.fluid[i,j]) Draw(e.Graphics,i,j,0.0,0.0,1.0);
            if(fl.surface[i,j]) Draw(e.Graphics,i,j,0.0,1.0,1.0);
            v=new Vector(0.5*(fl.vx[i,j]+fl.vx[i+1,j]),
            0.5*(fl.vy[i,j]+fl.vy[i,j+1]), 0);
```

```
        }
      }
      for(i=0;i<fl.np;i++) {
        DrawParticle(e.Graphics,fl.particles[i].x,
            fl.particles[i].y,1.0,0.0,0.0);
      }
    } else {
      if(right) { fl.fluid[mx,my]=true;  fl.boundary[mx,my]=false; }
      if(left)  { fl.boundary[mx,my]=true;  fl.fluid[mx,my]=false; }
      fl.compute_surface();
      for(i=0;i<fl.n;i++) {
        for(j=0;j<fl.n;j++) {
          d=fl.dye[i,j];
          if(d<0.0) d=0.0;  if(d>1.0) d=1.0;
          if(fl.boundary[i,j]) Draw(e.Graphics,i,j,0.0,1.0,0.0);
          if(fl.fluid[i,j]) Draw(e.Graphics,i,j,0.0,0.0,1.0);
          if(fl.surface[i,j]) Draw(e.Graphics,i,j,0.0,1.0,1.0);
        }
      }
    }
  }

  void CmdStartClick(object sender,EventArgs e)
  { active=true; fl.create_particles(); }
  }
}
```

Bibliography

[1] T. Akenine-Möller and E. Haines. *Real-Time Rendering*. A.K. Peters Ltd., Natick, Massachusetts, second edition, 2002.

[2] A. W. Bargteil, T. G. Goktekin, J. F. O'brien, and J. A. Strain. A semi-lagrangian contouring method for fluid simulation. *ACM Trans. Graph.*, **25**(1):19–38, 2006.

[3] M. F. Barnsley. *Fractals Everywhere*. Academic Press, San Diego, 1988.

[4] G. Beylkin. On the fast Fourier transform of functions with singularities. *Applied and Computational Harmonic Analysis*, **2**:363–381, 1995.

[5] P. Bézier. *Numerical Control: Mathematics and Applications*. Wiley, Chichester, UK, 1972.

[6] J. Bolz and P. Schröder. Rapid evaluation of Catmull-Clark subdivision surfaces. In *Web3D '02: Proceeding of the seventh international conference on 3D Web technology*, pages 11–17. ACM Press, 2002.

[7] O. P. Bruno and M. M. Pohlman. High order surface representation. In *Topics in Computational Wave Propagation, Direct and Inverse Problems*, volume **31** of *Lecture Notes in Computational Science and Engineering*, pages 47–53. Springer-Verlag, 2003.

[8] S. Buss. *3-D Computer Graphics*. Cambridge University Press, Cambridge, 2003.

[9] A. Calderbank, I. Daubechies, W. Sweldens, and B.-L. Yeo. Lossless image compression using integer to integer wavelet transforms. In *ICIP '97: Proceedings of the 1997 International Conference on Image Processing (ICIP '97) 3-Volume Set-Volume 1*, page 596, Washington, DC, USA, 1997. IEEE Computer Society.

[10] S. Campagna, P. Slusallek, and H.-P. Seidel. Ray tracing of spline surfaces: Bézier clipping, Chebyshev boxing, and bounding volume hierarchy - a critical comparison with new results. *The Visual Computer*, **13**(6):265–282, 1997.

[11] M. Carlson, P. J. Mucha, and G. Turk. Rigid fluid: animating the interplay between rigid bodies and fluid. In *SIGGRAPH '04: ACM SIGGRAPH 2004 Papers*, pages 377–384, New York, NY, USA, 2004. ACM Press.

[12] E. Catmull. *Subdivision Algorithm for the Display of Curved Surfaces*. PhD thesis, University of Utah, 1974.

[13] E. Catmull and R. Rom. A class of local interpolating splines. In R. Barnhill and R. Riesenfeld, editors, *Computer Aided Geometric Design*, pages 317–326, San Francisco, 1974. Academic Press.

[14] G. Celniker and D. Gossard. Deformable curve and surface finite-elements for free-form shape design. In *SIGGRAPH '91: Proceedings of the 18th annual conference on Computer graphics and interactive techniques*, pages 257–266, New York, NY, USA, 1991. ACM Press.

[15] G. Chaikin. An algorithm for high speed curve generation. *Computer Graphics and Image Processing*, **4**(3), 1974.

[16] F. Cheng and A. Goshtasby. A parallel B-spline surface fitting algorithm. *ACM Trans. Graph.*, **8**(1):41–50, 1989.

[17] B. V. Cherkassky, A. V. Goldberg, and T. Radzik. Shortest paths algorithms: theory and experimental evaluation. In *SODA '94: Proceedings of the fifth annual ACM-SIAM symposium on Discrete algorithms*, pages 516–525, Philadelphia, PA, USA, 1994. Society for Industrial and Applied Mathematics.

[18] F. C. Crow. The origins of the teapot. *IEEE Computer Graphics and Applications*, **7**(1):8–19, 1987.

[19] I. Daubechies. The wavelet-transform, time-frequency localization and signal analysis. *IEEE Trans. Inform. Theory*, **36**:961–1005, 1990.

[20] A. de Cusatis Junior, L. H. de Figuieredo, and M. Gattass. Interval methods for ray casting implicit surfaces with affine arithmetic. *Computer graphics forum*, **20**(3), 2001.

[21] T. DeRose, M. Kass, and T. Truong. Subdivision surfaces in character animation. *Computer Graphics*, **32**(Annual Conference Series):85–94, Aug. 1998.

[22] M. P. do Carmo. *Differential Geometry of Curves and Surfaces.* Prentice-Hall, 1976.

[23] D. Doo and M. Sabin. Behaviour of recursive division surfaces near extraordinary points. *Computer-Aided Design,* **10**(6):356–360, 1978.

[24] A. Dutt and V. Rokhlin. Fast Fourier transforms for nonequispaced data. *Siam Journal on Scientific Computing,* **14**(6):1368–1393, 1993.

[25] A. Dutt and V. Rokhlin. Fast Fourier transforms for nonequispaced data II. *Applied and Computation Harmonic Analysis,* **2**:85–100, 1995.

[26] N. Dyn, D. Levin, and J. A. Gregory. A 4-point interpolatory subdivision scheme for curve design. *Computer Aided Geometric Design,* **4**(4):160–169, 1987.

[27] D. S. Ebert, F. K. Musgrave, D. Peachey, K. Perlin, and S. Worley. *Texturing and Modeling: A Procedural Approach.* Academic Press, San Diego, second edition, 1998.

[28] M. Eck and H. Hoppe. Automatic reconstruction of B-spline surfaces of arbitrary topological type. *Computer Graphics,* **30**(Annual Conference Series):325–334, 1996.

[29] D. Enright, S. Marschner, and R. Fedkiw. Animation and rendering of complex water surfaces. In *SIGGRAPH '02: Proceedings of the 29th annual conference on Computer graphics and interactive techniques,* pages 736–744, New York, NY, USA, 2002. ACM Press.

[30] M. P. Epstein. On the influence of parametrization in parametric interpolation. *SIAM Journal of Numerical Analysis,* **13**(2):261–268, 1976.

[31] J. Erickson and S. Har-Peled. Optimally cutting a surface into a disk. In *SCG '02: Proceedings of the eighteenth annual symposium on Computational geometry,* pages 244–253, New York, NY, USA, 2002. ACM Press.

[32] G. Farin. *Curves and Surfaces for Computer Aided Geometric Design–A practical guide.* Academic Press Inc., fifth edition, 2002.

[33] R. Fedkiw, J. Stam, and H. W. Jensen. Visual simulation of smoke. In *SIGGRAPH '01: Proceedings of the 28th annual conference on Computer graphics and interactive techniques,* pages 15–22, New York, NY, USA, 2001. ACM Press.

[34] A. Finkelstein and D. H. Salesin. Multiresolution curves. In *Proceedings of the 21st annual conference on Computer graphics and interactive techniques*, pages 261–268. ACM Press, 1994.

[35] M. S. Floater. Parametrization and smooth approximation of surface triangulations. *Computer Aided Geometric Design*, 14:232–250, 1997.

[36] M. S. Floater. Mean value coordinates. *Comput. Aided Geom. Des.*, 20(1):19–27, 2003.

[37] M. S. Floater and K. Hormann. Surface parameterization: a tutorial and survey. In N. A. Dodgson, M. S. Floater, and M. A. Sabin, editors, *Advances in multiresolution for geometric modelling*, pages 157–186. Springer Verlag, 2005.

[38] J. D. Foley, A. van Dam, S. K. Feiner, and H. John F. *Computer Graphics, Principles and Practice*. Addison–Wesley, Reading, Massachusetts, second edition, 1995.

[39] A. R. Forrest. The twisted cubic curve: A computer-aided geometric design approach. *Computer Aided Design*, 12(4):165–172, 1980.

[40] N. Foster and D. Metaxis. Realistic animation of liquids. *Graphical Models and Image Processing*, 58(5):471–483, 1996.

[41] A. Fournier and J. Buchanan. Chebyshev polynomials for boxing and intersections of parametric curves and surfaces. *Computer Graphics Forum*, 13(3):127–142, 1994.

[42] I. Friedel, P. Schröder, and M. Desbrun. Unconstrained spherical parameterization. In *SIGGRAPH '05: ACM SIGGRAPH 2005 Sketches*, page 134, New York, NY, USA, 2005. ACM Press.

[43] R. Goldman. *Graphics gems*, chapter Matrices and transformations, pages 472–475. Academic Press Professional, Inc., San Diego, CA, USA, 1990.

[44] R. Goldman. The ambient spaces of computer graphics and geometric modeling. *IEEE Comput. Graph. Appl.*, 20(2):76–84, 2000.

[45] R. Goldman. Baseball arithmetic and the laws of pseudoperspective. *IEEE Comput. Graph. Appl.*, 21(2):70–78, 2001.

[46] R. Goldman. On the algebraic and geometric foundations of computer graphics. *ACM Trans. Graph.*, 21(1):52–86, 2002.

[47] R. Goldman. Deriving linear transformations in three dimensions. *IEEE Comput. Graph. Appl.*, **23**(3):66–71, 2003.

[48] C. Gotsman, X. Gu, and A. Sheffer. Fundamentals of spherical parameterization for 3d meshes. In *SIGGRAPH '03: ACM SIGGRAPH 2003 Papers*, pages 358–363, New York, NY, USA, 2003. ACM Press.

[49] A. Graps. An introduction to wavelets. *IEEE Computational Science and Engineering*, **2**(2), 1995.

[50] G. Greiner and K. Hormann. Interpolating and approximating scattered 3D-data with hierarchical tensor product B-splines. In A. L. Méhauté, C. Rabut, and L. L. Schumaker, editors, *Surface Fitting and Multiresolution Methods*, Innovations in Applied Mathematics, pages 163–172. Vanderbilt University Press, Nashville, TN, 1997.

[51] X. Gu. *Parametrization for surfaces with arbitrary topologies*. PhD thesis, Harvard University, 2002.

[52] X. Gu, S. Gortler, and H. Hoppe. Geometry images. *Computer Graphics Proceedings (SIGGRAPH 2002)*, pages 355–361, 2002.

[53] M. Halstead, M. Kass, and T. DeRose. Efficient, fair interpolation using Catmull-Clark surfaces. In *Proceedings of the 20th annual conference on Computer graphics and interactive techniques*, pages 35–44. ACM Press, 1993.

[54] A. Hardy and W.-H. Steeb. Harmonic interpolation and Lie groups. *International Journal of Theoretical Physics*, **43**(5):1261–1266, 2004.

[55] A. Hardy and W.-H. Steeb. Harmonic interpolation, Bézier curves and trigonometric interpolation. *Z. Naturforsch.*, **59a**:591–596, 2004.

[56] F. H. Harlow and J. E. Welch. Numerical calculation of time-dependant viscous incompressible flow of fluids with free surface. *Physics of Fluids*, **8**(12):2182–2189, 1965.

[57] M. J. Harris. *GPUGems*, chapter Fast Fluid Dynamics Simulation on the GPU, pages 637–663. Addison-Wesley, 2004.

[58] J. C. Hart. Sphere tracing: A geometric method for the antialiased ray tracing of implicit surfaces. *The Visual Computer*, **12**(10):527–545, 1996.

[59] P. S. Heckbert. Adaptive radiosity textures for bidirectional ray tracing. In *SIGGRAPH '90: Proceedings of the 17th annual conference*

on *Computer graphics and interactive techniques*, pages 145–154, New York, NY, USA, 1990. ACM Press.

[60] N. J. Higham. Stable iterations for the matrix square root. *Numerical Algorithms*, **15**(2):227–242, 1997.

[61] J. D. Hobby. Smooth, easy to compute interpolating splines. *Discrete and Computational Geometry*, **1**(2):123–140, 1986.

[62] J. D. Hobby. A user's manual for MetaPost. Technical Report 162, AT&T Bell Laboratories, Murray Hill NJ, 1992.

[63] H. Hoppe. *Surface Reconstruction from Unorganized Points*. PhD thesis, University of Washington, 1994.

[64] H. Hoppe, T. DeRose, T. Duchamp, M. Halstead, H. Jin, J. McDonald, J. Schweitzer, and W. Stuetzle. Piecewise smooth surface reconstruction. *Computer Graphics*, **28**(Annual Conference Series):295–302, 1994.

[65] J. Hoschek and D. Lasser. *Fundamentals of Computer Aided Geometric Design*. A.K. Peters Ltd., Natick, Massachusetts, 1993.

[66] A. Iones, A. Krupin, M. Sbert, and S. Zhukov. Fast, realistic lighting for video games. *IEEE Computer Graphics and Applications*, **23**(3):54–64, 2003.

[67] H. W. Jensen. *Realistic Image Synthesis Using Photon Mapping*. A. K. Peters Ltd., Natick, Massachusetts, 2001.

[68] H. Jiaxing. On a linear combination of S.N. Bernstein trigonometric interpolation polynomial. *Applied Mathematics and Computation*, **106**(2–3):197–203, 1999.

[69] L. W. Johnson and R. D. Riess. *Numerical analysis*. Addison Wesley, second edition, 1982.

[70] K. I. Joy and M. N. Bhetanabhotla. Ray tracing parametric surface patches utilizing numerical techniques and ray coherence. In *Proceedings of the 13th annual conference on Computer graphics and interactive techniques*, pages 279–285. ACM Press, 1986.

[71] J. T. Kajiya. Ray tracing parametric patches. In *Proceedings of the 9th annual conference on Computer graphics and interactive techniques*, pages 245–254. ACM Press, 1982.

[72] D. E. Knuth. *Computers and Typesetting*, volume **D**. Addison–Wesley, Reading, Massachusetts, 1986.

[73] D. E. Knuth. *The Art of Computer Programming - Fundamental Algorithms*, volume **1**. Addison–Wesley, Reading, Massachusetts, third edition, 1997.

[74] L. Kobbelt. $\sqrt{3}$ subdivision. *Computer Graphics Proceedings (SIGGRAPH 2000)*, pages 103–112, 2000.

[75] L. Kobbelt, K. Daubert, and H.-P. Seidel. Ray tracing of subdivision surfaces. In *Rendering Techniques '98 proceedings of the 9th Eurographics Workshop on Rendering*, Berlin, 1998. Springer Verlag.

[76] W. Koepf. Efficient computation of Chebyshev polynomials. In M. Wester, editor, *Computer Algebra Systems: A Practical Guide*, pages 79–99, Chichester, 1999. John Wiley.

[77] R. Krawczyk. Newton-Algorithmen zur Bestimmung von Nullstellen mit Fehlerschranken. In *Computing*, volume **4**, pages 187–201, 1969.

[78] E. Kreysig. *Advanced Engineering Mathematics*. John Wiley & Sons, Singapore, eighth edition, 1999.

[79] U. Labsik and G. Greiner. Interpolatory $\sqrt{3}$ subdivision. *Computer Graphics Forum (Proceedings of Eurographics 2000)*, **19**(3):131–138, 2000.

[80] H. Landis. Production-ready global illumination. In *Renderman in Production*, pages 87–101. ACM SIGGRAPH Course notes, 2002.

[81] S. Lee, G. Wolberg, and S. Shin. Scattered data interpolation with multilevel B-splines. *IEEE Transactions on Visualization and Computer Graphics*, **3**(3):228–244, 1997.

[82] S.-L. Lien, M. Shantz, and V. Pratt. Adaptive forward differencing for rendering curves and surfaces. In *SIGGRAPH '87: Proceedings of the 14th annual conference on Computer graphics and interactive techniques*, pages 111–118. ACM Press, 1987.

[83] D. Lischinski and J. Gonczarowski. Improved techniques for ray tracing parametric surfaces. *The Visual Computer: International Journal of Computer Graphics*, **6**(3):134–152, 1990.

[84] N. Litke, A. Levin, and P. Schröder. Fitting subdivision surfaces. In *VIS '01: Proceedings of the conference on Visualization '01*, pages 319–324. IEEE Computer Society, 2001.

[85] C. Loop. Smooth subdivision based on triangles. Master's thesis, University of Utah, 1987.

[86] C. Loop. *Generalized B-spline Surfaces of Arbitrary Topological Type.* PhD thesis, University of Washington, 1992.

[87] F. Losasso, F. Gibou, and R. Fedkiw. Simulating water and smoke with an octree data structure. In *SIGGRAPH '04: ACM SIGGRAPH 2004 Papers*, pages 457–462, New York, NY, USA, 2004. ACM Press.

[88] F. Losasso, H. Hoppe, S. Schaefer, and J. Warren. Smooth geometry images. *Eurographics Symposium on Geometry Processing*, pages 138–145, 2003.

[89] W. Ma and J.-P. Kruth. NURBS curve and surface fitting and interpolation. *Mathematical Methods for Curves and Surfaces*, pages 315–322, 1995.

[90] B. B. Mandelbrot. *The Fractal Geometry of Nature.* Freeman and Company, New York, 1982.

[91] D. Manocha and J. Demmel. Algorithms for intersecting parametric and algebraic curves I: simple intersections. *ACM Trans. Graph.*, 13(1):73–100, 1994.

[92] G. Miller. Efficient algorithms for local and global accessibility shading. In *SIGGRAPH '94: Proceedings of the 21st annual conference on Computer graphics and interactive techniques*, pages 319–326, New York, NY, USA, 1994. ACM Press.

[93] R. E. Moore. *The automatic analysis and control of error in digital computing based on the use of interval numbers*, volume 1, chapter 2, pages 61–130. John Wiley and Sons, 1965.

[94] H. P. Moreton and C. H. Séquin. Functional optimization for fair surface design. In *SIGGRAPH '92: Proceedings of the 19th annual conference on Computer graphics and interactive techniques*, pages 167–176. ACM Press, 1992.

[95] A. C. R. Newberry. Interpolation by algebraic and trigonometric polynomials (in technical notes and short papers). *Mathematics of Computation*, 20(96):597–599, 1966.

[96] A. C. R. Newberry. Trigonometric interpolation and curve-fitting. *Mathematics of Computation*, 24(112):869–876, 1970.

[97] T. Nishita, T. W. Sederberg, and M. Kakimoto. Ray tracing trimmed rational surface patches. In *Proceedings of the 17th annual conference on Computer graphics and interactive techniques*, pages 337–345. ACM Press, 1990.

[98] J. Peters. Constructing C^1 surfaces of arbitrary topology using biquadratic and bicubic splines. In N. Sapidis, editor, *Designing Fair Curves and Surfaces*, pages 277–293. SIAM, 1994.

[99] L. Piegl and W. Tiller. *The NURBS Book*. Springer Verlag, Berlin/Heidelberg, second edition, 1997.

[100] E. Praun and H. Hoppe. Spherical parametrization and remeshing. *Computer Graphics Proceedings (SIGGRAPH 2003)*, pages 340–349, 2003.

[101] W. H. Press, S. A. Teukolsky, W. T. Vetterling, and B. P. Flannery. *Numerical Recipes in C*. Cambridge University Press, second edition, 2002.

[102] P. Prusinkiewicz and A. Lindenmayer. *The Algorithmic Beauty of Plants*. Springer Verlag, New York, 1996.

[103] N. Ray, W. C. Li, B. Lévy, A. Sheffer, and P. Alliez. Periodic global parameterization. *ACM Trans. Graph.*, **25**(4):1460–1485, 2006.

[104] A. Razdan and G. Farin. Determination of end conditions for NURB surface interpolation. *Computer Aided Geometric Design*, **15**(7):757–768, 1998.

[105] U. Reif. A unified approach to subdivision algorithms near extraordinary vertices. *Computer Aided Geometric Design*, **12**(2):153–174, 1995.

[106] S. M. Roth, P. Diezi, and M. H. Gross. Ray tracing triangular Bézier patches. *Computer graphics forum*, **20**(3), 2001.

[107] P. V. Sander, J. Snyder, S. J. Gortler, and H. Hoppe. Texture mapping progressive meshes. In *SIGGRAPH '01: Proceedings of the 28th annual conference on Computer graphics and interactive techniques*, pages 409–416, New York, NY, USA, 2001. ACM Press.

[108] P. Schröder. Wavelets in computer graphics. *Proceedings of the IEEE*, **84**(4):615–625, 1996.

[109] W. Schuster. A closed algebraic interpolation curve. *Computer Aided Geometric Design*, **17**(7):631–642, 2000.

[110] W. Schuster. Erratum to: "a closed algebraic interpolation curve".
      Computer Aided Geometric Design, **18**(1):73–76, 2001.

[111] W. Schuster. Harmonische interpolation. In *Math. Semesterber.*, volume **48**, pages 1–27. Springer-Verlag, 2001.

[112] D. Schweitzer and E. S. Cobb. Scanline rendering of parametric surfaces. In *Proceedings of the 9th annual conference on Computer graphics and interactive techniques*, pages 265–271. ACM Press, 1982.

[113] T. W. Sederberg and D. C. Anderson. Ray tracing of Steiner patches.
      Computer Graphics Proceedings (SIGGRAPH 1984), **18**(3):159–164, 1984.

[114] A. Sheffer, C. Gotsman, and N. Dyn. Robust spherical parameterization of triangular meshes. *Computing*, **72**(1-2):185–193, 2004.

[115] A. Sheffer and J. C. Hart. Seamster: Inconspicuous low-distortion texture seam layout. In *VIS '02: Proceedings of the conference on Visualization '02*, Washington, DC, USA, 2002. IEEE Computer Society.

[116] A. Sheffer, B. Lévy, M. Mogilnitsky, and A. Bogomyakov. ABF++: fast and robust angle based flattening. *ACM Trans. Graph.*, **24**(2):311–330, 2005.

[117] L. A. Shirman and C. H. Séquin. Local surface interpolation with Bézier patches. *Computer Aided Geometric Design*, **4**(4):279–295, 1987.

[118] L. A. Shirman and C. H. Séquin. Local surface interpolation with Bézier patches: errata and improvements. *Computer Aided Geometric Design*, **8**(3):217–221, 1991.

[119] K. Shoemake. Animating rotation with quaternion curves. In *SIGGRAPH '85: Proceedings of the 12th annual conference on Computer graphics and interactive techniques*, pages 245–254, New York, NY, USA, 1985. ACM Press.

[120] J. M. Snyder. Interval analysis for computer graphics. In *Proceedings of the 19th annual conference on Computer graphics and interactive techniques*, pages 121–130. ACM Press, 1992.

[121] J. Stam. Stable fluids. In *SIGGRAPH '99: Proceedings of the 26th annual conference on Computer graphics and interactive techniques*, pages 121–128, New York, NY, USA, 1999. ACM Press/Addison-Wesley Publishing Co.

[122] W.-H. Steeb. *Matrix Calculus and Kronecker Product with Applications and C++ Programs*. World Scientific, Singapore, 1997.

[123] W.-H. Steeb. *Problems and Solutions in Theoretical and Mathematical Physics*. World Scientific, Singapore, 2002.

[124] W.-H. Steeb. *Mathematical Tools in Signal Processing with C++ and Java Simulations*. World Scientific, Singapore, 2005.

[125] W.-H. Steeb. *The Nonlinear Workbook*. World Scientific, Singapore, third edition, 2005.

[126] W.-H. Steeb. *Problems and Solutions in Introductory and Advanced Matrix Calculus*. World Scientific, Singapore, 2006.

[127] W.-H. Steeb, Y. Hardy, A. Hardy, and R. Stoop. *Problems and Solutions in Scientific Computing*. World Scientific, Singapore, 2004.

[128] E. J. Stollnitz, T. D. DeRose, and D. H. Salesin. Wavelets for computer graphics: A primer, part 1. *IEEE Computer Graphics and Applications*, **15**(3):76–84, 1995.

[129] E. J. Stollnitz, T. D. DeRose, and D. H. Salesin. Wavelets for computer graphics: A primer, part 2. *IEEE Computer Graphics and Applications*, **15**(4):75–85, 1995.

[130] G. Strang. Wavelets. *American Scientist*, **82**:250–255, 1994.

[131] W. Stürzlinger. Ray tracing triangular trimmed free-form surfaces. *IEEE Transactions on Visualization and Computer Graphics*, **4**(3):202–214, 1998.

[132] W. Sweldens and P. Schröder. Building your own wavelets at home. In *Wavelets in Computer Graphics*, pages 15–87. ACM SIGGRAPH Course notes, 1996.

[133] D. L. Toth. On ray tracing parametric surfaces. In *Proceedings of the 12th annual conference on Computer graphics and interactive techniques*, pages 171–179. ACM Press, 1985.

[134] A. Tucker. *Applied Combinatorics*. John Wiley & Sons, New York, third edition, 1995.

[135] A. Vlachos, J. Peters, C. Boyd, and J. L. Mitchell. Curved PN triangles. In *ACM Symposium on Interactive 3D Graphics 2001*, pages 159–166, 2001.

[136] S.-W. Wang, Z.-C. Shih, and R.-C. Chang. An efficient and stable ray tracing algorithm for parametric surfaces. *Journal of Information Science and Engineering*, **18**(4):541–561, 2002.

[137] J. Warren and H. Weimer. *Subdivision Methods for Geometric Design: A Constructive Approach.* Morgan Kaufmann Publishers, 2001.

[138] A. Watt and M. Watt. *Advanced Animation and Rendering Techniques.* Addison Wesley, New York, 1992.

[139] D. F. Wiley, M. Bertram, B. Hamann, K. I. Joy, N. Max, and G. Scheuermann. Hierarchical spline approximation. In G. Farin, B. Hamann, and H. Hagen, editors, *Hierarchical and Geometrical Methods in Scientific Visualization*, pages 63–88, Heidelberg, Germany, 2003. Springer-Verlag.

[140] S. Yoshizawa, A. G. Belyaev, , and H.-P. Seidel. A fast and simple stretch-minimizing mesh parameterization. *International Conference on Shape Modeling and Applications*, pages 200–208, 2004.

[141] S. Zhukov, A. Iones, and G. Kronin. An ambient light illumination model. *Rendering Techniques '98*, pages 45–56, 1998.

[142] D. Zorin. A method for analysis of C^1-continuity of subdivision surfaces. *SIAM Journal on Numerical Analysis*, **37**(5):1677–1708, 2000.

[143] D. Zorin, P. Schröder, T. DeRose, L. Kobbelt, A. Levin, and W. Sweldens. Subdivision for modelling and animation. In *Course Notes at SIGGRAPH 2000*, 2000.

[144] D. Zorin, P. Schröder, and W. Sweldens. Interpolating subdivision for meshes with arbitrary topology. *Computer Graphics Proceedings (SIGGRAPH 96)*, pages 189–192, 1996.

Index